Contexts of Early Intervention

Contexts of Early Intervention
Systems and Settings

edited by

S. Kenneth Thurman, Ph.D.
Temple University
Philadelphia, Pennsylvania

Janet R. Cornwell, Ph.D.
Southern New Jersey Regional Early Intervention Collaborative
Berlin, New Jersey

and

Sheryl Ridener Gottwald, Ph.D.
Child & Family Services
Exeter, New Hampshire

·P A U L·H·
BROOKES
PUBLISHING Cᵒ

Baltimore • London • Toronto • Sydney

Paul H. Brookes Publishing Co.
Post Office Box 10624
Baltimore, Maryland 21285-0624

Typeset by PRO-IMAGE Corporation, York, Pennsylvania.
Manufactured in the United States of America by
The Maple Press Company, York, Pennsylvania.

Case studies in this book are fictional or composites based on the authors'
experiences. Any similarity to actual individuals or circumstances is
coincidental, and no implications should be inferred.

Library of Congress Cataloging-in-Publication Data
Contexts of early intervention : systems and settings / edited by
    S. Kenneth Thurman, Janet R. Cornwell, and Sheryl Ridener Gottwald.
        p.   cm.
    Includes bibliographical references and index.
    ISBN 1-55766-260-6
    1. Handicapped children—Services for.   2. Child development.
3. Early childhood education.   I. Thurman, S. Kenneth.
II. Cornwell, Janet R.   III. Gottwald, Sheryl Ridener, 1953–
HV888.C65   1997
362.4'083—dc20   96-19845
                                                          CIP

British Library Cataloguing-in-Publication data are available from the British
Library.

Contents

Contributors

Wesley Brown, Ph.D.
Center for Early Childhood Learning and
  Development
East Tennessee State University
Box 70434
Johnson City, TN 37614-0434

Maureen Conroy, Ph.D.
Center for Early Childhood Learning and
  Development
East Tennessee State University
Box 70434
Johnson City, TN 37614-0434

Janet R. Cornwell, Ph.D.
Southern New Jersey Regional Early
  Intervention Collaborative
Winslow Professional Center
339 South Route 73, Suite 6
Berlin, NJ 08009

Susan E. Craig, Ph.D.
AGH Associates, Inc.
P.O. Box 130
Hampton, NH 03842

Angela G. Deal, M.S.W.
Burke County Partnership for Children
P.O. Box 630
Morganton, NC 28680

Carl J. Dunst, Ph.D.
Allegheny-Singer Research Institute
Medical College of Pennsylvania and
  Hahnemann University
Pittsburgh, PA 15212

Susan L. Golbeck, Ph.D.
Graduate School of Education
Rutgers University
10 Seminary Place
New Brunswick, NJ 08903

Sheryl Ridener Gottwald, Ph.D.
67 Mount Delight Road
Deerfield, NH 03037

Susan Harlan, M.S.
Graduate School of Education
Rutgers University
10 Seminary Place
New Brunswick, NJ 08903

Kathleen M. Hebbeler, Ph.D.
SRI International
333 Ravenswood Avenue
Menlo Park, CA 94025

Aquiles Iglesias, Ph.D.
Department of
  Communication Sciences
Temple University
Weiss Hall
Philadelphia, PA 19122

Rosemary Karabinos, M.Ed.
Special People in Northeast, Inc.
10521 Drummond Road
Philadelphia, PA 19154-3886

Donald A. Kates, M.B.A.
Center for Child Health and
  Mental Health Policy
Georgetown University
  Child Development Center
3307 M Street, NW
Washington, DC 20007

Constance Korteland, Ph.D.
Psychology Department
Neumann College
Concord Road
Aston, PA 19014-1297

Donald W. Mott, M.A.
Family, Infant and Preschool Program
Western Carolina Center
300 Enola Road
Morganton, NC 28655

P. Alan Pardy, Ed.D.
Sanborn Regional School District
178 Main Street
Kingston, NH 03840

Rosemary Quinn, Ph.D.
Communication Sciences and Disorders
San Jose State University
1 Washington Square—SH11J
San Jose, CA 95129-0079

S. Kenneth Thurman, Ph.D.
Department of Curriculum, Instruction,
   and Technology in Education
College of Education
Temple University
Philadelphia, PA 19122

Carol M. Trivette, Ph.D.
Family, Infant and Preschool Program
Western Carolina Center
300 Enola Road
Morganton, NC 28655

Preface

Several years ago, the three editors of this volume were involved in a study carried out to begin to describe what goes on in a neonatal intensive care unit (NICU). The basic questions that we were asking were as follows: What goes on here? And who does what? It was in discussing the results of this study (results that are fully presented in Chapter 7) that this book was born. We realized that the data from our study provided the basis for beginning to understand the nature of the NICU as an environmental unit. As a result of our discussion about our study, it occurred to us that early intervention as a process is influenced by the contexts and settings in which it is carried out. Furthermore, we realized that few sources examined these influences. Thus, we asked ourselves, "Why not develop a book that addresses how the nature of early intervention is influenced by the systems and settings in which it is carried out?" This book is our answer to this question.

The central purpose of this book is to describe the major systems and settings in which early intervention is practiced. While clearly there may be systems and settings that might have been included in this text that were not, we nonetheless feel that we have identified those that early intervention practitioners will most likely confront. In choosing colleagues to contribute to this book, we sought individuals who not only have an academic understanding of early intervention and the contexts in which it is carried out but also have clinical and experiential knowledge of the particular setting about which they were writing.

Each chapter of this book, save the first and last, provides background on a particular system or setting. Each chapter elucidates the influences that a system or setting typically has on the delivery of early intervention services and suggests some means by which hindrances to service provision within it might be overcome. Each chapter concludes with a case study designed to provide the reader with a "real life" look at how early intervention services are influenced by the particular system or setting being described.

It is our hope that these chapters will make each system or setting come alive for the reader. Our intent is to provide information to students and professionals who may have knowledge of and expertise in the implementation of early intervention but who are desirous of more information regarding the delivery of early intervention services in a particular system or setting. This book may be particularly useful to those who are starting out in the field and who want to make some decisions regarding the setting in which they would most like to work. Those who are working in a particular setting for the first time may also find the book useful. The book is also designed to give students and professionals a better understanding of how the context in which one works can influence the delivery of service. Essentially, the book provides an ecological systems view that allows the reader to see that early intervention practice does not happen in a vacuum but is highly dependent on the particular setting in which it occurs as well as on the systems in which those settings are embedded. Thus, university instructors may find this book useful for giving their students some understanding of the contexts in which early intervention happens. Practicing professionals, for their part, may find the book useful in broadening their knowledge of specific early intervention systems and settings.

We would be remiss if we did not acknowledge certain individuals without whom this book would not have become a reality. Although somewhat unorthodox, we would like to thank each other for the cooperation and collegiality that we enjoyed in completing this project. Clearly each of us made a unique contribution. Certainly we must thank each of the professionals who contributed chapters to this book. These individuals were without exception willing to work with us and to accept feedback to ensure that the book was as internally consistent as possible and that each chapter was well developed and thorough in its content. We owe also a special debt of thanks to Carol Martin, who was generous and timely in sharing her expert review with us. We also extend our thanks to our colleagues at Paul H. Brookes Publishing Co. In particular we would like to thank Sarah Cheney who helped to launch this project, Theresa Donnelly who nursed it along, and Roslyn Udris and Lynn Weber who oversaw and facilitated the final editing and production of this book. We appreciate all of your efforts! To Paul and Melissa, thanks for your ongoing trust and support. Finally, we want to thank our families who, as always, have been there to love and support us. Ken thanks Marcia, Shane, and Jada. Janet thanks Connie, Tina, Laura, and John. And Sheryl thanks Jeff.

Contexts of Early Intervention

. . . I
. . .
. . .
SYSTEMS

To some extent, the difference between systems and settings, as discussed in Chapter 1, is an artificial one. However, we have chosen to divide this book into two sections, the first addressing systems and the second addressing settings. While one could argue over the merits of this approach, we feel that it provides a meaningful structure to the book.

Bronfenbrenner's (1979) ecology of human development is discussed in some detail in Chapter 1. The divisions within the text are essentially based on his conceptualization. The systems discussed in Chapters 2, 3, and 4 would be characterized by Bronfenbrenner (1976) as *macrosystems*, which "are the overarching institutions of the culture or subculture such as the economic, social, educational legal and political systems" (p. 158). We also include Chapter 6 on families in this section of the book, even though technically families do not fall within the category of macrosystems as defined by Bronfenbrenner. Nonetheless we do so because we feel that, like macrosystems, families have an overarching effect not only on children in early intervention but also on how we deliver these services to them.

As you will discern after reading Chapter 1, Chapter 5 addresses what Bronfenbrenner (1976) would categorize as the *mesosystem*, or "the interrelationship among major settings containing the learner" (p. 157). The mesosystem is a system of settings that interact with and affect each other and thus form a larger system characterized by synergy. This idea is also discussed in Chapter 1.

Simply put, the chapters included in this section discuss the broader contexts of early intervention. Section 2, by contrast, addresses more specific environmental settings.

REFERENCES

Bronfenbrenner, U. (1976). The experimental ecology of education. *Teacher's College Record, 78*, 157–204.

Bronfenbrenner, U. (1979). *The ecology of human development: Experiments by nature and design.* Cambridge, MA: Harvard University Press.

... 1
.
.
.

Systems, Ecologies, and the Context of Early Intervention

S. Kenneth Thurman

Early intervention may be defined as an array of services that is put in place through a partnership with families for the purpose of promoting their well-being and the well-being of their infants, toddlers, and young children whose development may be at risk due to a combination of biological and environmental factors. To this end, Bailey and Wolery (1992) suggested that early intervention has the following primary goals:

1. To support families in achieving their own goals
2. To promote child engagement, independence, and mastery
3. To promote development in key domains
4. To build and support children's social competence
5. To promote the generalized use of skills
6. To provide and prepare for normalized life experiences
7. To prevent the emergence of future problems or disabilities (p. 35)

To these goals, Raver (1991) added the provision of information, support, and assistance to families in dealing with their child; the building of parental competence in facilitating child development and in advocating for their child; and the fostering of "effective interactions between the parent, family, and child that promote mutual feelings of competence and enjoyment" (p. 4).

According to public policy promulgated through the passage of the Education of the Handicapped Act Amendments of 1986 (PL 99-457) and its extension through the Individuals with Disabilities Education Act (IDEA) of 1990 (101-476) and the Individuals with Disabilities Education Act Amendments of 1991 (PL 102-119), *early intervention* is a term used only when speaking about services to children birth through 2 years and their families. These services are differentiated from early childhood and preschool special education services, which are focused on children in the 3- to 5-year age range. These latter services tend to be somewhat less family centered than early intervention services and are typically more school or center based. Whether this distinction in terminology is a meaningful one is open to question, although the literature clearly suggests that the training of personnel for work with the birth through 2-year-old population should take a somewhat different slant and focus from preparation programs designed for personnel desiring to serve the 3- to 5-year-old population (Bricker & Slentz, 1988; Burton, Hains, Hanline, McLean, & McCormick, 1992; Klein & Campbell, 1990; Miller, 1992). In a generic sense, the term *early intervention* can be applied to services to children birth through 5 years of age and their families. Some texts (e.g., Noonan & McCormick, 1993) have reflected this more generic usage. Within this book, this more generic use of the term is being applied; however, the reader is cautioned that *early intervention* technically is the term used only when referring to services to the birth through 2 years population.

During the 1990s, a series of "recommended practices" was developed and generally accepted by early interventionists (Division for Early Childhood [DEC], Task Force on Recommended Practices, 1993). These recommended practices, although not necessarily supported with strong empirical verification, have come to define the nature of early intervention and to provide standards against which programs are assessed (Snyder & Sheehan, 1993). Thus, to the extent that a consensus forms around these recommended practices and they are used in the rendering of early intervention services, they become defining parameters of that service. To reflect recommended practices in early intervention, McDonnell and Hardman (1988) suggested that programs should be the following: 1) integrated (i.e., include children with and without disabilities); 2) comprehensive (i.e., offer a full array of services); 3) normalized (i.e., offer instruction across a variety of settings); 4) adaptable (i.e., employ flexible procedures); 5) referenced to peers and family (i.e., employ a curriculum directly related to the child, family, and community); and 6) outcome based (i.e., place emphasis on skill development for the future). Table 1 further expands these categories.

For a more comprehensive view of recommended standards, the interested reader is referred to *DEC Recommended Practices: Indicators of Quality in Programs for Infants and Young Children with Special Needs and Their Families* (DEC, Task Force on Recommended Practices, 1993), which has been widely accepted by the field. Recommended practices or even typical practices evolve with time and are influenced by the sociopolitical contexts as well as by the accumulation of empirical data. A combination of ideology, which grows from the norms and mores of society, and empirical data, which grow from research, makes early intervention practice a dynamic entity and leads to its further development and evolution.

As suggested in the definition given previously, early intervention can be characterized as an array of services. These services are not only provided by a variety of professionals from a number of different disciplines but also occur in a variety of systems and settings. Although the above-mentioned goals and practices provide the general parameters of early intervention, the systems and settings in which early intervention occurs need to be considered. Each system or setting has unique characteristics that define how early intervention services are presented. In addition, the comprehensive approach of early intervention often requires the collaborative interaction among programs that operate in diverse settings (Bruder & Bologna, 1993; Swan & Morgan, 1992). Understanding early intervention and its practice requires an understanding of the nature of these systems and settings. Together they define the context in which early intervention occurs.

A *system* can be defined as a complex set of interacting entities whose collective function forms a synergy. A system is broad in nature and is guided by a set of parameters that govern its function across time. A *setting*, although displaying the

Table 1. Components of recommended practice

Integrated
  Supported placement in generic early childhood service sites
  Systematic contact with nonhandicapped peers
  Planned integration at all levels

Comprehensive
  Comprehensive assessment, planning, programming, service coordination, and evaluation
  Models theoretically and procedurally well defined
  Transdisciplinary approach to the delivery of related services
  Direct instruction of generalized responding

Normalized
  Support for parenting role
  Age-appropriate skills and instructional strategies
  Concurrent training across skill areas
  Distributed practice across settings
  Establishment of self-initiated responding
  Avoidance of artificial reinforcement and aversive control techniques

Adaptable
  Flexible procedures within noncategorical models
  Support of different family structures
  Emphasis on function rather than form of response
  Programming changes based on individual, formative evaluation

Referenced to peers and family
  Curriculum is referenced to individual child, family, peers, and community
  Parents are full partners in educational planning and decision making
  Systematic communication between family and service providers
  Planned enhancement of child's skill development within daily family routine

Outcome based
  Variety of outcome measures
  Preparation for future integrated settings
  Curricular emphasis on skills with present and future utility
  Transition planning

From McDonnell, A., & Hardman, M. (1988). A synthesis of "best practice" guidelines for early childhood services. *Journal of the Division for Early Childhood, 12,* 328–341; reprinted by permission.

features of a system, is more discrete and circumscribed. A setting typically is embedded within a larger system. Settings most often have time and physical boundaries that define them; a system is more flexible in these characteristics. Thus, the family represents a system, but the home represents a setting. That is not to say that a family does not have boundaries. Those boundaries, however, transcend physical location and time. A home, in contrast, is confined to a particular location and operates only during that time when the family members are present. This view of a setting draws heavily on the work of Barker (1968) and is elucidated further in this chapter's discussion of ecological psychology.

As reflected in the organization of this book, examples of systems are the economic, the cultural, and the sociopolitical systems. Examples of settings would be neonatal intensive care units, child care centers, and public schools. The purpose of this book is to facilitate a better understanding of early intervention practice by providing the reader with a better understanding of the nature of various systems and settings in which early intervention takes place.

ECOLOGICAL AND SYSTEMS APPROACHES

The term *ecology* was originally used in the biological sciences to denote the study of interactive systems or the mutual effects of organisms and their environments. Thus, rather than focusing on a single organism, ecology is concerned with the total system in which the organism lives and how it affects its environment and in turn how its environment affects it. Simply, ecology is concerned with the totality of a system. Ecology is consistent with general systems theory (von Bertalanffy, 1968) in that it recognizes that the interrelationship of each part of a system creates a whole that is greater than the sum of those parts. However, ecology is more concerned with understanding mutual effects of individuals and environments than is general systems theory, which is more concerned with the description of whole systems and the prediction of their behavior (Vetere, 1987).

To understand mutual effects, it is necessary to understand the characteristics of both the individual and the settings or systems in which an individual interacts. Human development researchers and human services providers typically have focused their efforts on the understanding of individuals and their development. They have been concerned with the prediction of human behavior and developmental outcome and how various factors within the environment can enhance that prediction or, in the case of service providers, can be modified to cause what is perceived to be a more desirable developmental outcome. Although this is a legitimate and important course of action, it falls short of an ecological perspective because it fails to recognize the importance of how individuals affect their environments. Any change in an individual effects change in those environments (i.e., systems and settings) in which that individual interacts. However, Sommer and Wicker (1991) suggested the importance of understanding individual settings and suggested that these entities are important to study as units. The ecology changes as a result of the changing of the environment, the individuals in that environment, or both; thus, an understanding of ecology comes from recognizing and analyzing these sources of change.

Early intervention is a human endeavor and as such results from the interaction of people with their environments. The ecology of early intervention can be defined as the interaction of various environments (settings) where early intervention takes place with individuals who, through their behavior, are engaged in the practices associated with early intervention. In subscribing to an ecological and systems view, it is assumed that these practices will be manifested somewhat differently depending on the nature of the setting in which they occur.

Although it is important to understand specific early intervention settings, it is equally important to recognize that these specific settings are embedded in larger systems with which they have an ecological relationship. In addition, because of the collaborative nature of early intervention, different early intervention settings tend to have ecological relationships with each other.

Several ecological approaches promoted in the literature can help provide a framework for understanding the relationship between early intervention practice and the systems and environments in which that practice occurs. These approaches emanate from the work of Bronfenbrenner on the ecology of human development (1979), Barker on behavior settings (1968), and Thurman on ecological congruence (1977). Each approach is described in the following sections.

The Ecology of Human Development

Bronfenbrenner (1979) has been credited with bringing an ecological perspective to the study of human development. He asserted the importance of natural environment in the determination of developmental outcomes in children and stressed the necessity of studying the factors in these environments that contribute to these outcomes. Bronfenbrenner suggested that any individual inhabits or operates as part of a number of different systems and settings that are embedded within each other and at the same time interactive with each other. Bronfenbrenner conceptualized these systems as a series of concentric circles, which he referred to as the "ecological environment" (p. 22). He maintained that developmental research must be ecologically valid and based on "the extent to which the environment experienced by the subjects in a scientific investigation has the properties it is supposed or assumed to have by the investigator" (p. 29). Bronfenbrenner's concern with how the features of these embedded ecological systems determine outcomes in human beings is important; however, of more relevance here is his codification and characterization of these systems. Bronfenbrenner identified what he called the *microsystem*, the *mesosystem*, the *exosystem*, and the *macrosystem*. Each of these systems is defined relative to a particular individual and grows from "the [individual's] phenomenological conception of the environment" (p. 32).

Microsystems are those most immediate to the individual, including specific behavior settings as well as somewhat broader systems that might include several behavior settings in them, such as home environments, preschools, and hospitals. Garbarino (1990) suggested that, although "the quality of the microsystem depends on its ability to sustain and enhance development, and to provide a context that is emotionally validating and developmentally challenging" (p. 81), at the same time the nature of the microsystem changes across time. He asserted that "the microsystem [is] a pattern experienced by the developing person" (p. 81). Thus, the microsystem and the individual develop simultaneously and mutually.

Mesosystems are represented by the interaction among microsystems. Although each microsystem is distinct, it also interacts and is linked with the other microsystems around it. As Garbarino (1990) suggested, "These links themselves form a system. We measure the richness of a mesosystem in the number and quality of its connections" (p. 81). Collaboration employed to provide early intervention along with the child's home and family would be an example of a mesosystem. These links can be important in determining the effectiveness of early intervention services in bringing about desirable outcomes in children and families.

Exosystems are represented by social structures that do not include the individual child directly. The school system, economic system, and the workplace would all be part of the exosystem. Factors in the exosystem would have a direct impact on the meso- and microsystems but not on the child. For example, changes in the economy may lead to decreased funding of early intervention services or the unemployment of a parent. These events could in turn have direct effects on several of the microsystems that included a particular child (e.g., the early intervention center he or she attends, the family's economic resources). These in turn might have a direct effect on the child. Garbarino (1990) noted that events in the exosystem can put children at increased risk or provide them with increased opportunity.

The *macrosystem* encompasses all of the previous systems and is defined as the general beliefs, values, and ideology of a particular culture or subculture. Garbarino (1990) stated that "macrosystems . . . serve as the master blueprints for the ecology of human development reflect[ing] a people's shared assumptions about how things should be done. [They] are ideology incarnate" (p. 83). A major ideological position that affects early intervention is inclusion, which states that all children, regardless of the degree of their disability, should be included fully in environments (mesosystems) that serve all children. Because public policy reflects society's shared view, various dimensions of the macrosystem may have profound effects on the delivery of early intervention services. Evidence for this is seen in the passage of the Education of the Handicapped Act Amendments of 1986, which grew from a societal assumption that early intervention services are important to young children with disabilities and their families.

Garbarino (1990) provided the following summation of the relationship of Bronfenbrenner's (1979) ecological view and early intervention:

> When all is said and done, an ecological perspective has much to contribute to the process of formulating, evaluating, and understanding early intervention. It gives us a kind of social mapping for navigating a path through the complexities of programming. . . . An ecological perspective provides a kind of checklist to use in thinking about what is happening, and what to do about it when faced with developmental problems and social pathologies that affect children. (Garbarino, 1990, p. 84)

Figure 1, taken from Fogel and Melson (1988), is a schematic of Bronfenbrenner's (1979) view of the ecology of human development.

Behavior Settings

Barker (1968) suggested the concept of a behavior setting. In his formulation of ecological psychology, he maintained that it was necessary to identify units of the environment that had a standard set of defining characteristics and could provide the basis for understanding molar patterns of human behavior. Building on Barker's work, Schoggen (1989) suggested that "an initial practical problem of ecological research is to identify the natural units of the phenomena studied" (p. 14). This was Barker's goal

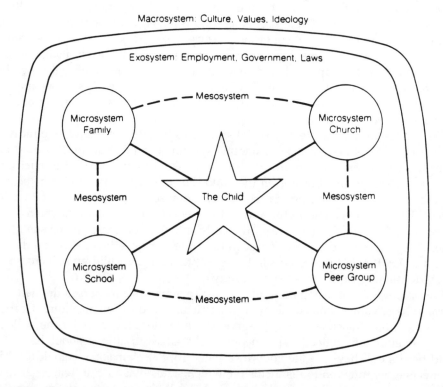

Figure 1. Schematic of Bronfenbrenner's ecological model of human development. (From Fogel, A., & Melson, J.F. [1988]. *Child development*, p. 50. St. Paul, MN: West Publishing Co.; reprinted by permission.)

in developing his behavior settings. According to Barker, in simple terms a *behavior setting* is a bound unit of the environment. Specifically he suggested that a behavior setting has two structural characteristics: 1) one or more standing patterns of behavior and 2) a milieu. Barker maintained that the standing pattern of behavior was extraindividual—that is, not dependent on the particular individuals who inhabit the setting at a point in time; rather, "it has unique and stable characteristics that persist even when current inhabitants of the setting are replaced by others" (Schoggen, 1989, p. 31). The standing pattern of behavior describes the program of behavior that characterizes the setting and is independent of inhabitants of the setting at any point in time. That is, the inhabitants of the setting will engage in the standing pattern of behavior because that is what the setting demands. For example, in a preschool classroom standing patterns of behavior would consist of instruction of children, children playing, toileting of children, gross motor activities, and so forth.

The *milieu* is defined as the physical features of the behavior setting, including props and paraphernalia as well as constructed and natural environments. The milieu represents the nonbehavioral elements of the setting. In a preschool classroom the milieu would include instructional materials, bulletin boards, tables, chairs, and "cubbies."

Barker (1968) contended that for a behavior setting to be operational the standing pattern of behavior and the milieu must come together in a way that is termed *synomorphic* and *circumjacent*. Synomorphy exists when the standing pattern of behavior and the milieu are juxtaposed in such a way as to be functional with each other. Thus, for example, in a preschool classroom if the tables were upside down there could be no synomorphy between the milieu and the standing pattern of behavior until the tables were righted. "The behavioral and milieu components of a behavior setting are not independently arranged; there is an essential fittingness between them" (Schoggen, 1989, p. 32). Circumjacent means that the standing pattern of behavior and the milieu surround each other. In essence they fill the same space and time concurrently. They typically remain circumjacent without interruption for a fixed interval of time (e.g., from 6 A.M. to 6 P.M. in a child care center). Milieu may continue to exist undisturbed when the behavior setting is not operational. For example, the milieu of the preschool classroom (its physical props, materials, and structure) is present at midnight even though the behavior setting (the preschool class) is not functional at that time. Schoggen (1989) concluded that the importance of behavior settings lies in their inclusion of both physical and behavioral aspects of "things and occurrences" (p. 33).

Although emanating from what Barker (1968) termed *ecological psychology*, behavior settings in large measure are not truly ecological because they do not consider the effect of the individual on the setting in general and on the nature of the standing pattern of behavior in particular. Wicker (1987) also made this observation and suggested that behavior settings have considerable more dynamic quality than was recognized by Barker (1968). Wicker (1987) suggested that "behavior settings can and do grow, shrink, and change their operating levels" (p. 616). He asserted that these changes are a function both of the individuals who operate in the setting and thus influence it and of the resources available both inside and outside of the setting. Outside resources result from the interaction of the setting in the larger system.

Each chapter in the second part of this book focuses on a particular setting and how early intervention manifests itself in that setting. These descriptions are generic and outline general parameters. Specific settings may vary and that variation is a function of the individual setting inhabitants, the resources available, and the influences the setting is subject to from the larger systems in which it is embedded. Furthermore, the degree and effect of these outside influences are likely interactive with inhabitants of the settings, who seek out, reject, or assign meaning to resources and influences. Although the development of the behavior setting theory was a significant contribution to understanding person–environment systems, it was limited in its assertion that behavior settings are static freestanding entities whose existence is unaffected by their inhabitants or by the greater system of which they are a part.

Ecological Congruence

The *ecological congruence model* was first promulgated by Thurman (1977) and was suggested as a model for providing special educational programming. The application of the model to the understanding of families with parents with disabilities also has been discussed (Thurman, 1985). The model's application to early intervention programming was elucidated by Thurman and Widerstrom (1990), and Benner (1992) suggested the model's application in carrying out ecologically valid assessments of young children with special needs. In Thurman's (1977) original conceptualization, the ecological congruence model consisted of three dimensions (deviance, competency, and tolerance for difference), as illustrated in Figure 2.

According to the original model, *deviance* is a label placed on the individual and his or her behavior by the social system when some behavior or characteristic that the person exhibits is deemed to be far outside of norms of the system. Simmons (1969) suggested that no human behavior is inherently deviant but that deviance is a social

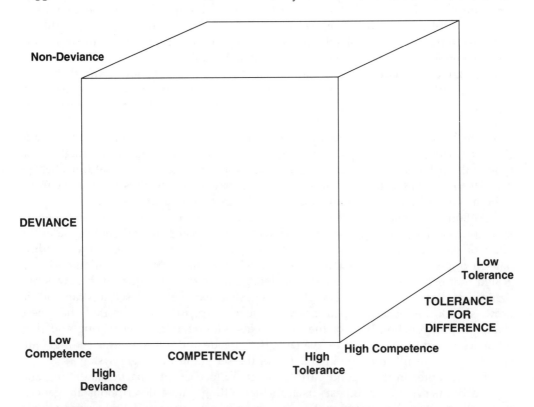

Figure 2. Ecological congruence model. (From Thurman, S.K. [1977]. The congruence of behavioral ecologies: A model for special education programming. *Journal of Special Education, 11*, p. 332; reprinted by permission.)

construction based on the beliefs and values of the social context. Such labeling may lead to the individual reconstructing his or her self in reaction to this label. As Davis (1975) postulated, "Labeling, then, is a social process that transforms one conception of self (normal) into another (deviant)" (p. 173). The effect of labeling on self may further exacerbate the deviant status of the individual and result in lowered self-acceptance. Thus,

> the judgment made about a particular behavior or set of characteristics can be made only relative to the social context in which it has occurred. [Therefore,] those conditions accounting for the label placed upon a behavior and subsequently on the individual himself [sic], lie within the environmental context in which that behavior occurs [and in which that individual interacts]. (Thurman, 1977, p. 330)

Competency can be simply defined as functional behavior or a person's ability to perform tasks. "Competency/incompetency, unlike deviance, is an attribute of the individual, since given a specific task a person either has or does not have the [ability] to perform the task" (Thurman, 1977, p. 330). Behavior setting theory, as previously discussed, associates a specific pattern of behavior with a given setting. The ecological congruence model ties competency to a given setting by recognizing that "every social setting defines . . . a certain set of functional behaviors, or behaviors that lead to the completion of a task or job, within that setting" (Thurman, 1977, p. 330). Ecological validity arises from assessing the competence of a child relative to the behavioral requirements of the particular ecological settings in which the child interacts (Benner, 1992; Thurman & Widerstrom, 1990).

Inability or incompetence should not be equated with nonperformance. In a given situation, motivational and social contextual features of the environment may inhibit the expression of individual competence. An example would be asking a 5-year-old child to swim in the bathtub. Clearly the physical constraints of the bathtub are such that even if this child could swim, she would be unable to demonstrate her ability in that context; nor would swimming be an ecologically relevant behavior in that context.

The third dimension of the ecological congruence model is *tolerance for difference*. In the original conceptualization of the model, tolerance for difference was seen solely as a function of the system. Thurman and Widerstrom (1990) suggested that

> within every social system there is a range of tolerance for difference. Each system defines its own range of what is and what is not acceptable. Individuals viewed as excessively different, either because of their assigned deviance or their lack of competence in performing tasks within the system, are not tolerated. (p. 211)

It also can be suggested that tolerance for difference is a social construction of the setting in the same way that deviance was seen as a social construction in the previous discussion.

The conceptualization of tolerance for difference in the original model overlooks an important aspect of interplay between an individual and the system with which that individual interacts. The individual creates a view of the system. In that view, attributes may arise that are unacceptable to the individual and subsequently lead to the individual's intolerance of the system. The interplay of the system's tolerance for the individual and the individual's tolerance for the system forms the critical dimension of *fit*. Fit or congruence is an attribute of a particular ecology that is a function of the degree of mutual tolerance between an individual and the environmental context with which that individual interacts. Thurman, Cornwell, and Korteland (1989) suggested that adaptive fit results from mutual acceptance between the individual and the environment. Germaine (1979) also asserted that adaptive fit represents a balance between individuals and their environment. A congruent ecology is one where there is a maximum level of adaptive fit. Adaptive fit is a result of the mutual construction of the individual's view of the environment with the construction of the environment's view of the individual. In an interactive system, each of these constructions affects and influences the other; thus, adaptive fit becomes a relative state that can be characterized as being in dynamic homeostatic flux. Wicker (1987, 1992) similarly argued that behavior settings are the social constructions of their inhabitants.

Adaptive fit has emerged as the critical dimension of the ecological congruence model, and thus it should be reflected in the schematic in Figure 2. The dimension of tolerance for differences should be labeled more precisely as adaptive fit. Adaptive fit is reflective of the degree of mutual acceptance between the individual and the environment whose interaction combines to form an ecological system.

Thurman and Widerstrom (1990) suggested that a goal of early intervention should be to increase the adaptive fit or congruence within the ecological systems that are the beneficiaries of early intervention services. Individuals who operate in systems with high degrees of adaptive fit are more likely to experience a sense of well-being. Whether the adaptive fit is normal, based, for example, on Bronfenbrenner's (1979) concept of the macrosystem previously discussed, may make less difference than whether there is mutual acceptance between the individual and the environment. Systems, according to this point of view, define their own fit and construct that fit based on the phenomenology of the interacting agents that make up that system. Thus, "congruence [i.e., high levels of adaptive fit] does not necessarily mean 'normal,' rather it can be seen as maximum adaptation [between the individual and the environment]" because adaptive fit is dynamic in nature and provides "the basis of further adaptation and development of [both] the individual and [the] environment [as well as their continued interaction with each other]" (Thurman, 1977, pp. 332–333).

The use of the ecological congruence model for the implementation of early intervention services has been discussed in detail by Thurman and Widerstrom (1990). In addition, Thurman et al. (1989) illustrated how the construct of adaptive fit was reflected in the implementation of a program to serve families with infants in neonatal intensive care units, an approach that was later modified and extended specifically to single, low-income adolescent mothers and their low birth weight babies (Thurman & Gonsalves, 1993).

Fit as a Unifying Construct

As a construct, fit is applicable not only when one examines the relationship between an individual and his or her environment, as suggested by the ecological congruence model, but also when one combines the three ecological approaches previously discussed. As pointed out above, earlier conceptualization of behavior setting theory did not focus on the interaction of the individuals and the environment as much as it was concerned with the features of the setting per se (e.g., Barker, 1968). Discussions of behavior setting theory now have recognized the effects that individual participants may have on the standing pattern of behavior within a setting (e.g., Wicker, 1987). Behavior setting theory is used in the implementation of the ecological congruence model (Thurman & Widerstrom, 1990). This implementation begins with the identification of the specific behavior settings, or in Bronfenbrenner's (1979) view microsystems, in which a particular child operates. Through its focus on fit, the ecological congruence model, which uses behavior setting theory, acknowledges the dynamic quality of individual settings and takes that into account as programs are developed and implemented. Further development of behavior setting theory could similarly make use of the construct of fit for enhancing understanding of person–environment systems.

Fit is also useful in considering the interrelationship of one setting with another as promulgated in Bronfenbrenner's (1979) conceptualization of the mesosystem. The meaningful and effective interrelationship of microsystems or behavior settings is likely dependent on the adaptive fit among these specific ecological units. Thus, an effective mesosystem would be one in which the individual microsystems exhibited a high degree of congruence with each other. The effective collaboration necessary for early intervention services would be a direct result of good adaptive fit, both within and among systems. It is even likely, although not empirically ascertained, that the degree of fit within a particular system may be instrumental in the facilitation or hindrance of fit in other microsystems within the same mesosystem.

Cultural differences often result from a lack of fit between individuals and the exo- and macrosystems as defined by Bronfenbrenner (1979). Sensitivity to cultural differences is necessary to help establish fit between individuals and families within various micro- and mesosystems. However, individuals may need to make accommodations in their patterns of behavior to facilitate greater fit as defined by the parameters of the dominant macrosystem.

In the final analysis, adaptive fit undergirds the smooth and effective functioning of any system. Systems, like individuals, are adaptable. Adaptation within and among systems occurs through the waxing and waning of fit and the tendency of systems to always move toward homeostatic balance. The degree of fit changes as a function of changes in either the individuals (separately or collectively) or in the environment.

ENVIRONMENTAL PSYCHOLOGY

Like the heuristic framework provided by the previous discussion of ecological models, some understanding of environmental psychology is useful to furthering the knowledge of the relationship between environment and behavior. Of the three models discussed previously, Barker's (1968) is most closely related to environmental psychology. Environmental psychology is concerned with the role of the environment in the determination of behavior, and it explores the relationship of environment and behavior but is somewhat less concerned with the reciprocity inherent in more ecologically oriented views. Stokols and Altman (1987b) have defined environmental psychology as "the study of human behavior and well-being in relation to the sociophysical environment" (p. 1). Any environmental setting or microsystem has both a social and a physical dimension. Environmental psychology is concerned with each of these dimensions and how they affect the behavior of human beings.

The Social Environment

The social environment of a setting is composed of the social objects in that setting. These objects include people, animals, and even inanimate objects that are engaged in or instrumental in maintaining social interactions (Lewis & Feiring, 1979). The interactions of these social objects are influenced by the norms and values of the particular setting as well as by the norms and values of the greater system (i.e., macrosystem). Barker (1968) maintained that the social behavior and social relationships within a setting are heavily influenced by the established standing pattern of behavior identified with that setting. The social environment also defines roles and expectations as well as standards for defining deviance and tolerance for difference, as previously discussed.

The social environment, when viewed from the perspective of any inhabitant of that setting, will be seen as supportive and facilitative, neutral, or hostile and hindering. These perceptions will be important in determining an individual's acceptance of (i.e., tolerance for) that setting and feelings of well-being in that setting. These perceptions will in turn contribute to the degree of fit between the individual and the setting.

The Physical Environment

The physical environment in any setting can be seen as roughly equivalent to Barker's (1968) concept of the milieu. The physical environment includes the furnishings and decorations in the setting. However, the actual arrangement and layout of these furnishings define the physical environment. Moreover, the physical environment includes features such as space, lighting, temperature, and noise. Each of these factors has been related to human behavior and performance (Moos, 1976; Stokols & Altman, 1987a).

The physical environment is affected by the social environment and how inhabitants of the setting behave, and the social environment is affected by the nature of the physical environment. As Barker's (1968) constructs of synomorphy and circumjacency suggest, the very essence of a setting is dependent on a fit between the social and the physical environments within that setting. All human behavior occurs in some specific context, and that context influences and is influenced by that behavior. To better understand early intervention and to effectively render early intervention services, the interaction between early intervention service behaviors and various settings in which they occur must be elucidated.

Subsequent chapters of this book provide rather generic descriptions of various settings. Although these descriptions are useful in gaining a general understanding of the social and physical environments in, for example, a neonatal intensive care unit, a child care center, or a family home, they do not provide a picture of any specific neonatal intensive care unit, child care center, or family home. Like human beings, no two environments within the same class of environment are exactly the same. The general parameters and frameworks provided in this chapter and throughout this book will be helpful to the practitioner who may be entering a particular setting for the first time or to those who may be seeking services for themselves or others in these settings.

The Individuality of Settings and Systems

Every setting or system is individually different from others in its same class. As an example, consider a culture in which the criminal justice system believes that a suspect is guilty until proven innocent rather than innocent until proven guilty, as is the custom in U.S. culture. How attorneys develop their cases and present their arguments is significantly affected by which of these premises is accepted. Although each culture has established rules for its criminal justice proceedings, the actual conduct of those proceedings can be significantly different depending on the rules established.

A similar phenomenon can be observed when two behavior settings (microsystems) of a like category (e.g., child care centers, neonatal intensive care units, Head Start centers) are compared. Each Head Start center operates under the same set of guidelines from the federal government, but each interprets and implements those guidelines in a unique and idiosyncratic manner. Take, for example, the Head Start curriculum. Head Start Performance Standards require that every Head Start program adopt a curriculum. However, they do not dictate which curriculum to adopt. Thus, a Head Start classroom in a program using the High Scope Curriculum (Hohmann, Banet, & Weikart, 1979), a cognitively based curriculum widely used with preschool children, would be considerably different from a Head Start classroom using a curriculum such as HICOMP (Willoughby-Herb & Neisworth, 1983), a curriculum based on direct teaching of specific skills.

Individual settings over time take on a set of values, norms, and ways of doing business that become institutionalized. Some authors (e.g., Louis, 1981, 1983; Pettigrew, 1979; Schein, 1990; Wilkins & Ouchi, 1983) have referred to the existence of organizational cultures that reflect the style and personality of a particular setting. As an overriding culture influences the behavior of an individual, organizational subgroups within a larger system also tend to mirror each other in their function (Wheelan & Abraham, 1993). Essentially, systems and settings exhibit mutual influences on each other and on the inhabitants within them. They also exhibit some degree of similarity to other systems while demonstrating unique ways of doing business. As suggested previously in this chapter, it is the dynamic fit within and among individuals, settings, and systems that accounts for their continued growth and adaptation.

THE INFLUENCE OF INDIVIDUALS ON SETTINGS

Although the emphasis of this book is on the nature of systems and settings rather than on individuals, within an ecological view it is also necessary to reflect on the influence that individuals exert on systems. In some instances, a specific person can have a profound influence on a system or setting. Consider, for example, Gandhi's influence in India, the influence of a child with autistic behavior on her family, or the program administrator who decides to save money by eliminating bus transportation to and from an early intervention center. Each actor within a setting, whether child or adult or student, teacher, therapist, parent, or administrator, has an impact on that setting. Each individual's state of mind, personality, stage of development, level of disability, temperament, and state of well-being help shape and influence the setting and his or her relationship with the setting. The fit between each individual and a setting will be determined partly by the characteristics that each individual brings to the setting.

Within any setting, people may act individually or as a group with a common link or purpose. For example, parents may individually press the system to provide more speech-language services for their child, or they may join with other parents to lobby state legislatures to allocate more funds for all early intervention services. Direct services personnel may invest significant effort in designing and implementing a program for a specific child while pressuring their agency's executive director to increase salary and benefits. Meanwhile, the early intervention coordinator may be developing her own agenda for advancement within the agency at the same time she is working closely with her supervisor and those from other agencies to increase transportation options for families served by the citywide early intervention system. Each of these actions individually or collectively is designed to have an impact on the system and could be instrumental in reshaping the setting and its function.

Settings and systems are complex dynamic entities that shape and are shaped by factors operating both within and outside of their boundaries. Thus, the best understanding of these complex entities may come from recognizing that ecologies are interactive and strive to achieve and maintain adaptive fit. Wheelan (in press) offers the following insight:

> Those who study systems composed of human beings may find the idea of complex adaptive systems composed of human beings disconcerting. Even as we seek to understand these systems we continue to call them human systems which implies that they are the sum of their human parts. However, if they are truly complex adaptive systems, referring to them as human systems is inaccurate just as it would be inaccurate to call organs "tissue systems" or tissues "cell systems."

Wheelan asserts that systems are living entities with their own capacity to learn, respond to feedback, and develop. Are they more than the sum of their parts as she suggests, or are they nothing more than the collective social construction of their inhabitants? The ensuing chapters begin to delineate the system that is called early intervention.

REFERENCES

Bailey, D.B., & Wolery, M. (1992). *Teaching infants and preschoolers with disabilities* (2nd ed.). New York: Macmillan.

Barker, R.G. (1968). *Ecological psychology.* Stanford, CA: Stanford University Press.

Benner, S.M. (1992). *Assessing young children with special needs: An ecological perspective.* New York: Longman.

Bricker, D., & Slentz, K. (1988). Personnel preparation: Handicapped infants. In M.C. Wang, M.C. Reynolds, & H.J. Walberg (Eds.), *Handbook of special education: Research and practice* (Vol. 3, pp. 319–345). Elmsford, NY: Pergamon.

Bronfenbrenner, U. (1979). *The ecology of human development: Experiments by nature and design.* Cambridge, MA: Harvard University Press.

Bruder, M.B., & Bologna, T. (1993). Collaboration and service coordination for effective early intervention. In W. Brown, S.K. Thurman, & L.F. Pearl (Eds.), *Family-centered early intervention with infants and toddlers: Innovative cross-disciplinary approaches* (pp. 103–128). Baltimore: Paul H. Brookes Publishing Co.

Burton, C.B., Hains, A.H., Hanline, M.F., McLean, M., & McCormick, K. (1992). Early childhood intervention and education: The urgency of professional unification. *Topics in Early Childhood Special Education, 11*(4), 53–69.

Davis, N.J. (1975). *Social constructions of deviance: Perspectives and issues in the field.* Dubuque, IA: William C. Brown.

Division for Early Childhood (DEC), Task Force on Recommended Practices. (1993). *DEC recommended practices: Indicators of quality in programs for infants and young children with special needs and their families.* Reston, VA: Council for Exceptional Children.

Education of the Handicapped Act Amendments of 1986, PL 99-457, 20 U.S.C. §1400 *et seq.*

Fogel, A., & Melson, G.F. (1988). *Child development.* St. Paul, MN: West Publishing Co.

Garbarino, J. (1990). The human ecology of early risk. In S.J. Meisels & J.P. Shonkoff (Eds.), *Handbook of early childhood intervention* (pp. 78–96). Cambridge: Cambridge University Press.

Germaine, C. (1979). *Social work practice: People and environments.* New York: Columbia University Press.

Hohmann, M., Banet, B., & Weikart, D.P. (1979). *Young children in action: A manual for preschool educators.* Ypsilanti, MI: High/Scope Educational Research Foundation.

Individuals with Disabilities Education Act (IDEA) of 1990, PL 101-476, 20 U.S.C. §§ 1400 *et seq.*

Individuals with Disabilities Education Act Amendments of 1991, PL 102-119, 20 U.S.C. §1400 *et seq.*

Klein, N.K., & Campbell, P. (1990). Preparing personnel to serve at-risk and disabled infants, toddlers and preschoolers. In S.J. Meisels & J.P. Shonkoff (Eds.), *Handbook of early childhood intervention* (pp. 679–699). Cambridge: Cambridge University Press.

Lewis, M., & Feiring, C. (1979). The child's social network: Social object, social functions, and their relationship. In M. Lewis & L.A. Rosenblum (Eds.), *The child and its family* (pp. 9–27). New York: Plenum.

Louis, M.R. (1981). A cultural perspective on organizations. *Human Systems Management, 2,* 246–258.

Louis, M.R. (1983). Organizations as culture bearing milieux. In L.R. Pondy, P.J. Frost, G. Morgan, & T.C. Dandridge (Eds.), *Organizational symbolism* (pp. 39–54). Greenwich, CT: JAI Press.

McDonnell, A., & Hardman, M. (1988). A synthesis of "best practice" guidelines for early childhood services. *Journal of the Division for Early Childhood, 12,* 328–341.

Miller, P.S. (1992). Segregated programs of teacher education in early childhood: Immoral and inefficient practice. *Topics in Early Childhood Special Education, 11*(4), 39–52.

Moos, R.H. (1976). *The human context: Environmental determinants of behavior.* New York: John Wiley & Sons.

Noonan, M.J., & McCormick, L. (1993). *Early intervention in natural environments: Methods and procedures.* Pacific Grove, CA: Brooks/Cole.

Pettigrew, A.M. (1979). On studying organizational cultures. *Administrative Science Quarterly, 24,* 570–581.

Raver, S.A. (1991). Trends affecting infant and toddler services. In S.A. Raver (Ed.), *Strategies for teaching at-risk and handicapped infants and toddlers: A transdisciplinary approach* (pp. 2–25). New York: Macmillan.

Schein, E.H. (1990). Organizational culture. *American Psychologist, 45,* 109–119.

Schoggen, P. (1989). *Behavior settings: A revision and extension of Roger G. Barker's ecological psychology.* Stanford, CA: Stanford University Press.

Simmons, J.L. (1969). *Deviants.* Berkeley, CA: Glendessary Press.

Snyder, S., & Sheehan, R. (1993). Program evaluation in early intervention. In W. Brown, S.K. Thurman, & L.F. Pearl (Eds.), *Family-centered early intervention with infants and toddlers: Innovative cross-disciplinary approaches* (pp. 269–302). Baltimore: Paul H. Brookes Publishing Co.

Sommer, R., & Wicker, A.W. (1991). Gas station psychology: The case for specialization in ecological psychology. *Environment and Behavior, 23,* 131–149.

Stokols, D., & Altman, I. (Eds.). (1987a). *Handbook of environmental psychology* (Vols. 1 & 2). New York: John Wiley & Sons.

Stokols, D., & Altman, I. (1987b). Introduction. In D. Stokols & I. Altman (Eds.), *Handbook of environmental psychology* (Vol. 1, pp. 1–4). New York: John Wiley & Sons.

Swan, W.W., & Morgan, J.L. (1992). *Collaborating for comprehensive services for young children and their families: The local interagency coordinating council.* Baltimore: Paul H. Brookes Publishing Co.

Thurman, S.K. (1977). The congruence of behavioral ecologies: A model for special education programming. *Journal of Special Education, 11,* 329–333.

Thurman, S.K. (1985). Ecological congruence in the study of families with handicapped parents. In S.K. Thurman (Ed.), *Children of handicapped parents: Research and clinical perspectives* (pp. 35–46). Orlando, FL: Academic Press.

Thurman, S.K., Cornwell, J.R., & Korteland, C. (1989). The Liaison Infant Family Team (LIFT) project: An example of case study evaluation. *Infants and Young Children, 2*(2), 74–82.

Thurman, S.K., & Gonsalves, S.V. (1993). Adolescent mothers and their premature babies: Responding to double risk. *Infants and Young Children, 5*(4), 44–51.

Thurman, S.K., & Widerstrom, A.H. (1990). *Infants and young children with special needs: A developmental and ecological approach* (2nd ed.). Baltimore: Paul H. Brookes Publishing Co.

Vetere, A. (1987). General system theory and the family: A critical evaluation. In A. Vetere & A. Gale (Eds.), *Ecological studies of family life* (pp. 18–33). New York: John Wiley & Sons.

von Bertalanffy, L. (1968). *General systems theory.* London: Penguin Press.

Wheelan, S. (in press). *Complex adaptive systems composed of human agents.*

Wheelan, S., & Abraham, M. (1993). The concept of intergroup mirroring: Reality or illusion. *Human Relations, 46,* 803–825.

Wicker, A.W. (1987). Behavior settings reconsidered: Temporal stages, resources, internal dynamics, context. In D. Stokols & I. Altman (Eds.), *Handbook of environmental psychology* (Vol. 1, pp. 613–653). New York: John Wiley & Sons.

Wicker, A.W. (1992). Making sense of environments. In W.B. Walsh, K.H. Craik, & R.H. Price (Eds.), *Person-environment psychology: Models and perspectives* (pp. 157–192). Hillsdale, NJ: Lawrence Erlbaum Associates.

Wilkins, A.L., & Ouchi, W.G. (1983). Efficient cultures: Exploring the relationship between culture and organizational performance. *Administrative Science Quarterly, 28,* 468–481.

Willoughby-Herb, S.J., & Neisworth, J.T. (1983). *HICOMP preschool curriculum.* New York: Psychological Corporation.

... 2
...

A System in a System
Sociopolitical Factors and Early Intervention

Kathleen M. Hebbeler

At its most basic level, early intervention is an interaction between one or more family members and a representative of a service agency. Many questions about these interactions can be raised: Why this family? Why this particular family member or members? Why this service? Why this setting? Why this service provider from this particular discipline? Why is this particular agency involved? Why did the service provider do what he or she did? How did the service provider know what to do? Why does the interaction last 1 hour and occur once a week? A simple answer to many of these questions is, "because of the unique characteristics of this particular child and family." Yet this answer is incomplete; the rest of the answer can be found in the sociopolitical system.

For purposes of this chapter, the "sociopolitical system" refers to the many social and political forces that interact to shape the delivery of early intervention services. The sociopolitical system includes the laws and regulations that set the parameters for the provision of early intervention; the history nationally, in each state, and at the local level of service provision to infants and toddlers with disabilities; the key players in early intervention at all levels (those who draft and pass legislation at the federal and state level; those who administer early intervention programs at all levels of government; faculty who train early intervention staff; frontline staff who provide services to children and families; and those who advocate for early intervention, including, and especially, families of children with disabilities); and a multitude of factors not directly related to infants and toddlers with disabilities and their families but that are significant influences on the provision of early intervention, such as the economy or society's values and priorities.

The discussion in this chapter of the sociopolitical system is based on a conceptual framework that depicts early intervention services as potentially shaped by myriad interacting factors at multiple levels of influence. The framework categorizes the major influences into those that are directly related to early intervention, such as the federal Part H legislation (Education of the Handicapped Act Amendments of 1986, PL 99-

457), and those that are external, such as the health of a state's economy, that may determine how much money is available for early intervention services. External factors are not connected to early intervention but can influence it significantly.

Figure 1 shows four levels of influence that can shape the early intervention services received by a child and family. These four influences are federal, national (but not related to the federal government), state, and local. The framework depicts a policy passing from the federal to the state to the local level and being susceptible to factors at each of these levels, which is a common theme in studies of policy implementation (Albritton & Brown, 1986; Dokecki & Heflinger, 1989; Elmore, 1979–1980; Greene, 1980). The federal-to-state-to-local policy relationship is often discussed as unidirectional. Within early intervention, however, there are examples of bidirectional influence (e.g., not only did the federal factors influence the state factors but the state factors influenced federal activity). The framework thus shows the potential for influences in both directions.

Examples of potential factors in these four sectors are also shown in Figure 1. The exact nature of the influence of many of these factors has not been well researched; thus, much of the discussion here posits them as hypothesized factors. This list is also by no means exhaustive. Not all factors appear at each level of administration, but many do, such as leadership and funding. Some of these factors are policies, but other factors relate to people (e.g., leadership) or circumstances (e.g., history of service provision). The particular factors shown in Figure 1 are derived from the general literature on policy implementation (Elmore, 1978; Lipsky, 1980; Mazmanian & Sabatier, 1983; Weatherley, 1979); the work of the Carolina Policy Studies Program on state policy development for Part H (Gallagher, 1993; Harbin, Eckland, Gallagher, Clifford, & Place, 1991; Harbin, Gallagher, Clifford, Place, & Eckland, 1993); and the author's work on Part H, especially an evaluation of Part H implementation in California (Chambers et al., 1995; Hebbeler, 1993, 1994).

The nature of early intervention services, however, may be affected by more than the policies directed at it, the players at various levels of government who are implementing those policies, or other factors listed in Figure 1. Early intervention is also pushed, pulled, expanded, and contracted by factors totally outside the realm of early intervention. These are referred to as external factors. Figure 2 shows potential external factors that can shape early intervention. As depicted in the figure, these factors can operate at the federal, state, and local levels.

One way to identify the potential elements of the sociopolitical system is to imagine a factor, such as listed in Figure 1, with a completely different embodiment. What would early intervention look like if funding were doubled? Halved? What would it look like if it were one of the governor's top priorities? What would it look like if services historically had been provided by Agency B rather than Agency A? If no services had ever been provided and the task was to design a comprehensive system to best meet the needs of children and families? If early intervention would look different in some way by changing any particular factor, then it is likely this factor has exerted some influence on the current form of service delivery and is operating as part of the sociopolitical system.

Central to any discussion of sociopolitical influences is the concept of *system* (for further detail, see Chapter 1). *Webster's New Collegiate Dictionary* defines a system as "a regularly interacting group of items forming a unified whole" (p. 1175). Sociopolitical factors interact to create the phenomenon known as early intervention. Understanding the influence of any one factor requires understanding how this factor

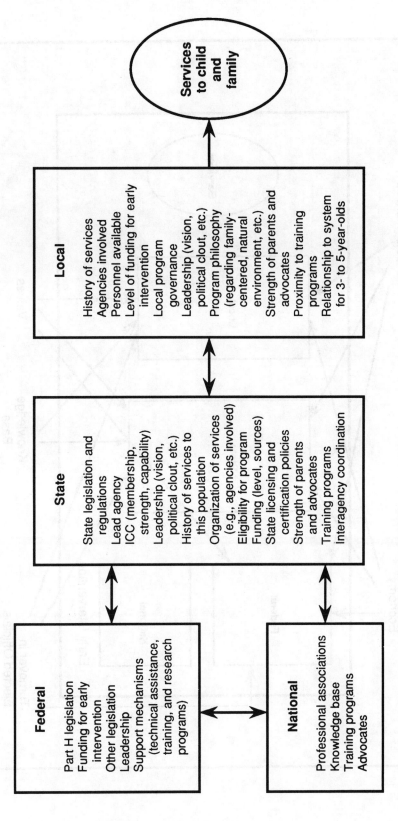

Federal

Part H legislation
Funding for early
intervention
Other legislation
Leadership
Support mechanisms
(technical assistance,
training, and research
programs)

National

Professional associations
Knowledge base
Training programs
Advocates

State

State legislation and
regulations
Lead agency
ICC (membership,
strength, capability)
Leadership (vision,
political clout, etc.)
History of services to
this population
Organization of services
(e.g., agencies involved)
Eligibility for program
Funding (level, sources)
State licensing and
certification policies
Strength of parents
and advocates
Training programs
Interagency coordination

Local

History of services
Agencies involved
Personnel available
Level of funding for early
intervention
Local program
governance
Leadership (vision,
political clout, etc.)
Program philosophy
(regarding family-
centered, natural
environment, etc.)
Strength of parents and
advocates
Proximity to training
programs
Relationship to system
for 3- to 5-year-olds

**Services
to child
and
family**

Figure 1.   Examples of potential sociopolitical influences on early intervention services.

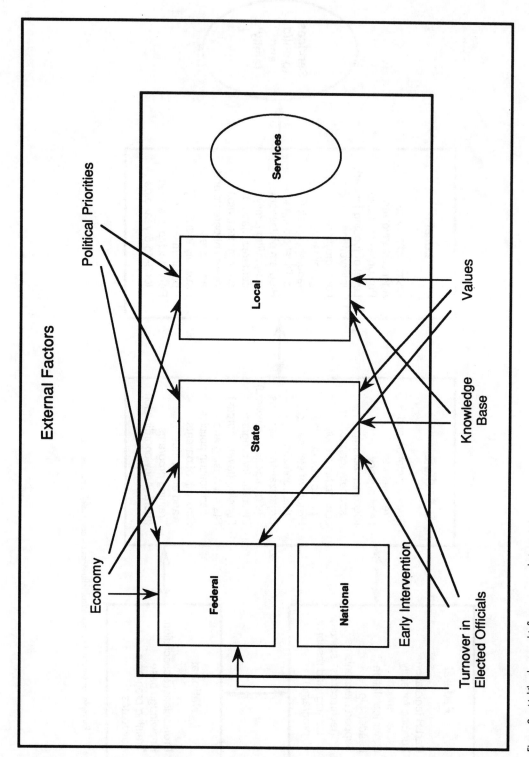

Figure 2. Multilevel external influences on early intervention.

influences and is influenced by other forces. Understanding early intervention involves understanding federal legislation and the corresponding state legislation. Understanding why the federal legislation is worded as it is involves identifying sociopolitical influences on the legislation itself. The same is true for all elements listed in Figure 1. Each has shaped early intervention but also has been shaped by its own particular set of interacting sociopolitical factors.

The interactive nature of the elements in the system means that a change in one element could affect others, often resulting in unanticipated consequences. Figure 3 shows a hypothesized model of how some of the factors might interact to influence the quality and type of personnel available to provide early intervention services.

A second concept is the difference that exists between programs as described in policy and as they are implemented. Early intervention, like any other social program, exists in many forms at many levels. It exists in an idealized form in statute and regulations, in vision and mission statements, in textbooks and training materials. However, the reality often deviates from the ideal. In the ideal, the individualized family service plan (IFSP) was intended to be the written product associated with a partnership between parents and professionals that builds on families' strengths and respects their beliefs and values (McGonigel, Kaufman, & Johnson, 1991). Unfortunately, in reality, a lack of sufficient resources, understanding, or commitment to the intent of the law could reduce the IFSP to a bureaucratic requirement.

Weatherley and Lipsky (1977) used the term "street-level bureaucrat" in a 1970s study of special education implementation. They observed that, although policy is crafted in Washington, D.C., and in state capitals, policy is ultimately controlled at the street level where the program is actually delivered. The researchers noted discrepancies between the provision of special education as written in law and regulation and its provision to children in schools. They concluded that those providing the service ultimately made policy, regardless of what was written in laws and regulations.

The opening section of this chapter presented some general concepts about sociopolitical influences. The second and third sections discuss specific influences on early intervention services. The fourth section addresses three specific facets of early intervention to show how the sociopolitical system has influenced them. Specifically, this section discusses eligibility for services, the personnel providing the services, and transition to a preschool program. The last section briefly describes some factors external to early intervention and their contribution to the current service system.

The power and complexity of the sociopolitical system can go unrecognized by those involved in early intervention at any level. The impacts of factors close at hand may be obvious, but it may be harder to see the influence of more distal factors. However, it is the overall system of sociopolitical factors that explains why early intervention may take one form in one locale and a different form in a different locale. Understanding these factors is not just an academic exercise. Knowing what they are and how they operate is absolutely essential for anyone committed to building a better system of services for children and families.

FEDERAL INFLUENCES

The federal role in early intervention is often considered synonymous with Part H of the Education of the Handicapped Act Amendments of 1986 (PL 99-457). Part H, the Program for Infants and Toddlers with Disabilities, modified in subsequent reauthorizations of the Individuals with Disabilities Education Act (IDEA) of 1990 (PL 101-476)

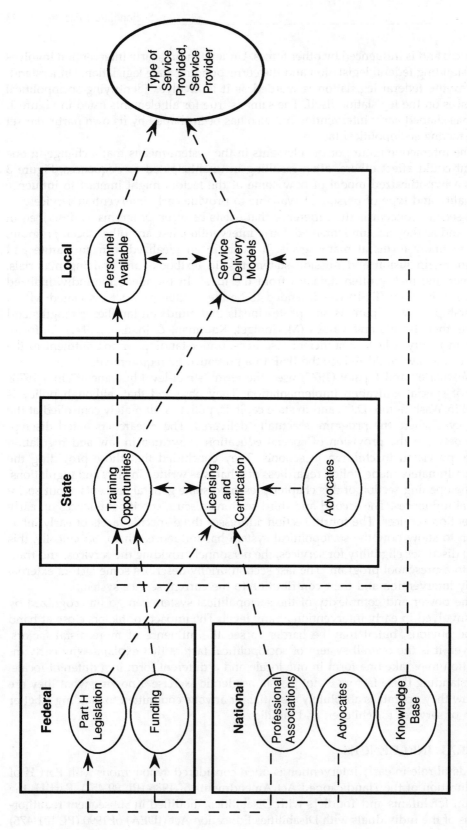

Figure 3. Possible interacting influences on service delivery from factors at multiple levels related to personnel.

24

and the Individuals with Disabilities Education Act Amendments of 1991 (PL 102-119), was intended to fundamentally alter the provision of early intervention services nationwide. The law was designed to make major changes in nearly every aspect of service delivery for children younger than 3 years of age with disabilities and their families. However, the federal influence on early intervention extends beyond Part H and its regulations to encompass federal support for services, technical assistance, training programs, knowledge development in the form of model demonstration programs and research, and administration of these programs by the federal government. The Part H legislation and some other federal influences are described briefly in the following sections.

Part H

Part H was designed to assist states in developing a statewide, comprehensive, coordinated, multidisciplinary, interagency system for infants and toddlers with disabilities and their families. The legislation provides financial assistance for states on the condition that they comply with certain requirements. To receive a grant under Part H, a state is required to name a lead agency for the program, establish an interagency coordinating council (ICC), have the mandatory program components in place (see Table 1), and provide services to all eligible infants and toddlers. PL 99-457 provided a 5-year phase-in during which states could move to full implementation of the law's requirements. This phase-in period was lengthened with the passage of IDEA.

Federal special education legislation had supported various facets of early intervention since the late 1960s (Hebbeler, Smith, & Black, 1991; Smith, 1988). Congress had been funding the development of model demonstration programs for services to young children with disabilities since the passage of the Handicapped Children's Early Education Act of 1968 (PL 90-538). Services for 3- to 5-year-olds with disabilities were included under the Education for All Handicapped Children Act of 1975 (PL 94-142), but were made optional for states. This act did not include services for infants and toddlers. Subsequent legislation provided several different state grant programs to build a nationwide system for services for children younger than 6 with disabilities. By 1986, the political case could be made for mandating free appropriate public education for all 3- to 5-year-olds with disabilities. A House of Representatives report (1986) noted the importance of the early years for later development. The extension

Table 1. Components for a statewide system of early intervention as required by Part H

Definition of developmental delay
Time table for serving all in need
Comprehensive, multidisciplinary evaluation of children and families
Individualized family service plan and service coordination
Child Find and referral system
Public awareness
Central directory of services and resources
Comprehensive system of personnel development
Single line of authority established in a lead agency
Policy pertaining to contracting for services
Procedures for timely reimbursement
Procedural safeguards
Policies and procedures for personnel standards
Data system

of services downward to birth was the next step, although the speed with which the legislation for the extension was drafted, passed, and signed came as a pleasant surprise even to the staunchest advocates (Gilkerson, Hilliard, Schrag, & Shonkoff, 1987).

The influence of Part H on the nature of early intervention services was intended to be all-encompassing. As Dokecki and Heflinger (1989) observed, many hoped that PL 99-457 would be among the watershed events in the social ecology of families of children with disabilities. Harbin et al. (1993) noted that Part H required changes in six major areas of service delivery: 1) the law changed who was eligible for service by moving states from serving some infants and toddlers with disabilities to serving all of them, 2) the law addressed the structure of the service system through its emphasis on interagency coordination, 3) the law promoted a family-centered rather than the more traditional child-centered approach and entitled families to a comprehensive set of early intervention services provided from a multidisciplinary focus, 4) the law changed how services were to be funded by requiring states to coordinate multiple funding sources, 5) the law required states to develop policies including interagency agreements to address this new approach to service provision, and 6) the law required changes affecting personnel to produce a work force qualified to work with this population and trained in a multidisciplinary perspective.

In setting the sociopolitical context for implementation, Part H established aspects of early intervention that would be the same in all states and aspects that would be different. By law, the required program components (see Table 1) would be found in all states. For example, all states would have policies for contracting for services or a data system. The statute also specified the components of the IFSP, and the regulations added some time lines and additional guidance. Thus, in some ways, the federal government set the stage for uniform nationwide implementation.

However, the law also provides for substantial state discretion. First, states can name the lead agency for the program. As of the fall of 1992, 38% had named the education department as the lead agency, 38% had named health, and the rest had named another agency (U.S. Department of Education, 1993). Some states have changed lead agencies since the inception of the program. Second, states have discretion in the determination of the eligible population. States develop a definition of the term "developmentally delayed" and decide whether to include infants and toddlers who are at risk for developmental delay. This has resulted in various eligibility criteria being used by states for determining developmental delay. Furthermore, there is little agreement from state to state on the specific conditions that constitute eligibility for early intervention (Harbin & Maxwell, 1991). By 1994, only 10 states reported that children at risk were included in their eligible population for Part H, although far more had indicated earlier they intended to do so (Harbin & Maxwell, 1991; Shackelford, 1994). Third, states can develop their own personnel standards. All states must set standards, but the content remains the individual discretion of each state. These standards, where they existed, varied before the passage of Part H, and continued variation can be expected (Bruder, Klosowski, & Daguio, 1991).

Part H was also based on hypotheses and assumptions, some of which were unstated or at least unprinted (Gallagher, 1989; Gallagher, Harbin, Eckland, Clifford & Fullagar, 1992). A critical assumption behind its passage was that Part H funds were to be "glue money" rather than support for services (Silverstein, 1989). Part H was passed long after the Great Society programs of the 1960s when the federal government expended large sums of money to expand social services (Garwood, Phillips, Hartman, & Zigler, 1989). The federal government's contribution to providing early intervention was meant to be small because it was assumed that the program only needed to provide financial assistance to allow states to "glue together" the many components of early intervention services that already existed. States were assumed to have services available; the major problem was that services were provided by several different agencies, resulting in duplication and major inconveniences for families. The federal dollar was to be the interagency glue that would correct this problem (Silverstein, 1989).

The events of the 5 years after the passage of PL 99-457 would show the fallacy of the glue money assumption. Many states were not ready to fully implement Part H within the 5-year time line because they could not provide a full array of services to all eligible children (National Association of State Directors of Special Education, 1991). Many states considered discontinuing their participation in the program because they feared the price tag attached to full implementation. Many states needed more than glue; they needed the pieces to glue together.

The relatively low level of funding attached to Part H continues to be of concern among states (Division of Early Childhood, Council for Exceptional Children, 1990; National Association of State Directors of Special Education, 1991). Many states saw Part H as one more federal program with a lot of requirements and very little money. Education agencies, in particular, were sensitized by their experiences with PL 94-142, which had held out the promise of up to 40% of the cost of special education for older children being picked up by the federal government. In fact, the federal government's share has never been more than 8% (Parrish & Verstegen, 1994). For these agencies, the sociopolitical context of Part H included a long and costly experience with previous federal mandates. The key policy question became and remains the following: Could a relatively small amount of money serve as an incentive to states to fundamentally restructure their system of early intervention services and serve all eligible children?

Other Federal Influences

Although Part H constitutes the most visible federal influence on the delivery of early intervention services, it is not the only influence. IDEA also authorizes the Early Education Program for Children with Disabilities (EEPCD), which is the largest single source of discretionary funding for children 8 years of age and younger with disabilities. This program has supported early childhood activities such as demonstration projects, outreach projects, experimental projects, technical assistance, research projects, research institutes, and in-service training projects since 1968, when it was first funded. For example, the National Early Childhood Technical Assistance System (NEC*TAS) is the latest in a series of major technical assistance projects designed to assist states and other entities in providing services to young children with disabilities. The network of professionals that emerged from the early demonstration projects was part of the core that established the Division of Early Childhood of the Council for Exceptional Children (Black, 1990). The EEPCD projects, along with other IDEA programs in research and personnel preparation, have helped establish the infrastructure that made the provision of early intervention possible (Hebbeler et al., 1991). These programs have helped to build the knowledge base, develop and disseminate program models, and establish training programs without which Part H would have been meaningless.

Other federal programs, including those outside the Department of Education, address the needs of the birth-to-3 population (Fraas, 1986; Smith, 1986). A joint study conducted by the U.S. Department of Education and the Department of Health and Human Services (1989) identified 15 programs in addition to Part H with the potential to contribute resources toward a statewide system of early intervention. These programs have legislative authority that includes early intervention services among possible uses of funds or that directly authorizes one or more early intervention services. A second group of programs was identified with legislative authorities broad enough to include projects aimed at improving the quality of early intervention services.

The federal contribution to early intervention services has taken many forms. However, the actual impact of Part H and other federal programs on early intervention is an empirical question for which few data are available. It remains to be seen whether or when the vision of family-centered, coordinated multidisciplinary services for all eligible children and their families will be realized nationwide.

STATE INFLUENCES

Long before the passage of Part H, states were involved in the provision of early intervention services. A few states already had developed comprehensive systems of services with some of the key features later required by Part H. Most state systems were far less comprehensive, however. These varied histories became important to the translation of federal policy to service provision because each state faced the challenge of incorporating the federal vision and requirements into its existing system.

It is difficult to succinctly discuss the sociopolitical system at the state level because states vary widely in the provision of early intervention services. The important elements, for example, history of services or leadership, may be the same from state to state, but the form they take and how they influence local programs differ significantly among states.

Before Part H

The unique constellation of sociopolitical influences in each state produced tremendous variation from state to state before the passage of PL 99-457. Some states had developed relatively comprehensive systems. Some already had mandates to provide services for children with disabilities. Others had very little in place in the way of systems or services (Fraas, 1986; Meisels, Harbin, Modigiliani, & Olson, 1988; Upshur, Hauser-Cram, Shonkoff, Krauss, & Divitto, 1987). These state-to-state variations were extremely important because they would become key sociopolitical factors that would shape the evolution of early intervention in each state (Harbin et al., 1991).

In the year before the passage of PL 99-457, seven states mandated the provision of special education services from birth (Fraas, 1986). In these states, infants and toddlers with disabilities were provided special education and related services and were entitled to all the rights of a school-age child with disabilities. In other states, only infants and toddlers with certain types of disabilities were eligible for special education from birth. In most states, the mandated age of eligibility for special education was 3 years or older. Most states permitted special education to be made available before the age at which services were required (Fraas, 1986). In most states, some infants and toddlers were being served under a second special education program, PL 89-313, Chapter 1 of the Education Consolidation and Improvement Act, State Operated Programs (U.S. Department of Education, 1986).

Special education services were provided through an education agency that was (and still is) only one of the many players involved in early intervention across the states. Both Texas and Massachusetts had legislatively mandated early intervention services but not as special education. Wyoming required health and social services but not education services (Fraas, 1986). A survey of states conducted in 1986 found that states with entitlements had one or two state-level agencies with overall responsibility for the delivery and coordination of services (Meisels et al., 1988). The researchers noted that

> Many other states had no single agency or pair of agencies with primary responsibility for managing intervention services, but relied instead on a loosely defined confederation of stage agencies or even local agencies. In some states, early intervention services were managed by as many as seven different types of agencies all operating semiautonomously. (pp. 160–161)

The study found an average of three to four agencies with primary responsibility for managing birth-to-6 services. These clearly were not well-planned systems designed from the ground up with the interests of children and families in mind.

A case study of the restructuring of early intervention in Massachusetts provides numerous insights into how the sociopolitical forces interact within a state to affect the delivery of services (Meisels, 1985). In this case, the forces interacted to bring about much-needed improvements. In 1982, early intervention programs in Massachusetts were funded by either the Department of Mental Health (DMH) or the Department of Public Health (DPH). Seven state agencies had some formal or informal responsibility for early intervention; 19 federal or state statutes governed these agencies. A recently completed study had concluded that early intervention in the state was beset by problems including fragmented policy, no overall leadership, unstable funding, lack of a mandate for services, high-level officials unaware of the importance of the first 3 years of life, and responsibility distributed among too many agencies with too little administrative, policy, or fiscal direction. As Meisels (1985) pointed out, the public policy context for early intervention in Massachusetts resembled the problems experienced nationwide by many programs for children who were poor, were at high risk, or who had disabilities.

Early intervention service providers were becoming increasingly dissatisfied. One program director sought help from her state legislators and helped to transform early interventionists into an effective political constituency. Meanwhile, a state senator who was a former special educator and children's advocate had become a member of the powerful Ways and Means Committee. He formed a task force to address interagency issues and later introduced a bill to formally establish an interagency coordinating committee. Subsequently, the chair of the Ways and Means Committee became interested in early intervention. He heard the message of the study, the early interventionist, and the state senator on his committee: Early intervention is a cost-effective enterprise that was being impaired by inadequate funding and interagency disputes. His response was to transfer early intervention services out of DMH's budget and into DPH's. DMH had a reputation for weak leadership, lack of accountability, inefficiency, and an unwillingness to follow directions from the legislature. DPH had a clear focus on maternal and child health issues and a respectable administrative reputation. In addition to receiving DMH's funds for early intervention, DPH was also given additional monies for program expansion. The political backdrop against which these events occurred included a state tax-cutting law and a governor who was losing credibility; these events resulted in the Ways and Means Committee becoming extremely powerful. As the budget transfer went into effect, the two senators from the Ways and

Means Committee also introduced a bill mandating early intervention services that became law.

The Massachusetts case study is an excellent example of the sociopolitical system at work. Early intervention in Massachusetts was permanently changed because of the interaction of a unique set of factors, including documented inadequacies in the existing system; a cause that was politically a "winner"; and the readiness of individuals with vision, vested interest, and influence to take action. A good cause was backed by individuals with sufficient political influence to enact change. The Massachusetts case study does not document the impact of the state-level changes on the delivery of services, but the outlook appears considerably brighter. In 1987, Upshur et al. reported that "early intervention in Massachusetts has come to mean an integrated, community-based program of educational, therapeutic, and support services for developmentally vulnerable or disabled children from birth to 3 years of age and their families" (pp. 7–8).

The case study in Massachusetts highlights some of the problems that the federal legislation was designed to address. Few states were like Massachusetts, however, which represented the extreme end of the implementation spectrum before Part H. Many, if not most, states were providing far less in the way of early intervention services. For these states, the challenge of coordinating services across agencies would be faced after the passage of Part H. Thus, when federal legislation that allowed states substantial discretion was placed on 50 unique variations on the early intervention theme, the outcome was considerable diversity in the state systems.

After Part H

Understanding a state's early intervention system requires a grasp of at least three elements: 1) the requirements of the federal legislation, 2) the state's history of services, and 3) the current state sociopolitical context in which early intervention is operating. The first element was previously discussed. Both the second and third elements can be very complicated, as the Massachusetts case study illustrated.

Harbin et al. (1991) conducted case studies of six states during the planning phase for Part H. The researchers identified various combinations of eight factors that served to facilitate or impede the development of Part H policies. These factors were the following: 1) the state's history, including the state's interest in and service to this population, the political support in the legislature for this population, and the continued presence of several key decision makers; 2) the willingness of key people to influence action and state administrators with the needed skills; 3) a shared vision of the desired service system and a set of strategies for moving the state to the vision; 4) a process of policy development that involved multiple levels of agencies and staff; 5) mechanisms for planning and program coordination that existed prior to PL 99-457; 6) a political climate of trust among state agencies and a general political climate of a public commitment to young children; 7) a base of state resources on which to build a system of services; and 8) existing policies that established the process and structure for early intervention programs. The same factor that acted as a facilitator in one state acted as a barrier in another where it was absent. Additional barriers identified included a tradition of local autonomy within the state and certain types of governmental structures, including in some cases the existence of early intervention services before Part H. Taken together, these factors begin to address the complexity behind the success of some states in their attempts to build comprehensive early intervention systems.

Policy development was only the beginning of state activity related to Part H. The ultimate goal was to build or revise the service delivery system to be consistent with the vision of the federal legislation. The sociopolitical factors affected this goal in many ways across the states. Berman (1991) conducted a study of job satisfaction among Part H coordinators and uncovered several important findings about how Part H was being implemented at the state level. Some Part H coordinators had not been given clear directives or allowed to assume responsibility. Some were receiving directives from too many authorities, which is a risk inherent in attempts at interagency coordination. Other problems included bureaucratic red tape and a lack of control over important matters such as budget and personnel decisions. Some Part H coordinators worked for lead agencies that lacked interest in the program or were openly hostile to it. Not surprisingly, Part H coordinators who left their jobs were more likely to report hostile relationships between the lead agency and the ICC than were those who stayed. Advocates were found to be critically important to many Part H coordinators because the lead agency lacked interest in the program and the coordinator lacked access to the legislature or legislative staff, staff in the governor's office, or the media without going through agency officials.

To illustrate the organizational diversity among states in the early intervention system, consider the structure of service delivery in three states in the early 1990s. In Maryland, the lead agency for early intervention was the Governor's Office of Children and Youth. The State Department of Education, the Department of Human Resources, and the Department of Health and Mental Hygiene participated in the delivery and provision of early intervention services. Services also were available through private providers. Local ICCs and lead agencies had been designated in each of the 23 local jurisdictions. In Texas, the ICC served as the lead agency. The Departments of Health, Human Services, and Mental Retardation and the Texas Education Agency participated in the early intervention system. The Council funded 77 local programs through a competitive bidding process. At the local level, agencies such as mental health/mental retardation agencies, local school districts, state schools, and private nonprofit organizations operated early intervention programs. In North Carolina, three state agencies and six divisions within those agencies were involved in early intervention. The lead agency was the Division of Mental Health, Developmental Disabilities and Substance Abuse in the Department of Human Resources. Programs included a network of developmental evaluation centers that provided evaluation and service coordination, a program that provided services to infants with risk indicators for developmental delay, and an intervention program that provided various kinds of early intervention services (Hebbeler, 1993).

As states move to build comprehensive systems, these influences will shape the provision of early intervention services. Factors that facilitate bringing early intervention systems in line with the vision of the federal legislation are competing with factors that advocate the status quo or even reductions in service. The final vision of early intervention service systems remains to be seen.

LOCAL INFLUENCES

In addition to federal and state factors, local sociopolitical factors also affect the interaction between the early intervention system and families. This section discusses three specific facets of early intervention to illustrate some of the ways sociopolitical factors could potentially affect early intervention. Eligibility, personnel, and transition are each discussed.

Eligibility

Eligibility is determined by federal legislation, the state definition of the eligible population, the application of the state's definition at the local level, and the professionals who make up the diagnostic team. These and other factors interact to raise or lower the number of children and families eligible for early intervention.

As mentioned previously, Part H set the stage for state-to-state variation in the eligible population by allowing each state to develop its own definition of developmental delay and to decide whether to include children who are at risk in the eligible population. The result? States use a variety of criteria for determining eligibility. Harbin and Maxwell (1991) found that 16 states used test-based criteria only, 4 states used professional judgment, and 22 states used a combination of test and nontest criteria. There was little agreement among states as to which specific "established conditions" made a child eligible for early intervention. By 1994, only 10 states reported providing early intervention services for infants and toddlers who were at risk (Shackelford, 1994).

Do these differences matter to children and families? Hawaii and Florida reported serving more than 5% of their birth-to-3 population in early intervention in 1991. Twenty-two states served less than 1% that same year (U.S. Department of Education, 1993). The states serving the most children were serving more than five times as many children as the states serving the fewest. State of residence has a great deal to do with whether a family receives early intervention services.

In theory, the same eligibility criteria apply across the state, but it is highly likely that some communities in any given state serve a much higher percentage of their birth-to-3 population. Some of this can be explained by differences in demographics and incidence rates. Other possible contributors are the extensiveness of efforts to locate and serve infants and toddlers with disabilities, the eligibility criteria of local programs, and the shared understanding of the service providers as to which type of children the program serves. Variation from community to community in children served is almost inevitable given the technical and professional problems with identifying developmental problems in very young children (Gallagher, 1993). Families of children with significant or unmistakable disabilities have a high probability of being determined eligible for services regardless of where they live (provided that there are early intervention services). In states serving less than 1% of infants and toddlers in early intervention, the families of children with less severe or less easily identifiable problems may or may not receive services.

Personnel

Qualified personnel are integral to a good early intervention system. A shortage of personnel has been a long-standing problem in early intervention programs, and there is no indication that the situation is improving (Hebbeler, 1994; Meisels et al., 1988). The sociopolitical factors that affect the availability of qualified personnel originate in several different arenas, as was illustrated in Figure 3.

The type of personnel that programs need is determined by the particular staffing model being used. Are services provided by an early intervention team composed of various professionals, such as an occupational therapist, a physical therapist, an infant development specialist, and a social worker? Are services provided by transdisciplinary personnel who consult with specialists? Are services provided by staff who are aides or assistants working under the supervision of a more highly trained professional? The answers to these questions determine a program's staffing needs. The answer to why a particular constellation of staff is used can be found in the social, political, and geographical factors that have influenced the delivery of early intervention services in the community and in the state.

A second arena that affects the availability of qualified staff for early intervention programs is institutions of higher education. The number of training programs, where they are located, how many and what type of professionals they produce, and what skills and knowledge those professionals have are within the sociopolitical realm of colleges and universities. Given that institutions of higher education are responding to a different set of sociopolitical factors than legislators or program administrators, incongruities sometimes arise between the types of personnel universities train and the types of personnel programs need. Gallagher and Staples (1990) reported that fewer than half of the deans of education they surveyed were willing to expand programs for training staff for young children with disabilities. Bailey, Simeonsson, Yoder, and Huntington (1990) found that entry-level students in eight disciplines involved in early intervention received little specialized training in the infancy period or working with families.

Another example comes from the field of physical therapy. According to the Bureau of Labor Statistics, 79,000 more physical therapists will be needed in the United States by the year 2005 (Silvestri, 1993). Early intervention is only one of many areas that compete for these professionals. Despite predictions of severe shortages, the number of graduates from physical therapy programs is barely sufficient to replace those who leave the field annually due to retirement, death, or career changes (Hebbeler, 1994). Early intervention will continue to feel the effects of this shortage.

Another personnel issue is the role of professional standards in controlling the availability of personnel. Ideally, licensing and certification policies operate to ensure that only qualified personnel are practicing in the field. Key players in setting the standards for each discipline traditionally have included professional associations, state staff, and universities. All states have examined or are still examining personnel standards for early intervention personnel because setting personnel standards is one of the required components of an early intervention system under Part H. Each state's decision on standards will be a key sociopolitical factor contributing to the availability of personnel. High standards reduce the supply of personnel; low standards allow unqualified people to provide early intervention. The challenge for each state will be to find the right balance. However states set standards, service delivery at the local level will be directly affected.

Transition

Early intervention services as defined by federal legislation are for infants and toddlers and their families up to the child's third birthday. Upon turning 3, all children who meet the eligibility requirements receive special education and related services through their local school system. Those who do not meet the requirements may receive no services or a more limited set of services than previously received. The experiences of those families who make the transition to special education and of those who do not have been heavily influenced by sociopolitical factors.

One service delivery system exists for infants and toddlers with disabilities and a radically different system exists for 3- through 21-year-olds. The reason why 3- through 5-year-olds are served by school systems and the manner in which they are served are interconnected with the history of the IDEA. Advocates had been pushing for a downward extension of the right to a free appropriate public education for 3- to 5-year-olds for a decade prior to PL 99-457. Congress had responded through a variety of programs designed to move states in this direction (Hebbeler et al., 1991; House of Representatives, 1991). The preschool mandate in PL 99-457 was the successful culmination of the push to extend the rights afforded school-age children to younger children. Part H, however, was a program designed explicitly for this age group. Inadvertently, these two sections of the same legislation made the child's third birthday an event of enormous significance.

What is the impact of having one program for infants and toddlers with disabilities and another for preschoolers? In all likelihood, it depends on where the family lives. Presumably families who live in a state with a mandate for special education from birth or in a state where education is the lead agency for Part H have an easier transition than families in other states. Even in states where the agencies are the same, many other differences remain, including differences in eligibility, differences between the IFSP and the individualized education program (IEP), the absence of service coordination for preschoolers, the emphasis on family-centered programs in Part H, differences in the program year with early intervention operating year-round and school programs operating on a school calendar, and the requirement that preschool services be provided free whereas fees can be charged for services provided under Part H.

Legislative and administrative activity undertaken since the passage of PL 99-457 has been designed to bridge the two programs. Some states have been trying to design "seamless systems" to minimize the transition from early intervention to preschool services (U.S. Department of Education, 1993). Congress amended the preschool provisions of IDEA with PL 102-119 to allow states to include "developmental delay" as an eligible category for preschool services. The amendments also required states to develop transition policies and gave states the discretion of using IFSPs with children ages 3–5 and using preschool grant funds to provide free appropriate public education to 2-year-olds who turn 3 during the school year.

The children and families who make the transition to preschool services are the lucky ones. The families of the children who have grown too old for early intervention and who still need services but are no longer eligible for them are the unfortunate ones. There are no good national data on the frequency of this phenomenon, but there are strong suggestions that it is a reality. Harbin, Danaher, and Derrick (1992) analyzed states' eligibility criteria for Part H and preschool services. They found 27 states in which there was a discontinuity between the two programs' criteria. In addition to inclusion of children who are at risk in Part H only, other areas of concern were preschool criteria that required a higher level of delay, the inability to rely solely on professional judgment for preschool eligibility, the incompatibility of different scoring procedures and instruments used in the two programs, and the possible elimination of disabilities in the eligible preschool population that are difficult to document using test scores.

The differences between early intervention and special education for preschoolers will mean different things to different families. In communities where a seamless system has been implemented, the child's third birthday may be just another birthday. In communities where disjunctures exist, a family may lose their eligibility for service, lose some services, or lose the service providers with whom they are familiar. Sociopolitical activity created two systems; sociopolitical activity now will try to put them together. All families involved in early intervention will experience the outcome firsthand.

EXTERNAL FACTORS

This chapter has focused on sociopolitical factors directly linked to early intervention. However, early intervention, like many other programs, is significantly affected by factors completely external to the program itself. These external factors can have a positive or negative impact. Four such factors are the knowledge of the importance of early development, the general consensus on the need to coordinate human services across agencies, the economy, and turnover in elected officials.

The importance of early experience and early development has been widely recognized in public policy since the 1960s. This shared knowledge that now borders on conventional wisdom bolsters political and public support for early intervention programs. Lessons from research on the importance of the early years were an integral part of the House Report on Part H (House of Representatives, 1986). It was only in 1965, however, that policy makers designed an innovative program called Head Start based on what was then new knowledge about the importance of early experience to later development (Zigler & Valentine, 1979). Head Start and the associated knowledge base on child development paved the way for early intervention for infants and toddlers with disabilities.

Another external factor is the emerging acceptance of interagency coordination and the realization of the problems associated with fragmented services (Kusserow, 1991). Task forces and panels have given credibility to the idea of integrating services across public and private agencies to better meet the needs of children and families (Levy & Copple, 1989; National Resource Center for Family Support Programs, 1993; National School Boards Association, 1991). Early intervention will benefit from its generally positive association with concepts such as interagency coordination and service coordination. (However, early intervention for children with disabilities and their families is rarely cited in the integrated services literature despite a number of philosophical similarities.)

The downturn in the nation's economy in the late 1980s had a significant negative impact on the expansion of early intervention services. Congress was forced to extend the phase-in period for Part H when it became clear that a number of states were unable to achieve full implementation within the 5-year time line (U.S. Department of Education, 1993). Repeatedly, states cited their economies as the reason. The following are excerpts from letters written by governors requesting an extension for Part H implementation (U.S. Department of Education, 1993, pp. 49–50):

> significant economic and demographic hardships have prevented the state from meeting all of the fifth year requirements (Bob Miller, Nevada)

> Given Vermont's continuing austere economic climate, we cannot fully participate in Part H at this time (Howard Dean, Vermont)

> New Jersey is currently facing fiscal hardships and a budget deficit (Jim Florio, New Jersey)

> the fiscal reality in South Dakota does not allow us to proceed this year with full entitlement (George S. Mickelson, South Dakota)

One last example of an external factor that shapes early intervention, especially at the federal and state level, is turnover in elected officials (Harbin et al., 1993). Early intervention is an emerging service delivery system and thus extremely vulnerable to changes in the agendas of political leadership. There is no substitute for support for early intervention from people in positions of influence, and there is no estimating the extent of possible harm when they are no longer in those positions.

SUMMARY

This chapter has discussed some of the possible sociopolitical factors that influence the provision of early intervention services. Some of these factors emanate from the federal government in the forms of legislation, regulations, and financial support for specific types of activities. Some can be traced to state-level influences, including the history of service provision to young children, the political climate, the funding available, and the definition of the eligible population. Some come from institutions of higher education that exert an influence at community, state, and national levels. Others come from associations and advocacy groups that exert influence at a variety of levels. Local programs add their own sociopolitical circumstances. These factors are interrelated at one point in time, but the relationships change as time passes. For example, the passage of PL 99-457 gave a great deal of importance to federal influences, whereas previously state influences had been the most important. Intentional efforts to shape early intervention will continue to encounter enabling forces, opposing forces, and historical accidents. The final outcome for early intervention services remains to be seen. Every aspect of the provision of early intervention services can be changed through action at the appropriate level. Knowledge, vigilance, and persistence are needed to ensure that these changes will be positive.

REFERENCES

Albritton, R.B., & Brown, R.D. (1986). Intergovernmental impacts of policy variations within states: Effects of local discretion on general assistance programs. *Policy Studies Review, 5*(3), 529–535.

Bailey, D.B., Simeonsson, R.J., Yoder, D.E., & Huntington, G.S. (1990). Preparing professionals to serve infants and toddlers with handicaps and their families: An integrative analysis across eight disciplines. *Exceptional Children, 57*(1), 26–35.

Berman, C. (1991). *Job satisfaction of Part H coordinators.* Unpublished doctoral dissertation, Walden University, Minneapolis, MN.

Black, T. (1990). *Early education for all children with handicaps: Eighteen years of getting ready.* Unpublished manuscript.

Bruder, M.B., Klosowski, S., & Daguio, C. (1991). A review of personnel standards for Part H of PL 99-457. *Journal of Early Intervention, 15*(1), 66–79.

Chambers, J., Cook, R., Hebbeler, K., Montgomery, D., Padilla, C., Parrish, T., & Spiker, D. (1995). *Early Start program evaluation: Research plan.* Palo Alto, CA: American Institutes for Research.

Division of Early Childhood, Council for Exceptional Children. (1990). *Public Law 99-457. Early childhood hearings: Recommendations for the Education of the Handicapped Act, Part B and Part H.* Reston, VA: Author.

Dokecki, P.R., & Heflinger, C.A. (1989). Strengthening families of young children with handicapping conditions: Mapping backward from the "street level." In J.J. Gallagher, P.L. Trohanis, & R.M. Clifford (Eds.), *Policy implementation and PL 99-457: Planning for young children with special needs* (pp. 59–84). Baltimore: Paul H. Brookes Publishing Co.

Education for All Handicapped Children Act of 1975, PL 94-142, 20 U.S.C. §1400 *et seq.*

Education Consolidation and Improvement Act (ECIA), PL 89-313, State Operated Programs, 20 U.S.C. §241 *et seq.*

Education of the Handicapped Act Amendments of 1986, PL 99-457, 20 U.S.C. §1400 *et seq.*

Elmore, R.F. (1978). Organizational models of social program implementation. *Public Policy, 26*(2), 185–228.

Elmore, R.F. (1979–1980). Backward mapping: Implementation research and policy decisions. *Political Science Quarterly, 94*(4), 601–616.

Fraas, C.J. (1986). *Preschool program for the education of handicapped children: Background, issues, and federal policy options*. Washington, DC: Congressional Research Service.

Gallagher, J.J. (1989). A new policy initiative: Infants and toddlers with handicapping conditions. *American Psychologist, 44*(2), 387–391.

Gallagher, J. (1993). *The study of federal policy implementation with infants/toddlers with disabilities and their families: A synthesis of results*. Chapel Hill, NC: Carolina Policy Studies Program.

Gallagher, J., Harbin, G., Eckland, J., Clifford, R., & Fullagar, P. (1992, Winter). Policy implementation of services for infants and toddlers with developmental delays. *OSERS News in Print*, pp. 23–26.

Gallagher, J., & Staples, A. (1990). *Available and potential resources for personnel: Preparation in special education: Dean's survey*. Chapel Hill, NC: Carolina Policy Studies Program.

Garwood, S.G., Phillips, D., Hartman, A., & Zigler, E.F. (1989). As the pendulum swings: Federal agency programs for children. *American Psychologist, 44*(2), 434–440.

Gilkerson, L., Hilliard, A.G., Schrag, E., & Shonkoff, J.P. (1987). Commenting on P.L. 99-457. *Zero to Three, 7*(3), 13–17.

Greene, D. (1980). *Local implementation of P.L. 94-142: The crucial role of "boundary crossers."* Menlo Park, CA: SRI International.

Handicapped Children's Early Education Act of 1968, PL 90-538, 20 U.S.C. §621 *et seq.*

Harbin, G., Danaher, J., & Derrick, T. (1992). *Comparison of infant/toddler and preschool eligibility criteria*. Chapel Hill, NC: Carolina Policy Studies Program.

Harbin, G., Eckland, J., Gallagher, J., & Clifford, R., & Place, P. (1991). *State policy development for P.L. 99-457: Initial findings from six case studies*. Chapel Hill, NC: Carolina Policy Studies Program.

Harbin, G., Gallagher, J., Clifford, D., Place, P., & Eckland, J. (1993). *Case study report #2*. Chapel Hill, NC: Carolina Policy Studies Program.

Harbin, G., & Maxwell, K. (1991). *Progress toward developing a definition for developmentally delayed: Report #2*. Chapel Hill, NC: Carolina Policy Studies Program.

Hebbeler, K. (1993). *Data systems in early intervention*. Chapel Hill, NC: Carolina Policy Studies Program.

Hebbeler, K. (1994). *Shortages in professions working with young children with disabilities and their families*. Chapel Hill, NC: National Early Childhood Technical Assistance System, (NEC*TAS).

Hebbeler, K.M., Smith, B.J., & Black, T. (1991). Federal early childhood special education policy: A model for the improvement of services for children with disabilities. *Exceptional Children, 58*(2), 104–112.

House of Representatives. (1986). *House Report #99-860. Report accompanying the Education of the Handicapped Act Amendments of 1986*. Washington, DC: Author.

House of Representatives. (1991). *House Report #102-188. Report accompanying the Individuals with Disabilities Education Act Amendments of 1991*. Washington, DC: Author.

Individuals with Disabilities Education Act (IDEA) of 1990, PL 101-476, 20 U.S.C. §1400 *et seq.*

Individuals with Disabilities Education Act Amendments of 1991, PL 102-119, 20 U.S.C. §1400 *et seq.*

Kusserow, R.P. (1991). *Services integration: A twenty-year retrospective*. Washington, DC: U.S. Department of Health and Human Services, Office of the Inspector General.

Levy, J.E., & Copple, C. (1989). *Joining forces: A report from the first year*. Alexandria, VA: National Association of State Boards of Education.

Lipsky, M. (1980). *Street level bureaucracy*. New York: Russell Sage.

Mazmanian, D.A., & Sabatier, P.A. (1983). *Implementation and public policy*. Glenview, IL: Scott, Foresman.

McGonigel, M.J., Kaufman, R.K., & Johnson, B.H. (1991). *Guidelines and recommended practices for the individualized family service plan* (2nd ed.). Bethesda, MD: Association for the Care of Children's Health.

Meisels, S.J. (1985). A functional analysis of the evolution of public policy for handicapped young children. *Educational Evaluation and Policy Analysis, 7*, 115–126.

Meisels, S.J., Harbin, G., Modigliani, K., & Olson, K. (1988). Formulating optimal state early intervention policies. *Exceptional Children, 55*(2), 159–165.

National Association of State Directors of Special Education. (1991). *Statement to the House Subcommittee on Select Education on the reauthorization of Part H of the Individuals with Disabilities Education Act*. Alexandria, VA: Author.

National Resource Center for Family Support Programs. (1993). *Family support programs and school-linked services.* Chicago: Author.

National School Boards Association. (1991). *Link-up: A resource directory—Interagency collaboration to help students achieve.* Baltimore: Author.

Parrish, T.B., & Verstegen, D.A. (1994). *Fiscal provision of the Individuals with Disabilities Education Act: Policy issues and alternatives. Policy paper #3.* Palo Alto, CA: Center for Special Education Finance.

Shackelford, J. (1994). *State/jurisdiction eligibility definitions for Part H, NEC*TAS Notes.* Chapel Hill, NC: National Early Childhood Technical Assistance System (NEC*TAS).

Silverstein, R. (1989). A window of opportunity. In *The intent and spirit of P.L. 99-457: A sourcebook.* Washington, DC: National Center for Clinical Infant Programs.

Silvestri, G.T. (1993). Occupational employment: Wide variations in growth. *Monthly Labor Review, 116*(11), 58–86.

Smith, B.J. (1986). *A comparative analysis of selected federal programs serving young children: Steps toward making these programs work in your state.* Chapel Hill: University of North Carolina.

Smith, B.J. (1988). Early intervention public policy: Past, present, and future. In J.B. Jordan, J.J. Gallagher, P.L. Hutinger, & M.B. Karnes (Eds.), *Early childhood special education: Birth to three* (pp. 213–228). Reston, VA: Council for Exceptional Children.

Upshur, C., Hauser-Cram, P., Shonkoff, J., Krauss, M.W., & Divitto, B. (1987, August). *A multistate review of early intervention services and programs.* Paper presented at the meeting of the American Psychological Association, New York.

U.S. Department of Education. (1986). *Eighth annual report to Congress on the implementation of the Education of the Handicapped Act.* Washington, DC: Author.

U.S. Department of Education. (1993). *Fifteenth annual report to Congress on the implementation of the Individuals with Disabilities Education Act.* Washington, DC: Author.

U.S. Department of Education & the Department of Health and Human Services. (1989). *Meeting the needs of infants and toddlers with handicaps: Federal resources, services, and coordination efforts in the Departments of Education and Health and Human Services.* Washington, DC: Authors.

Weatherley, R.A. (1979). *Reforming special education: Policy implementation from state level to street level.* Cambridge, MA: MIT Press.

Weatherley, R., & Lipsky, M. (1977). Street-level bureaucrats and institutional innovation: Implementing special education reform. *Harvard Educational Review, 47*(2), 171–197.

Webster's New Collegiate Dictionary. (1979). Springfield, MA: G&C Merriam Co.

Zigler, E., & Valentine, J. (Eds.). (1979). *Project Head Start.* New York: Free Press.

... 3

Funding Context of
Early Intervention

Donald A. Kates

The theoretical basis for the Part H early intervention program of the Education of the Handicapped Act Amendments of 1986 (PL 99-457; reauthorized as the Individuals with Disabilities Education Act [IDEA, PL 101-476] in 1990) was that services and funding for infants and toddlers would continue to be available in many forms. Congress believed all that was needed was a small amount of funds to develop and support systems to publicize and coordinate these resources and to serve as "payer of last resort" when existing resources were not available. Because there is no mandate for or history of government-sponsored education and/or developmental services for all children under 5 years of age, a variety of programs and service systems have been developed to target particular groups of young children and, in some cases, their families. These specialized efforts include Head Start for young children in poor families; prekindergarten classes for children who need extra preparation for public school; Title V Maternal and Child Health (MCH) programs for children with special health care needs; and early intervention programs for children with developmental delays, or who are at risk for developmental delays, and their families.

This chapter first presents a framework of the organizational and economic contexts of early intervention systems. It then discusses various economic forces, and their impact on early intervention systems and the families who qualify for these services, from three perspectives: 1) government funding at the federal, state, and local levels; 2) early intervention providers; and 3) the economic effects on families. Each section reviews the forces that comprise the economic context for early intervention, implications for providing services, examples of family and provider experiences, and some recommendations for maximizing funding resources for early intervention services in light of various economic factors. Two case studies are then presented to highlight the impact of economic forces and funding decisions on families of children with special needs. The final section summarizes the contextual discussion and recommendations for current and future policy makers.

FRAMEWORK

Funding for early intervention can be viewed from both a systemic and an economic framework. Several key components must be in place to assemble a funding system that supports an array of early intervention services. These include public agencies from different levels of government; private agencies and companies, both for profit and nonprofit; coordination mechanisms; and dedication to family-centered services, recognizing that the family is the main decision maker for the team when specifying services needed (see Figure 1). The financing resources that support early intervention programs are a patchwork. Funds are combined from numerous sources, including public and private health insurance (Medicaid, Civilian Health and Medical Program of the Uniformed Services [CHAMPUS], health maintenance organizations, etc.); federal, state, and local education moneys (Parts B and H of IDEA, state and local tax levies, etc.); social services budgets (Title XX Social Services Block Grants, Child Welfare Funds, etc.); private foundations; charitable organizations; and the families of these young children. The array of resources that must be tapped constitutes the core of an early intervention funding system.

The major mechanisms for coordinating these resources are interdisciplinary development of the individualized family service plan (IFSP) and service coordination. Once the child's and family's service needs are identified during the IFSP process, most teams will specify a funding source for each service. In a small number of states the IFSP actually serves to authorize most services, allowing the family and service coordinator to bypass many preauthorization requirements. For example, Louisiana

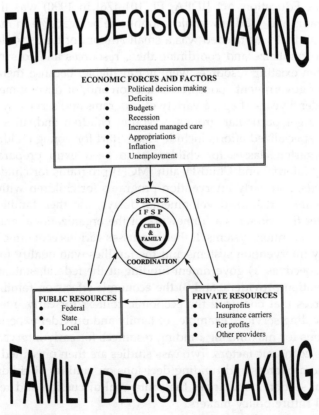

Figure 1. Funding context framework.

uses the IFSP to authorize a number of service categories for Medicaid and other funding sources, including physical therapy, occupational therapy, speech and hearing services, and psychological services (Orloff, Rivera, Harris, & Rosenbaum, 1992).

Through IDEA, both Parts B and H, Congress recognized that parents must join with other experts in child development, medicine, and education in determining what and how services will be provided to themselves and their children. No longer do parents quietly accept the recommendations of physicians and other professionals; rather they discuss and evaluate them in light of their own priorities, concerns, and family resources. Parents also play an important role in decisions about reimbursement of IFSP services. Certain resources are available at parents' discretion (e.g., sliding fees, private insurance) while others are controlled by government decision makers (e.g., Medicaid, Title V MCH Programs, block grants). Family members can affect these policy decisions through voting and lobbying/education activities. Thus, parents play a central role in early intervention funding systems.

In Chapter 1 Thurman defines a system as "a complex set of interacting entities whose collective function forms a synergy" (p. 4). The economic system is based on the production and use of resources, often expressed in terms of dollars or rates of change in amounts of dollars or other resources. The economic system interacts closely with the sociopolitical system in this country, and trends in both are related and often difficult to separate (see Chapter 2 for further details on the impact of sociopolitical factors). Changes in the economic system affect all elements of society and early intervention systems at many different levels.

Federal and state appropriations for Part H programs, and for other programs that support Part H services, are subject to economic influences, such as inflation, recession, deficit levels, and unemployment rates. Other trends, such as the movement toward managed health care and two-parent working families, also change the economic environment and the need for and availability of early intervention resources to support the delivery of services in different locations. Local government revenues and appropriations can also be a major influence, although they may provide pressure in the opposite direction from state and federal effects. For example, a decrease in state budgets may result in the need for increased property taxes to support county or city agencies or school systems, or private agencies may see increased donations and better insurance coverage in a time of lower unemployment. Also, the availability of funding for preservice and in-service training has a direct effect on the quality and quantity of available personnel to provide services to young children and their families.

Individual families are affected by these economic forces in different ways. Unemployment or a disability may force one family to increase their reliance on government assistance and other community resources whereas wise investments in a time of economic growth may increase another family's choices when a family member is identified as having a disability. Therefore, two families who live in the same neighborhood and each have a 6-month-old son with a diagnosis of cerebral palsy will likely use a very different set of resources to provide and pay for a similar set of services.

GOVERNMENT FUNDING

This section examines theoretical principles for the establishment of early intervention programs by PL 99-457 and how these principles are operationalized under various economic and political factors. One principle included the idea that numerous resources were already available for early intervention funding and that families could benefit from increased coordination of these resources (see also Chapter 2). A second principle included the projection of long-term monetary savings for public programs by addressing actual and potential disabilities early in the child's life. Some evidence has been produced to support this theory, and longitudinal studies are now under way to examine it more closely (Clifford, 1991; Clifford, Bernier, & Harbin, 1993). A third principle was that states should be given the option of using family resources (when this would not place a burden on the family) as one source of financing for early intervention services. Approximately one third of the states and other jurisdictions are using or are considering sliding fee scales under Part H (Greer, 1994). The use of sliding fee scales is discussed in a later section of this chapter.

The number of federal programs that can support a portion of each state's early intervention program is large and growing. Table 1 (based on the National Early Childhood Technical Assistance System [NEC*TAS] financing workbook [Williams & Kates, 1991]) shows the array of potential federal resources available to most states. Each of

Table 1. Federal funding resources for early intervention

Department of Education
Individuals with Disabilities Education Act, Part B: Assistance for Education of All Children with Disabilities
Individuals with Disabilities Education Act, Part B: Section 619, Preschool Grants
Individuals with Disabilities Education Act, Part C: Services for Deaf-Blind Children and Youth
Individuals with Disabilities Education Act, Part H: Infants and Toddlers with Disabilities
Chapter 1: Financial Assistance to Meet Special Educational Needs of Children, Part A: Basic Programs Operated by Local Educational Agencies
Chapter 1: Financial Assistance to Meet Special Educational Needs of Children, Part B: Even Start Family Literacy Programs
Chapter 1: Financial Assistance to Meet Special Educational Needs of Children, Part D: Programs Operated by State Agencies, Programs for Migratory Children
Bilingual Education Act, Part A: Financial Assistance for Bilingual Education Programs
Technology-Related Assistance for Individuals with Disabilities Act, Title 1: Grants to States
Department of Health and Human Services
Social Security Act, Title XIX: Grants to States for Medical Assistance Programs, Sections 1901-1926, Medicaid
Social Security Act, Title XIX: Grants to States for Medical Assistance Programs, Sections 1902 (a)(43) and 1905 (a)(4)(b), Medicaid's Early and Periodic Screening, Diagnosis and Treatment Program (EPSDT)
Social Security Act, Title V: Maternal and Child Health Service Block Grant
Social Security Act, Title IV-B: Child and Family Services
Social Security Act, Title XX: Block Grants to States for Social Services
Developmental Disabilities Assistance and Bill of Rights Act, Part B: Basic Grants to States for Planning and Services
Developmental Disabilities Assistance and Bill of Rights Act, Part D: Grants to University Affiliated Programs
Head Start Act, including Early Head Start
Indian Health Care Improvement Act
Public Health Service Act, Title XIX, Part B: Block Grants for Community Mental Health Services
Public Health Service Act, Section 329: Migrant Health Centers
Public Health Service Act, Section 330: Community Health Centers
Stewart B. McKinney Homeless Assistance Act, Title VI-A: Categorical Grants for Primary Health Services and Substance Abuse Services
Stewart B. McKinney Homeless Assistance Act, Title VI-B: Block Grant for Community Mental Health Services
Developmental Disabilities Assistance and Bill of Rights Act, Part C: Grants to Protection and Advocacy Groups
Comprehensive Community Mental Health Services for Children with Serious Emotional Disturbances
Child Care and Development Block Grant
Family Support for Families of Children with Disabilities
Other Federal Programs
Civilian Health and Medical Program of the Uniformed Services (CHAMPUS)
Special Supplemental Food Program for Women, Infants, and Children (WIC), Child Nutrition Act, Section 17

Adapted from Williams and Kates (1991).

these programs has its own eligibility requirements and covered services. Most programs are found within the Departments of Education and Health and Human Services. Many are categorical, providing specific services to a limited number of children and families, whereas others are general (e.g., block grants), giving states more freedom in the use of funds. The number of such programs will vary in reaction to changes in the economic and political environment. A growing economy with an increasing tax base can lead to an increase in social and educational programs. Recessionary pressures and increasing deficits often result in combining federal programs and capping their growth via block grants and program consolidation.

As part of the reauthorization of the Elementary and Secondary Education Act of 1965 (PL 89-10) by the Improving America's Schools Act of 1994 (PL 103-382), Congress merged the Chapter 1, Handicapped Program, into IDEA, Parts B and H. This is a typical example of program consolidation in response to economic and political changes. As a result of the November 1994 election, the change in Congress to a Republican Party majority, and promises of balanced budgets and deficit reduction, this consolidation of federal programs is expected to continue. A similar consolidation process occurred in the early and mid-1980s during the Reagan presidency. For example, many specialized health programs for children and pregnant women were merged into the MCH Block Grant. Although states gained flexibility in operating these programs, the combined appropriation was reduced. As pressures changed in the mid- to late 1980s, due to such factors as inflation and increases in social unrest and poverty, Congress again began targeting appropriations to special populations and very specific programming, such as IDEA, Part H, and Even Start Family Literacy programs.

Many of these trends can be observed by looking at the Medicaid program (Title XIX of the Social Security Act [1965]), which is designed to provide health and medical care to poor families. Medicaid has become the single largest payer of Part H early intervention services (Bergman, 1994). The percentage of a state's Part H participants who are also enrolled in Medicaid ranges from 30% in some states to 80% in others, and many early intervention services are currently being reimbursed by Title XIX in all states.

The Medical Assistance program was enacted in 1965 by the Social Security Act Amendments (PL 89-97) as part of a broad increase in the role of the federal government in financing health and social programs (including Medicare, also enacted by PL 89-97, and the Economic Opportunity Act [PL 88-452] [1964], which enacted Head Start). During the mid-1960s the economy was booming and the federal budget grew rapidly. Despite cyclic changes in the economy the Medicaid program grew steadily through the mid-1990s. In times of economic growth the additions were broad, such as the enactment of the Early and Periodic Screening, Diagnosis and Treatment (EPSDT) Program in 1966, which requires medical and developmental screening and follow-up treatment services for all children enrolled in Medicaid (Social Security Act Amendments of 1967; PL 90-248). During the 1980s, when inflation was high and deficits were rising, Medicaid expansions were more targeted, such as increasing Medicaid eligibility for pregnant women and infants under 1 year of age, mandatory in families up to 133% of the federal poverty level (FPL) and, at state option, up to 185% of the FPL.

Medicaid and its EPSDT program were further strengthened in 1989 to require screening (both comprehensive and partial) for all children enrolled in Medical Assistance programs and treatment for all conditions confirmed by diagnosis. State Medical Assistance programs must both arrange and reimburse for all needed treatment services, including traditional medical and nursing services and therapies as well as health education, nutritional counseling, assistive technology, and other counseling services. These changes have resulted in increasing reliance on Medicaid funding to pay for early intervention services.

There has been an unparalleled growth in the Medicaid program since the mid-1980s as states became increasingly sophisticated in leveraging state dollars to increase the federal Medicaid funds available to serve children with disabilities (Fox & Neiswander, 1990; Orloff et al., 1992; Williams & Kates, 1988). The trend toward Medicaid managed care in many states is a result of the increase in state appropriations for Medical Assistance and is part of cost-containment efforts at the federal and state levels. Early intervention programs are thus facing new impediments in their access to Medicaid. Managed care is also a growing issue for those states relying on private insurance to finance part of this program. In both public and private managed care systems there is a blurring of the distinction between which services can be considered "medical" or "health" as opposed to "educational." Third-party payers cover most health and medical services but do not reimburse for educational services. Several early intervention services can fit into either category, and decisions on whether to reimburse for a given service are being made by these payers independently and repeatedly.

Case Study 1 is an example of the reliance on Medicaid to cover early intervention services in the absence of private insurance.

Case Study 1

The Johnson family consists of the father who works for a local dry cleaner and the mother who is at home with her two children, 6-year-old Jill and Kyle, a funny and smart 2-year-old. Kyle is deaf and has poor gross motor abilities. The father earns slightly more than $16,000 per year, which is about 125% of the FPL for a family of four. The father has insurance for himself for which he contributes $11.50 per month, but he has not signed up for a family policy because he would have to contribute an additional $175 per month. Jill and her mother currently have no private medical insurance. However, as Kyle is under 6 years of age and their family income is less than 133% of the FPL, his parents successfully applied for Medicaid coverage for him. Kyle received an EPSDT screening as well as diagnostic and assessment procedures paid for by Medicaid/EPSDT, which were used to develop an IFSP. Because of his Medicaid coverage and the fact that he has no other third-party insurance, all of Kyle's services except special instruction are being reimbursed by Medicaid. Part H funds are being used for the special instruction as payer of last resort because no other resources were identified to cover that service.

A series of studies by researchers at the Frank Porter Graham Child Development Center at the University of North Carolina, Chapel Hill, is looking at both the public and private resources being used by early intervention programs as well as the long-term financial outcomes for early intervention systems. Data from the Carolina Policy Studies Project on the first 4 years of implementation of state Part H programs show a surprisingly small number of resources being tapped into as a significant payer of Part H services (Clifford et al., 1993). The "new" policy institute is working on a longitudinal study of Part H programs, including the financing of services in three states. This will allow a comparison of funding resources under changing economic conditions.

Administrators of early intervention programs at the state level also face economic pressures that may mimic what is occurring at the federal level or that may work in different directions. For example, staffing levels in key state agencies fluctuate, and a governor and/or cabinet secretary can have a strong influence on various financing options that are under state control. If staffing for Medicaid is insufficient for making changes in the state plan or in procedures for reimbursing services (e.g., during a change in state-level leadership), then access to increased Medicaid funding may be delayed or blocked. This can occur even if sufficient state and local funds are available to match federal Medicaid dollars, and, therefore, increased state appropriations would not be required. Most states are also affected by state taxing policies and traditions. Some states do not impose sales or income taxes, thus limiting growth in state budgets. States such as California and Oregon have been told by voters via ballot initiatives that they must reduce property taxes and state budgets. This can mean that state Part H programs must look to existing resources for growth as more infants and toddlers are identified and qualify for services.

Part H of IDEA is notably different from most other state programs in that it is truly interagency in planning, financing, and service delivery. In all states, some early intervention services are financed or provided by both health and education agencies and, in most states, by the developmental disabilities and Medicaid agencies. Generally one or more additional agencies are responsible for some early intervention services as well, such as child welfare, mental health, social services, and agencies responsible for special populations (e.g., Native Americans, migrants, children who are blind or deaf). To foster collaboration between these various agencies, Congress and the Department of Education require that states use a variety of mechanisms including interagency coordinating councils, interagency agreements, and the involvement of the governor and state legislature.

Sharing or combining funds from different state agencies often proves to be a difficult task. Managers are reluctant to give up any control of their budgets to officials in other agencies. When lead agencies transfer funds to other state departments (e.g., Medicaid to use as state match), they may not receive equivalent value in service reimbursement and thus experience a net loss. If, in the above example, the lead agency designated its own state or local dollars that pay for early intervention services for Medicaid-enrolled infants and toddlers as certified Medicaid match, they would maintain control over all of its appropriated funds while the same services were submitted to the Health Care Financing Administration for reimbursement of the federal share of Medicaid services.

Administrators of local early intervention programs may not have access to the financing resources discussed in this chapter. In some states (e.g., Massachusetts, Tennessee), early intervention is controlled mostly at the state level with relatively little decision-making power at the local level, whereas other states (e.g., Virginia, California) give significant authority to county or regional agencies to operate early intervention programs. In addition, economic or political factors may limit access to certain resources. For example, when a local lead agency for Part H is within a health department or a developmental disabilities agency, some school systems, faced with insufficient funds, may not make educational funds available to early intervention programs. Or, established provider agencies in some communities may try to keep their traditional funding for their staff and facilities, thus lessening the potential flexibility of some funding sources. An intensive educational campaign may be needed to inform service coordinators and providers of the resources that can be garnered to provide early intervention services to infants and toddlers with disabilities and their families.

EARLY INTERVENTION PROVIDERS

Early intervention providers range from independent practitioners (e.g., occupational, physical, and speech therapists) working in client homes, to community facilities such as child care centers, to specialty agencies (e.g., United Cerebral Palsy Associations, The Arc, Easter Seals chapters) and large institutions (e.g., hospitals, school systems) serving one or more communities. Changes in health care delivery and insurance affect many types of early intervention providers. The massive growth in the health care sector of the economy since the 1970s has caused government payers and private insurance companies to make major changes aimed at cost containment and economic survival.

The major trend affecting early intervention (now that all 50 states and the District of Columbia have entered the full implementation phase of Part H) is the move toward increased managed care. A review of growth in managed care activity in the states by the National Governors' Association revealed that many states were addressing similar issues: "A number of states implemented private market insurance reforms, such as restricting the use of preexisting condition exclusions and waiting periods, establishing some form of modified community rating, and ensuring the portability of benefits" (National Govenors' Association, 1994, p. 1). Many states have obtained waivers from the federal government to expand their Medicaid programs to provide coverage for previously uninsured residents and to contain costs through various managed care entities. These include health maintenance organizations, preferred provider organizations, point of service plans, and primary care case management plans.

Providers must now negotiate with many managed care plans to maintain their caseloads. Because providers must now make arrangements to participate in one or more of these managed care plans, often at significantly reduced rates, they may have to see a greater number of children and families to generate sufficient income. They also may need additional approvals from gatekeepers, referral clerks, or case managers who are part of various managed care systems before initiating services, further delaying the onset of services. Parallel changes are occurring in the public and private sectors, leading toward consolidation of providers into a smaller number of larger organizations with a potential improvement in cost containment but a reduction of flexibility in service delivery. Providers must also deal with the everchanging managed care marketplace, both public and private, and frequent changes in the managed care plan in which a given family participates. Many providers are considering adding less costly staff to their teams, such as certified occupational therapy assistants, physical therapy assistants, or speech and language aids, to lower the cost of providing services.

Personnel preparation is another area of concern for many early intervention administrators. Providing specialized services to infants and toddlers with disabilities and their families requires additional training beyond what is covered in many academic programs. Thus, a strong need exists for preservice and in-service training in the particular skills and procedures that are effective for early intervention. However, funds for this specialized training are scarce and unlikely to increase in the economic environment of the mid-1990s. Creative models of personnel training are being developed with funding support from the Early Education Program for Children with Disabilities in the Department of Education. Funding for similar discretionary programs is likewise seriously threatened during times of economic downsizing. When funds for program growth become scarce, many administrators will divert funds from non–direct service purposes to client services. Although this is understandable as a short-term strategy, in the long term there may not be a sufficient number of trained personnel to meet the expected need. The same result can affect other administrative functions, such as monitoring and technical assistance.

In many communities across the country, the majority of early intervention services were traditionally provided by center-based programs run by nonprofit agencies, such as the Easter Seals societies, The Arc, and United Cerebral Palsy Associations chapters. These agencies have met an important need in these communities for a long time. Based on research and demonstrations sponsored by the Department of Education, Office of Special Education Programs (OSEP), and others, PL 99-457 required the principles of family-centered care and least restrictive environments (now referred to as using "natural environments") to be incorporated into all Part H programs (Gallagher, Trohanis, & Clifford, 1989). Although some traditional providers have adopted policies based on the principles of family-centered care and natural environments, a significant number have resisted making the necessary changes to their programs. In some instances, these agencies have retained most of their funding from government as well as private sources to continue to use their facilities and not lay off employees. This usually results in early intervention programs that do incorporate the principles of Part H having to proceed with limited or insufficient funding. In other common scenarios, these providers attempt to use political pressure or other means to influence the establishment of other early intervention programs that incorporate family-centered concepts emphasizing natural environments. Again, the limited funding and other economic factors hinder the ability of these communities to provide the individualized services envisioned by PL 99-457.

ECONOMIC EFFECTS ON FAMILY DECISION MAKING

Families enter the early intervention system in many different ways, bringing with them varying economic resources. This chapter previously discussed one of the principles established by PL 99-457, that numerous resources were already available for intervention funding. This section discusses two other principles: 1) access to and determination of the need for early intervention services must be available at no cost to the family; and 2) lack of resources may never be a barrier to an infant, child, or family member obtaining any needed early intervention service as listed on an IFSP. The first principle means that the following components of the Part H system are provided at no cost to the family: Child Find, evaluation and assessment, the development of an IFSP, service coordination, and procedural safeguards. The second allows parent participation in paying for IFSP services but only if there is federal or state legislation allowing such fees to be imposed and a reasonable schedule of charges. Theoretically, therefore, a family's resources should not be a factor in the early intervention services they receive. However, practical considerations and economic factors play an important role in the development and implementation of IFSPs.

Unlike in Part B of IDEA, under Part H, if families do not want any or all early intervention services for themselves or their young children, then they will not be provided. Because parents have this right to refuse any service, they also can decide whether to use their own funds to reimburse according to a sliding fee schedule. If parents decide that they disagree with the early intervention program's determination of their ability to pay, then they can decline one or more of the services discussed during the IFSP meeting. As long as the early intervention program can document that the family has sufficient resources to pay for the service, it has no further obligation to provide the service. However, if there is some question or dispute regarding ability to pay, then the early intervention program must pay for the service until the question is answered or the dispute resolved.

The important distinction to be made is whether the family is "unable" or "unwilling" to participate financially in paying for IFSP services. "Unable" to pay means that, even when the criteria used in a sliding fee scale indicate a financial obligation on the part of the family, other factors felt to be important by the family preclude the use of limited resources in this way. "Unwilling" to pay means that, even though the family has sufficient resources, they voluntarily choose not to pay for early intervention services. In the first case, Part H requires that the service must be provided (services cannot be denied based on an inability to pay). In the second situation, the early intervention program does not have an obligation to provide services. The distinction between "unable" and "unwilling" remains a difficult concept to operationalize. Who has the authority to make this distinction? At what level should it be made? How much personal information may and must be collected from the family? Although a few states are attempting to address these issues, they have not developed satisfactory answers to date. Because only a few states have instituted sliding fee scales (Greer, 1994), it will be some time before all states arrive at practical solutions to these problems.

Discussions with family members in Pennsylvania (which does not use sliding fee scales) and Indiana (which is planning to implement a system of charges and sliding fees) revealed some surprising information. Many families in both states said that fees should be charged as long as they do not become a hardship or barrier for the family. Some families expressed their feelings that people place more value on something they pay for than on something given to them. Others feel just as strongly that families of children with disabilities or delays have enough problems and extra costs to handle and that the government-sponsored Part H program should not impose any additional financial burdens on the family.

Another difficult issue is the use of private insurance to collect reimbursement for early intervention services. Again, for the purpose of this discussion, a distinction must be made between the five services that must be provided at no cost to the family (Child Find, etc.) and early intervention services listed on the IFSP that may require a family to participate financially. For the first group of services, Part B is illustrative because all services under Part B must be provided at no cost to the family. Both federal court rulings (*Chester County Intermediate Unit v. Pennsylvania Blue Shield*, 1990; *Shook v. Gaston County Board of Education*, 1990) and OSEP policy interpretations (*Federal Register*, 1980) agree that a family's private insurance can only be tapped when it can be demonstrated that there will be no cost of any kind to the family. Costs are defined as including deductibles, copayments, reduction of annual or lifetime caps (on any category of services or total dollars), and increases in premiums. It is not sufficient to cover copayments and deductibles incurred by families if there will be other costs incurred by the family. And if a family with an indemnity insurance plan has no obligation to pay for early intervention services (due to the "no cost to families" provision), then the insurance carrier is not obligated to reimburse for those services. (Indemnity plans cover only those costs that would otherwise be incurred by the family.) Therefore, private insurance is not a significant source of revenue for Child

Find, evaluations and assessments, development of the IFSP, service coordination, and procedural safeguards.

However, health care insurance plans can be a significant source of revenue for early intervention programs in some states. If a schedule of charges and a sliding fee scale is in place, then many families will have an obligation to pay part or all of the cost of the services. When these same IFSP services are covered by the family's private insurance, then the indemnity plan will be responsible for some or all of the cost of those services. The family then has the choice of allowing their insurance carrier to be billed or of paying for the services themselves. This policy is now under review by OSEP.

Public programs such as Medicaid present a different set of issues. As discussed earlier in this chapter, Title XIX can be used to pay for most early intervention services. Although parent approval to bill Medicaid is not required (or even allowed), it should be listed as a source of payment for each covered service included on an IFSP. When an infant or toddler has both Medicaid and private insurance, Medicaid cannot be billed for any service covered by the insurance policy. The decision on whether to bill Medicaid must be made separately for each IFSP service. In situations in which families or young children have dual coverage, the family or provider must document for Medicaid that the service is not reimbursable under the health insurance policy. This can be done by furnishing a copy of the policy or a written refusal to reimburse for a given service (via a claims denial form or letter) from the insurance carrier.

Decisions on resource utilization are best made by families as part of the IFSP development process. When fees are not charged and private insurance is not available as a significant payer of early intervention services, the responsibility for identifying a funding source for each service listed on the IFSP must be assumed by the early intervention program through the family's service coordinator. However, when fees may be charged and the family's insurance coverage includes some early intervention services, the family must share the responsibility for specifying a funding source for each IFSP service. If the family has an obligation under a sliding fee scale, then, for each service they choose to list on their IFSP, they must decide whether to pay for the services themselves, seek reimbursement from their insurance carrier, or determine if another public or private resource is available. The availability of government programs varies with changes in the economy. When economic forces such as a recession result in higher levels of unemployment or decreased personal savings, family resources will decrease and fewer families will be assessed charges through application of a sliding fee scale. Lower levels of family resources are usually associated with increased pressure on public programs to serve more individuals and families without concurrent increases in their budgets. The job of the service coordinator of identifying resources for each IFSP service becomes even more difficult.

To allow timely identification of funding services during the IFSP process, a great deal of information must be easily accessible to the service coordinator. The NEC*TAS financing workbook (Williams & Kates, 1991) recommends several methods for making information on financing resources readily available to service coordinators. First, there must be initial and ongoing training provided on financing issues and resources. Some states have specific staff in place centrally or regionally to accept telephone or on-line inquiries concerning sources for providing or reimbursing IFSP services. This information can also be provided on a computer disk or in a loose-leaf notebook format that the service coordinator can use during IFSP meetings. The Family Centered Financing Project in Richmond, Virginia, has produced such a binder for use by early intervention service coordinators in Richmond and other Virginia communities (Buck & Yoder, 1993). As resources and priorities change in response to economic and political pressures, these resource compilations must be updated and distributed to all users. The availability of this type of information during the IFSP process helps make family participation in the process of selecting providers and funding sources possible.

Economic and financial factors can affect the provision of family-centered care. For example, the cost of providing a service is generally less in an early intervention facility than delivering the same services in a home, child care setting, or other community setting. By setting differential rates for center- and community-based services, the full cost of both can be met. An alternative is to reimburse directly the provider's time and expenses for travel to deliver community-based care. If a state wants to discourage facility-based services and encourage home-based delivery, it can set the community rate at cost while setting the facility-based rate at just below cost. (Setting rates at above the actual cost to provide a premium in certain situations is not advised because Medicaid and most other third-party payers will not reimburse at a rate higher than the actual cost of delivering the service.)

When a child turns 3 and must prepare for transition from an early intervention program to a preschool special education program (if he or she qualifies) or another program in the community, the family must adjust to a new set of rules. Families are not required to assume any of the costs of special education and related services. However, schools can and should tap into other community resources, such as Title V MCH, Medicaid, and private agencies, to cover some of the cost of providing special education-related services. Many non-school programs will require families to pay for services, either at full cost or according to a sliding scale. Families who have been part of the process of assigning financial responsibility for IFSP services will be better prepared to make similar decisions as their child grows older.

CASE STUDIES

Case Studies 2 and 3 exemplify the range of funding options available through early intervention systems and the types of decisions faced by families and professionals in determining how to fund implementation of IFSPs.

Case Study 2

Jason is an attractive 15-month-old boy living with his mother in an urban community. His father moved out of state before Jason's birth and provides no financial support to Jason or his family. His mother works 28 hours per week at the neighborhood grocery store, earning about $800 per month. She exchanges child care with her sister who lives nearby and works evenings and weekends. Jason was born prematurely at 30 weeks' gestation. Following a lengthy hospitalization and daily visits to be with her son, Jason's mother is pleased with his development. He enjoys the limited interaction he has with his cousins. He held up his head without support at 9 months and just recently began to sit up alone. He has not begun crawling yet. He is generally withdrawn from his social surroundings and exhibits poor eye contact. His developmental delays in both the gross motor and emotional domains qualify him for Part H services. An interdisciplinary team recommends physical therapy two times per week at 30–45 minutes per session and psychological services once per week for 45 minutes to provide developmental guidance and strategies to strengthen parent–child interaction.

Although Jason's mother's income is too high for her family to qualify for either Aid to Families with Dependent Children or Medicaid, Jason can qualify for Medicaid benefits for himself only because the family income is less than 133% of the FPL and he is under 6 years of age. When his service plan is sent by the pediatrician at the community health center to Medicaid for approval before initiating services, the response is mixed. Medicaid indicates that it would reimburse for two units of physical therapy per week. Because the state's Medicaid policy allows services to be delivered in private homes and other locations in the community, the IFSP team accepts Jason's mom's suggestion that the physical therapist come once a week to the home and once a week to her sister's home. This way both caregivers can follow up with appropriate activities between visits.

The psychological services for Jason are determined not to be medically necessary by the state Medicaid office and, therefore, not reimbursable by Medicaid. The service coordinator knows that similar psychological services are reimbursed by a neighboring state's Medicaid program, but because the responsibility for determination of medical necessity is given by federal statute to the states, she cannot argue or appeal her state's decision. The outpatient center of the local hospital can provide the psychological services in Jason's IFSP but cannot cover the cost. The service coordinator checked several other options, including a community mental health center and a family services agency to see if they could provide or reimburse for the needed services, but she drew a blank. Thus, federal Part H funds were made available under the payer of last resort provision to the hospital outpatient center.

Case Study 3

Latitia is a cheerful 21-month-old girl living with her parents in a suburban community. Both of her parents work full time in white-collar positions for medium-size firms. Their annual income is approximately $40,000. Latitia spends 4 days per week with a neighbor who runs a licensed child care home. Latitia enjoys running around with other children in the neighborhood and is often seen mimicking their actions. Latitia has frequent episodes of otitis media and currently exhibits a mild to moderate hearing loss. She has no expressive language, limited use of gestures to communicate, and minimal receptive language. She also has fine motor delays of 6–8 months. After finding Latitia eligible for early intervention services, the multidisciplinary assessment team determined that she needs 30 minutes of speech therapy twice a week and 30 minutes of occupational therapy once a week. In addition, an audiologic evaluation every 3 months is specified.

The decisions concerning the funding of Latitia's IFSP are also complicated. When her family's income and resources are applied to the county's sliding fee scale, the family is responsible for 75% of the cost. Checking the insurance policy provided by the father's company reveals that the occupational therapy is covered but the speech therapy and audiologic testing are not. Latitia's family decides not to use any of their lifetime health insurance coverage (which is capped at $500,000). They are concerned that the otitis media will continue and that she will require surgery and other potentially expensive medical care. In addition, they feel that 75% of the cost of occupational and speech therapy is more than they can afford. Latitia's older brother has learning disabilities and attention-deficit/hyperactivity disorder. When this is taken into account and expenses for the brother's medicine and other health care are subtracted from the family's available resources, they are found to be responsible for only 40% of the cost of early intervention services.

The funding specialist from the regional early intervention office is asked to review the case to determine if any other resources may be available. The state school for the deaf operates a regional hearing screening program and will perform an audiologic assessment every 3 months at no cost to the family. The local United Cerebral Palsy Associations chapter has a small endowment that it agrees to use for occupational therapy if the family can bring Latitia to their center once a week. As Latitia's mother is home on Wednesdays, she agrees. The family then agrees to pay their share of speech therapy services, which are provided twice a week in the child care home.

SUMMARY

Although significant new appropriations for early intervention programs and services are always welcome, they are not likely in times of economic downsizing. Reducing the deficit, balancing the budget, and maintaining budget levels for essential government functions (Social Security, defense, debt payment, etc.) all will work to produce level or reduced appropriations for federal programs that provide or reimburse early intervention services and to create pressure in state legislatures to maintain services without increasing taxes. Increases in property taxes, often the largest source of revenue for cities and counties, have been prohibited by voter referenda in many states. In difficult economic times, families often cannot make up the losses from reduced government spending from their own resources. Thus, maximizing existing revenue is essential if the early intervention needs of young children with developmental delays and their families are going to be met.

The single largest source of funding for early intervention services is the Medicaid program. Many potential changes are being discussed at the state and federal levels due to the unparalleled growth in state Medicaid expenditures and their effect on state budgets. States that can identify existing state or local tax revenue to serve as a match for federal Medicaid funds will be able to bring in more federal dollars without increasing the states' line item for matching funds. For infants and toddlers who have both Medicaid and private insurance coverage, all services must be submitted to the insurance carrier for reimbursement before billing Medicaid. If the insurance company does not pay or if it can be demonstrated that the policy does not cover a particular service, then that service can be reimbursed by Medicaid. (These decisions can be made on a service-by-service basis for each child.)

The one change that is under way and sure to continue is the adoption of managed care approaches to health services delivery. To continue using Medicaid to the same degree, all of the agencies participating in a state's early intervention program must work collaboratively with the state's Medicaid agency to ensure that early intervention services are included in all managed care contracts and capitation rates set for young children. Those states that are reimbursing (or planning to reimburse) early intervention services outside of their managed care systems should look at this as a short-term solution. If managed care meets its goals of cost containment, then services are not likely to remain available on a fee-for-service basis.

Both families and providers will have to adapt to private and public managed care systems for early intervention and other needed services. Providers will likely need to negotiate rates with a number of plans and learn to work with their gatekeeping mechanisms. Families will have to inquire about which services are covered, and to what extent, before selecting a managed care plan and may need to advocate for coverage of early intervention services they believe are necessary.

The decision to establish a schedule of charges and a sliding fee scale will allow a state's early intervention program to collect a small amount of money from families and simultaneously to tap into the private insurance resources of these and other families. Some states use differential rate schedules to provide incentives for delivering services in natural settings such as homes, child care centers, and other locations in the community. Other important resources in most states include Title V Services for Children with Special Health Care Needs; the Child Care and Development Block Grant; Even Start; the Special Supplemental Foods for Women, Infants and Children (WIC) Program; and voluntary agencies such as Easter Seals, United Cerebral Palsy Associations, and The Arc. States with significant ethnic populations or other groups of families in need of early intervention services may use specialized resources such as CHAMPUS, Migrant Health and Education Programs, and the Indian Health Service.

Families and service coordinators must work together to learn about and understand the array of potential resources for early intervention services in their communities. Because each child and family has their own sets of strengths, priorities, and concerns, distinct and separate IFSPs must be developed for each. Because personal and community resources also differ in each situation, the funding resources identified and selected for each IFSP service will also differ. When various economic factors result in decreased personal resources for families, the pressure to identify and use more community funding sources increases. Under any economic scenario, the process of joint family/professional meetings to develop an IFSP must be used to allow families a choice in what services will be provided and how each of these services will be reimbursed.

REFERENCES

Bergman, A. (1994). *Testimony respectively submitted to the U.S. House of Representatives, Committee on Education and Labor, Subcommittee on Select Education and Civil Rights at a hearing on the impact of health care reform on individuals with disabilities*. Washington, DC: United Cerebral Palsy Associations, Inc.

Buck, D., & Yoder, T. (1993). *Optimizing financial resources for family centered early intervention services: A guide for local interagency coordinating councils*. Richmond: Virginia Institute for Developmental Disabilities.

Chester County Intermediate Unit v. Pennsylvania Blue Shield, 1990 U.S. App. Lexis 2692 (3d Cir. 1990), *aff'g* 1988–89 Educ. for the Handicapped L. Rep. (CRR) 441:535 (M.D. Pa. 1989).

Clifford, R. (1991). *State financing of services under P.L. 99-457, Part H*. Chapel Hill: University of North Carolina, Carolina Policy Studies Program, Frank Porter Graham Child Development Center.

Clifford, R., Bernier, K., & Harbin, G. (1993). *Financing Part H services: A state level view*. Chapel Hill: University of North Carolina, Carolina Policy Studies Program, Frank Porter Graham Child Development Center.

Economic Opportunity Act of 1964, PL 88-452, 42 U.S.C. § 2701 *et seq.*

Education of the Handicapped Act Amendments of 1986, PL 99-457, 20 U.S.C. § 1400 *et seq.*

Elementary and Secondary Education Act of 1965, PL 89-10, 20 U.S.C. § 2701 *et seq.*

Federal Register. (1980). *Nondiscrimination on the basis of handicap in programs and activities receiving or benefiting from federal financial assistance; and assistance to states for education of handicapped children*, 86390 (34 CFR Part 104 and 300).

Fox, H., & Neiswander, L. (1990). *The role of medicaid and EPSDT in financing early intervention and preschool special education services*. Washington, DC: Fox Health Policy Consultants.

Gallagher, J., Trohanis, P., & Clifford, R. (Eds.). (1989). *Policy implementation & PL 99-457: Planning for young children with special needs*. Baltimore: Paul H. Brookes Publishing Co.

Greer, M. (1994). *Part H sliding fee survey*. Unpublished manuscript, Indianapolis, IN.

Improving America's Schools Act of 1994, PL 103-382, 20 U.S.C. § 630 *et seq.*

Individuals with Disabilities Education Act (IDEA) of 1990, PL 101-476, 20 U.S.C.A. § 1400 *et seq.*

Kates, D. (1990). *NEC*TAS information packet on the financing of early intervention and preschool services.* Chapel Hill: University of North Carolina, National Early Childhood Technical Assistance System, Frank Porter Graham Child Development Center.

Medicaid Early and Periodic Screening, Diagnosis and Treatment Program Act of 1966, 42 U.S.C. § 1396 *et seq.*

Medicaid Early and Periodic Screening, Diagnosis and Treatment Amendments of 1989, Omnibus Budget Reconciliation Act of 1989, PL 101-239, 42 U.S.C.A. § 1396 *et seq.*

Medical Assistance Fund of 1965, PL 85-97, 42 U.S.C. § 1396 *et seq.*

National Governors' Association. (1994). *Update: state progress in health care reform.* Washington, DC: Author.

Orloff, T., Rivera, L., Harris, P., & Rosenbaum, S. (1992). *Medicaid and early intervention services: Building comprehensive programs for poor infants and toddlers.* Washington, DC: Children's Defense Fund.

Shook v. Gaston County Board of Education, 882 F.2d 119 (4th Cir. 1989), *cert. denied,* 58 U.S. L.W. 3528 (1990).

Social Security Act Amendments of 1965, PL 89-97, 42 U.S.C. § 101 *et seq.*

Williams, S., & Kates, D. (1988). *Using Medicaid to increase funding for home and community-based mental health services for children and youth with severe emotional disturbances.* Washington, DC: Georgetown University Child Development Center.

Williams, S., & Kates, D. (1991). *NEC*TAS financing workbook: Interagency process for planning and implementing a financing system for early intervention and preschool services.* Chapel Hill: University of North Carolina, National Early Childhood Technical Assistance System, Frank Porter Graham Child Development Center.

... 4
Culture as a Context
for Early Intervention

Aquiles Iglesias and Rosemary Quinn

Early intervention services are provided in a variety of organizational settings that are embedded in a much larger sociocultural environment. In each of these settings, a set of loosely shared values and beliefs—a culture—guides the action of participants. This organizational culture emerges as members (parents and staff) accept, accommodate, or reject the values and beliefs that are brought to a particular setting. The culture is neither a monolithic nor a static entity but rather is composed of multiple loci of shared values and beliefs. These multiple loci of agreement lead to similar perspectives when viewing particular events and, as a consequence, result in similar actions. Harmony exists when the culture of the organization and the subcultures of its members are similar. However, the potential for conflict increases when the values and beliefs that lead to successful actions within an organization are inadequate or inconsistent with those needed by its members to function adequately in other environments. Rather than allowing potential differences to escalate into conflict, attempts to understand these points of differences and, where possible, to accommodate these differences should be made. In no place is this need for understanding and accommodation more evident than in the area of early intervention.

Changes in the demographic characteristics of the U.S. population and legislative and judicial mandates have resulted in the increasing number of cross-cultural and, sometimes, cross-linguistic encounters faced by early intervention professionals and by the families served by these professionals. These experiences have greatly increased since the 1960s as a result of three co-occurring trends:

1. Futurists predict that by the year 2080, Americans of European descent will likely be the largest minority in the nation (Bouvier & Gardner, 1986; Spencer, 1984). In 1996, in one U.S. state, in 25 cities, and in numerous counties, the "minority" population represents more than half of the total population. Given that the birth rate of the minority population is presently 50% higher than that of the general population (Public Health Service, 1990), the minority population should increase faster than the majority.

55

2. Racial-ethnic minorities are overrepresented in statistical categories that may place their infants at higher risk for disabilities or developmental delays (Center for the Study of Social Policy, 1994). The U.S. minority population is younger, poorer, and less educated than the majority. Minority women bear more children at younger ages, are more likely to be single parents (Bureau of the Census, Ethnic and Hispanic Branch, 1988), and often receive late or no prenatal care (National Center for Clinical Infant Programs, 1986).

3. Federal laws more frequently mandate service providers to incorporate diverse linguistic, social, and cultural factors into service delivery practices. Relative to early intervention, Part H of the Education of the Handicapped Act Amendments of 1986 (PL 99-457; reauthorized as the Individuals with Disabilities Education Act [IDEA], PL 101-476, in 1990) mandated that families play an active role in the multidisciplinary team. The individualized family service plan (IFSP), which lists intervention goals for the child and family, is to be generated by service delivery professionals in collaboration with family members, many of whom are members of nonmainstream cultural-linguistic minority groups.

To a large extent cross-cultural/linguistic encounters have always existed, but they have been neither seen with such frequency nor reacted to with such sensitivity. The increasing awareness that differences, across and within cultural-linguistic groups, need to be accounted for has led to a rethinking of previous practices that unwittingly defined "good" interventions as those in which the clients incorporated the values, beliefs, and behaviors congruent with middle-class European American culture. The challenge posed to early interventionists is how to provide intervention programs that are consistent with the research literature, based on professional knowledge, and at the same time respect the culture of the families who are served. This challenge is not unidirectional. Families must also understand the perspective of the professionals if they are to develop a partnership in early intervention.

The process of providing culturally sensitive programs begins with professionals becoming aware of and sensitive to their own cultural heritage and how their own biases can affect interactions with others and approaches to assessments and interventions. The process further requires a familiarization with the literature on cultural variations and a value of and respect for differences. Finally, providers need to gain the skills necessary to implement cross-cultural intervention programs.

THE CULTURAL FRAMEWORK

A person is usually defined in terms of what he or she values and how he or she acts. These values and ways of being are deeply rooted and culturally based. This cultural framework is dynamic and changing and is the result of adaptations that individuals make to various social, economic, and physical environments. An examination of personal values, beliefs, and choices is the first step in developing a philosophy conducive to culturally sensitive, family-focused intervention.

Values and beliefs, which are deeply ingrained in each culture, serve as a template to guide a person's actions and judgment of the action of others. This alterable template begins to develop in the home and continues to expand and change throughout life. The development of this template evolves as a result of the social interactions in which children and their significant others engage, what Rogoff (1990) refers to as guided participation. During this period, children learn the cultural norms of their community—that is, the rules of appropriate behavior as well as the values and beliefs that underlie overt behavior. The children's acquisition of these skills is gradual and undergoes transformation as a function of the social and cognitive demands they encounter in various social situations.

The moment children enter any kind of formal program (early intervention, preschool, kindergarten) the specific goal of the socialization process changes. Rather than learning the cultural norms of their community, children are often expected to learn and abide by the cultural norms of the programs, which are too often consistent only with the values, traditions, and expectations of the dominant group in the society (Iglesias, 1994). Neither the social and cognitive skills nor the process by which this array of skills is acquired is universal (Garcia-Coll, 1990; Lin & Fu, 1990). Early interventionists must acknowledge these multiple paths as well as the fact that competency should be decided by the individuals receiving services, taking into consideration their communities and the adaptations required to function within them. This self-determination is the true meaning of empowerment.

Providers may at times assume that certain features of their socialization are part, or should be part, of the socialization process of other people. This ethnocentric view often leads to the postulation of certain hypotheses on what constitutes "adequate" socialization practices. For example, it might be assumed that mother–child interactions should be child centered (follow the child's lead) or that parents should be active participants in all interactions (encourage parents to be active participants in daily interactions with their children). Although these aspects of child socialization might be consistent with the providers' experiences, they are not necessarily consistent with the socialization practices of other families and other cultures (Heath, 1982; Ochs, 1983). Asking families to follow the providers' "path" has the potential for creating conflict and stress, especially when the behaviors are incongruent with the families' socialization practices or when these behaviors are maladaptive for their particular community.

A philosophy that supports and enables culturally sensitive, family-focused practices would minimally incorporate self-awareness of values and beliefs about a variety of family-related issues; the knowledge that families are uniquely composed of individuals and that this uniqueness influences how they define and adapt to events; and a commitment to honoring family diversity and an array of family definitions, styles, and coping strategies through intervention practices.

Broadening the Cultural Framework

Legislative and judicial mandates tend to focus on statistically "at-risk" groups, with the dimensions most often used to define these groups being racial/ethnic, economic, and linguistic. However, too often in research and in practice it is forgotten that children are not "at risk" but rather that they are members of "statistically at-risk" groups. Variations in skin color, wealth, and fluency in the language spoken by the majority are not, in and of themselves, challenging conditions to be overcome. By themselves, these characteristics present no risk for maladaptive behavior. However, statistical data suggest that some groups of individuals who share any of these characteristics have a higher than average probability of negative outcomes. Because the individual characteristics are not the cause of the undesirable outcome, it must be assumed that some of the experiences these individuals have in common are the cause of their elevated probability for negative outcomes.

Describing the social and cultural characteristics that result from shared experiences is not an easy task. There must be a balance between the polar positions of overconsciousness of differences or denial of these effects altogether. If sociocultural variables are overemphasized, the provider is guilty of stereotyping. If they are underemphasized, the provider is guilty of insensitivity. A more productive approach might be to acknowledge that some groups are at a greater risk than others, and as a result more resources, both human and capital, need to be allocated. Similarly, a family-focused orientation looks at families as unique groups that demonstrate particular clusters of behaviors. Rather than dwelling on specific behaviors that particular groups display, it looks at the belief systems that guide the actions of families. Thus, the focus shifts from describing and assigning, often incorrectly, a myriad of behaviors to particular groups to the continuum of beliefs that guide behavior, the template.

The template can be described as a series of discrete points along continua from which an individual makes choices. These choices may be planned or unplanned, constituting a class of tacit knowledge or folkways. For example, belief continua may deal with the nature of infants or the roles of family members in the process of child socialization. The remainder of this section discusses various examples of beliefs about the nature of infants and the nature of adult–infant interaction in terms of continua from which choices may be made. Generally, the extremes of each belief continuum are discussed. Most families fall between the two ends of the continuum.

Several examples of groups demonstrating a particular point in the continuum are presented. These are illustrative points from the research literature and should not be considered as characteristics of any particular racial, ethnic, or linguistic group. As is often the case, intragroup differences are as great as intergroup differences. Second, cross-cultural research has tended to study people from more remote areas or to examine groups fairly isolated from the more dominant or mainstream societies, which can render the findings easily discountable. Conversely, the numerous examples may be viewed as evidence that serves to broaden the range of acceptable variation.

The Nature of Infants

Beliefs about the nature of infants dictate who interacts with an infant and why, as well as what adults teach and infants learn. Figure 1 lists five illustrative examples of belief continua concerning the nature of infants.

Bundle of Potentialities—Preordained Character At one end of this continuum, the infant is considered a bundle of potentialities. Adults view themselves as facilitators of the development of these potentials and assume the role of a teacher (Sameroff & Feil, 1985). Infants are viewed as active learners and hypothesis testers. This view subsumes a particular Western European philosophy of child development, based on Piaget's sensorimotor stages. At the other end of the continuum, the infant is believed to have a preordained character. A more extreme form of this belief was found by Whiting and Edwards (1988) among a caste group in India. If infants are

Figure 1. Continua concerning the nature of infants.

viewed as incapable of thinking or hypothesizing about their environment, parents see their primary role as caretaker. Therefore, infant appearance, health (weight), and cleanliness become important manifestations of parental skill in this role and sources of pride.

Willful—Innocent Groups differ in the degree to which they believe infants are willful or behave willfully. Ward (1971) found that some rural African American families in Louisiana view young children as basically "bad," in that their immaturity prevents them from acting in a socially responsible manner. Adults can punish them for misbehaving, but cannot really change or control them. They must simply outgrow this state of willfulness. Among Hispanics in New Mexico (Briggs, 1984), infants and young children are referred to as "inocentes" (innocents). From this view, babies are thought to have no control over their behavior. Therefore, adults show great tolerance for and patience with infant behavior. Similarly, Kessen (1975) reported that parents on mainland China speak of young children as "helpless treasures."

Independent—Dependent This dimension refers to whether infants are seen as dependent with independence as a desirable goal to be attained or as independent with dependence as a desirable goal. Independence/dependence refers to a mature adult state and implies the degree of dependence on the family or group for social, emotional, or economic support. Preference for independence is seen when adults show pleasure when infants express their wants, likes, and dislikes (e.g., *"She* knows what she wants"). Infants are encouraged to explore actively. They sleep alone in their own rooms and are assigned personal possessions (Munroe, Munroe, & Whiting, 1981). Other researchers (Minturn & Lambert, 1964; Whiting & Edwards, 1988) have described the pride with which some American parents talk about "the terrible twos." They anticipate the infant's expressions of increasing independence and discuss the behavior with considerable pleasure. However, Shimizu (1984) found that Filipino infants are exposed to a dependent socialization pattern through which they learn to enjoy being taken care of and realize that they can make others happy by being dependent on them.

Intentional—Nonintentional Adults vary as to whether they believe infants are intentionally using vocalizations, body language, or eye contact to communicate. Accordingly, there is variation in the degree to which adults "map" intentions onto infant vocalizations and adapt their speech to infants and young children. Ferguson (1971) reported findings of "baby talk" in adults' speech among many unrelated and geographically distinct languages. Most of us are familiar with a pattern in which the baby says "nana" and the mother responds, "What? You want a banana with your cereal?" In this case, the adult's response may far exceed the infant's intent. At the other end of the continuum, some adults do not perceive infants' behavior as intentional and do not adapt their speech. Beliefs about the nature of adults and infants, infant intentionality, and social status issues account for the lack of adaptation found in adult–child interaction among groups such as Samoans (Blount, 1972a, 1972b; Ochs, 1982), rural Guatemalans (Harkness, 1971), and southern African Americans (Werner, 1984). Rural Guatemalan mothers were found to use rapid, monotonic speech to young children. They rarely expanded young children's utterances but occasionally echoed them. Werner (1984) reported that African Americans from a working-class community in the southeastern United States did not believe infants are able or need to communicate.

Possession of Parents—Possession of (Extended) Family This continuum defines to whom the infant "belongs." It reflects the definition of family (nuclear vs. extended) and the degree to which independence at this level or dependence (interdependence) is valued. Young (1970) described a rural African American community in which adults show great pleasure in young children. Everyone with the slightest claim to do so would hold and play with a baby. Shimizu (1984) reported that Filipino children are exposed to complex, dyadic relationships with various parenting figures through which they learn to respond actively to people and communicate intimately with them. Brukman (1973) was surprised to find among research groups in Kenya, India, and Samoa that socialization is a "grand family affair" involving uncles, aunts, and cousins in daily routines and group activities. Similar practices are found among Native American families (Burgess, 1980; Chisholm, 1981). In contrast, there are many middle-class European American families in which relatives, even grandparents, will not pick up a baby without asking permission and no adult will scold someone else's child.

This continuum has given examples of beliefs about the nature of infants that play a crucial role in determining the kinds of social input an infant receives. From the earliest interactions, adults begin communicating to infants who they are, want to be, or ought to be. This is the process of socialization.

Adult–Infant Interactions

Through their interactions with others, infants learn a set of social and cultural values and beliefs that will make them members of the group and identify them as such for life. Four belief continua that may influence the nature of adult–infant interactions are shown in Figure 2. As in the previous section, the majority of families fall between the two ends of the continuum, and the examples are to be thought of as illustrative, not characteristic, of any group.

Talking to Learn—Learning to Talk This continuum reflects beliefs about the roles of infants and adults in infant learning, as well as the way language should be used. For instance, language may be used to regulate thinking or to regulate social interaction. If infants are viewed as bundles of potentialities who actively form hypotheses about sensory input and if parents view themselves as teachers, talking becomes another vehicle for the learning–teaching process. These parents engage children in "conversations" through labeling routines ("This is a book; what's that?"), pseudo-questioning (requesting known or shared information: "What's your name?"), and recounting shared events ("When you and I went to …"). If infants are seen as learning to talk, parents may encourage the repetition of socially relevant language that reflects adult beliefs about how different individuals should be addressed. Schieffelin and Eisenberg (1986) reported that young Kaluli children in Papua New Guinea are taught appropriate language forms in a variety of social situations (e.g., teasing, threatening, asserting) through use of the directive "Say this." Hispanic parents frequently frame socially relevant language with "Dile" ("Tell him/her"). A familiar pattern is the parental response to a child's complaint of teasing: "Tell him: 'Stop it! Leave me alone.' "

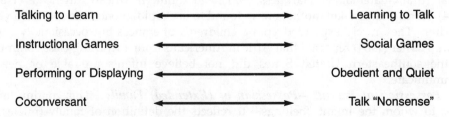

Figure 2. Continua concerning adult–infant interactions.

   Instructional Games—Social Games   Play may be viewed as consisting of instructional games (e.g., counting or singing the "ABCs"), social games (e.g., "peekaboo," "Gotcha!", giving kisses), or an activity in which adults do not engage at all. This dimension is also related to beliefs about adult–infant roles in the learning process, infant communicative competence, and the use of language. For instance, parents who see their primary role as caretaker most likely do not regard themselves as playmates for children. Field and Widmayer (1981) studied mother–infant interactions among lower socioeconomic African American, Cuban, Puerto Rican, and South American immigrants in Miami. They found evidence for "hidden agendas" in parental styles of play. African American mothers expressed concerns about "spoiling" the child by giving too much attention. Cuban mothers, who talked the most and used polysyllabic words and long utterances, said that parents had a duty "to educate" children. Puerto Rican and South American mothers engaged in more social and interactive games, in which mutual enjoyment was the primary goal.

   Performing or Displaying—Obedient and Quiet   Children may be expected to perform or display knowledge and skills for adults. Alternatively, the preference may be for a child who is obedient and quiet in the presence of adults. Some families value verbal displays of information, and young children are encouraged to talk to and initiate conversations with adults. Parents and other adults rehearse these skills with young children, helping them to relate their experiences and retell stories. For the family that values an obedient, quiet child, nonverbal means of communication may be stressed, including eye contact, proximity, and body language. Fajardo and Freedman (1981) studied mother–infant interactions among African American, Caucasian, and Navajo dyads. In 25% of the Navajo dyads selected for study, the mothers were totally silent. Nevertheless, Navajo infants spent as much total time looking at their mothers as the other infants did. Similar results were reported by Callahan (1981) in a comparison study of Anglo, Hopi, and Navajo dyads. Furthermore, they reported that the Anglo mothers relied primarily on vocalization and repositioning in interactions with their infants. Distinct differences were found between Japanese and European American mothers' styles of interaction with their infants (Caudill & Weinstein, 1972; Otaki, Durrett, Richards, Nyguist, & Pennebaker, 1986). European American mothers spent less time with their babies; emphasized verbal interactions; and preferred active, self-assertive infants. Japanese mothers spent more time with their infants; emphasized physical contact versus verbal interaction; and had as a goal a passive, contented baby. Among Hong Kong Chinese parents, the well-bred child is described as obedient, unspoiled, unemotional, and polite (Wang, 1984).

   Coconversant—Talk "Nonsense"   Along this belief continuum, young children are seen as conversational partners and are encouraged to learn appropriate skills, or conversely adults view children's talk as immature or unworthy of adult attention. For instance, some Hispanics refer to young children's talk as "basurita" (garbage/nonsense). Adults may discourage the use of baby talk and sound play among infants and toddlers in the belief that these forms interfere with learning the more adult, socially appropriate form of language (Schieffelin, 1983). These adults will not imitate infants' sounds or engage in vocal turn taking or "conversations" with infants. Whiting and Edwards (1988) were particularly impressed with the efforts of European American mothers they studied to engage their children in conversations throughout daily activities, even when the children seemed unwilling or uninterested in doing so. A different pattern was reported among Southern African Americans in the United States (Hale, 1982; Heath, 1982; Ward, 1971). Young children were included in most daily activities with adults and were immersed in rich multiple examples of adult talk.

However, language input was not modified for children, topics were not addressed to them, and adults did not direct questions to children to engage them in conversations or elicit known responses. This shared view is expressed succinctly by a rural Guatemalan mother: "I never talk with my child. I just tell him to do something and he does it. When he talks, it's to other children" (Harkness, 1971, p. 497). At this end of the continuum, infant vocalizations do not require an adult response and are not particularly attended to by adults.

Common Clusters of Shared Experiences

The selection of specific points within a particular continuum by an individual, a family, or a group of families is not a random event. The point or points selected are those that are perceived by individuals and families to best buffer the stresses caused by changes in the environment. It is not surprising that groups of families often select the same point(s) on the continuum when faced with similar events; it is probably the best adaptation that can be made given the context and available resources. When successful, these adaptations are then taught to newer members of the group as the correct way to perceive, think, and act.

To illustrate this adaptation process, assume that you moved into a society in which inhabitants walked twice as fast as your normal rate. If you ventured into the streets and walked at your own normal rate, you would be trampled. You have the option of staying in your house forever and walking at your own rate or you can select, from the "rate continuum," a faster rate and venture out into the streets. Selecting the second option is an adaptation that you and other "slower" walkers make as a result of events that require you to make changes. As a conscientious adult, the changes you have selected will be passed on to your children to ensure the survival of your progeny. The adaptation you make is not necessarily a conscious one, is not a group decision, and is not one that makes you lose your cultural identity. Your decision just guaranteed living in a less life-threatening situation.

The same general principles can be seen when groups of individuals are marginalized in a society as a result of any characteristic, be it their race, their income, or their lack of specific abilities. Faced with similar stress-causing environments, they select particular ways of buffering the stress. If the strategies are successful, the parents will pass these on to their children as the appropriate way to feel, think, and act. For example, one common adaptation to marginalization is the development of interdependence among marginalized individuals. Thus, the immediate social network plays a much more critical role in the provision of information, social norms, and crisis assistance. As a result, these marginalized families do not rely on formal organizations and turn instead to other marginalized families and friends as their source of information (Harrison, Wilson, Pine, Chan, & Buriel, 1990; Sontag & Schacht, 1994).

Variations in Language Use

One factor often linked to culture that can result in the marginalization of families is the degree to which family members speak English, especially the standard dialect of English. The acquisition of English is perhaps the greatest adaptation made by many cultural groups and is the one viewed by many as the true measure of Americanization. As families vary with respect to their values and beliefs, so too do families vary with respect to their ability to speak English. Some individuals are monolingual speakers of the minority language, some are monolingual speakers of the majority language, but the majority fall between the two ends of the continuum. From a linguistic point of view, no language (or dialect of a language) is superior to any other because any particular thought can be expressed using any dialect of any language. This is not to say that all varieties of a language carry the same prestige. Some varieties of a language, specifically those used by the dominant groups in any socially stratified society, will be considered to have higher prestige (Wolfram, 1986), promulgated within the educational system (Adler, 1984), and valued by the private sector of the society (Shuy, 1972; Terrell & Terrell, 1983). The acknowledgment by the courts of the rights of linguistic minority populations has resulted in greater acceptance of dialects other than Standard American English. In addition, there has been a realization that, although English is the most common and dominant language spoken in the United States, other languages have a right to exist in its linguistically pluralistic society.

Historically, the general trend was for immigrants to come to this country, lose their language, and embrace English as their mother tongue. To a large extent, this trend was only followed by some immigrant groups; other groups maintained the use of their mother tongue from generation to generation with reinforcement by new immigrants and by their movement to and from their country of origin. One example of this trend is the Hispanic population in the United States; more than 20% of the population do not speak English well or at all (U.S. Department of Commerce, 1991). As a result of immigration and maintenance, Spanish has become the second most common language spoken in the United States; more than 11 million individuals, or 5% of the U.S. population, speak the language. The percentage of individuals who do not speak English well or at all is even greater if the numerous other languages spoken in the United States are taken into consideration.

IMPLICATIONS AND RECOMMENDATIONS

From an ecological perspective, there can be no one blueprint for a culturally appropriate early intervention program. Each program's content and approach must be sensitive to the ecology in which the families served live. What is significant to and appropriate for a family living in a particular environment may not be for the same family living in a different environment. From this ecological perspective, it can be argued that looking at the characteristics and practices of those individuals who are successful (generally middle-class Caucasian families) and attempting to transfer those skills and attitudes to individuals who are less successful is inappropriate and might lead, in some situations, to counterproductive outcomes. However, for the most part, this transfer of skills and attitudes is exactly how early intervention programs have been organized.

An intervention program must begin by implementing culturally sensitive screening and assessment procedures that are both family and child centered. Most existing assessments have as their purpose the sorting of children, either by comparing their performance with the performance score obtained from a standardized sample (norm referenced) or on the basis of their mastery of specific skills (criterion referenced). Both procedures could result in biased assessments if careful consideration is not given to the standardization procedures and the interpretation of results. Knowledge and behaviors valued by one culture are not necessarily those valued, and thus encouraged and trained, by others. The assessment procedure is further complicated when the family speaks a language other than English. Although some assessment tools are available in languages other than English, they are often direct translations without separate norms.

Ideally, the most appropriate professional to carry out the assessment, and to some degree the intervention, of families for whom English is not the dominant language is a bilingual-bicultural professional. Although this may be the most appropriate choice, this may not be a realistic option. Therefore, until there is a significant increase in the number of bilingual-bicultural professionals, alternative approaches must be considered. However, these alternative approaches should be viewed as temporary alternatives and not as permanent solutions to the problem. The following options are suggested for service providers who are not fluent in the language spoken by the family:

1. Assistance from a bilingual aide, other professional, or student in training
2. Assistance from family member or friend
3. Assistance from a member of the community

The first option assumes that in addition to bilingual skills, the individual knows the relevance of the information to be obtained, can administer the assessment appropriately, and can provide accurate and unbiased information. Although the second approach appears to be a viable alternative, and sometimes the only alternative, using bilingual individuals from the familial or social environment of the parent introduces possible problems. In addition to their lack of training in the areas being assessed, the personal nature of the questions in a case history may violate cultural values. The interviewer also will be unaware of when to probe for further information, or the helpers may insert their own interpretations of information, particularly if they are family members. The desire to help the child perform well or to modify the evaluation procedures and test items may occur as a result of "being helpful." A bilingual community member would appear to be a viable choice to assist in the interview or assessment. However, the evaluator must be aware of the issues of confidentiality, status of the individual in the community, dialect variations, and language ability, as well as the limited knowledge that these individuals might bring with respect to the content and approaches used in the assessment process.

The use of translators or interpreters may appear, on the surface, to solve the problem of assessing children and families who speak a language other than English, but they cannot be used without caution. Furthermore, a problem inherent in a monolingual professional's selection and use of bilingual interpreters to assist in an assessment is that the professional is in no position to evaluate the interpreter's communication skills in the other language. Extensive training of the interpreter, ensuring that the interpreter understands the particular assessment procedure to be used, and using the same interpreter over time would ameliorate the inherent problems that monolingual professionals routinely encounter.

The next step in the process, if necessary, is the planning and implementation of an intervention plan. By its definition, intervention creates changes in attitudes, behaviors, or both. Successful interventions empower families by providing the knowledge they want and need to make informed decisions, even the decision not to seek services, and the skills to make desired changes. Unsuccessful interventions are those that fail to help families or that force families to make changes that are not adaptable to their situations. Each failure reinforces the idea of differences and widens the span of misunderstanding between interventionists and the families they are attempting to help.

Intervention programs should be tailored to the individual needs of each family. Because no two families are alike and what has worked for one family will not necessarily work with another, it is important that providers set aside the inclination to categorize families according to preconceived notions of what these families are or what their needs are. It is essential to provide families with what they want and not only with those services immediately available.

Families are more likely to be invested in intervention goals congruent with high-priority family goals, and they are more likely to implement those professional recommendations that fit with their values and beliefs (Bernheimer, Gallimore, & Weisner, 1990). Techniques that programs might use to ensure sensitivity to individual families' goals include conducting personal values clarification by program staff, gathering ethnographic information on the group with which the family identifies, understanding the degree of transcultural identification, and selecting intervention goals that are congruent with family and cultural values (Hanson, Lynch, & Wayman, 1990).

A pluralistic society requires that services be guided by a vision of cultural sensitivity. This sensitivity requires the use of service delivery options that are individually tailored to match family needs and styles. The ethnocentric view that proposes that all families will benefit from a single set of intervention practices, even if they are recommended practices, must be discarded. Bruder, Anderson, Schutz, and Caldera (1991) discussed modifications to an early intervention program that have proven successful in providing services to inner-city Puerto Rican families. These modifications include addressing a significant number of family needs and an increased awareness of culturally based values related to family relationships, child-rearing practices, support networks, and societal responsibilities. At the outset of this program, IFSP goals were primarily in the family support category, followed by informational goals and child intervention goals. After 1 year, the composition of the IFSP goals reflected fewer support and informational goals and more child intervention goals, suggesting that, as these families' support and informational needs were met, more attention could be focused on child intervention.

Cultural sensitivity also means a nonjudgmental recognition that families take many forms and that individual values and beliefs shape each family's perceptions of events and their unique responses to them. Providing services to diverse families requires programs to develop and use a menu, battery, or array of service delivery options (home based, center based, hospital based, and combinations of these) individually tailored to match family needs and styles. Families also should be encouraged to participate at whatever level they deem appropriate. Simeonsson and Bailey (1990) suggested a seven-level hierarchy or continuum of family involvement in early intervention (from Level 0, elective, in which the family rejects available services or elects not to be involved, through Level III, involvement focusing on information and skills needs, to Level VI, psychological involvement, in which family members seek psychological change at the family or personal level). From this perspective, the program must incorporate a broad-based service delivery model that uses all community resources and identifies the specific intervention program as one such resource.

The concept of a belief continuum in terms of values and beliefs about infants and their caregivers was discussed previously in this chapter. Similarly, cultural or family sensitivity constitutes one end of a continuum of program policies and practices. There is an ethnocentric view at the opposite end of this continuum that proposes that all families will benefit from a single set of intervention practices, which are generally derived from the values and beliefs of early interventionists (predominantly, Caucasian, middle-class females). This practice, in everyday terms, is referred to as "putting the round peg in the square hole."

A common example of the "round peg in the square hole" practice is a young child who repeatedly tries to force the wrong piece into one space on a puzzle board. He or she may push the piece with increasing force, bang the piece against the board, or turn the piece persistently into the wrong space. The provider then usually encourages the child to look at the individual puzzle piece more closely or to move the board or puzzle piece to fit. Yet providers sometimes resort to this strategy when their beliefs and practices are challenged by the needs of diverse families. A program rule stating that an enrolled mother and infant must attend a weekly 2-hour center-based parent–infant group to receive services is meaningless to a young, single mother of three toddlers, who has no family nearby, is afraid of her inner-city neighbors, and feels embarrassed because the baby has no socks. An intervention goal such as "the mother will use simple language to talk to Moisés throughout daily activities about what he sees and is doing" is not likely to be a high priority for a mother who believes that her job is to keep the baby clean, well-fed, and safe and that babies learn by observing what others do. Similarly, a diagnosis of developmental delay and a recommendation for early intervention may be incomprehensible to a family whose members believe that their infant with Down syndrome is a special gift from God, who will always remain childlike and innocent.

A common practice in early intervention programs is providing families with "parenting classes." Many early intervention programs are based on the assumption that the information families receive during training will change their behavior and, indirectly, affect the behavior of their children. This belief, coupled with the "unidirectional path to success" perspective, has led many program developers to focus on providing parents with the knowledge base the developers feel parents need to enhance the children's development. For the most part, these programs focus on what are considered to be the parents' gaps in knowledge and assume that providing parents with these often disconnected bits of information will change their present practice. However, the degree to which parents will be successful at changing their own and their children's behavior depends on a number of variables, some of which are parent related and some of which are program related. The change parents are asked to make is often an immense task that cannot be accomplished without unsustained and long-lasting support. Some program participants must not only reorient their way of thinking but must also persuade other members of their immediate network to at least support this change. Wachs and Gruen (1982) speculated that the effects of intervention can only be maintained if the parents have the time and social support to continue intervention and the necessary motivation and skills. The skills, and to some extent the motivation, that parents possess will be a direct result of the effectiveness of the individual procedures and methods used in the program in which they are enrolled.

Finally, culturally sensitive policies and practices need to incorporate the goals of advocacy and education. All program announcements, public awareness campaigns, forms, and parent information materials should be translated into the primary languages of the families served. Pictures of children representative of the surrounding communities should be included in program fliers, announcements, training videotapes, and advertisements. Furthermore, community leaders need to be involved in planning services that affect their communities. Programs can work with community leaders and advocates to ensure representation and meaningful involvement of families from diverse cultural and linguistic backgrounds in internal advisory and policy-making groups and at various levels, including local and state interagency coordinating councils. Because people from diverse cultural and linguistic groups are underrepresented among professionals in early childhood fields, programs should consider how to make staff ratios more reflective of the families served and what strategies can be used to involve more people from diverse cultural backgrounds in all aspects of service provision.

CASE STUDIES

This section presents two case examples from the authors' experiences, and for each case an alternative response from the perspective of culturally sensitive, family-focused early intervention services is discussed.

Case Study 1

A middle-age man and his wife moved from Puerto Rico to the "barrio" in a major northeastern city with the goal of finding help for their 16-month-old son. The man had worked as a mechanic in Puerto Rico, and the family was self-sufficient. They left behind a large extended family, including several teenage children from their previous marriages. The baby had big brown eyes and an infectious smile. He was microcephalic, hearing impaired, and blind in one eye. He had multiple seizures daily and feeding problems. They were referred to an early intervention program by the pediatrics clinic of the local children's hospital. During the program's evaluation, the father explained through a translator that his wife was completely dedicated to the baby and seldom put him down. For instance, while she cooked dinner or did the laundry she balanced him on her hip and rocked him. He said they would do whatever the team suggested: "God gave him to us, we're his parents, and we'll take care of him." They wanted to learn how to make the baby more comfortable (he had muscle spasms in both arms and legs), so that when he wasn't having a seizure he would be happy and could interact with them. The father said that the baby smiled at them intentionally, liked to watch the television, searched for them with his eyes and head when he heard their voices, and was afraid of strangers. They were enrolled in the program and assigned to a weekly, center-based parent–infant group.

The parents never came back to the center. Program team members went to the home several times with a translator to encourage, cajole, and nag them to attend the group session. Each time, the father politely and patiently asked if someone could come to the house and show them how to do exercises to help relax the baby's muscles. He said that was all they really wanted to know, and they were not interested in meeting other Spanish-speaking parents. The mother was concerned that the baby would cry for the 2 hours of the group and saw that as unnecessary suffering for him. The team members repeatedly explained to them that program therapists did not make home visits and that the baby would receive physical therapy when they came to the parent–infant group. During one such visit to the home, the father said that the baby was getting worse. He choked more frequently, took hours to drink a bottle, and seemed to be hungry all the time. Shortly after that visit, the baby developed pneumonia, began having seizures more frequently, and was hospitalized. He recovered and went home. During the last home visit, the father said they were moving back to Puerto Rico. "We came here looking for a miracle for our little boy. Now I know that there are no miracles, and perhaps there never were," he explained.

Obviously, the outcome would have been different if the program had been responsive to this family's stated values and needs. They wanted to learn how to make the baby more comfortable, and they wanted to do it themselves, in their own home. Their perceptions and needs seemingly were based on their religious beliefs ("God gave him to us"), a strong sense of family, and a sense of personal responsibility to protect and nurture their baby ("we're his parents, and we'll take care of him").

The program's response was based on the belief that center-based services (parent–infant groups) are best for all children with disabilities and that "good" or "caring" parents will adapt their lives to fit that model. In contrast, culturally sensitive, family-focused practices would incorporate the family's values and beliefs and respond to the need the family identified. A therapist might visit the home, teach the parents techniques to relax the baby's muscles, and make periodic home visits to monitor their effectiveness or modify the techniques. Thus, a relationship of mutual trust and respect could begin to evolve. Other needs or issues might be identified over time and matched to resources or solutions that were congruent with family values and goals and in a manner consistent with recommended practices.

Case Study 2

María Peña is an 18-month-old child with severe language delays. The family, who is Spanish speaking, resides in a rural county of Pennsylvania. The father is a migrant worker presently employed at a mushroom farm and the mother is a homemaker, taking care of María and her two older brothers, ages 3 and 4 years. Mrs. Peña describes María as a happy, loving baby. She is learning to blow kisses and dances when someone holds her hand. María receives home-based services once a month from a monolingual (English) speech-language pathologist using an interpreter and a bilingual early interventionist. The service coordinator is concerned that María is not making significant progress compared with other children from Spanish-speaking homes who receive center-based services primarily in English with some interpreter support. The service coordinator and the family would like María to continue to receive home-based services but with greater frequency. Due to budgetary and logistic problems, any increased services would have to be provided in English, which the local early intervention program refuses to do on the grounds that the law and the research literature suggest that children must be served in their native language. The service coordinator, who is aware of the advantages of providing services in the family's native language, would prefer to see an increase in services, even if they were provided in English. To gain support for more frequent services, the service coordinator contacted one of the authors for "research evidence which would support the notion that teaching a language-delayed child in English would be beneficial and would enhance, or at least not interfere with, the child's acquisition of her parents' native language."

On the surface, the main issue appeared to be one of language of intervention, which is a common concern of early intervention professionals who find it difficult to implement agreed-upon goals as a result of the lack of personnel competent to provide services in a language other than English. There is no question that the issue of language of intervention is important, but it is not the only factor to be considered in this case. As further discussion revealed, the agency was ill-equipped to deal with the large number of Spanish-speaking children in the county. Rather than helping families identify the best possible situations for themselves and their children, the agency indirectly forced families to choose options from limited services. Not only were there a limited number of staff members who lacked the necessary linguistic skills to communicate with these families, but they also lacked knowledge of child socialization practices and of the natural support systems that existed among these migrant families. Rather than empowering families, the program was fostering dependency. The county agency, which had always prided itself on the quality of its services, is presently undergoing a thorough evaluation of its practices.

SUMMARY

The "face" of America is changing rapidly and dramatically. Americans of European descent must provide services to families that increasingly challenge their personal values and beliefs. This chapter discussed a vision-based model in which the provisions of PL 99-457 serve as the vision for culturally sensitive, family-focused services. The model's three components, the knowledge base, policies and practices, and an enabling philosophy, were also reviewed and applied to family service delivery.

The terms *culturally sensitive* and *family focused* have been used to describe recommended practices in early intervention. In fact, family-focused services are, inherently, culturally sensitive, provided that interventionists are aware of their own values and beliefs, acknowledge the range of diversity in families' values and beliefs, and are committed to honoring that diversity through the services they provide to families. The merging of cultural sensitivity with family-focused practices is the vision for a multicultural society. Above all, culturally sensitive, family-focused practices promote an environment in which dreams and visions for children are shared by both families and professionals.

REFERENCES

Adler, S. (1984). *Cultural language differences: Their educational and clinical-professional implications.* Springfield, IL: Charles C Thomas.

Bernheimer, L.P., Gallimore, R., & Weisner, T.S. (1990). Ecocultural theory as a context for the individual family service plan. *Journal of Early Intervention, 14*(3), 219–233.

Blount, B.G. (1972a). Aspects of socialization among the Luo of Kenya. *Language in Society, 1,* 235–248.

Blount, B.G. (1972b). Parental speech and language acquisition: Some Luo and Samoan examples. *Anthropological Linguistics, 14,* 119–130.

Bouvier, L.F., & Gardner, R.W. (1986). *Immigration to the U.S.: The unfinished story.* Washington, DC: Population Reference Bureau.

Briggs, C.L. (1984). Learning how to talk: Native metacommunicative competence and the incompetence of fieldworkers. *Language in Society, 13,* 1–28.

Bruder, M.J., Anderson, R., Schutz, G., & Caldera, M. (1991). Niños especiales program: A culturally sensitive early intervention model. *Journal of Early Intervention, 15*(3), 268–277.

Brukman, J. (1973). Language and socialization: Child culture and the ethnographer's task. In S.T. Kimball & J.H. Burnett (Eds.), *Learning and culture: Proceedings of the American Ethnological Society.* Seattle: University of Washington Press.

Bureau of the Census. (1991). *National data books and guides to resources: Statistical abstracts of the U.S.* (112th ed.). Washington, DC: U.S. Government Printing Office.

Bureau of the Census, Ethnic and Hispanic Branch. (1988). *Current population reports: Population characteristics* (Series P-20, No. 431). Washington, DC: U.S. Government Printing Office.

Burgess, B.J. (1980). Parenting in the Native American community. In M.D. Fatina & R. Cardenas (Eds.), *Parenting in a multicultural society.* New York: Longman.

Callahan, J.W. (1981). A comparison of Anglo, Hopi and Navajo mothers and infants. In T.M. Field, A.M. Sostek, P. Vietze, & P.H. Leiderman (Eds.), *Culture and early interactions.* Hillsdale, NJ: Lawrence Erlbaum Associates.

Caudill, W., & Weinstein, H. (1972). Maternal care and infant behavior in Japan and America. In C.S. Lavatelli & F. Stendler (Eds.), *Readings in child behavior and development.* San Diego: Harcourt Brace Jovanovich.

Center for the Study of Social Policy. (1994). *Kids count data book: State profiles of child well-being.* Greenwich, CT: Annie E. Casey Foundation.

Chisholm, J.S. (1981). Residence patterns and the environment of mother-infant interaction among the Navajo. In T.M. Field, A.M. Sostek, P. Vietze, & P.H. Leiderman (Eds.), *Culture and early interactions.* Hillsdale, NJ: Lawrence Erlbaum Associates.

Education of the Handicapped Act Amendments of 1986, PL 99-457, 20 U.S.C. §1400 *et seq.*

Fajardo, B.F., & Freedman, D.G. (1981). Maternal rhythmicity in three American cultures. In T.M. Field, A.M. Sostek, P. Vietze, & P.H. Leiderman (Eds.), *Culture and early interactions.* Hillsdale, NJ: Lawrence Erlbaum Associates.

Ferguson, C.A. (1971). Baby talk as a simplified register. In C.A. Snow & C.A. Ferguson (Eds.), *Talking to children.* Cambridge, MA: Cambridge University Press.

Field, T.M., & Widmayer, S.M. (1981). Mother-infant interactions among lower SES Black, Cuban, Puerto Rican and South American immigrants. In T.M. Field, A.M. Sostek, P. Vietze, & P.H. Leiderman (Eds.), *Culture and early interactions.* Hillsdale, NJ: Lawrence Erlbaum Associates.

Garcia-Coll, C.T. (1990). Developmental outcome of minority infants: A process-oriented look into our beginnings. *Child Development, 61*(2), 270–289.

Hale, J. (1982). *Black children: Their roots, culture and learning style.* Salt Lake City, UT: Brigham Young University Press.

Hanson, M.J., Lynch, E.W., & Wayman, K.I. (1990). Honoring the cultural diversity of families when gathering data. *Topics in Early Childhood Education, 10*(1), 112–131.

Harkness, S. (1971). Cultural variations in mothers' language. *Word, 27,* 495–498.

Harrison, A.O., Wilson, M.N., Pine, C.J., Chan, S.Q., & Buriel, R. (1990). Family ecologies of ethnic minority children. *Child Development, 61*(2), 347–362.

Heath, S.B. (1982). Questioning at home and at school: A comparative study. In G. Spindler (Ed.), *Doing the ethnography of schooling: Educational anthropology in action.* New York: Holt, Rinehart & Winston.

Iglesias, A. (1994). Communication in the home and classroom. In A. Iglesias (Ed.), *Cross-cultural perspective in language: Assessment and intervention* (pp. 15–27). Rockville, MD: Aspen Publishers.

Kessen, W. (Ed.). (1975). *Childhood in China.* New Haven, CT: Yale University Press.

Lin, C-Y.C., & Fu, V.R. (1990). A comparison of child-rearing practices among Chinese, immigrant Chinese, and Caucasian-American parents. *Child Development, 61*(1), 429–433.

Minturn, L., & Lambert, W.W. (1964). *Mothers of six cultures: Antecedents of child-rearing.* New York: John Wiley & Sons.

Munroe, R.L., Munroe, R.H., & Whiting, B.B. (Eds.). (1981). *Handbook of cross-cultural human development.* New York: Garland Press.

National Center for Clinical Infant Programs. (1986). *Infants can't wait: The numbers.* Washington, DC: Author.

Ochs, E. (1982). Talking to children in Western Samoa. *Language in Society, 11,* 77–104.

Ochs, E. (1983). Cultural dimensions of language acquisition. In E. Ochs & B.B. Scheiffelin (Eds.), *Acquiring conversational competence.* London: Routledge and Kegan Paul.

Otaki, M., Durrett, M.E., Richards, P., Nyguist, L., & Pennebaker, J.W. (1986). Maternal and infant behavior in Japan and America. *Journal of Cross-Cultural Psychology, 17*(3), 251–268.

Public Health Service. (1990). *National Center for Health Statistics: Vital statistics of the United States 1988: Vol. 1. Natality.* (DHHS Publication No. PHS 90-1100). Washington, DC: U.S. Government Printing Office.

Rogoff, B. (1990). *Apprenticeship in thinking. Cognitive development in social context.* New York: Oxford University Press.

Sameroff, A.J., & Feil, L.A. (1985). Parental concepts of development. In I.E. Sigel (Ed.), *Parental belief systems.* Hillsdale, NJ: Lawrence Erlbaum Associates.

Schieffelin, B.B. (1983). Talking like birds: Sound play in a cultural perspective. In E. Ochs & B.B. Schieffelin (Eds.), *Acquiring conversational competence.* London: Routledge and Kegan Paul.

Schieffelin, B.B., & Eisenberg, A.R. (1986). Cultural variations in children's conversations. In R. Schieffelbusch & J. Pickar (Eds.), *The acquisition of communicative competence.* Baltimore: University Park Press.

Shimizu, H. (1984). Filipino children in family and society: Growing up in a many-people environment. In N. Kabayashi & T.B. Brazelton (Eds.), *The growing child in family and society.* Tokyo: University of Tokyo Press.

Shuy, W.R. (1972). Social dialect and employability: Some pitfalls of good intentions. In L.M. Davis (Ed.), *Studies in linguistics* (pp. 145–156). Birmingham: University of Alabama Press.

Simeonsson, R.J., & Bailey, D.B. (1990). Family dimensions in early intervention. In S.J. Meisels & J.P. Shonkoff (Eds.), *Handbook of early childhood intervention* (pp. 428–444). New York: Cambridge University Press.

Sontag, J.C., & Schacht, R. (1994). An ethnic comparison of parent participation and information needs in early intervention. *Exceptional Children, 60,* 422–433.

Spencer, G. (1984). *Projections of the population of the United States by age, sex and race: 1983 to 2080* (Current Population Reports, Series P-25, No. 952). Washington, DC: U.S. Department of Commerce, Bureau of the Census.

Terrell, S.L., & Terrell, F. (1983). Effects of speaking Black English upon employment opportunities. *Asha, 25*(6), 27–29.

Wachs, T.D., & Gruen, G.E. (1982). *Early experience and human development.* New York: Plenum Press.

Wang, S. (1984). Child rearing training in Hong Kong Chinese society. In N. Kobayashi & T.B. Brazelton (Eds.), *The growing child in family and society.* Tokyo: University of Tokyo Press.

Ward, M.C. (1971). *Them children: A study in language learning.* New York: Holt, Rinehart & Winston.

Werner, E.E. (1984). *Child care: Kith, kin, and hired hands.* Baltimore: University Park Press.

Whiting, B.B., & Edwards, C.P. (Eds.). (1988). *Children of different worlds: The formation of social behavior.* Cambridge, MA: Harvard University Press.

Wolfram, W. (1986). Language variation in the United States. In O. Taylor (Ed.), *Nature of communication disorders in culturally and linguistically diverse populations* (pp. 73–117). San Diego: College-Hill Press.

Young, V.H. (1970). Family and childhood in a Southern Negro community. *American Anthropologist, 72,* 269–287.

. . . 5
. .
.

Resource-Based Approach to Early Intervention

Carol M. Trivette, Carl J. Dunst, and Angela G. Deal

This chapter describes an approach to identifying and mobilizing community resources and services that can be used to meet child and family needs in ways that support and strengthen competence. This approach is one component of a model (see Dunst, Trivette, & Deal, 1988, 1994) that defines the goals of family-centered assessment and intervention as 1) identifying family needs, priorities, or concerns; 2) locating the formal and informal resources for meeting needs; and 3) helping families identify and use their strengths and capabilities to procure resources in ways that strengthen family functioning (see Hobbs et al., 1984).

In 1985, Dunst proposed an expanded definition of early intervention as the "provision of support (and resources) to families of young children from members of informal and formal social support networks that impact both *directly* and *indirectly* upon parent, family, and child functioning" (p. 179). Such a definition recognizes that families of young children experience events in addition to those provided by early intervention programs that can and do influence child development and family functioning (Bronfenbrenner, 1979). Dunst and colleagues have continued the study of the relationship between social support and its effects on children and families and the implications of this research for practice (Dunst & Trivette, 1987, 1988a, 1988b, 1990; Trivette & Dunst, 1992; Trivette, Dunst, & Hamby, in press). Their work as well as that of others (e.g., Affleck, Tennen, Allen, & Gershman, 1986; Affleck, Tennen, & Rowe, 1991; Colletta, 1981; Crnic, Greenberg, Ragozin, Robinson, & Basham, 1983;

The work described in this chapter was supported, in part, by the North Carolina Children's Trust Fund (Grant Nos. C1130, C1912, C7753, and C9514); Pennsylvania Department of Public Welfare, Office of Mental Retardation; and U.S. Department of Health and Human Services, Administration on Developmental Disabilities (Grant Nos. 90DD0144 and 90DD0113). Appreciation is extended to Michelle Davis, Nancy Gordon, Deborah Hamby, Lynda Pletcher, Dolores Richardson, Faye Rhodes, Lauren Starnes, Sherra Vance, and Darlene Wilson for data collection and analysis; Carol Whitacre and Kristen Buchan for editing the chapter and verifying the references; and Pat Condrey, Norma Hunter, and Mary Brown for preparation of the manuscript.

Crnic, Greenberg, & Slough, 1986; Crockenberg, 1981, 1985; Dean & Lin, 1977; Garbarino & Kostelny, 1993; Kahn, Wethington, & Ingersoll-Dayton, 1987; McCubbin et al., 1980; McGuire & Gottlieb, 1979; Pascoe, Loda, Jeffries, & Earp, 1981; Wandersman, Wandersman, & Kahn, 1980; Weinraub & Wolf, 1983) has led to additional insights and considerations of the best ways to conceptualize early intervention practices to maximize their benefits. The emphasis of the strategy described in this chapter is based on a conceptual and procedural distinction between resource-based and service-based approaches to mobilizing supports to meet child and family needs. The call for adoption of resource-based practices derives from a human ecology framework (Bronfenbrenner, 1979; Cochran & Brassard, 1979) that considers the manner in which a range of community experiences influence both directly and indirectly child, parent, and family functioning.

An expanded perspective of human services practices, including early intervention, that moves beyond only professional services as sources of support for meeting child and family needs has been voiced by a number of authorities (see Kretzmann & McKnight, 1993). For example, Sarason and colleagues (Sarason, Carroll, Maton, Cohen, & Lorentz, 1977) made the following observations about the restrictive orientation of thinking about solutions to people's problems solely in terms of professional services:

> We have never known of a human service agency of any kind that asserted that it had the resources to accomplish its goals. That is to say, the demand for the agency's services always exceeds what the agency feels it can and should supply. The solution, far more often than not, is put in terms of obtaining more money to hire more staff. Occasionally, it is put not in terms of obtaining more money but of being unable to locate and attract personnel who are in known short supply. However it is put, it always reflects a concept of "the market," in which it is competing for limited resources. Put in another way, the agency defines resources as those it can purchase and, therefore, control and distribute, consistent with definition of its task. The agency usually knows where the additional resources are located, but unless it has the funds to purchase them (in whole or in part), the resources do not, so to speak, exist. (pp. 19–20)

As is evident from this quote, defining human services practices in terms of service-based solutions can be problematic. For example, there probably will never be enough public funds to provide all the services children and families need when solutions to meeting needs are defined solely or primarily in terms of professional supports. To meet the most needs among the greatest number of children and families, human services programs in general, and early intervention programs in particular, will most likely have the greatest positive impact if resource-based rather than service-based approaches are used to meet needs and address child- and family-related concerns. As described below, this alternative way of thinking about resources does not "box one into a corner" in terms of limiting the options best suited for creating opportunities for promoting child and family competence.

COMMUNITY CONTEXT OF RESOURCE-BASED PRACTICES

A central feature of resource-based human services practices in general and early intervention practices specifically is the importance and emphasis placed on community support. Resource-based practices recognize that families are embedded within a broader-based community and that this community is a major source of support and resources for meeting child and family needs.

In their description of the meaning of community, Hobbs and colleagues (1984) stated that

> A community is an immediate social group that promotes human development . . . .
> In communities, individuals experience a sense of membership, influence members of
> the group and are themselves in turn influenced by others, have personal needs ful-
> filled, and share psychologically and personally satisfying connections with other peo-
> ple . . . . Community basically involves the coming together of people around shared
> values and the pursuit of common cause. (p. 41)

A sense of community in turn promotes the exchange of resources and supports including various experiences and assistance necessary for enhancing and maintaining
individual, family, and community well-being. Bronfenbrenner (1979), for example,
noted that

> whether parents can perform effectively in their child-rearing roles within the family
> depends upon the role demands, stresses, and supports emanating from [community]
> settings . . . . The availability of supportive settings is, in turn, a function of their
> existence and frequency in a given culture or subculture. (p. 7)

Although communities are often defined as geographical entities (Garbarino &
Kostelny, 1993; Schwirian, 1983), community in the social, cognitive, and affective
sense (Chavis & Wandersman, 1990; Unger & Wandersman, 1985) transcends circumscribed physical boundaries (Wellman, 1979). People in general and families in particular belong to multiple communities, although, according to Garbarino and Kostelny
(1993), "people belong to only one neighborhood [or locale], based on where they
live" (p. 301). This distinction is important, especially with regard to resource-based
practices, because community in the broader sense and not neighborhood in the nar-
rower one is the focus of efforts to promote the flow of resources to children and their
families.

Because children and families belong to multiple communities, resource-based
early intervention practices will, by necessity, occur not in a single but rather in multiple locations. Consequently, the context of resource-based early intervention will depend on, and differ according to, the community people, groups, organizations,
programs, and so forth providing learning opportunities and experiences for children
and their families participating in early intervention programs.

CONCEPTUAL BASES OF RESOURCE-BASED PRACTICES

Contemporary early intervention practices are to a large degree conceptualized primarily in terms of service-based solutions to meeting child and family needs. That is,
early intervention programs generally define their relationships with children and
their families in terms of particular services (e.g., physical therapy, speech therapy,
service coordination, developmental therapy, special instruction, respite care) that the
program offers and sometimes that other human services programs provide (hence
interagency coordination). This way of conceptualizing early intervention practices is
both limited and limiting because it fails to explicitly consider the value of sources of
support other than formal professional services. In contrast, a resource-based approach
to meeting child and family needs is both expansive and expanding because it focuses
on mobilization of a range of community supports.

Distinguishing between a service and a resource is a first step in understanding
the benefits of resource-based over service-based approaches to early intervention.
Operationally, a service is defined as a specific or particular activity employed by a
professional or professional agency to assist an individual or group, such as occupational therapy or special instruction. Generally, but not always, services are the "unit
of intervention" used by programs to provide assistance to the children and families

served by an agency or program. In contrast, resources are operationally defined as the full range of possible types of community help or assistance—potentially useful information, experiences, opportunities, and so forth—that might be mobilized and used to meet the needs of an individual or group. Resources are a means to accomplishing a desired outcome, including, but not limited to, different kinds of community learning opportunities for enhancing child and family competence. Consequently, a resource-based approach to intervention does not rely on a single type of (professional) help or assistance but rather promotes the mobilization and utilization of multiple sources of informal and formal community resources.

The term *community resources* is used in this chapter to mean community people, groups, organizations, programs, and so on that can be used by families of preschool-age children to provide both the children and the parents with opportunities and experiences that positively influence child, parent, and family behavior and development. These experiences include, but are not limited to, story times at a local library, swimming classes at a YM/YWCA or recreation center, "hands-on" science activities at a nature museum, music programs at a community church, child care services at a mothers-day-out program, and play groups organized by parents. In resource-based approaches to early intervention, any and all potential sources of community support are seen as options for meeting child and family needs. The goal of early intervention practices from a resource-based perspective is the increased utilization of these sources of support, and the experiences they provide, as one way of influencing child, parent, and family functioning.

DIFFERENCES BETWEEN
RESOURCE-BASED AND SERVICE-BASED PRACTICES

Table 1 lists five major characteristics that operationally differentiate resource-based from service-based early intervention practices. These characteristics are largely based on the work of Katz (1984), Kretzmann and McKnight (1993), McKnight (1987, 1989), McKnight and Kretzmann (1984, 1990), Rappaport (1981, 1987), and Sarason et al. (1977), as well as Dunst and colleagues' work with children and families (Dunst, 1985; Dunst, Trivette, & Deal, 1988, 1994; Dunst, Trivette, Gordon, & Pletcher, 1989; Dunst, Trivette, Starnes, Hamby, & Gordon, 1993).

First, service-based approaches tend to be limited and constricted because they are defined primarily in terms of what professionals do and thus are largely professionally centered in nature (Katz, 1984). Additionally, services that programs and practitioners provide are generally made available to certain people under certain conditions dictated by professionals. In contrast, resource-based approaches view a wide array of community people and organizations as sources of support with important resources for meeting child and family needs. Resources are viewed as potentially unlimited and broadly available; that is, they exist in abundance and are ready to be used at almost any time.

Second, service-based approaches are underscored by the adoption of a "scarcity paradigm" in which assistance is assumed to be scarce and therefore distributed to only those determined to be in need by professionals (Katz, 1984). In contrast, resource-based approaches are derived from a "synergistic paradigm" in which assistance, supports, and resources, are assumed to be expandable and renewable. Moreover, resources are not distributed based on means-tested eligibility criteria but rather are made available to all community members because "what is good for one is good for all and the whole is greater than the sum of its parts" (Katz, 1984, p. 201).

Table 1. Differential features of service-based and resource-based early intervention practices

Service based		Resource based	
Characteristic	Feature	Characteristic	Feature
Professionally centered	Solutions are defined in terms of centralized professional expertise or interdisciplinary professional expertise.	Community centered	Solutions are defined in terms of a range of resources available from an array of community people and organizations.
Scarcity paradigm	Professional services are seen as scarce and made available to people using means-tested eligibility criteria.	Synergistic paradigm	Community resources are seen as varied, rich, expandable, and renewable.
Formal support emphasis	Efforts to meet child and family needs focus on what professionals and professional programs and agencies do best.	Informal and formal support emphasis	Efforts to meet child and family needs focus on mobilization of informal and formal community social network members.
Deficit focused	Interventions focus on correcting weakness.	Asset focused	Interventions are strengths based and build on individual and collective capacity.
Outside-in solutions	Solutions tend to be prescribed by "outsiders" as an infusion of expertise.	Inside-out solutions	"Outside" resources are used in ways that are responsive to local agenda building.

Third, service-based practices are typically described in terms of what professionals and professionally oriented organizations offer as help and assistance. This is generally referred to as formal support. In contrast, resource-based practices are defined in terms of the assistance that both informal and formal support network members can provide. Moreover, communities are viewed as rich in untapped resources that can benefit all community members, including children with or at risk for disabilities and their families who are participating in early intervention programs.

Fourth, in contrast to most service-based approaches to solving problems, which are generally deficit based, resource-based practices employ what Kretzmann and McKnight (1993) call *asset-focused approaches* to building and mobilizing community capacity. Asset-focused intervention practices focus on the strengths, skills, gifts, and capabilities of community people and groups and employ these capacities to create opportunities for promoting individual and collective behavior and development.

Fifth, resource-based practices develop solutions to meeting needs from an inside–out rather than from an outside–in perspective. According to Swift (1984), the latter process

> has been to seek "expert" opinion about the needs of target populations, to back this expert opinion with an infusion of funds (and services) administered by a bureaucracy of experts, and to wonder at the resistance of indigenous populations to our efforts to improve their lives. (p. xi)

In contrast, resource-based practices encourage communities and community members to set their own agenda for what they want to accomplish and then ask how professional helpers and agencies can provide services to realize this agenda (see Kretzmann & McKnight, 1993).

Resource-based human services practices constitute at least one alternative way of conceptualizing and implementing child- and family-level interventions. Mobilizing community support systems that include formal and informal resources for meeting child and family needs would seem indicated because a primary goal of early intervention is crafting learning opportunities that can positively influence child and family functioning (Meisels & Shonkoff, 1990).

EMPIRICAL RATIONALE OF RESOURCE-BASED PRACTICES

Does it make a difference whether a resource-based or service-based approach is employed to address child and family needs and concerns? This section briefly presents data from three studies that indicate that the benefits of resource-based practices are significantly greater than those of service-based practices.

The first study involved 22 families from 11 states who participated in extensive case studies aimed at identifying the characteristics and effects of different practices employed by human services programs for people with disabilities, including early intervention programs (see Dunst et al., 1993). The case study protocol elicited descriptions of the ways that programs and practitioners provided supports and resources to families, including the extent to which practices were either service or resource based. The families' descriptions of interactions with service providers obtained during the interviews, together with investigator observations and other information provided by program personnel, were used as a basis of classifying the practices as highly consistent, somewhat consistent, neither consistent nor inconsistent, somewhat inconsistent, or highly inconsistent with resource-based practices. The classification of the practices was done independently of, and without reference to, the families' descriptions of the outcomes associated with the different practices.

Following each description or example, the family was asked to describe the reaction they had or feelings they experienced as a result of the practice used by the service provider. The families' descriptions of the effects (outcomes) were classified as highly or somewhat positive, neither positive nor negative, or somewhat or highly negative. Positive outcomes were operationally defined as descriptions that included both positive feelings experienced by the respondent and specific reference to the characteristics of the practices that produced the reported effects (e.g., "I felt good having the decision about the resources I could have") or descriptions that included positive feelings experienced by the respondent but no reference to the characteristics of the practices that were associated with the effects (e.g., "I really was happy about what happened"). Negative outcomes were defined as descriptions that included negative feelings only (e.g., "I was really upset about what they did") or descriptions that included both negative feelings and reference to the characteristics of the practices that produced the effects (e.g., "I was very angry that they didn't follow through on getting the information they promised"). (Responses were classified as neither positive nor negative if they did not meet the criteria for any of the other four outcomes.)

Figure 1 shows the results in terms of the percentage of resource-based and service-based practices that was associated with the two classes of positive and negative outcomes. Resource-based practices were associated with more positive outcomes compared with service-based practices. A Two Type of Practice × Two Type of Outcome chi-square analysis was highly significant, $\chi^2 = 47.12$, $p < .0001$. The results indicated a very strong relationship between the characteristics of program practices and the families' descriptions of effects associated with the practices, providing support for the contention that resource-based practices were associated with more positive outcomes than were service-based practices.

The second study involved a sample of 30 families of children with disabilities who were participating in an early intervention program, all of whom indicated a need for child care. The families were randomly assigned to either a service-based or a resource-based approach to meeting child care needs (Dunst, 1992; Raab, 1994). The service-based approach involved the provision of formalized respite care in response to family requests to a project staff member, who was responsible for identifying a

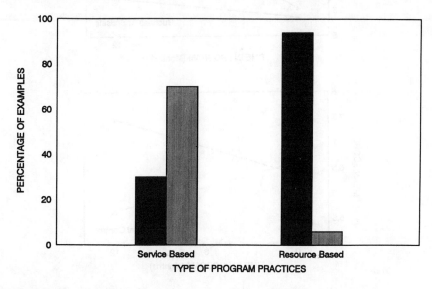

Figure 1. Percentage of resource-based and service-based practices associated with positive and negative outcomes. (■ = positive outcome; ▦ = negative outcomes.)

respite care provider and scheduling the delivery of respite care. The resource-based approach involved a project staff member and a parent working collaboratively to identify community-based child care options and to develop and implement strategies to build a child care network by promoting parent knowledge about, and skills for, mobilizing community-based child care experiences.

Telephone surveys conducted three to four times per family over 12 months by a person unfamiliar with each family's experimental condition were used to gather information about child care experiences and outcomes. The dependent measures included changes in both kinds of child care and the respondents' appraisals of child care procurement experiences. Intraindividual change across time was ascertained using growth modeling (Willett, 1989) to assess the impact of the two approaches. Nonparametric Mann-Whitney tests were used to compare change rates between groups. The results indicated that the parents participating in the resource-based approach demonstrated the greatest positive changes across time, including increases in the number of people caring for their children ($z = 1.85$, $p < .05$), frequency of provision of child care ($z = 1.52$, $p < .07$), the appraisals of how successful attempts to obtain child care were ($z = 1.78$, $p < .05$), perceived control over child care procurement experiences ($z = 2.00$, $p < .05$), and overall satisfaction with child care ($z = 1.57$, $p < .07$). Figure 2 graphically shows the results for the success appraisal and personal control outcomes. The benefits of a resource-based over a service-based approach to mobilizing child care are quite apparent.

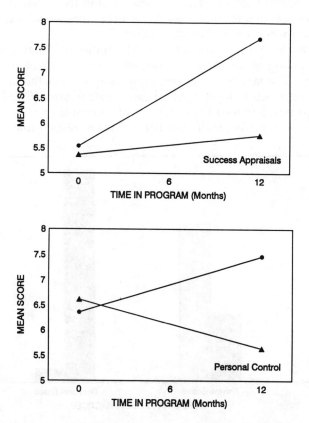

Figure 2. Mean success appraisals and personal control scores for resource-based and service-based child care procurement practices. (● = resource based; ▲ = service based.)

The third study involved almost 1,300 parents of children participating in a variety of early intervention programs in Pennsylvania. The participants completed a survey of early intervention program practices, including the resource-based nature of these practices, and the outcomes associated with them. The resource-based practices measure included a number of individual items assessing the extent to which the programs and practitioners emphasized the use of community resources (in addition to professional services) as part of meeting child and family needs. Each item was rated on a 5-point scale ranging from "never" to "almost always." The sum of the ratings was used to divide the sample into quartiles for purposes of establishing four levels of resource-based practices: very low, low, high, and very high. The dependent measures included the degree to which parents indicated their children had made developmental progress since being involved in the early intervention program (rated on five 7-point scales ranging from "made much less progress than expected" to "made much more progress than expected" for five different developmental domains) and the extent to which the parents indicated they had control over the kinds of services and activities provided to their family by the early intervention program (rated on a 10-point scale ranging from "very little control" to "a great deal of control"). One-way ANOVAs (analyses of variance) with the resource-based practices groups as the blocking variable yielded highly significant findings for both the child progress, $F(3, 1281) = 66.00$, $p < .00001$, and the personal control, $F(3, 1281) = 92.96$, $p < .00001$, outcomes. The findings, displayed in Figure 3, show linear ascending trends between the degree to which practices were resource based and families' assessment of the benefits associated with these practices.

Collectively, the findings from the three studies briefly described here as well as relevant research published elsewhere (Dunst & Leet, 1987; Dunst, Leet, & Trivette, 1988; Dunst et al., 1989, 1993) provide corroborating evidence that resource-based practices are associated with a number of positive outcomes and that the effects of resource-based practices are better than those of more traditional service-based approaches. The findings are particularly robust because the studies yielding empirical evidence included both qualitative and quantitative and experimental and nonexperimental investigations.

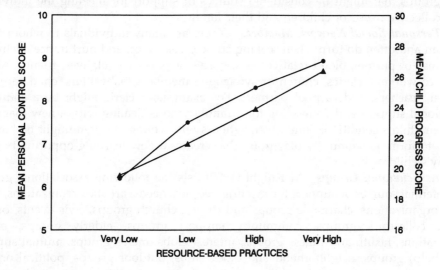

Figure 3. Relationship among use of resource-based practices, children's progress, and parents' self-efficacy appraisals. (◆ = personal control; ▲ = child progress.)

FRAMEWORK FOR IMPLEMENTING RESOURCE-BASED APPROACHES

The ability to identify community resources for meeting needs necessitates that the provider first have an idea of what families might require for stable functioning, individual and family growth, and day-to-day coping and well-being. It is useful to organize family resources into broad categories for guiding both assessment and intervention practices. Dunst, Trivette, and Deal (1988, 1994), Hartman and Laird (1983), and Trivette, Deal, and Dunst (1986) provided lists of resource categories. The list provided by Dunst, Trivette, and Deal (1988) includes the following 12 groups of resources: 1) economic resources, 2) physical and environmental resources, 3) food and clothing, 4) medical and dental care, 5) employment and vocational resources, 6) transportation and communication, 7) adult education and enrichment, 8) child education and intervention, 9) child care, 10) recreation, 11) emotional resources, and 12) cultural and social resources. Table 2 gives examples of resources often required and requested by families for meeting needs in each of these categories. This table provides a framework both for assessing needs, concerns, and desires and for identifying possible resources and supports that might be mobilized to achieve stated outcomes (Deal, Dunst, & Trivette, 1994; Dunst & Deal, 1994).

Figure 4 shows the three major components of the resource-based approach to early intervention that have evolved from efforts to better understand the optimal conditions for supporting and strengthening families. The components include the sources of support for meeting child and family needs; procedures for locating these sources in a family's immediate and broader-based communities (community resource mapping); and the strategies used to build the capacity of community people, groups, and organizations to provide resources to young children and their families (Weissbourd, 1994).

Major Sources of Support

A resource-based approach looks toward various community people, groups, organizations, and programs as potential sources of support for meeting needs (Dunst et al., 1994; Katz, 1984). The following represents some but certainly not all of the people and groups that might be considered sources of support for meeting the individual and collective needs of children and their families.

Personal Social Network Members   There are many individuals to whom families can and often do turn when seeking advice, assistance, and nurturance, including a spouse or partner, blood relatives, a spouse's or partner's relatives, friends, neighbors, co-workers, clerics, church or synagogue members, babysitters, child care personnel, teachers, and carpool partners. For example, a cleric might be a source of emotional support and counseling for a family who is dealing with a new diagnosis of their child's condition. Similarly, neighbors with young children might be "organized" to form a community playgroup that creates a new learning opportunity for a family's children.

Associational Groups   McKnight (1989) lists the following associational groups as potential sources of support for meeting people's needs: artistic organizations, business organizations, charitable groups and drives, church groups, civic events, organizers, collector's groups, community support groups, elderly groups, ethnic associations, health and fitness groups, interest clubs, men's groups, mutual support (self-help) groups, neighborhood and block clubs, outdoor groups, political organizations, school groups, service clubs, social cause groups, sports leagues, study groups, veteran groups, women's groups, and youth groups. For example, artistic organiza-

Table 2. A taxonomy of resources for meeting family needs

Resource category	Examples
Economic	Money for necessities Money for emergencies Money for special needs or project Money for the future Stable income level
Physical and environmental	Clean environment Adequate housing (space, safety, furnishings) Safe neighborhood (protection) Adequate heat, water, plumbing Housing accessible to other resources Resources for home repairs and maintenance
Food and clothing	Adequate food for two meals a day Enough clothes for each season Reliable means for laundering clothes
Medical and dental	Trustworthy medical and dental professionals Available general or emergency health care Accessible medical and dental care Means of acquiring medical and dental care
Employment and vocational	Opportunity to work Satisfaction with work (in or out of home) Job security Available and accessible work
Transportation and communication	Means of getting family members where they need to go Means of contacting relatives, friends, and other sources of support
Adult education and enrichment	Available adult education opportunities Accessible educational opportunities
Child education and intervention	Accessible child education opportunities Opportunities and activities to help, teach, and play with children Appropriate toys and other educational materials
Child care	Help in routine daily care Emergency child care Child care/babysitting for employment purpose Respite child care
Recreational	Opportunities for recreational activities for individual family members, couples, total family Available recreational facilities for individual members, couples, total family
Emotional	Positive intrafamily relationships Positive relationships outside the family Companionship Sense of belonging to family or group Opportunities to spend time with significant people
Cultural and social	Opportunities to share ethnic or value-related experiences with others Opportunities to be involved with community and cultural affairs Accessible community and cultural affairs

Adapted from Dunst, Trivette, and Deal (1988).

tions might be asked to assist with the development of preschool art classes that include children with and without disabilities. Likewise, a service group might be recruited to make the necessary modifications to a family's home to accommodate a young child learning to use a wheelchair.

   Community Programs and Professionals   Almost every community in the United States has at least some of the following types of people, programs, and agencies that provide services and supports to members of their communities: public and private schools, family resource programs, child care centers, older-adult programs,

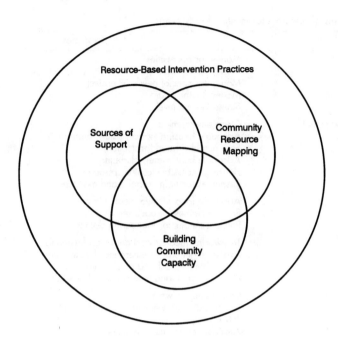

Figure 4. Three major components of resource-based early intervention practices.

financial planning programs, community colleges, institutions of higher education, recreational programs and camps, libraries, community health care centers, family planning clinics, police and fire departments, hospitals, family physicians and nurses, social workers and counselors, community officials, employment agencies, legal assistance agencies, social services agencies (public and private), and housing programs (e.g., Habitat for Humanity, public housing). For example, individuals participating in a senior citizen program might be asked to serve as "buddies" to children with disabilities participating in different kinds of community activities. Additionally, a family resource program might sponsor a series of "family fun days" for all children and their families in a community.

Specialized Professional Services Many child and family needs can be met by particular professionals and professional programs and agencies, including public health clinics; home health agencies; mental health programs and agencies; early intervention programs; special education programs; vocational rehabilitation programs; child welfare agencies; family preservation programs; special health care clinics; adult basic education programs; resource and referral programs; parent education programs; child development specialists (physicians, special education teachers, psychologists, developmental specialists, physical and occupational therapists, speech therapists); substance abuse programs; specialized transportation services; emergency, crisis, and disaster relief services; hospice programs; respite care; and case management and care coordination programs. For example, service coordinators from early intervention programs might be involved in "expanding" their view of the community resources that can be used to meet the needs of a family dealing with the death of a child with disabilities to include resources such as hospice care.

The above-mentioned lists of support categories include more than 75 potential sources of support and resources for meeting child and family needs. Providers often say that communities are limited in resources needed by children and families for strengthening functioning and promoting competence. This is perhaps true if a service-based approach is used, but not if a resource-based approach is used. The resource-based model provides a wider view of the best ways to create opportunities for supporting and strengthening child and family functioning.

Community Resource Mapping

According to Katz (1984), Kretzmann and McKnight (1993), McKnight and Kretzmann (1990), and others interested in increasing the use of community resources, the assumption is often made (erroneously) that community resources and supports are generally limited. Network mapping specialists (e.g., McKnight, 1987, 1989; McKnight & Kretzmann, 1984, 1990) often prove this assumption wrong when they engage people in the process of mapping community resources. Procedures for doing so constitute one major strategy for increasing awareness and utilization of resources and supports for children with disabilities and their families.

The process of community resource mapping has been used extensively in the community development field (Daley & Poole, 1985; Hasenfeld, 1983; Kaufman, 1985; McKnight & Kretzmann, 1990; Mulford, 1975; Rothman & Gant, 1975; Warren & Warren, 1977). To the best of the authors' knowledge, the procedures have not been widely or systematically used in early intervention. They would appear to have special utility, however, as the process of community resource mapping has proven effective in increasing awareness of community resources (Kretzmann & McKnight, 1993) and, if done collaboratively between families and early intervention staff members, should promote utilization of these resources coupled with capacity-building strategies (see the following section) (see especially Hasenfeld, 1983, for a review of relevant research). Therefore, the process and procedures can function as an important tool in mobilizing resources to meet needs.

Community resource mapping involves developing a complete listing of particular kinds of resources and the location (placement) of these resources in a physical space such as a neighborhood or county map. Community mapping literally identifies target community resources (e.g., child care, recreation opportunities, counseling) and pinpoints the location of these resources on a large map of the catchment and surrounding areas of the early intervention program wanting to employ resource-based practices. Starting points for beginning the network mapping process include the yellow pages of a telephone directory, knowledge of the community, or county and city resource guides. A completed map provides a visual display of what resources are available and where they are within a community. A complete network map promotes collection of information for identifying, mobilizing, and developing resources for families of young children with disabilities and their families. Fear, Carter, and Thullen (1985) and Kaufman (1985) included sources of community development models and described frameworks for translating network mapping information into action steps (see also Kretzmann & McKnight, 1993). Booth and Owen (1985) and Daley and Poole (1985) included descriptions of case studies that illustrate community development "in action."

Building Community Capacity

According to McKnight and Kretzmann (1990), efforts to successfully build the capacity of community people, organizations, and programs to serve children with disabilities and their families must focus on the strengths of communities as well as those of children and families. A modified set of procedures developed by McKnight and

Kretzmann (Kretzmann & McKnight, 1993; McKnight & Kretzmann, 1990) has proven useful as the building block for the development of strategies for building community capacity to serve children with disabilities and their families. The approach involves the development and use of a capacity inventory to identify the strengths of community programs and organizations in meeting the needs of children and families. The process of developing a capacity inventory can lead practitioners and program builders to recognize community assets and the meaningful contributions that community people and groups can make toward meeting child and family needs. Once strengths have been identified, any concerns that might interfere with serving children with disabilities and their families are identified. At this point, an important role of a community resources practitioner is to try to alleviate these concerns and make different sources of support viable resources for meeting child and family needs.

The following example of this strategy will help illustrate its applicability. The mother of a 3-year-old child with cerebral palsy indicated a desire for her child to participate in the "tadpole" swimming class at their community recreation center. A meeting with the swimming class instructor began with a description of the things the instructor did to promote child (swimming) competence. This resulted in a fairly detailed description of different strategies and past successes. The mother then described her desire for her child, which was followed by a request for any concerns the instructor had about a child with a disability participating in the swimming class. The only concern that was raised was for the child's safety (i.e., not drowning). The instructor was asked if having a volunteer in the water with the child at all times would alleviate his concern. The answer was yes, and a student on the high school swim team was recruited as a "buddy" for the child. This simple, yet highly effective, capacity-building process can work in a variety of situations. The three-step process involves 1) identifying the strengths of community people and groups, 2) demonstrating how these strengths address child and family desires, and 3) eliminating barriers through use of other resources.

Examples of Resource-Based Practices

The differences between service-based and resource-based early intervention practices perhaps are best illustrated by several additional examples. The examples presented are real and not hypothetical. They come from the authors' experiences of working with children and their families in an early intervention program that employs resource-based intervention practices.

Families of children with disabilities often indicate a need for a break from day-to-day child-rearing demands (actually most parents need this!). A service-based solution would meet this need through use of a professional or formal respite care program. In contrast, a resource-based approach would look to babysitters, mothers' morning-out programs, babysitting co-ops, or child care programs as ways of meeting this need. The latter approach will most likely prove more successful because a resource network is being built and mobilized rather than depending on a single source of support that may be labor intensive to create or unavailable when the family needs access to the resource (see Dunst et al., 1989).

The need for transportation is often requested by families of children with disabilities participating in early intervention programs. Service-based solutions to meeting transportation needs generally involve the development of some type of transportation system operated by the early intervention program or its host agency. In contrast, a resource-based approach would look to friends and relatives, volunteer organizations, or a bartering program as sources of transportation. This approach not only builds on the capacity of community people and groups to provide a needed resource but also builds a broader-based support system for families.

Children with disabilities participating in early intervention programs are often seen as needing particular kinds of services provided by particular kinds of professionals (e.g., speech pathologists, teachers, physical therapists). This is a service-based approach for meeting child needs. In contrast, resource-based approaches define needs not in terms of what professionals do but rather in terms of the full range of experiences that children require that promote child competence. For instance, in the case of a child who has motor development needs, a resource-based approach would not define efforts to meet needs only in terms of physical therapy but in the broad-based experiences (e.g., community play groups, YMCA exercise programs, early intervention programs) that can be used to enhance this aspect of child behavior.

A second example of a child-level resource-based approach comes from experiences promoting the communicative competence of young children with disabilities. In contrast to a service-based approach that might define a solution in terms of only speech therapy, a resource-based approach would consider all the possible community experiences that could be used to enhance communication skills. These might include, but not necessarily be limited to, a range of settings (e.g., libraries, petting zoos, preschool classrooms, mothers' morning-out programs) and experiences and activities within settings (e.g., promoting interactions between children and animals in a petting zoo) that can enhance children's behavior by building on their interest in things they find engaging (see Dunst & McWilliam, 1988).

The descriptions provided here and those throughout earlier sections of this chapter give numerous examples of what resource-based early intervention practices can look like when developed for a synergistic paradigm that considers communities as potentially rich in valuable resources and as important to the lives of children with disabilities and their families. Resource-based approaches to early intervention, as corroborating evidence indicates, tend to produce the greatest positive impact and therefore seem indicated as the method of choice for mobilizing resources to meet child and family needs.

Implications for Developing Individualized Family Service Plans

The methods and strategies described in this chapter for implementing resource-based practices are easily adapted and incorporated into the development of individualized family service plans (IFSPs). As described in Dunst et al. (1994, especially Chapters 5 and 6), effective and efficient IFSPs are those that promote the process of identifying family needs and mobilize a range of resources and supports to meet those needs. The resource-based approach considers informal as well as formal supports as legitimate resources. A simple yet efficient approach of identifying resources to meet needs is described in the next paragraph.

The first step in the IFSP process is the identification of the family's needs, concerns, or priorities. Once concerns have been identified and prioritized, the next step is to identify resources for meeting each of them. This is accomplished using a community network map and adding the people and institutions with which a target family and its members come in contact, either directly or indirectly. This activity provides a visual display of potential resources that can be explored to respond to identified concerns. A general rule is followed at this individualized level of network mapping: Potential resources are mapped separately for each identified concern to focus the resource identification and mobilization process. This ensures that the information gathered is specifically related to a family-identified concern and that the identification of resources does not become intrusive. This process often results in the development of a variety of resources that can be used to meet a concern or priority identified by the family.

BARRIERS TO ADOPTING RESOURCE-BASED PRACTICES

Adoption of resource-based early intervention practices is partly dependent on the elimination of a number of conceptual and pragmatic barriers. First, resource-based early intervention will become a reality when the necessary paradigm shift is made in terms of the five conceptually based characteristics described earlier in this chapter (see also Table 1). However, unless professionals begin to view their work with families through a different lens, changes in the ways child and family needs are met are not likely to occur.

A second barrier has attitudinal underpinnings and in many ways is the linchpin between theory and practice. Adoption of practices derived from a resource-based model requires a shift in how professionals view their roles and responsibilities. This shift necessitates that professionals view their expertise as a means of creating opportunities and experiences that promote child and family development (i.e., the end or outcome). Providers have to value mobilizing community resources as much as directly providing a service as a way of influencing behavior outcomes.

A third barrier concerns the expanded vista of where interventions can and should occur. Early intervention to a large degree has been defined and described as either home based or center based, or a combination of the two. Resource-based early intervention necessitates that a broad range of settings be the context for ensuring that children have multiple and varied learning experiences and opportunities. Reconfiguring early intervention in this manner requires determining where such practices are best implemented.

A fourth barrier is also attitudinal but concerns the ways communities view (and respond to) children with disabilities, as well as how they see their own capabilities and confidence in working with these children. Often, but not always, community people and groups initially respond to participation of children with disabilities in community activities with trepidation and anxiety. Unfortunately, apprehension is sometimes heightened when professionals, employing service-based approaches, convey the message that these people and groups need to be knowledgeable about multiple aspects of the child's disability. This focus on the "differences" in the child can undermine the success of the effort. Focusing on the strengths and successes of community people and groups and identifying the supports they need to feel capable and confident are often sufficient for breaking down most attitudinal barriers on the part of community people and groups.

SUMMARY

Resource-based early intervention programs define interventions not only in terms of specific kinds of professional services (e.g., respite care) but also in the range of community supports and resources (e.g., respite care, child care, sitter or companion services) that can be mobilized for meeting specific child and family needs (e.g., child care assistance). Resource-based approaches view sources of support as renewable and expandable, whereas service-based approaches view program-specific services as generally scarce and limited (Katz, 1984). Evidence described earlier in this chapter contrasting resource-based and service-based early intervention practices found the former associated with better outcomes compared with the latter.

Based on both research evidence and clinical experience, it is clear that early intervention practices are more likely to be successful if meeting child and family needs is defined in terms of the broad-based resources and supports required for typical community life and stable family functioning. This includes, but is not limited to, the provision and mobilization of the following resources: economic, physical and environmental, life necessities, medical and health, employment and vocation, transportation and communication, child and adult education, child care, recreational, emotional, and cultural and social (see Dunst, Trivette, & Deal, 1988, 1994; Hartman & Laird, 1983; Trivette et al., 1986; Turnbull, Summers, & Brotherson, 1986). It should be noted, however, that defining the targets of intervention in terms of these various resource categories does not mean being "everything to everybody," as some have interpreted resource-based family-centered intervention practices (see Dunst et al., 1994). It does mean being responsive to all family needs and in some cases providing resources and supports to families, while in other cases linking families with appropriate resources and services. It means never dismissing what families voice as their needs and priorities. Strengthening community support systems for meeting child and family needs will be beneficial in the long term, as community supports tend to be more stable than professional support systems and are often more easily accessible to children and families.

REFERENCES

Affleck, G., Tennen, H., Allen, D.A., & Gershman, K. (1986). Perceived social support and maternal adaptation during the transition from hospital to home care of high-risk infants. *Infant Mental Health Journal, 7*, 6–18.

Affleck, G., Tennen, H., & Rowe, J. (1991). *Infants in crisis: How parents cope with newborn intensive care and its aftermath.* New York: Springer-Verlag.

Booth, N., & Owen, F. (1985). The relevance of formal and informal networks for community development. *Research in Rural Sociology and Development, 2*, 159–172.

Bronfenbrenner, U. (1979). *The ecology of human development: Experiments by nature and design.* Cambridge, MA: Harvard University Press.

Chavis, D., & Wandersman, A. (1990). Sense of community in the urban environment: A catalyst for participation and community development. *American Journal of Community Psychology, 18*, 55–81.

Cochran, M., & Brassard, J. (1979). Child development and personal social networks. *Child Development, 50*, 601–616.

Colletta, N. (1981). Social support and the risk of maternal rejection by adolescent mothers. *Journal of Psychology, 109*, 191–197.

Crnic, K.A., Greenberg, M.T., Ragozin, A., Robinson, N., & Basham, R. (1983). Effects of stress and social support on mothers of premature and full-term infants. *Child Development, 54*, 209–217.

Crnic, K.A., Greenberg, M.T., & Slough, N.M. (1986). Early stress and social support influences on mothers' and high-risk infants' functioning in late infancy. *Infant Mental Health Journal, 7*, 19–48.

Crockenberg, S.B. (1981). Infant irritability, mother responsiveness and social influences on the security of infant-mother attachment. *Child Development, 52*, 857–865.

Crockenberg, S.B. (1985). Professional support and care of infants by adolescent mothers in England and the United States. *Journal of Pediatric Psychology, 10*, 413–428.

Daley, J., & Poole, D. (1985). Community development insights for planning public social service innovations. *Research in Rural Sociology and Development, 2*, 143–157.

Deal, A.G., Dunst, C.J., & Trivette, C.M. (1994). A flexible and functional approach to developing individualized family support plans. In C.J. Dunst, C.M. Trivette, & A.G. Deal (Eds.), *Supporting and strengthening families: Vol. 1. Methods, strategies and practices* (pp. 62–72). Cambridge, MA: Brookline Books.

Dean, A., & Lin, N. (1977). Stress-buffering role of social support. *Journal of Nervous and Mental Disease, 165,* 403–417.

Dunst, C.J. (1985). Rethinking early intervention. *Analysis and Intervention in Developmental Disabilities, 5,* 165–201.

Dunst, C.J. (1991, February). *Empowering families: Principles and outcomes.* Paper presented at the Fourth Annual Research Conference, "A System of Care of Children's Mental Health: Expanding the Research Base," Tampa, FL.

Dunst, C.J., & Deal, A.G. (1994). A family-centered approach to developing individualized family support plans. In C.J. Dunst, C.M. Trivette, & A.G. Deal (Eds.), *Supporting and strengthening families: Vol. 1. Methods, strategies and practices* (pp. 73–88). Cambridge, MA: Brookline Books.

Dunst, C.J., & Leet, H.E. (1987). Measuring the adequacy of resources in households with young children. *Child: Care, Health and Development, 13,* 111–125.

Dunst, C.J., Leet, H., & Trivette, C.M. (1988). Family resources, personal well-being and early intervention. *Journal of Special Education, 22,* 108–116.

Dunst, C.J., & McWilliam, R.A. (1988). Cognitive assessment of multiply handicapped young children. In T.D. Wachs & R. Sheehan (Eds.), *Assessment of developmentally disabled children* (pp. 213–238). New York: Plenum.

Dunst, C.J., & Trivette, C.M. (1987, April). *Social support and positive functioning in families of developmentally at-risk preschoolers.* Paper presented at the symposium "Every Cloud Has a Silver Lining: Successful Adaptations to the Care of a Handicapped Child," held at the biennial meeting of the Society for Research in Child Development, Baltimore.

Dunst, C.J., & Trivette, C.M. (1988a). A family systems model of early intervention with handicapped and developmentally at-risk children. In D. Powell (Ed.), *Parent education in early childhood intervention: Emerging directions in theory, research, and practice* (pp. 131–180). Norwood, NJ: Ablex.

Dunst, C.J., & Trivette, C.M. (1988b). Determinants of caregiver styles of interaction used with developmentally at-risk children. In K. Marfo (Ed.), *Parent-child interaction and developmental disabilities: Theory, research, and intervention* (pp. 3–31). New York: Praeger.

Dunst, C.J., & Trivette, C.M. (1990). Assessment of social support in early intervention programs. In S. Meisels & J. Shonkoff (Eds.), *Handbook of early intervention* (pp. 326–349). New York: Cambridge University Press.

Dunst, C.J., Trivette, C.M., & Deal, A.G. (Eds.). (1988). *Enabling and empowering families: Principles and guidelines for practice.* Cambridge, MA: Brookline Books.

Dunst, C.J., Trivette, C.M., & Deal, A.G. (Eds.). (1994). *Supporting and strengthening families: Vol. 1. Methods, strategies and practices.* Cambridge, MA: Brookline Books.

Dunst, C.J., Trivette, C.M., Gordon, N.J., & Pletcher, L.L. (1989). Building and mobilizing informal family support networks. In G.S. Singer & L.K. Irvin (Eds.), *Support for caregiving families: Enabling positive adaptation to disability* (pp. 121–142). Baltimore: Paul H. Brookes Publishing Co.

Dunst, C.J., Trivette, C.M., Starnes, A.L., Hamby, D.W., & Gordon, N.J. (1993). *Building and evaluating family support initiatives: A national study of programs for persons with developmental disabilities.* Baltimore: Paul H. Brookes Publishing Co.

Fear, F., Carter, K., & Thullen, M. (1985). Action research in community development: Concepts and principles. *Research in Rural Sociology and Development, 2,* 197–216.

Garbarino, J., & Kostelny, K. (1993). Neighborhood and community influences on parenting. In T. Luster & L. Okagaki (Eds.), *Parenting: An ecological perspective* (pp. 297–320). Hillsdale, NJ: Lawrence Erlbaum Associates.

Hartman, A., & Laird, J. (1983). *Family-centered social work practice.* New York: Free Press.

Hasenfeld, Y. (1983). *Human service organizations.* Englewood Cliffs, NJ: Prentice Hall.

Hobbs, N., Dokecki, P.R., Hoover-Dempsey, K.V., Moroney, R.M., Shayne, M.W., & Weeks, K.H. (1984). *Strengthening families.* San Francisco: Jossey-Bass.

Kahn, R.H., Wethington, E., & Ingersoll-Dayton, B. (1987). Social support and social networks: Determinants, effects, and interactions. In R.P. Abeles (Ed.), *Life-span perspectives and social psychology* (pp. 139–165). Hillsdale, NJ: Lawrence Erlbaum Associates.

Katz, R. (1984). Empowerment and synergy: Expanding the community's healing process. In J. Rappaport, C. Swift, & R. Hess (Eds.), *Studies in empowerment: Steps toward understanding and action* (pp. 201–226). New York: Haworth Press.

Kaufman, H. (1985). An action approach to community development. *Research in Rural Sociology and Development, 2,* 53–65.

Kretzmann, J., & McKnight, J. (1993). *Building community from the inside out.* Evanston, IL: Northwestern University, Center for Urban Affairs and Policy Research.

McCubbin, H.I., Joy, C.B., Cauble, A.E., Comeau, J.K., Patterson, J.M., & Needle, R.H. (1980). Family stress and coping: A decade of review. *Journal of Marriage and the Family, 42,* 855–871.

McGuire, J.C., & Gottlieb, B.H. (1979). Social support groups among new parents: An experimental study in primary prevention. *Journal of Clinical Child Psychology, 8,* 111–116.

McKnight, J. (1987, Winter). Regenerating community. *Social Policy,* pp. 54–58.

McKnight, J. (1989, April). *Beyond community services.* Unpublished manuscript, Northwestern University, Center for Urban Affairs and Policy Research, Evanston, IL.

McKnight, J., & Kretzmann, J. (1984, Winter). Community organization in the 80's: Toward a post-Alinsky agenda. *Social Policy,* pp. 145–147.

McKnight, J., & Kretzmann, J. (1990). *Mapping community capacity.* Unpublished manuscript, Northwestern University, Center for Urban Affairs and Policy Research, Evanston, IL.

Meisels, S.J., & Shonkoff, J.P. (Eds.). (1990). *Handbook of early childhood intervention.* Cambridge, MA: Cambridge University Press.

Mulford, C. (1975). Interorganization relations: Implications for community developers. In R. Warren (Ed.), *Studying your community.* New York: Russell Sage.

Pascoe, J.M., Loda, F.A., Jeffries, V., & Earp, J. (1981). The association between mothers' social support and provision of stimulation to their children. *Developmental and Behavioral Pediatrics, 2,* 15–19.

Raab, M.M. (1994, August). *Supporting families of young children with disabilities through child care assistance.* Paper presented at the 1994 SUNRISE Summer Institute, Hilton Head, SC.

Rappaport, J. (1981). In praise of paradox: A social policy of empowerment over prevention. *American Journal of Community Psychology, 9,* 1–25.

Rappaport, J. (1987). Terms of empowerment/exemplars of prevention: Toward a theory for community psychology. *American Journal of Community Psychology, 15*(2), 121–148.

Rothman, J., & Gant, L.M. (1975). Approaches and models of community intervention. In R. Warren (Ed.), *Studying your community* (pp. 35–44). New York: Russell Sage.

Sarason, S.B., Carroll, C., Maton, K., Cohen, S., & Lorentz, E. (1977). *Human services and resources networks: Rationale, possibilities, and public policy.* Cambridge, MA: Brookline Books.

Schwirian, K.P. (1983). Models of neighborhood change. *Annual Review of Sociology, 9,* 83–102.

Swift, C. (1984). Empowerment: An antidote for folly. In J. Rappaport, C., Swift, & R. Hess (Eds.), *Studies in empowerment: Steps toward understanding and action* (pp. xi–xv). New York: Haworth Press.

Trivette, C.M., Deal, A.G., & Dunst, C.J. (1986). Family needs, sources of support, and professional roles: Critical elements of family systems assessment and intervention. *Diagnostique, 11,* 246–267.

Trivette, C.M., & Dunst, C.J. (1992). Characteristics and influences of role division and social support among mothers of handicapped preschoolers. *Topics in Early Childhood Special Education, 12*(3), 367–387.

Trivette, C.M., Dunst, C.J., & Hamby, D. (in press). Social support and coping in families of children at risk for developmental disabilities. In M. Brambring, A. Beelmann, & H. Rauh (Eds.), *Intervention in early childhood: Theory, evaluation, and practices.* Berlin/New York: de Gruyter.

Turnbull, A.P., Summers, J.A., & Brotherson, M.J. (1986). Family life cycle: Theoretical and empirical implications and future directions for families with mentally retarded members. In J.J. Gallagher & P.M. Vietze (Eds.), *Family of handicapped persons: Research, programs, and policy issues* (pp. 45–66). Baltimore: Paul H. Brookes Publishing Co.

Unger, D., & Wandersman, A. (1985). The importance of neighbors: The social, cognitive, and affective components of neighboring. *American Journal of Community Psychology, 13,* 139–169.

Wandersman, L., Wandersman, A., & Kahn, S. (1980). Social support in the transition to parenthood. *Journal of Community Psychology, 8,* 332–342.

Warren, R., & Warren, D. (1977). How to diagnose a neighborhood. In R. Warren & D. Warren (Eds.), *The neighborhood organizer's handbook* (pp. 173–195). South Bend, IN: University of Notre Dame Press.

Weinraub, M., & Wolf, B. (1983). Effects of stress and social supports on mother-child interactions in single- and two-parent families. *Child Development, 54,* 1297–1311.

Weissbourd, B. (1994). The evolution of the family resource movement. In S. Kagan & B. Weissbourd (Eds.), *Putting families first: America's family support movement and the challenge of change* (pp. 28–47). San Francisco: Jossey-Bass.

Wellman, B. (1979). The community question: The intimate networks of East Yonkers. *American Journal of Sociology, 84,* 1201–1231.

Willett, J.B. (1989). Some results on reliability for the longitudinal measurement of change: Implications for the design of studies of individual growth. *Educational and Psychological Measurement, 49,* 587–602.

... 6
.
.
.

The Family as a System and a Context for Early Intervention

Janet R. Cornwell and Constance Korteland

The concept of "family" is challenging both to define and to understand. The family as a unit is invisible, with its form inferred and its reality described through ongoing interactions that are dynamic and everchanging (Bell & Bell, 1989). The family as a social system has been defined as a group of individuals who are in the process of constructing their own reality (Handel & Whitchurch, 1994). A family is founded in diverse, experiential activities that develop into a unified whole. The concept of "family" is a theoretical construct that is often characterized as a system (Hess & Handel, 1994).

Multiple paradigms compete in defining and describing families in America today. The "modern" paradigm describes the family as an ancient, essential, and endangered institution: "an intact nuclear household composed of a male breadwinner, his full-time homemaker wife, and their dependent children" (Stacey, 1994, p. 644). This paradigm holds family as a static and accepted structure, attributing to this structure what is moral and right and describing existing family units in terms of their discrepancy with this sanctioned form. It also includes value judgments and denies economic, social, and cultural realities. The modern paradigm is exemplified by the viewpoint of the National Commission on Children (1993): "Families formed by marriage—where two caring adults are committed to one another and to their children—provide the best environment for bringing children into the world and supporting their growth and development" (p. 18). This paradigm accepts the "family" as a system, yet defines this system in such a way that the majority of Americans are not included in the definition of a healthy, functional family. These definitions also affect the way in which "help" (possibly in the form of early intervention services) is delivered to those in need of services and influence the stigma and response cost that accompany the need for formal support and assistance.

The emerging "postmodern" paradigm attempts to make sense of the reality of the family as a dynamic, interactive unit existing within a world where arrangements are "diverse, fluid, and unresolved" (Stacey, 1994, p. 646). Family diversity is intrinsic to contemporary families and is not a temporary deviation from the norm. Stacey further described the perspective of the postmodern paradigm: "Americans today have crafted a multiplicity of family and household arrangements that we inhabit uneasily and reconstitute frequently in response to changing personal and occupational circumstances" (Stacey, 1994, p. 645).

To meet the goals of early intervention, it is necessary to function under the postmodern paradigm. If a family is to be empowered through early intervention services to better care for and cope with a child who has special needs, then service providers should accept and support the family as a unit that is whole and authentic on its own terms and that cannot be looked at in terms of its flaws or differences from the norm.

This chapter describes the family in all its complexities and discusses the implications for providing early intervention services. A framework for early intervention is outlined that can provide the services needed for positive outcomes for both children with special needs and their families. Recommendations for early intervention providers follow. The chapter concludes with a case study describing a "nontraditional" family involved in early intervention services that illustrates the points made throughout the chapter.

FAMILIES IN AMERICA IN THE 1990s

The National Commission on Children (1993) reviewed the statistics concerning families and drew the conclusion that "Dramatic social, demographic, and economic changes [since the 1960s] have profoundly affected the American family and altered the routines of family life and the roles of many parents and children" (p. 1). The statistics reveal that children are now a smaller proportion of the U.S. population than they were in the early 1960s. In general, families are smaller, with fewer children.

In addition, since the 1970s, the number of children living in homes with one parent has increased to include more than 25% of the children living in America (Galston, 1993). The major explanations for these figures are the rising divorce rates and the increased number of unmarried mothers, especially teenagers (Carnegie Corporation of New York, 1994). Children are also cared for more often by relatives or other caring adults who become surrogate parents in either a short-term or lifelong role.

An increasing number of mothers are in the work force, thereby increasing the number of children receiving care from others in child care or informal babysitting arrangements. Approximately 60% of mothers with children under the age of 6 work outside of the home. The roles of mothers and fathers have changed somewhat at the same time, with many fathers taking a more active caregiving role with their children.

Another outcome of these changes is the reduction in the amount of time families spend together. Eisenberg (1990) stated that since 1955 the amount of time children spend with their parents has declined by more than 10 hours per week.

Families with young children have a higher chance of living in poverty than they did in the past (Zill, 1993), especially if the family is headed by a single mother and/or the family is African American or Latino (National Commission on Children, 1993). Approximately 43% of families headed by mothers alone are labeled as poor compared with 7% of two-parent families. In addition, in 1991, the income of the poorest 20% of families in America had declined by 9% since 1973 (average annual income $9,734), whereas the income of the wealthiest 20% of families had increased by 18% over the same period (average annual income $95,530). Also, the income of families with children has fallen overall since the early 1970s while the income of families without children has continued to rise (National Commission on Children, 1993).

These findings are sometimes interpreted as an indictment of nontraditional families (e.g., single-parent families) and as justification for exaggerating the requirements to form a family or developing government programs to correct the problem. However, the findings can also be interpreted as a redefinition of the complexity and diversity of the family unit in America today. This interpretation heralds a need for the social, economic, and political systems surrounding the family system to be responsive and supportive to families as they continually change and evolve. This is the interpretation on which this chapter's discussion of family-centered early intervention is based. Families are everchanging units, and early intervention must be designed as a responsive, flexible system to support families of young children with developmental delays and disabilities, promoting their well-being and independent functioning.

THE FAMILY AS A SYSTEM

An ecological perspective of human development was proposed by Bronfenbrenner (1979), who suggested that the individual develops within a series of environmental systems—the microsystem, mesosystem, exosystem, and macrosystem—that interact with the individual and each other (see Chapter 1 of this book for a detailed explanation of these systems). Bronfenbrenner (1986) also included the chronosystem, which is the pattern of events over the course of a lifetime. Bronfenbrenner views the individual as developing within multiple environmental contexts with direct and indirect influences of each system and the interaction among systems over time. The family fits his description of a microsystem, the most immediate system surrounding the individual. Understanding the complex, reciprocal influences of the family on the individual is only a part of understanding the interrelationships among the various systems.

Minuchin (1985) synthesized the key principles of systems theory, applying it to family functioning. He proposed the following:

> The family as a system is an organized whole whose members are interdependent. . . .
> The patterns of these members' interactions within the family system are circular rather than linear. . . .
> Families have homeostatic features that maintain the stability of their patterns of interactions. . . .
> Evolution and change are inherent in family systems. . . .
> Family systems are composed of subsystems separated by boundaries and governed by rules and patterns of interaction. (pp. 289–291)

Limitations to this systems model of family functioning have been explored (Handel & Whitchurch, 1994; Roberts, 1992). Roberts (1992) stated that descriptions of families as systems are mechanistic and impersonal, ignoring the human dimension of family. Handel and Whitchurch (1994) asserted that describing the family as a system is misleading because it exaggerates the inevitability of outcomes of interaction within it. Families are composed of people who not only function within systems but interpret the multiple forces of those systems. "They construct their lives in interaction" (Handel & Whitchurch, 1994, p. 494).

This chapter uses the structure and terminology of family systems theorists while attempting to move past the confining aspects of this model. A popular conceptual framework of family systems as it applies to families who have children with special needs was proposed by Turnbull, Summers, and Brotherson (1983). This model includes four elements that can be examined separately but that interrelate and interact with each other. These components are family structure, family interaction, family functions, and family life cycle. These elements will be used to frame further discussion on families and their complexities.

Family Structure

The structure of families comprises those aspects that describe the family, including composition, size, socioeconomic status, family and ethnic cultures, and geographical location. Families have as their members a diverse constellation of people, sometimes including the traditional husband, wife, and two children, but often including assorted relatives and individuals who function as family for short or long periods of time. Some families also have family members who are defined by their exceptionality. Turnbull et al. (1993) considered the exceptionality, including the nature, severity, and demands of the exceptionality, and other aspects of individual functioning, such as coping style, health, and well-being, as part of family structure.

The size of families can vary from one person (some individuals with pets may define themselves as family) to a large number of people. Size of the family unit also varies over the family life cycle. Another variable is socioeconomic status (SES), which is defined by education and income of household wage earners. The significance that accompanies these figures is relative to the interpretation given by the family. Families living in poverty are often categorized by the larger society as exhibiting a variety of deficiencies. Closer study has revealed that families in poverty often exhibit a high degree of competence in managing their complex lives (Rosier & Corsaro, 1993).

The examination of culture as it defines and affects family systems is complex and challenging to discuss. Family members interact within one or more large cultural systems. Members have ethnic and religious backgrounds that contain assorted beliefs and attitudes (Anderson, 1992). Families also develop their own cultures, defined by interrelated norms shared by members, including values, rules, and expectations (Handel, 1994). Some families who have children with special needs appear to become a part of the "world of exceptionalities" with its own cultural aspects. Another aspect of family structure is geographical location. Geographical location influences the family's culture and includes aspects of rural and urban influences, as well as regional differences.

Family Interaction

Family interaction examines the subsystems of the family unit, traditionally described as the marital, parental, sibling, and extrafamilial subsystems. This model suggests that these subsystems are encompassed by three processes: cohesion, adaptability, and communication.

Cohesion refers to the close emotional bonding that members have as well as the level of autonomy members feel within the family system (Olson et al., 1983). Cohesion can vary along a continuum from total disengagement to total enmeshment with dysfunction appearing to occur on each end of the continuum. *Adaptability* refers to family members' abilities to respond to stress (Olson et al., 1983). Adaptability varies across a continuum from rigid with a high degree of control and structure to chaotic with a low degree of control and structure. Again, families functioning at either end of the continuum are traditionally seen as pathological. *Communication* is the third process through which a family functions. Handel and Whitchurch (1994) stated that communication is the central process that a family uses to construct their reality.

Family subsystems hold traditional labels that depict the various relationships that exist for family members. In families headed by a single parent, the marital subsystem will not be present. However, the other parent may function as a member of the parental subsystem. Other family members may also function as members of the parental subsystem.

In families with more than one child, the sibling subsystem plays a dynamic and lifelong role for each of its members. Issues of this subsystem include equity, maturity, loyalty, and individuality (Handel, 1994). Sibling relationships present multiple challenges due to siblings sharing their parents, being of different ages and possibly different genders, and having unique, individual traits. When one of the siblings has a disability, challenges become even more complex (Powell & Ogle, 1993).

The extrafamilial subsystem can be an indispensable source of informal support for a family. This subsystem can provide resources that are "vital for the well-being of families" (Rosier & Corsaro, 1993, p. 173). Family subsystems can best be understood if the service provider develops a sensitivity to the family unit, its members, and their interactions. Family interactions are interrelated with family structure and will differ depending on the family's values, ethnic background, resources, and so forth.

Family Functions

Family systems exist within a context of ongoing activities and tasks. These activities vary as to importance, intensity, and the amount of time they require from family members. Family functions include economic, domestic, health care, recreation, socialization, affection, self-definition, and education and vocation. These functions are defined as needs by the family and serve to prompt family activity.

Family needs and functions construct a locus of concern that is placed into a context of feelings, motives, and fantasies, described by Hess and Handel (1994) as "family themes." Family themes influence family behavior and become the lens through which the family sees the results of their activities. For example, one family may have a theme of "you and me against the world," and all activities and their outcomes serve to reinforce that theme as they are interpreted by the family through that perspective.

Family Life Cycle

Family life cycle may be defined as a series of developmental changes over time experienced by the family unit and its members. Family life cycle changes are defined by Turnbull and Turnbull (1990) in terms of children's developmental progress, including birth of the child, early childhood, school entry, adolescence, and young adulthood. When a family system includes a child with special needs, the expectations for and the reality of the family life cycle may differ.

Handel and Whitchurch (1994), in describing the family as a political unit representing a set of power dynamics, discussed the changes in these power dynamics through the family life cycle. For example, children gain power as they grow and develop while parents yield their authority and power. Family life cycle changes affect and interrelate with family composition, interactions, and priority functions of the family. Children are born, grow up, and leave their family to become independent adults, thereby affecting membership and roles within the system. Functions and themes of families vary over time as their members develop and change. Interactions among family members may vary in cohesion and adaptability at different points in the family life cycle.

Steinglass, Bennett, Wolin, and Reiss (1994) examined family maturation through three phases. The early phase establishes a structure and identity of the family as an independent system. The middle phase establishes a commitment of the family to a number of themes, and the final phase is focused on clarification and legacy. It might be concluded, then, that the family, as well as each member of the family, goes through developmental changes.

FAMILY-CENTERED EARLY INTERVENTION

As outlined in Chapter 1, the goals of early intervention include supporting families of young children with disabilities to achieve their own goals and enabling family members to have positive interactions that promote shared feelings of competence and success. To achieve these goals, as well as the goals focusing on children's development and learning, early intervention should be family centered, working with the family as a system that deserves to be accepted, respected, and supported. Families embrace their children with the care and nurturance needed for them to grow and thrive. Even when, or perhaps especially when, the child has been identified as being in need of early intervention services, families need to be supported to continue providing this most essential function.

The following section of this chapter describes aspects of family-centered early intervention designed to achieve the goals of early intervention. Initial discussion centers around a description of several models of helping and their outcomes for families. The relationships and interactions necessary for early interventionists to be helpful to families receiving early intervention are then outlined. Finally, the family system context in which these relationships function is described.

Models of Helping Families

To achieve positive outcomes for young children in early intervention programs, the major focus of intervention needs to include the family system. Help in the form of early intervention must be offered in a way that results in the family feeling an increased sense of empowerment (Dunst, Trivette, & Deal, 1994). Brickman et al. (1982) described four helping models and examined the degree to which people are held responsible for the cause of their problems, the level of expectation for solving their own problems, and the effect of both on feelings of self-efficacy. Brickman et al. employed attribution theory (Zuckerman, 1979), which predicts that if one makes an external attribution for the onset of problems but yet takes the responsibility to solve them, the results will be an increased sense of empowerment, enhanced well-being, and internalized locus of control.

The four helping models of Brickman et al. (1982) were moral, medical, enlightenment, and compensatory. Brickman et al. found that when help is given through the moral model, as in advice columns, families are perceived as the cause of their problems and should be held responsible for their solutions. The outcome is that the family may feel competent if they solve their problems. However, the family may suffer loneliness, exhaustion, and guilt in being blamed for the problem and in seeking their own solutions without support.

The medical model, typical in health care systems, relieves the family of responsibility for both the cause and solution of their problems. The helper is seen as the expert and, when and if the problem is solved, the family realizes their need for expert intervention and their own lack of ability to handle issues. Family outcomes may include feelings of incompetence, passivity, and dependency.

The enlightenment model, as in various 12-step programs, suggests that the family is responsible for their problems but also that they do not have the power or the skills to solve them without help. When the family concedes to the power of the helper, solutions will be found. For some families, this model may result in a sense of incompetence and lowered self-esteem.

The compensatory model seems to achieve the most effective outcomes for families in early intervention. In this model, central to Head Start philosophy, the helper is seen as a facilitator or a resource to offer the family support and assistance to their identified needs. Families experience positive behavior change, while feelings of competence and well-being are increased (Dunst, Trivette, & Deal, 1988). The family is not held responsible for causing their problems in this model, but is seen as capable of solving them with support and assistance given in the process.

Dunst and colleagues (1988) have adapted the compensatory model for the field of early intervention, labeling their model a "promotion" model. The promotion model is not deficit oriented in that the family is not blamed for being in need of early intervention services. Once the child is found to meet the criteria for early intervention services, the focus of service delivery shifts to supporting the family's strengths and capabilities to promote the most positive outcomes. In this model, the family is able to credit themselves for their successes and achievements.

Basic to this model of helping are the following principles, adapted from Rappaport's (1981) reflections on empowerment:

- Every family has strengths, capabilities, and competencies, which are already present or are possible.
- If a family displays poor functioning, it is the result of the lack of resources and supports that promote the use of existing competencies and/or the acquisition of new skills.
- Where new competencies need to be learned, they are best acquired within the context of the family's daily life, guided by the family's priorities, goals, and aspirations.

Effective helping, as defined by Dunst (1987), is the

> act of enabling families to become better able to solve problems, meet needs, or achieve aspirations by promoting acquisition of competencies that support and strengthen functioning in a way that permits a greater sense of individual and family control over its developmental course. (p. 1)

In early intervention, this help appears to be best given in collaborative partnerships between families and early interventionists (Crutcher, 1991; Dunst & Paget, 1991; Dunst, Trivette, & Johanson, 1994; Roberts & Magrab, 1991). These partnerships are described in detail in the following section.

Partnerships within Early Intervention

The definition of parent–professional partnerships (Dunst & Paget, 1991) is "an association between a family and one or more professionals who function collaboratively using agreed upon roles in pursuit of a joint interest and common goal" (p. 29). In these partnerships, it is expected that families will make their own final decisions and take credit for solving their problems with the support of their partner, the early interventionist.

Dunst, Trivette, Davis, and Cornwell (1994) studied families receiving a variety of early intervention services to identify the characteristics needed in professional partners to achieve positive family outcomes. These characteristics included prehelping attitudes and beliefs, helping behaviors, and posthelping responses and consequences. Dunst, Trivette, and Johanson (1994) investigated these characteristics to assess their impact on family outcomes. They concluded their study with an organizational scheme of partnership characteristics that includes beliefs, attitudes, communicative style, and behavioral actions. Cornwell and Korteland (1994) selected key elements of partnership relationships from the findings in these studies and from their experiences in early intervention. These elements can be found in Table 1 and are discussed below.

1. Partnerships should be based on mutual acceptance, respect, and caring. Early interventionists should be able to put aside their own biases developed through their life experiences (Harry, 1992). They need to appreciate the diversity of life experiences and work within the multiple contexts that family systems provide. For example, early interventionists should understand and respect the families' cultures and how families experience and even create their own cultures (Anderson, 1992).

2. Partners should be able to trust each other. Early intervention relationships should exist at a level of intimacy and shared understanding that denotes trust (Sonnenschein, 1981). Families should be able to assume that confidentiality will be respected at all times.

3. Partnership relationships take time to develop. The relationship between a family and an early interventionist is at the core of the early intervention process. However, early interventionists cannot expect families to enter these relationships immediately prepared to work collaboratively and openly. Early interventionists should establish themselves as consistent and available partners with the expectation that relationships will develop.

4. Partnerships are reciprocal relationships. In early intervention, partnerships work best if families feel that it is acceptable, but not required, for them to contribute to the relationships. There should be different opportunities for families to contribute in their partnerships with early interventionists. Families' contributions may reach farther than their individual interventionists; that is, contributions may include hints and information that can be compiled and shared with other families. Because power lies in the provider role in relationships, if families are limited only to receiving, feelings of incompetence and powerlessness may be the outcomes of early intervention.

5. Partners should be open to sharing some of themselves in their relationships. Early interventionists are often trained to maintain professional distance in their relationships with clients. The concept of professional distance does not contribute to a working partnership and may actually be more detrimental than beneficial to effective family partnerships (Turnbull & Turnbull, 1990). Sonnenschein (1981) indicated that, in early intervention, professional distance leads to a relationship in which

Table 1. Key elements of family–professional partnerships

1. Partnerships should be based on mutual acceptance, respect, and caring.
2. Partners should be able to trust each other.
3. Partnership relationships take time to develop.
4. Partnerships are reciprocal relationships.
5. Partners should be open to sharing some of themselves in their relationships.
6. Families maintain the final decision-making authority in partnerships.
7. Partners should share responsibility for their work together to achieve their goals.
8. Partners offer help to families in response to their identified needs and concerns.
9. Open and effective communication is needed in partnerships.
10. Disagreement and negotiation are allowed in partnerships.

families sense that empathy is withheld by the professional. As partnerships develop, early interventionists should risk sharing their personal selves with the families they serve.

6. Families maintain the final decision-making authority in partnerships. In many types of partnerships, decision making is a shared pursuit. In early intervention, families should maintain the ability, after information and opinions are shared, to make the final decisions. Also, however the decision is made, families should be able to credit themselves with their decisions and their successful actions. Families should not feel any risk of losing the support and assistance of their early interventionists by making certain decisions.

7. Partners should share responsibility for their work together to achieve their goals. The primary focus of partnerships in early intervention should be on the solutions to, and not the causes of, problems. Families should receive assistance and support in meeting their own needs (Bailey, 1987). Early interventionists should work with families to use available resources to meet their needs. These resources should be composed primarily of systems and services most meaningful in families' ongoing lives.

8. Partners offer help to families in response to their identified needs and concerns. At times, help should be offered before it is requested to be supportive of the give-and-take of partnership relationships. This help should be aligned with the priority needs and concerns of families. Early interventionists should frequently check with families to ensure their help fits the families' current direction.

9. Open and effective communication is needed in partnerships. Early interventionists should communicate clearly and honestly with families (Dunst, Trivette, & Deal, 1994). The focus of problem-oriented communication should be on solutions rather than blame (Turnbull & Turnbull, 1990). Reflective and empathetic listening is the most essential communication skill that early interventionists can possess. Early interventionists should maintain an awareness of qualitative and cultural differences among families and among individuals within families as to their pace, phrasing, and pauses in verbal and nonverbal communication patterns (Wayman, Lynch, & Hanson, 1990). Early interventionists need to adjust their own styles to fit families' comfort and expectations.

10. Disagreement and negotiation are allowed in partnerships. In a functioning partnership, families and early interventionists should be able to "agree to disagree." The respect and acceptance that this requires take time to develop. Conflicts often can produce growth when both parties need to negotiate to reach a conclusion. The final decision should belong to the family, fitting with their priorities and beliefs, or the intervention being planned will not result in positive outcomes (Bailey, 1987).

Partnerships within the Family System

Partnership relationships in early intervention need to be based within the context of the family system. As described earlier in this chapter, the major components of the family system include family structure, family interaction, family functions, and family life cycle. Each of these components is discussed next as it relates to the delivery of early intervention services. Although the goals of early intervention include many with a specific child focus, early intervention services are best delivered by working with families of these young children. Early intervention will not be successful over the long term if the family does not maintain the authority to direct and participate in the intervention given.

Family Structure   Several aspects of family structure are crucial and should be attended to when bringing early intervention services to families. Composition of the family system is information early interventionists should gather when first entering the relationship. Learning the functions of the various family members as well as the specific roles they play and how the individuals are labeled can help clarify the family structure. A family may be composed of a number of people who do not fit traditional expectations. Furthermore, composition of the family and the roles family members play may change over time. It is important to realize that this understanding emerges with the development of the partnership and cannot be obtained before initiating early intervention. Observing the family interact in their home setting is an effective way to enhance the development of this partnership.

Family values differ among cultures concerning issues such as autonomy, competition, achievement (Turnbull & Turnbull, 1990), gender, time, and individual power within the family. It is important to avoid cultural stereotypes when attempting to understand a family system. Early interventionists should discern family members' perceptions of their culture and the meaning that the family has attributed to these perceptions (Ronnau & Poertner, 1993).

Another important aspect of family structure is the family's SES and the assumptions and stereotypes that come with it. The early interventionist should not presume that lower-SES families will lack the skills, abilities, and resources to work successfully in partnership.

Families are diverse in terms of their strengths and coping styles in dealing with stress. Boyce, Behl, Mortensen, and Akers (1991) studied the relationship between family structure and the impact of stress when a child has special needs. They proposed stress as a variable to be considered when providing early intervention services.

Family Interaction   In early intervention, it is important that the interventionist not only become acquainted with the individuals making up the family system but also understand how they interact within the various subsystems. The early interventionist may focus on an individual subsystem within the family as a consequence of strengths and capabilities that are observed or due to concerns of family members. For example, the interactions within the sibling subsystem may reveal optimal intervention opportunities through engagement and enjoyment of devised play and games. Members of the sibling subsystem may also need extra support and attention in terms of information or listening when they have questions about special needs or prognosis.

The extrafamilial subsystem, made up of extended family members, may provide a great source of support and strength for the family with a child with disabilities. Early interventionists should become familiar with the members of this subsystem and their interactions with other family members. This subsystem may need support and information when questions occur and should receive the attention of the early interventionist when necessary. Direct intervention may be desired by members of the extended family, for example, to learn how to be most helpful to the family.

The processes used by the family to maintain their interactions, identified in the model proposed by Turnbull et al. (1993) as cohesion, adaptability, and communication, should be observed and respected by early interventionists because the processes often demonstrate the family's strengths and capabilities. Care should be taken not to label families as pathological because of the manner in which they interact. Families with a young child with special needs may appear to the early interventionist as pathologically enmeshed when in reality the family is using their closeness as a way of coping with this stressful situation. Families display unique and diverse capabilities in their interactions.

Family Functions Families strive to perform their multiple functions. Family functions are driven by needs as they are identified and responded to by the family. It is a misconception that a family can focus on and work toward meeting only one need at a time (Geary, 1992). Families cannot move in a linear fashion, working on one issue at a time, if they are going to successfully juggle the complex functions that must be maintained. Early intervention as a helping system must have the same flexibility if it is going to be helpful to families.

By understanding how the family meets its needs, the early interventionist can gain an appreciation of the competencies the family displays, as well as a sense of the family's themes. The family's themes, the meaning that the family attaches to their concerns, may motivate family activity in diverse directions (Handel & Whitchurch, 1994). The early interventionist should work with the family to identify their needs and themes to best provide supportive services to the family. However, identified needs and the family's focus on meeting them change over time and are influenced by the availability of resources and other priorities of the family (Dunst & Deal, 1994).

Family Life Cycle Early intervention typically occurs when the family is in the early childhood phase of development. Normative and nonnormative occurrences can affect the family life cycle. Most of the time raising a child with special needs is a nonnormative event. Families involved in early intervention may be grieving the shattering of an illusion—the expectation that children are always born perfect. These families may be attempting to adapt to their new family members and, possibly, to the beginning of an unexpected lifestyle. They may also have to come to terms with the knowledge that they will be raising children with special needs (Turnbull & Turnbull, 1990).

Early interventionists should not draw their conclusions too quickly. The life complexities and structural systems changes of many families can bring about life cycle transitions that are overlapping and complicated. Family well-being is enhanced when the changes that occur over time meet their expectations. Early interventionists can help by being proactive with families and by providing normative help whenever possible. Also, early intervention that is grounded in families' strengths and capabilities is most likely to promote the most positive outcomes for families (Dunst, Trivette, & Mott, 1994).

RECOMMENDATIONS AND SOLUTIONS

The partnerships that form the infrastructure of early intervention cannot survive without the support of the systems that surround them (Powell, 1988). Federal, state, and local systems, enforcing mandates and developing policies designed to achieve the goals of early intervention, should examine the philosophy and practices within their own systems to assess how consistent they are compared with the tenets of partnerships (see Chapter 2 of this book for further detail on federal, state, and local systems). Questions designed to assist in such an examination are outlined in Table 2.

The practice of early intervention needs to exist in a supportive and flexible environment. Early interventionists should see themselves as learners and creators of service delivery that uniquely fits the families they serve. Early interventionists need to be able to take risks and implement new ideas. They need to work in environments that give them time to reflect on their practice. Professional development should be

Table 2. Questions for federal, state, and local systems providing support and guidance for early intervention

1. Are systems based on mutual acceptance, respect, and caring among their members, and is that reflected in their policies?
2. Is trust present among members of these systems and reflected in policies developed by these systems?
3. Are evaluation plans designed from bottom up across these systems, cognizant of the time needed to develop a model of early intervention that promotes positive family outcomes through partnerships? Is that reflected in the rules and policies that regulate early intervention?
4. Do these systems work reciprocally across systems to loosen the boundaries between them and develop shared policy?
5. Are the members of these systems open and honest in their sharing across systems and willing to learn from those in practice?
6. Do these systems leave decision making to those working closest to families by providing much flexibility and autonomy in early intervention?
7. Is there a sense of shared responsibility across systems for the success of early intervention?
8. Do these systems offer help and support to practitioners that fit their identified needs and concerns?
9. Are the channels of communication open and able to withstand honest and in-depth discussion that requires listening to multiple perspectives?
10. Are disagreement and negotiation allowed among members of multiple systems, and is the learning that follows able to inform future policy and program development?

integrated into service delivery as an ongoing process with many opportunities for mentorship relationships, guided discussion, and practice.

Early intervention appears to work best when programs are organized into transdisciplinary teams of professionals who develop relationships based on their knowledge, skills, and personal talents more than the credentials they possess. Team members should provide support and recognition to each other, so that early interventionists are assured of their own competence and power. Families cannot be expected to take care of and fulfill the needs of their professional partners for recognition and status.

Early interventionists cannot serve large numbers of families in partnerships. They need to have flexibility to remain available when families need their support. The documentation required in early intervention, the individualized family service plan (IFSP), needs to be seen as a process that defines and documents the growing and developing partnership, its goals, and accomplishments:

> The IFSP is a promise to children and families—a promise that their strengths will be recognized and built on, that their needs will be met in a way that is respectful of their beliefs and values, and that their hopes and aspirations will be encouraged and enabled. (McGonigel, Kaufmann, & Johnson, 1991, p. 46)

As the field of early intervention matures, history and experience should reinforce and focus these recommendations. Early intervention conducted through partnerships to promote positive outcomes for young children with special needs and their families should be nurtured in a workplace that values and promotes the worth and diversity of its staff members.

CASE STUDY

Introduction   A hospital-based early intervention program at a large urban medical center received a referral for an infant girl who was born prematurely at 32 weeks' gestational age. The baby, who had been admitted to the intensive care nursery, was having difficulty breathing independently and appeared to have a lack of motor responses after experiencing perinatal anoxia. Jean, the family coordinator with the early intervention program, met with the baby's mother in her hospital room to introduce the program, discuss how it might be helpful to the family, and determine the mother's interest in the program. Jean also used this time to begin to get to know the baby's mother and her family.

Jean found that Ella, the baby's mother, was an attractive young woman of 17 with an outgoing personality and great sense of humor. Ella had another daughter, Tanika, who was 16 months old. Ella was planning to name the baby Shymanla, a name that Ella's father had created. Jean and Ella visited Shymanla together and designed a name card to be displayed on the baby's isolette. They scheduled a meeting with the medical team to ask questions and to learn more about the doctors' concerns before Ella was discharged from the hospital.

As Ella and Jean became better acquainted, Ella talked about her relationships with other family members. Her children came from two different short-term relationships with young men from her neighborhood. She was not interested in either of the fathers playing a role in raising the children, but she did plan to look into child support from these men.

Jean offered to give Ella a ride home from the hospital when she was discharged and found that Ella and her daughter lived with Ella's teenage brother and her grandmother in a neighborhood near the medical center. This neighborhood consisted mostly of two-story attached houses, many of which were apparently abandoned. There was graffiti on the houses, corner stores, and bars. The occupied houses gave the appearance of being protected from the streets with drawn blinds and curtains. As Jean listened to Ella talk about her home situation, she found that Ella's grandmother was not actually a relative but a woman who had lived for a short time with Ella's uncle, who was now deceased. The stability of Ella's home was dramatically affected by her "grandmother" having a severe drinking problem. Ella talked about how she and her brother planned to pay the bills using her welfare check and his disability payment so that they would continue to have a place to live. Ella had no other siblings with whom she was connected. She shared with Jean her dream for a home for her and her daughters.

Ella's mother, Joan, periodically joined Ella in her visits to the baby. During some of these visits, Joan's loud and boisterous behavior indicated that she was under the influence of alcohol. Joan told Jean that she wanted to do whatever she could to help her daughter but that she lived in another part of the city with her boyfriend. Ella appeared uncomfortable with her mother's involvement. Ella did not share her feelings about her relationship with her father, although she did visit him periodically. He gave many gifts to Tanika and often took Ella and Tanika out to dinner.

Intervention Phase   A major focus of this intervention was to engage Ella as the major decision maker for Shymanla's care. During the infant's stay in the intensive care nursery, she received physical therapy and developmental interventions. Ongoing medical testing continued to identify the cause of Shymanla's lack of motor responses, which affected her ability to bottle-feed.

After Shymanla had been at the medical center for 2 months, the intensive care team requested that Jean set up a meeting between the team and Ella. At the meeting, the topic of Shymanla's care was discussed. It was decided that the baby should be cared for at a children's rehabilitation center where Ella and other family members could receive the necessary training to achieve Ella's long-term goal for Shymanla to live at home.

Jean worked closely with the interdisciplinary team at the rehabilitation center, which was headed by the social worker. The social worker voiced her concern that Ella and her family members missed training sessions and meetings. Ella told Jean that she had a difficult time getting transportation to that part of the city. Jean gave Ella a ride to meet with the team to discuss this issue. Jean found that Ella was living in another house in the same neighborhood with the family of her new boyfriend. The team offered Ella tokens as a resource to help her transportation problems. They also discussed the need for other family members to help in the care of this infant.

It became apparent that Ella would not be able to meet her goal of bringing Shymanla home. Ella's mother offered to care for Shymanla in her home. The focus of training broadened to include Joan. As time went on, Joan's inconsistent attendance made this goal also appear unlikely. Jean and Ella discussed the option of temporary foster care with the team as Shymanla's discharge was imminent. Ella agreed with this course of action.

Jean accompanied Ella to family court to temporarily give up custody of Shymanla. On the way home from court, Ella told Jean that she was relieved that a child advocate had been appointed for her baby. During this same period, Jean also assisted Ella in applying for Supplemental Security Income benefits for Shymanla to provide needed funds when the baby came to live with Ella.

The focus of intervention became one of trying to keep Ella involved in communicating with the foster care agency as decisions were being made concerning Shymanla's care. Ella's new boyfriend and his father appeared to be supportive of Ella's role with her baby. Ella's other daughter, Tanika, was now staying with relatives of the child's father. Jean offered support to Ella by going with her to visit Tanika and bring her clean clothes.

Approximately 2 months after Shymanla was placed in foster care, Jean received an emergency message to visit Ella. Upon arriving at Ella's current residence, she was told that Shymanla had died a few days earlier. Representatives from the foster home had already visited Ella and discussed what had happened and had made funeral arrangements for Shymanla. Ella had agreed with their arrangements but spoke of her concerns to Jean. Jean attempted to gather more information about the situation and to involve the court-appointed child advocate to discover under what circumstances the baby had died.

Jean and her colleagues offered to drive the family to the funeral. Ella indicated that her father had his own car but that her mother, brother, and boyfriend's family would need rides. Ella chose for her and her boyfriend to ride with Jean. Neighbors provided the other needed rides.

Arriving at the funeral, Ella chose not to approach the casket. Joan took her daughter by the hand and walked with her to view Shymanla. Joan told Jean later that she realized that her daughter, although not physically caring for Shymanla, still needed the opportunity to grieve. With members of the foster care agency and the early intervention program in attendance at the funeral, family members surrounded this young mother and helped her mourn the death of her baby.

Conclusions   This case study aptly illustrates the complexities of understanding family systems and providing family-centered early intervention. Ella's family system was in constant motion and challenging to engage in providing support services. Any attempt to use preconceived ideas or past information on membership and use of "family" resulted in inaccurate focuses of interventions. Biological relationships were not necessary to function as family in Ella's case. Poverty and substance abuse as well as adolescence and its developmental impact on functioning added to the complexity of this family.

SUMMARY

This chapter focused on the family as a system and a context for early intervention services. The diversity and complexity of families means that many subsystems are interrelating in each family and must be accounted for when early interventionists provide services. Family-centered early intervention provided within a compensatory model of helping appears to be the most effective means of garnering resources while maintaining a family's sense of competence.

Equally important to maintaining family competence and empowerment is a dedication to working in partnerships with families. Partnerships must be based on acceptance, trust, long-term durability, reciprocity, equal openness in both parties, family decision making, work toward solutions rather than emphasis on causes, an emphasis on family needs and priorities, open communication, and an ability to accept disagreement and negotiation. Components from the framework of family systems and the elements of partnerships in early intervention must be integrated to achieve the goals and outcomes of early intervention for young children and their families.

REFERENCES

Anderson, J.D. (1992). Family-centered practice in the 1990's: A multicultural perspective. *Journal of Multicultural Social Work, 1*(4), 17–29.

Bailey, D.B. (1987). Collaborative goal setting with families: Resolving differences in values and priorities for services. *Topics in Early Childhood Special Education, 7*(2), 59–71.

Bell, D.M., & Bell, L.G. (1989). Micro and macro measurement of family systems concepts. *Journal of Family Psychology, 3*(2), 137–157.

Boyce, G.C., Behl, D., Mortensen, L., & Akers, J. (1991). Child characteristics, family demographics, and family processes: Their effects on the stress experienced by families of children with disabilities. *Counseling Psychology Quarterly, 4*(4), 273–288.

Brickman, P., Rabinowitz, V., Karuza, J., Coates, D., Cohn, E., & Kidder, L. (1982). Models of helping and coping. *American Psychologist, 37*, 368–384.

Bronfenbrenner, U. (1979). *The ecology of human development: Experiments by nature and design.* Cambridge, MA: Harvard University Press.

Bronfenbrenner, U. (1986). Ecology of the family as context for human development. *Developmental Psychology, 22*, 723–742.

Carnegie Corporation of New York. (1994, April). *Starting points: The report of the Carnegie task force on meeting the needs of young children.* New York: Author.

Cornwell, J.R., & Korteland, C. (1994, November). *Working in partnerships with families of young children.* Paper presented at the annual National Association for the Education of Young Children Conference, Atlanta.

Crutcher, D.M. (1991). Family support in the home: Home visiting and Public Law 99-457. *American Psychologist, 46*(2), 138–140.

Dunst, C.J. (1987, December). *What is effective helping?* Paper presented at the fifth Biennial National Training Institute of the Zero to Three/National Center for Clinical Infant Programs, Washington, DC.

Dunst, C.J., & Deal, A.G. (1994). Needs-based family-centered intervention practices. In C.J. Dunst, C.M. Trivette, & A.G. Deal (Eds.), *Supporting and strengthening families: Vol. 1. Methods, strategies and practices* (pp. 90–104). Cambridge, MA: Brookline.

Dunst, C.J., & Paget, K.D. (1991). Parent-professional partnerships and family empowerment. In M. Fine (Ed.), *Collaborative involvement with parents of exceptional children* (pp. 25–44). Brandon, VT: Clinical Psychology Publishing Co.

Dunst, C.J., Trivette, C.M., Davis M., & Cornwell, J.R. (1994). Characteristics of effective helpgiving practices. In C.J. Dunst, C.M. Trivette, & A.G. Deal (Eds.) *Supporting and strengthening families: Vol. 1. Methods, strategies and practices* (pp. 171–186). Cambridge, MA: Brookline.

Dunst, C.J., Trivette, C.M., & Deal, A.G. (1988). *Enabling and empowering families: Principles and guidelines for practice.* Cambridge, MA: Brookline.

Dunst, C.J., Trivette, C.M., & Deal, A.G. (Eds.). (1994). *Supporting and strengthening families: Vol. 1. Methods, strategies and practices.* Cambridge, MA: Brookline.

Dunst, C.J., Trivette, C.M., & Johanson, C. (1994). Parent-professional collaboration and partnerships. In C.J. Dunst, C.M. Trivette, & A.G. Deal (Eds.), *Supporting and strengthening families: Vol. 1. Methods, strategies and practices* (pp. 197–211). Cambridge, MA: Brookline.

Dunst, C.J., Trivette, C.M., & Mott, D.W. (1994). Strengths-based family-centered intervention practices. In C.J. Dunst, C.M. Trivette, & A.G. Deal (Eds.), *Supporting and strengthening families: Vol. 1. Methods, strategies and practices* (pp. 115–131). Cambridge, MA: Brookline.

Eisenberg, L. (1990). What's happening to American families? *ERIC Digest.* Urbana: ERIC Clearinghouse on Elementary and Early Childhood Education, University of Illinois.

Galston, W.A. (1993, Winter). Causes of declining well-being among U.S. children. *Aspen Quarterly*, pp. 52–77.

Geary, M. (1992, November). *Overview of linkage and transition issues.* Paper presented at the National Forum on Transitions and Continuity, Washington, DC.

Handel, G. (1994). Central issues in the construction of sibling relationships. In G. Handel & G.G. Whitchurch (Eds.), *The psychosocial interior of the family* (4th ed., pp. 493–523). New York: de Gruyter.

Handel, G., & Whitchurch, G.G. (Eds.). (1994). *The psychosocial interior of the family* (4th ed.). New York: de Gruyter.

Harry, B. (1992). Developing cultural self-awareness: The first step in values clarification for early interventionists. *Topics in Early Childhood Special Education, 12*(3), 333–350.

Hess, R.D., & Handel, G. (1994). The family as a psychosocial organization. In G. Handel & G.G. Whitchurch (Eds.), *The psychosocial interior of the family* (4th ed., pp. 3–17). New York: de Gruyter.

McGonigel, M.J., Kaufmann, R.K., & Johnson, B.H. (1991). A family-centered process for the individualized family service plan. *Journal of Early Intervention, 15*(1), 46–56.

Minuchin, P. (1985). Families and individual development: Provocations from the field of family therapy. *Child Development, 56*, 289–302.

National Commission on Children. (1993). *Beyond rhetoric: A new American agenda for children and families.* (Final report of the National Commission on Children.) Washington, DC: Author.

Olson, D.H., McCubbin, H.I., Barnes, H., Larsen, A., Muxen, M., & Wilson, M. (1983). *Families: What makes them work.* Beverly Hills: Sage Publications.

Powell, D.R. (1988). Emerging directions in parent-child intervention. In D.R. Powell (Ed.), *Annual advances in applied developmental psychology* (Vol. 3, pp. 1–23). Norwood, NJ: Ablex.

Powell, T.H., & Ogle, P.A. (Eds.). (1993). *Brothers and sisters: A special part of exceptional families* (2nd ed.). Baltimore: Paul H. Brookes Publishing Co.

Rappaport, J. (1981). In praise of paradox: A social policy of empowerment over prevention. *American Journal of Community Psychology, 9*, 1–25.

Roberts, M. (1992). Systems or selves? Some ethical issues in family mediation. *Mediation Quarterly, 10*(1), 3–19.

Roberts, R.N., & Magrab, P.R. (1991). Psychologists' role in a family-centered approach to practice, training, and research with young children. *American Psychologist, 46*(2), 144–148.

Ronnau, J., & Poertner, J. (1993). Identification and use of strengths: A family system approach. *Children Today, 22*(2), 20–23.

Rosier, K.B., & Corsaro, W.A. (1993). Competent parents, complex lives: Managing parenthood in poverty. *Journal of Contemporary Ethnography, 22*(2), 171–204.

Sonnenschein, P. (1981). Parents and professionals: An uneasy relationship. *Teaching Exceptional Children, 14*(1), 62–65.

Stacey, J. (1994). Backward toward the postmodern family: Reflections on gender, kinship, and class in the Silicon Valley. In G. Handel & G.G. Whitchurch (Eds.), *The psychosocial interior of the family* (4th ed., pp. 643–659). New York: de Gruyter.

Steinglass, P., Bennett, L.A., Wolin, S.J., & Reiss, D. (1994). The three phases of systemic maturation. In G. Handel & G.G. Whitchurch (Eds.), *The psychosocial interior of the family* (4th ed., pp. 129–138). New York: de Gruyter.

Turnbull, A.P., Summers, J.A., & Brotherson, M.J. (1983). *Working with families with disabled members: A family systems approach.* Lawrence: University of Kansas.

Turnbull, A.P., & Turnbull, H.R. (1990). *Families, professionals, and exceptionality: A special partnership* (2nd ed.). New York: Macmillan.

Wayman, K.I., Lynch, E.W., & Hanson, M.J. (1990). Home-based early childhood services: Cultural sensitivity in a family systems approach. *Topics in Early Childhood Special Education, 10*(4), 56–75.

Zill, N. (1993, Winter). The changing realities of family life. *Aspen Quarterly*, pp. 27–51.

Zuckerman, M. (1979). Attribution of success and failure revisited, or: The motivational bias is alive and well in attribution theory. *Journal of Personality, 47,* 245–287.

... II
.
.
.

SETTINGS

Section I discussed the broader contexts within which early intervention services are developed and delivered. These are systems that are overarching in nature. In this second section of the book, attention is shifted to specific settings—what Barker (1968) would refer to as a behavior setting or Bronfenbrenner (1979) would deem a microsystem. Thus, we began broadly in Section I and narrow our focus in Section II.

While reading Section II, it is important to keep in mind that, although each specific setting is discussed as if it were an isolated unit of the environment, in fact, these settings are affected by the broader contexts discussed in Section I. In addition, for certain children and families, these settings may interact much in the manner that Bronfenbrenner (1979) has described as the mesosystem.

The last chapter of the book focuses on collaboration. Viewed from Bronfenbrenner's perspective, collaboration may be seen as the development of a mesosystem designed to meet the needs of particular child and family. The notion of resource-based early intervention promulgated by Trivette, Dunst, and Deal in Chapter 5 (Section I) may be similarly characterized.

We hope that this book will provide you with useful information about specific settings and at the same time demonstrate the complexity involved in the delivery of early intervention services. Certainly, as we go about the practice of early intervention, the contexts within which we find ourselves, whether broad or specific, will shape the nature of our services to children and families.

REFERENCES

Barker, R.G. (1968). *Ecological psychology.* Stanford, CA: Stanford University Press.
Bronfenbrenner, U. (1979). *The ecology of human development: Experiments by nature and design.* Cambridge, MA: Harvard University Press.

. . . 7

Neonatal Intensive Care Units

S. Kenneth Thurman, Sheryl Ridener Gottwald,
Janet R. Cornwell, and Constance Korteland

This chapter discusses the nature and operation of neonatal intensive care units (NICUs) as settings and addresses how early intervention services are implemented in these settings. With the passage of the Education of the Handicapped Act Amendments of 1986 (PL 99-457) and subsequent federal and state legislation, more concern has been directed at the delivery of early intervention services within the NICU. The legislative requirements that early intervention services begin at birth set the stage for introducing specific developmental and family-centered programs into the NICU setting. The success of medical treatment of critically ill newborns, which continues to evolve rapidly, has further underscored the necessity to address their developmental needs (Gilkerson, Gorski, & Panitz, 1990) as well as the needs of their families (Thurman, 1991, 1993, 1994). The brief history of neonatal intensive care that follows should help the reader understand the evolution of NICUs.

In the 1880s, Etienne Tarnier developed the first incubators. These early incubators were based on those used for young animals in zoos and recognized the importance of maintaining body temperature in the survival of preterm newborns (Sammons & Lewis, 1985). A student of Tarnier's, Pierre Budin, established the first nursery for preterm and ill babies at the Paris Maternité Hospital in 1893. Budin's special care unit for "weaklings" was the original forerunner of what is now the modern NICU. Furthermore, it was Budin who first established guidelines for the treatment of these children and who recognized that a birth weight below 2,500 grams put infants at considerably increased risk (Ensher & Clark, 1986).

Martin Couney was instrumental in promulgating the principles developed by Budin. He began to put preterm infants on display much in the manner of a side show. The infants were cared for in incubators by specially trained nurses.

> Because preterm infants were generally not expected to live under usual circumstances, there were few objections [to Couney's tactics] from families. . . . Interestingly, Dr. Couney complained of difficulty in reuniting infants with their families [when they were medically stable enough to do so]. (Hodgman, 1985, p. 1)

Eventually, Couney established a permanent exhibit for these babies at Coney Island, where he even cared for his own daughter (Sammons & Lewis, 1985). Despite the sensationalism and "freak show" nature of his approach, Couney was quite instrumental in advancing the treatment of preterm infants.

As a result of observing one of Couney's exhibits, Dr. Julian Hess established the first special care nursery for premature infants in the United States at the Sarah Morris Hospital in Chicago during the 1920s (Sammons & Lewis, 1985). He worked closely with a skilled nurse named Evelyn Lundeen. Hodgman (1985) related that "the doctor was not even allowed to enter [the nursery] and instead routinely examined babies in an anteroom, into which they were slid through a 'pass through' constructed specifically for this purpose" (p. 2). The babies Hess and Lundeen treated were routinely kept in incubators and were given oxygen to aid their respiration. Visitation was highly controlled, parents were kept from the unit, and a number of procedures were put into place to help decrease the probability of infection. Anecdotal reports suggest that to minimize infection Lundeen maintained such tight control of the unit "that the only duty delegated to house officers . . . was signing the death certificate" (Hodgman, 1985, p. 2). However, the approach used by Hess and Lundeen was also very nurturant, and it has been suggested that "perhaps some of the high-tech nurseries of today could benefit from infusion of this superb nurturing orientation" (Avery, 1994, p. 3). As a result of their efforts and their success in reducing the mortality rates in preterm infants, the model established by Hess and Lundeen spread throughout the United States during the 1940s and 1950s. These pioneers were the first to recognize that premature infants have difficulty with temperature control and feeding and that they are more susceptible to disease and infection. These same issues are central in the treatment of premature infants in the 1990s.

During the 1950s and 1960s, neonatologists gained a better understanding of the pathophysiology of preterm newborns. They developed a number of interventions such as resuscitation, more sophisticated diagnostic procedures, improved methods to help with thermoregulation, blood transfusion technology, better laboratory techniques, improved monitors, and antibiotics. The 1970s saw even greater improvements with the development and introduction of infant ventilators, intravenous feeding, and neonatal surgery. In 1975, the recognition of neonatology as a distinct subspecialty within pediatrics was formalized (Bucciarelli, 1994), thus increasing its credibility and leading to the proliferation of accredited fellowship training programs throughout the country. The 1980s brought the development of computerized axial tomography (CAT) and ultrasound technology, both of which aid in diagnosis and treatment. The 1980s also saw the advent of methods for continuous monitoring of an infant's physiological state and additional technology such as jet ventilation and extracorporeal membrane oxygenation (ECMO), which saved some infants who previously would have died. Replacement of surfactant, a compound missing from the lungs of very premature infants, was also introduced and measurably improved the treatment of their respiratory distress. The 1990s have seen further development of imaging techniques such as magnetic resonance imaging (MRI) and experimentation with liquid as opposed to mechanical ventilation.

In the 1940s–1960s, babies weighing less than 2,000 grams did not have much chance of survival. By the 1970s babies weighing 1,500 grams routinely survived, and by the 1980s survival of those weighing 1,000 grams was common. Not uncommon in the 1990s is the survival of infants weighing as little as 600–700 grams. As Avery

(1994) pointed out, this has led to concern with ensuring survival that results in an intact child later.

During the 1970s and 1980s, psychologists and other developmental specialists conceived and tested interventions designed to improve the developmental outcomes in premature and ill newborns. These techniques have been expanded and further assessed during the 1990s. Many of these approaches have been discussed and critiqued elsewhere (e.g., Bennett, 1987, 1990; Thurman, 1993), and the interested reader is referred to these resources. Many of these interventions provided the initial introduction of early intervention into the NICU and have been incorporated into more family-centered models of services (Brown, Pearl, & Carrasco, 1991; Thurman, 1991, 1993, 1994; Thurman, Cornwell, & Korteland, 1989; Thurman & Gonsalves, 1993).

The NICU today is a highly technical and sophisticated environment dedicated exclusively to the care and survival of critically ill newborns. Today's NICUs are graded by levels depending on the types of services they have available. A Level I NICU is equipped to serve infants with relatively mild problems who may need observation and monitoring or specialized interventions such as phototherapy (described later in this chapter) or antibiotic therapy. The Level II NICU is equipped to provide resuscitation and mechanical ventilation to infants. The Level III NICU is the most sophisticated and is equipped to provide a full range of medical services using state-of-the-art technology. Typically Level III NICUs are in large teaching hospitals or regional medical centers (Avery, 1994; Bucciarelli, 1994) and can use the expertise of a variety of physicians and therapists. This is not to suggest that the quality of service is necessarily better at a Level III NICU but rather that it is equipped to serve more critically ill infants or those with more complex or difficult-to-diagnose illnesses.

In 1990 it was estimated that there were 792 NICUs in the United States (Ross Laboratories, 1990). This compares with only 703 units in 1988, which accounted for 11,020 beds and more than 2.8 million patient days. Bucciarelli (1994) reported that the average occupancy rate for NICUs across the nation was only 71.26%, although the average rates for Level III units were about 95%. Thus, Bucciarelli (1994) concluded that "available data suggest that most excess capacity appears to be in level II units that care for moderately ill neonates, but most level III units, which care for the most complex patients, remain at or near capacity" (pp. 13–14). The growth of NICU beds during the 1980s, especially Level II beds, seems to have outpaced the demand for these beds. This "excess capacity can become an engine driving resource consumption and cost without improving outcome [in infants]" (Bucciarelli, 1994, p. 14).

NATURE OF THE NEONATAL INTENSIVE CARE UNIT

The typical NICU is active 24 hours a day and often gives the uninformed visitor a feeling of chaos and disorganization. In reality, however, they are highly organized and staffed by well-trained professionals who specialize in the care of critically ill newborns. Avery (1994) provided the following definition of the NICU, which summarizes its purpose, structure, and function. The NICU

> is a therapeutic environment, a collection of equipment, and a multidisciplinary team that is guided by dedicated leadership, by a group of specific protocols, and by a body of relevant scientific knowledge. It is the [NICU] as an integrated organism, rather than any single person or collection of people, that takes care of the sick neonate [and her family]. (p. 4)

Physical Aspects of the NICU

Sophisticated monitoring and treatment devices are employed to ensure that each infant is given the highest level of care. Each of these devices has a specialized function, and each is employed based on the needs of a particular infant.

Warmer Bed Because premature infants often have difficulty in maintaining adequate body temperature, they may require the assistance of a warmer bed. The warmer bed provides radiant heat to the infant and is controlled by a sensor attached to the baby's skin. If the baby's temperature drops below a specific level, the heat from the warmer increases. The warmer bed also provides open access to the infant so that necessary medical and caregiving procedures can be carried out efficiently. When infants improve they are moved to isolettes or incubators, which provide continuous circulation of warm air to help maintain body temperature. Finally, when the infants are able to maintain their own body temperature, they are moved to a bassinet such as is found in the typical newborn nursery.

Cardiorespiratory Monitor Premature babies are often subject to lapses of more than 15–20 seconds in breathing called *apnea*. Often this apnea is accompanied by a significant decrease in the heart rate known as *bradycardia* (heart rate less than 100 beats per minute). Either of these conditions can be life threatening to an infant. Cardiorespiratory monitors continuously assess an infant's respiration and heart rates. The monitor is attached to the skin by means of a sensitive lead. If the respiration stops for more than a few seconds or if the heart rate falls too low, an alarm will sound, alerting NICU staff that the infant requires immediate attention.

Blood Gas Monitors To know whether an infant's respiration is adequate, NICU staff must monitor not only the baby's breathing but also the amount of oxygen and carbon dioxide in the blood. This may be done by drawing small amounts of blood from the infant and testing the blood directly. A more continuous means of assessing blood gases is through the use of a transcutaneous monitor. This monitor uses a heated electrode that is attached to the infant's skin. This electrode increases the blood flow to the area and provides an assessment of the levels of oxygen and carbon dioxide via the skin.

Ventilator Many preterm babies have lungs that are not mature enough to sustain adequate breathing independently. These babies must be placed on ventilators or respirators to maintain sufficient oxygen levels throughout the body. The respirator is attached by means of a tube placed into the infant's throat and trachea. The respirator can be set to control the percentage of oxygen delivered to the infant as well as the number of respirations per minute. A more recent advance is the jet ventilator, which can be set to breathe for a baby several hundred times per minute through rapid pulsed breaths that avoid extreme expansion of the lungs. Jet ventilators are found only at selected hospitals and require specially trained staff to ensure their proper use.

Intravenous (IV) Pumps IV pumps are used to control the amount of medication or nutrients given to the infant through a line attached to a vein. These lines may be attached by a needle into the veins of the scalp, feet, or hands, or they may be attached by means of a catheter directly into a major vessel such as the umbilical or jugular veins. Alarms on the pumps will sound when the flow of fluids is interrupted.

Chest Tubes and Suction Chambers Often the pressure applied to a premature infant's lung through the use of mechanical ventilation causes it to develop a hole, which results in a leak leading to a *pneumothorax* or collapsed lung. When this occurs the neonatologist will insert a tube into the infant's chest that is then attached to a special suction chamber. This suction chamber removes air from the chest cavity so that the collapsed lung can reinflate.

Phototherapy Lights Prematurity in infants can result in decreased liver function. When this happens a substance called *bilirubin*, which comes from the breakdown of red blood cells, can build up in the system, causing the baby to become jaundiced. Left uncorrected, increased bilirubin levels can cause permanant damage to an infant's nervous system. When the blood bilirubin level is too high, the infant is placed under phototherapy lights to help remove the excess bilirubin through the skin. When phototherapy lights are in use, the infant's eyes are protected by covering them with cotton pads.

Sensory Aspects of the NICU

The physical environment of the NICU is replete with technical devices that are critical to maintaining infants and sustaining their lives. However, the application of this technology is not without negative consequence, and it is used with the assumption that its benefits outweigh its costs. The emerging field of environmental neonatology (Gottfried & Gaiter, 1985; Wolke, 1987) has focused on studying the effects of the NICU environment on the infant. Wolke (1987) defined environmental neonatology as "the study of newborn special care units and their impact on the medical and developmental status of sick infants" (p. 17). The interested reader is referred to P. Glass (1994) for discussion of the effects of the NICU environment on the sensory development of critically ill newborns.

Noise The machines used to treat infants in NICUs can create a noisy environment. Gottfried (1985) reported that the mean sound level in the NICU studied was 77.4 decibels (dB) and at times reached a level as high as 109 dB. Low-frequency sounds were characterized as having the highest intensities. Lawson and Turkewitz (1985) reported a mean sound level of 72.2 dB in the NICU they studied. Wolke (1986) reported somewhat lower (i.e., 60–69 dB) average sound levels in a British NICU. When infants are housed within an incubator, their sound environment is somewhat different from that of the NICU in general. Only low-frequency sounds tend to penetrate the walls of the incubators. Because human speech is often in a higher frequency range, it can be masked or obscured by the incubator. Gottfried (1985) reported the mean noise level within the incubator as being 81.1 dB. He attributed this higher noise level to the constant running of the motor in the incubator. Furthermore, throughout his observations, Gottfried found that nonspeech sounds were present 100% of the time, speech sounds were present 92.2% of the time, and the radio was on 79.4% of the time.

Although there is no firm evidence that noise levels in the NICU lead to permanent hearing loss in infants, the acoustic environment does have an effect. First, as several authors (Gottfried, 1985; Gottfried et al., 1981; Wolke, 1987) have indicated, infants have no control over the sounds in the NICU nor are they able to easily match a sound with its source. Thus, the sources, intensities, types, and fluctuations in sound are all outside the control of the infant. Although this may also be the case to some extent with any newborn or young infant, their environments are generally less noisy, and they are more easily able to link sounds with their sources. Wolke (1987) speculated that babies hospitalized in NICUs may be less able to associate a particular voice with a particular face because they do not have the frequent opportunities to do this that a home-reared newborn has. Lawson and Turkewitz (1985) also suggested that the constancy of sound in the NICU may impede the infants' opportunities "to form an association between a particular sound and its visual and tactile referents" (p. 168). Wolke (1987) also suggested these "infants are exposed to the described noises for weeks and sometimes months" (p. 26). He asserted furthermore that "the noise and sound is [sic] not under the control of the infant and cannot be avoided by the infant, a classical learned helplessness situation" (p. 26).

Lawson and Turkewitz (1985) presented data showing a relationship between speech in the room and infant state in neonatal intensive care. They reported a correlation of −.54 between the infant state of quiet sleep and speech sounds in the room. At the same time, correlations indicated a moderate relationship ($r = .47$) between speech in the room and infant in a quiet awake state. Peabody and Lewis (1985) indicated that the noise levels in the typical NICU are intense enough to wake infants from sleep. They concluded that "hospital personnel [should] eliminate unnecessary noise, including radios, in the nursery [and that] more carefully controlled studies are needed to evaluate the effects of this environmental factor on the outcome of preterm and sick infants" (p. 205).

Light Another environmental factor in the NICU is light. Like noise, light can be a constant in the NICU, and there is often little variation in the levels of light. P. Glass and colleagues (1985) reported that the intensity of light has increased markedly in NICUs since the 1960s, and they presented evidence suggesting that the light levels in NICUs may be a contributing factor to retinal damage in very low birth weight infants. There is also speculation that the continuous bright lights of the NICU interfere with the establishment of natural diurnal rhythms. Gottfried (1985) reported an average illumination in the NICU of 530 lumen/m². This figure is somewhat higher than that reported by Mann, Haddow, Stokes, Goodley, and Rutter (1986), who reported an average of 200 lumen/m². Although infants' eyes are patched to protect them from the light, especially during periods of phototherapy, this practice is not without side effects. Rao and Elhassani (1981), for example, reported that eye patches can cause distortions of the face and corneal injury or conjunctivitis. Because the full extent of the effects of high levels of light is not known, Wolke (1987) suggested that lighting in the NICU be flexible and reduced when possible. He also suggested that infants be protected from direct sunlight and that light levels be altered to simulate day and night rhythms.

Touching and Handling To be treated, babies in the NICU must be touched and handled. Much of this touching is related to the medical maintenance of the infant. Jones (1982) presented data that indicated that ill and premature infants are given both medical and general care at rates that are as much as eight times higher than that of their full-term healthy peers. Murdoch and Darlow (1984) reported that babies under 1,500 grams in their study received a mean of 234 handling procedures in a 24-hour period. Thus, on average, infants were being handled about once every 6 minutes. Although much of this handling is necessary to ensure proper care of the infant, data from other researchers suggest that handling may be disruptive of sleep patterns (Gabriel, Grote, & Jonas, 1981) and of physiological states (Gorski, 1984; Gorski, Hole, Leonard, & Martin, 1983; Murdoch & Darlow, 1984) and may be related to increases in intraventricular hemorrhage (Volpe, 1990). Much of the touching and handling received by infants in the NICU can be done in clusters and spread out at intervals (Lawhon & Melzar, 1988). By using a clustering technique some of the adverse effects of handling may be reduced. In summary, Wolke (1987) suggested that "there is a bad fit between the infant's need for behavioural [sic] and physiological organization and the handling in the NICU. [Furthermore], the sicker the infant, the more adverse are the procedures and the higher the stress for the baby" (p. 30).

Social Aspects of the NICU

The complexity of the NICU environment does not stop with its physical or sensory features. The NICU is also a complex social environment. Of importance is not only the social environment of the infants with their caregivers but also the social environment of the caregivers themselves.

In the mid-1970s, largely owing to the work of Klaus and Kennell (1976), interest began to focus on bonding between hospitalized newborns and their mothers. It was hypothesized that the separation brought about by hospitalization interfered with the development of the bonding or the initial attachment between a mother and her infant. Although later research has not clearly substantiated this position, the work of Klaus and Kennell can be credited with establishing concern with the social interactions and environments of infants in NICUs.

A number of studies have suggested that relatively little social contact occurs between parents and infants during NICU hospitalization. According to Jones (1982), about 90% of the touching an infant receives in the NICU comes from individuals other than the baby's parents. Linn, Horowitz, Buddin, Leake, and Fox (1985) reported that mothers were seen interacting with their NICU-confined infants, on average, less than 5% of the time that the infants were hospitalized. However, these data were collected only during daytime hours rather than during the evening when parents are more likely to visit.

Jones (1982) reported that NICU staff were in contact with infants with respiratory distress 22% of the time of her observation; those with surgical problems 28.5% of the time; and those with complex histories 30.7% of the time. These figures are for personal contact only and do not include contact for medical or general care. In contrast, Jones reported that total staff contact with infants in the term nursery occurred 13.3% of the time. Mother–infant contact occurred .9%, 2.9%, 2.9%, and 23.3% (including the time when infants were taken to the mothers' rooms for feeding) of the time for these four groups of infants (including infants in term nursery), respectively. Parental contact was even lower, being .7%, .7%, and 2.5% of the time for the three groups of NICU babies. Jones (1982) reported that no direct contact was noted between fathers and their infants in the term nursery and that no data were available for fathers' visits in mothers' rooms where contact would have occurred. As previously noted, much of the contact and interaction between the infant and his or her environment is not within the infant's control (Linn et al., 1985). Thus, not only is the infant's social environment limited in the NICU, but the infant's control of that environment is also restricted. Marton, Dawson, and Minde (1980) reported that premature infants received slightly more than 8 minutes per hour of contact from NICU staff. They further noted that most of this contact was devoted to medical procedures rather than to strictly social interaction.

Gottwald and Thurman (1990) discussed parent–infant interaction within the context of the NICU. They concluded that relatively little research has been done in this area. They pointed to the link between social interaction and infant arousal, cautioning that "caregivers must respond to an infant's need for frequent respites from active interaction [and] they must tailor their interaction style so that infants can integrate new behaviors" (p. 5). They suggested that a number of factors may affect the nature of the parent–infant interaction in the NICU. Infant factors included medical status, degree of prematurity, and neurological integrity; parental factors included stress and emotional reactions, altered roles in caring for the infant, psychological well-being, and degree of social support; and NICU factors included noncontingent stimulation in the environment, medical interventions, lack of privacy, and flow of activity.

The NICU as a Work Environment

Regardless of the discipline or role, working in a NICU can create a high degree of stress. This is especially true for physicians and nurses who are confronted daily with significant crises that often require immediate, sometimes life-and-death, decisions. Sammons and Lewis (1985) summarized some of the challenges and expectations that confront NICU staff. Some of these challenges are self-created, but others are clearly determined by the hospital or even by society. These challenges and expectations include

Long hours of intense effort in restricted surroundings
Acquisition of complicated technical skills
Uncertainties over optimal therapy and unforeseen harm from new techniques
Ethical dilemmas
Dealing with their own intense emotional reactions and those of the parents and infants
Coping with infants whose rapidly changing condition demands immediate correct decisions and rapid intervention
Frequent frustration because of the inability to accurately define prognosis (p. 102)

In addition to these challenges, NICU staff must also learn to cope with the death of an infant as it affects both them and the family. As Marshall, Roberts, and Walsh (1985) suggested, it is important for those working in the NICU to provide mutual support to one another by becoming what they refer to as professional friends or having a colleague on whom to depend (B. Glass, Gretz, Fisher, & Speaks, 1985). If NICU staff do not receive enough emotional support, the stresses of the environment can become unbearable and lead to high degrees of staff burnout, increased turnover, reduced job satisfaction, and impaired job performance (Duxbury, Armstrong, Drew, & Henly, 1984; Duxbury, Henly, & Armstrong, 1982; B. Glass et al., 1985; Gribbons & Marshall, 1982; Jacobson, 1978; Norbeck, 1985). Those who choose to work in a NICU will be confronted with a number of significant challenges and frustrations, but they can also be the recipients of significant rewards.

What Goes on in a NICU?

To better understand an environmental setting, ecological psychologists (Barker, 1968; Schoggen, 1989; see also Chapter 1 of this volume) often raise the question, "What goes on here?" They then proceed to observe the setting to identify its behavioral features. We completed an observational study of a NICU to gain insight into the questions, "What goes on here?" and "Who does what?" To some extent the preceding discussion provided this insight by describing the physical, sensory, and social environment found in a NICU. This study, however, was more detailed and gathered data on all of the individuals within the NICU and what they did. These results are shared here to provide insight into the "behavior" of the NICU and elucidate the patterns of behavior associated with particular classes of individuals who inhabit the NICU.

The NICU that provided the site for this study was a Level III unit at a tertiary care major children's hospital. Open access to the unit was gained through discussion with the unit's director and the nurse managers. All attending physicians and neonatology fellows as well as the entire nursing staff were made aware of the study and offered their cooperation in carrying out the study. Other physicians, therapists, technicians, custodial staff, clerks, parents, and family members were not directly told of the study.

The NICU had 16 beds for the most critically ill infants and 6 additional beds for less ill infants and those who were approaching discharge. Half of the critical beds were arranged around two hexagonally shaped lazy susans that housed needed medical supplies and caregiving materials. The six additional beds were in an area separated from the remainder of the unit by a glass wall. These beds were placed perpendicular to the walls and encircled the entire room. Figure 1 provides an approximate layout of this NICU.

The researchers divided the NICU into 11 observation sites. Each of these sites provided a clear, unobstructed view of a section of the unit. These observation positions are indicated on Figure 1. Areas 1–4 were nonpatient areas and Areas 5–11 were

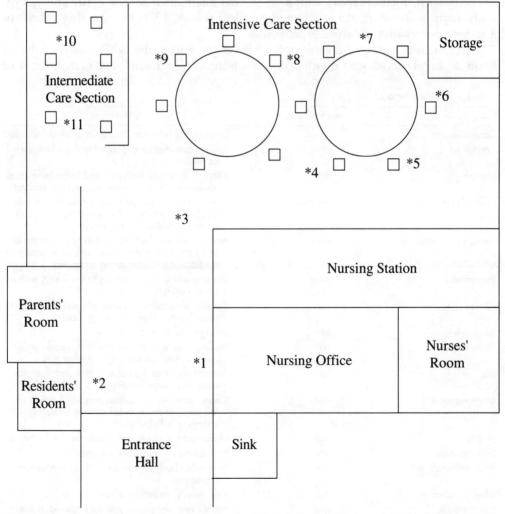

Figure 1. Diagram of the NICU site. Observation positions are indicated with a numbered star, and patient beds are indicated with rectangles.

patient areas. In respect for personal privacy, the parents' room and the nurses' room were not included in the observations. Closed-door meetings sometimes held in the residents' room were likewise excluded. Observations were carried out in all other areas.

Before beginning the study, several informal observations of the unit were conducted to develop a coding scheme and a data collection strategy. As a result of these informal observations, 16 activity categories were identified as well as 9 participant categories. Tables 1 and 2 respectively list and define these codes. These preliminary observations also assisted in making the more frequent inhabitants of the NICU more comfortable with being observed.

Observations were conducted during three 24-hour periods that commenced at 6:00 A.M. one day and continued until 6:00 A.M. the next. Observations began on a Thursday, Friday, and Sunday, all within a 4-week period during the winter. All data were collected by the authors and an additional graduate student. All observers reached a level of reliability with every other observer of at least .85 based on Cohen's kappa (Cohen, 1960). A mean kappa of .88 was maintained for the entire study. Typically, kappas above .75 are considered excellent (Fleiss, 1981) because they represent a rather conservative measure of reliability.

To obtain a representative sample of behavior within the NICU, each of the 72 hours to be observed was divided into ten 6-minute segments. For each hour, 5 of

Table 1. Activity categories

Category label	Abbreviation	Description
Communication	comm	Oral/verbal behavior directed to another individual
Caretaking	crtk	Routine custodial care directed to the infant, such as feeding
Nurturing	nurt	Attempts to soothe the infant and foster behavioral integration, such as touching, stroking, rocking
Medical procedure	medpro	Any medical activity performed directly on the infant for diagnostic or therapeutic reasons, such as drawing blood or suctioning
Therapeutic procedure	txpro	Any nonmedical therapeutic activity performed directly on or near the infant, such as adjusting medication and monitoring equipment
Preparation	prep	To get ready to do something to the infant, such as hand washing, gowning
Clerical	cler	Keeping of records and accounts, such as medical record notes, filing, reviewing reports
Telephone	tele	Engaged on the telephone
Observation	obs	Study or pay special attention to a specific occurrence without performing any other task
Idle	idl	Any activity other than observation that does not contribute to the functioning of the NICU
Maintenance	main	Clean, improve, or facilitate ongoing function of the physical environment such as sweeping, changing light bulbs
Mobile	mob	Movement from one place to another in the NICU
Infant inactive	ina	No observable infant body movement
Infant physically active	act	Noticeable body movement, such as arm or leg movement
Infant vocalization	voc	Any sounds emitted by infant
Infant gazing	gaz	Infant's eyes are partially or fully opened at the moment of observation

Table 2. Participant categories

Category label	Abbreviation	Description
Physician	phy	Specialists, primary care doctors, interns, and residents
Nurse	nur	Any nurse or nursing student
Parent	par	Mother or father
Family	fam	Siblings, grandparents, aunts, uncles, and cousins of the ill infant
Professional support staff	prosup	Physical, respiratory, occupational, or speech-language therapists; audiologists; social workers; psychologists
Technical support staff	tech	X-ray and lab technicians
Nonprofessional support staff	nonpro	Clerical and custodial personnel
Infant	inf	Intensive or intermediate care patient
Other	oth	Any person not readily identifiable or who does not fit into previously defined category

those segments were randomly selected to become observation periods. Thus, 36 of the 72 hours were actually observed using randomly selected 6-minute intervals. A time-sampling data collection method was employed. The first observation in any 24-hour period began at observation Site 1, the second at Site 2, the third at Site 3, and so on for the 24-hour period. Observers moved from site to site sequentially every 30 seconds. Observers used an audiotape as a cue for moving from site to site as well as a means to know when to observe. The word "ready" was heard on the tape 25 seconds into each 30-second interval. Five seconds later the word "record" was heard. This gave the observer 25 seconds to record what was seen and to move to the next site and prepare to record again. At the instant that observers heard "record," they recorded the classification category of each person at the observation site and in what behavior each person was engaged. This technique was equivalent to snapping a photograph at each observation site every 30 seconds. No observer recorded consecutively for more than 3 hours. A total of 10% of all 6-minute observation segments were done by two observers so that reliability could be established.

Data were analyzed to provide a descriptive picture of the activity in the NICU in terms of what went on and who did it. To analyze the data, the total number of behavioral incidents was calculated and the percentage of each category of behavior was computed by forming a ratio between the number of occurrences in each category and the total number of behavioral incidents observed. This was done individually for each category of adult inhabitant within the unit. Figure 2 presents the results of this analysis. Figures 3–14 show the proportion of each behavior attributable to each category of adult inhabitant.

Figure 2 shows that, as might be expected, nurses as a group were responsible for more of what went on in the NICU than any other class of inhabitants. Clearly, nurses constitute the largest class of inhabitants of the NICU and the group with the most responsibility for keeping the unit running and caring for infants and their families. It is also interesting to note that the highest percentage of any category of nurses' behavior was doing clerical work. In general, nurses were doing other things (e.g., clerical tasks, telephoning, maintenance, preparation) that did not involve direct interaction with infants. Although nurses had more opportunity to nurture infants, a higher percentage of nurturance was attributable to parents, who had less opportunity

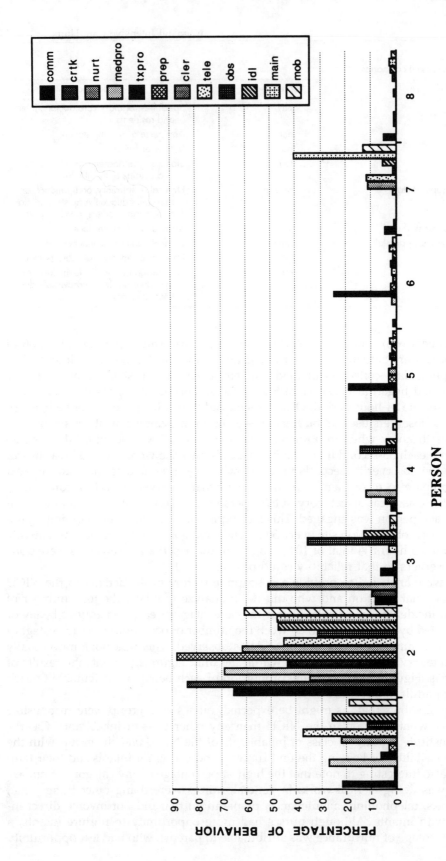

Figure 2.   Behaviors in the NICU. (1 = doctor, 2 = nurse, 3 = parent, 4 = family member, 5 = professional support, 6 = technician, 7 = nonprofessional, 8 = other.)

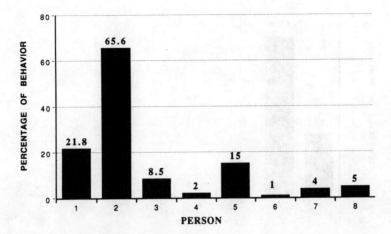

Figure 3. Communication in the NICU. (See Figure 2 for legend.)

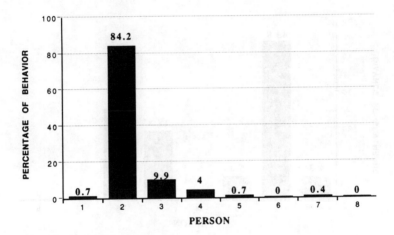

Figure 4. Caretaking in the NICU. (See Figure 2 for legend.)

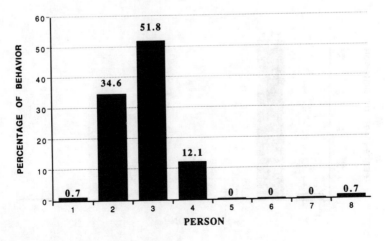

Figure 5. Nurturing in the NICU. (See Figure 2 for legend.)

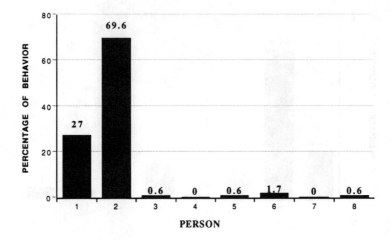

Figure 6. Medical procedures in the NICU. (See Figure 2 for legend.)

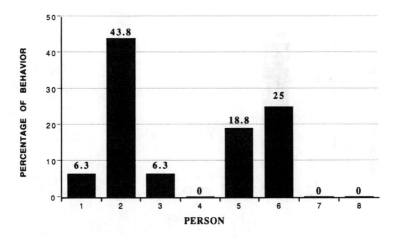

Figure 7. Therapeutic procedures in the NICU. (See Figure 2 for legend.)

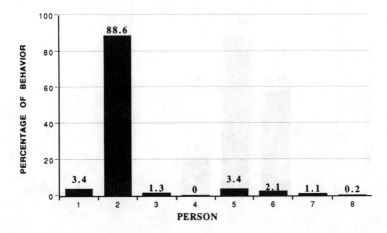

Figure 8. Preparation in the NICU. (See Figure 2 for legend.)

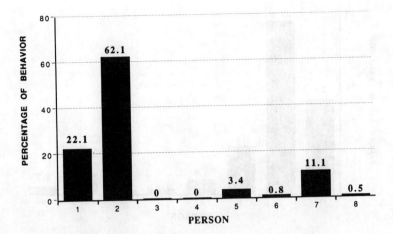

Figure 9. Clerical work in the NICU. (See Figure 2 for legend.)

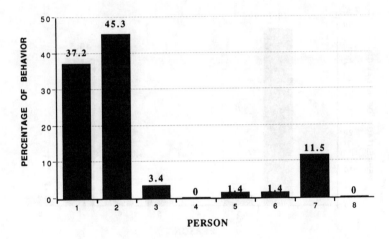

Figure 10. Telephoning in the NICU. (See Figure 2 for legend.)

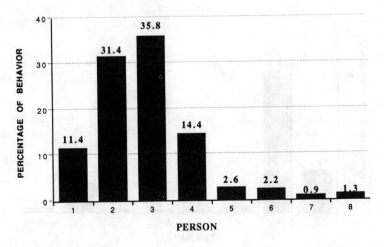

Figure 11. Observation in the NICU. (See Figure 2 for legend.)

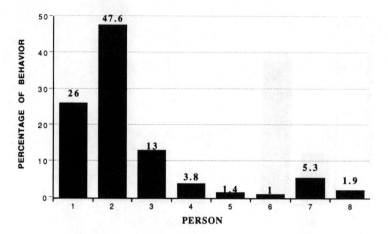

Figure 12. Idle behavior in the NICU. (See Figure 2 for legend.)

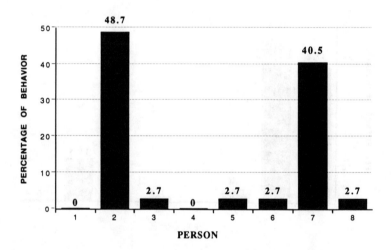

Figure 13. Maintenance in the NICU. (See Figure 2 for legend.)

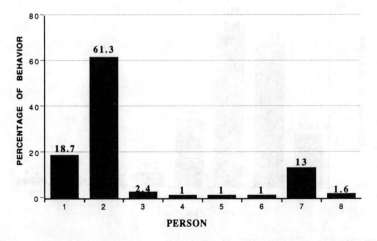

Figure 14. Mobile behavior in the NICU. (See Figure 2 for legend.)

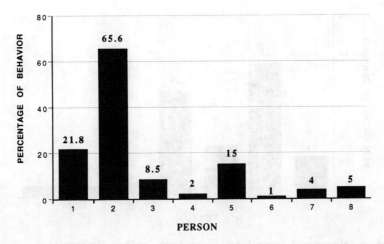

Figure 15. Percentage of NICU behaviors by participant that involved talking. (See Figure 2 for legend.)

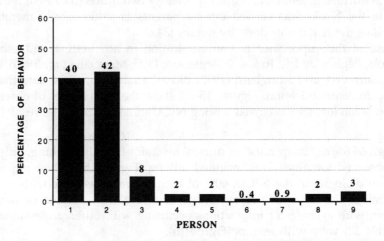

Figure 16. Percentage of doctor communication behavior by participant. (See Figure 2 for legend.)

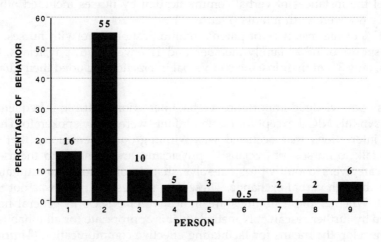

Figure 17. Percentage of nurse communication behavior by participant. (See Figure 2 for legend.)

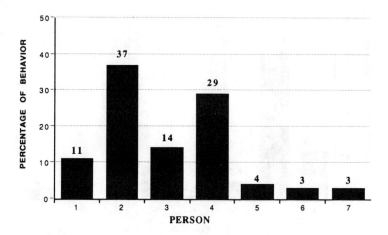

Figure 18. Percentage of parent communication behavior by participant. (See Figure 2 for legend.)

to engage in nurturing behaviors (Figure 5). Nearly two thirds (63.9%) of the nurturing observed in the NICU was carried out by parents or other family members, with virtually all of the remainder done by nurses (34.6%).

Because of the importance of communication in any setting and especially in NICUs (Cole, Begish-Duddy, Judas, & Jorgensen, 1990; Marshall et al., 1985), Gottwald, Thurman, Cornwell, and Korteland (1992) did an analysis of these data that focused exclusively on communication. Figures 15–18 show the percentages of observed communication behaviors that occurred among NICU inhabitants. These results are quite revealing:

- Although 65.6% of "snapshots" of nurses' behavior included talking, only 21.8% of those observed for physicians included talking (Figure 15). When physicians did engage in dialogue in the NICU, 40% of their interactions were with other physicians and 42% were with nurses. Only 10% were with parents or other family members, with even fewer interactions occurring with other professional support staff. Only 3% were with infants (Figure 16).
- Nurses also evidenced a limited number of verbal interactions with professional support staff (3%) and with parents and family members (15%). More than half (55%) of the instances of verbal communication by nurses included other nurses, and only 6% were with infants (Figure 17).
- Some 37% of the instances of parent communication were with nurses, 43% were with a spouse or other family member, and 11% were with physicians. Even with parents, only 3% of their instances of verbal interaction included their infant (Figure 18).

Despite its acknowledged importance, verbal interaction occurred infrequently among inhabitants in this NICU except for nurses. Infants were rarely spoken to. The majority of verbal interactions that occurred was within-group interactions; that is, nurses tended to talk to nurses, physicians to physicians, and families to themselves. It is useful for caregivers to jointly problem-solve, share information, and mutually support each other through verbal exchange. These data suggest that this was not the case in this NICU. Whether these findings are indicative of NICUs in general needs to be determined by further research. Nonetheless, it is appropriate for all inhabitants of the NICU to develop the means for facilitating effective communication (Thurman, 1991, 1994).

PROVIDING EARLY INTERVENTION IN THE NICU

In general, individuals working in NICUs are highly trained and dedicated to preserving the lives of critically ill newborns in a manner that will ensure the best developmental outcome. In one sense for these infants and their families, what goes on in NICUs is "early intervention." However, the practices and procedures carried out in NICUs more clearly fit within the parameters of acute and critical care medicine and focus on getting babies well. Thus, early intervention as it has been more commonly defined is often seen as a secondary concern of professionals working in NICUs. Some may even see it as a hindrance to the effective medical interventions being performed. NICU personnel may view early intervention as an afterthought and something to concern parents with only at the time of discharge. NICU environments are not necessarily hostile to early intervention, but they often do not see early intervention services as being the highest priority. Although this may not be an unreasonable stance, especially when infants are critically ill, it does present a challenge and a certain tension for those who see the benefits of introducing early intervention into the NICU.

Recommended practices in the delivery of early intervention services forcefully promulgate a family-centered approach. Although several authors (e.g., Harrison, 1993; Rushton, 1990; Thurman, 1991, 1993, 1994; Thurman et al., 1989) have advocated for the implementation of family-centered approaches in NICUs, data suggest that adoption of this approach has yet to become commonplace (Cardinal & Shum, 1993; Dobbins, Bohling, & Sutphen, 1994; O'Brien & Dale, 1994). One explanation for this lies in the orientation of the NICU toward the infant. Characteristically, NICU staff have a strong tendency to be infant centered and thus view the infant outside the broader family context. Their concern is for the welfare of the infant with less acknowledgment of the interactive relationship between infant and family well-being.

The data on communication previously presented suggest that there may be relatively little direct communication between NICU staff and family members. If this is in fact the case, then an additional barrier has been set up for implementation and delivery of family-centered early intervention services. Effective early intervention is dependent on meaningful team function and communication among staff from a variety of disciplines. Consequently, effective early intervention in the NICU environment requires a commitment to team function. Although effective team function may be used in NICUs to treat the medical and physical problems of infants, these efforts are often not extended to the broader goal of family-centered early intervention. A typically held view, for example, is that the neonatal social worker is exclusively responsible for working with families and offering them support (Korones, 1985). Although each discipline has a unique contribution to the provision of early intervention services in the NICU, all staff must act collaboratively as a team if effective family-centered services are to be carried out (Thurman, 1993). A team approach based on various roles and functions that are necessary to carry out family-centered early intervention in the NICU has been described by Thurman and colleagues (Thurman et al., 1989; Thurman & Widerstrom, 1990). This approach may be useful regardless of the disciplines involved.

Although the technology available in a NICU is important for maximizing the life chances of preterm and critically ill infants, successful family-centered early intervention in the NICU requires additional attention to the environment. Essentially, the NICU environment must be made more family friendly. Family accommodations should include warm, homelike sleeping and bathroom facilities. Not only can such facilities be important for families' sense of well-being, they may also be useful environments for teaching family members and other caregivers home-care techniques for infants with ongoing medical needs (Rushton, 1990). In addition, provisions are necessary to ensure family privacy. These provisions can include curtains that can be drawn between isolettes and quiet, pleasantly decorated side rooms for breast-feeding or family discussions. Bedside seating for family members and their guests should be available. Especially important are rocking chairs, which can provide parents an opportunity to be close to their infant and to help facilitate the attachment process.

A family-centered approach in the NICU does not overlook the developmental or medical needs of the infant. In fact, addressing these needs is an integral part of a family-centered approach. Als et al. (1986) stressed the importance of individualized behavioral and environmental care for babies in the NICU. They suggested a pattern of developmental care for infants that is based on the cues provided by individual infants. They also pointed to the importance of reducing sound and light levels and clustering the care of infants into contiguous time periods to decrease the necessity to touch the infants and disturb their physiological states. Their approach is clearly compatible with a family-centered approach because most families want the best care possible for their infant. Other approaches have been discussed in the literature that have been shown to be effective in bringing about improved developmental outcomes in babies who are hospitalized in NICUs (cf. Bennett, 1987, 1990).

The following case study illustrates the use of a family-centered approach in neonatal intensive care.

Case Study

Maria and Todd Cater were concerned when Maria went into labor with their first child unexpectedly during her 33rd gestational week. Everything had been fine until now, and they were scared as they drove to their community hospital. By the time they had arrived Maria was dilated 8 centimeters. An hour and a half later she delivered 3.5-pound Ronald. The staff at this Level II NICU immediately recognized that Ronald needed to be transferred to the university children's hospital 30 miles away in the city. This particular NICU had recently adopted a family-centered approach and focused as much on the needs of the family as it did on giving the infant the best medical and developmental interventions possible.

Todd was torn between staying with Maria or following the ambulance in their car. Maria insisted that Todd go with the baby to make sure everything would be all right. This was the beginning of 6 weeks of hospitalization for Ronald and a journey through the hills and valleys of intense feelings and emotions that parents travel while their infant is in neonatal intensive care.

At the university hospital the neonatologist, the nurse that was to be Ronald's primary nurse, and the NICU social worker met Todd as he came into the NICU. He looked pale and bewildered, and the professional staff assured him they would give Ronald the best possible care. On examination, the neonatologist suspected that Ronald had a heart lesion. He also suspected from Ronald's physical appearance that he might have Down syndrome. Within the next hour, an ultrasound confirmed that Ronald had a heart lesion.

The social worker had stayed with Todd in the parents' room while Ronald was examined. Several times the nurse came by and asked Todd if he would like to see Ronald, but he was too upset to respond. All he wanted to do was talk to Maria. The social worker showed him to the telephone. Todd and Maria spent the next half hour on the phone crying and praying. As he hung up, the neonatologist came to tell Todd about Ronald's heart problem. The social worker stayed in the room and listened with Todd. When the neonatologist left, the social worker asked Todd if he had any questions and then asked him what she could do to help. With tears in his eyes he said he wanted to be with Maria and tell her about Ronald's heart. The social worker asked Todd if he was all right to drive back to the hospital where Maria was. When he said he didn't know, she said she could get one of the hospital's volunteer transportation aides to go with him. Todd liked that idea and felt that having company would make the trip back to Maria easier.

The next morning Maria was discharged, and she and Todd immediately went to see Ronald. Although Todd had notified both his and Maria's families about Ronald and his condition, no one from either side was available to come and give support. Maria and Todd were on their own. As they entered the NICU, the social worker saw them and came over to meet Maria. She asked if they would like to see Ronald and then escorted them to Ronald's warmer bed. This was the first time that they had seen him since his birth. He was surrounded by tubes and monitors and seemed lost in all the equipment. Todd whirled around and ran from the NICU, leaving Maria in "shock" with Ronald, his nurse, and the social worker.

The next few hours would be emotionally intense. Maria was angry and hurt that Todd had run off, and Todd was too upset to even begin to comfort her, let alone explain his behavior. After a short meeting, the nurse and the social worker decided to concentrate on providing individual support to Maria and to Todd. The social worker found Todd in the waiting room, staring into space. The nurse stayed with Maria at Ronald's bedside.

While the nurse encouraged Maria to express her feelings and to ask questions, she periodically pointed out how cute Ronald was and how he seemed to know that Maria was there with him. Simultaneously, the social worker helped Todd regain some sense of well-being. After an hour or so, she asked if he would like to join Maria and Ronald and he said yes. Todd embraced Maria as he approached the bedside. The NICU staff suggested that they sit down together and spend some time with Ronald.

Now that things had settled down a bit, the social worker suggested that a team meeting be scheduled for the next morning. Maria and Todd agreed that this would be a good idea. The nurse invited them to stay in the unit as long as they wanted to and told them that they could come and go 24 hours a day and could bring any friends or family whom they wanted. She also told them that they could stay overnight in one of the family efficiencies if that suited them better.

The attending neonatologist, primary nurse, social worker, and Maria and Todd met the next day. They discussed Ronald's condition and told Maria and Todd that heart surgery should be scheduled in the next several days, because without it Ronald's chances of survival were greatly reduced. The neonatologist also explained that they were conducting tests to determine if Ronald had Down syndrome. This upset Maria and Todd because they had always heard that people with Down syndrome were "hopelessly retarded." At this point, the social worker stepped in and suggested that maybe she should talk more with Maria and Todd about their immediate concerns. The other team members left at this point. After further discussion, Maria and Todd decided it would be useful to get support from the NICU parent support group. That afternoon one of the group's parent peer counselors met with Maria and Todd.

When Maria arrived at the unit the next day, both the social worker and Ronald's nurse were there to meet her. Her peer support counselor was due later. After spending several hours at Ronald's bedside and asking question after question, Maria left to go home and rest.

When Todd came home from work, they ate a quick dinner and returned to the hospital. The neonatologist met them as they were coming through the door. He suggested that they talk for a while and asked if they would like to have their peer counselor present. The four of them went to the parent conference room and the neonatologist told Maria and Todd that Ronald's Down syndrome had been confirmed.

They spent the next few hours bewildered, very emotional, and unsure of their next course of action. Their peer counselor stayed with them to provide support.

Two days later Ronald had his heart lesion repaired. Throughout the day, NICU personnel kept Maria and Todd informed about his progress and their peer counselor took them to lunch. Ronald's heart repair went splendidly. He continued to make progress over the next several weeks.

Maria and Todd continued to meet with the team weekly. These meetings were scheduled in the evening so that Todd could attend after work. During the third week of Ronald's hospitalization, the team discussed the possibility of beginning early intervention with Ronald. Maria and Todd thought that this would be appropriate as it would help lessen their concerns about Ronald's Down syndrome. The early intervention specialist joined the team and an individualized family services plan (IFSP) was developed.

All of his NICU caregivers as well as his parents actively participated in providing Ronald with several developmentally based interventions. The peer counselor and the social worker continued to give Maria and Todd emotional support, and they even arranged to visit at Maria and Todd's house several times as the daily 60-mile round-trip to the hospital was beginning to take its toll, especially on Todd, who was working a full schedule at the office.

After 6 weeks of hospitalization Ronald was discharged. He and his family continued to receive home-based early intervention services. Maria and Todd also continued to receive support from their peer counselor as well as semimonthly follow-up telephone calls from the NICU social worker for the next several months.

SUMMARY

This chapter discussed the NICU as a setting in which early intervention is carried out. The physical, sensory, and social environments of the NICU were described. In addition, the chapter discussed barriers to implementing family-centered early intervention in the NICU, in hopes that such barriers will begin to be overcome.

REFERENCES

Als, H., Lawhon, G., Brown, E., Gibes, R., Duffy, F.H., McAnulty, G., & Blickman, J.G. (1986). Individualized behavioral and environmental care for the very low birth weight preterm infant at high risk for bronchopulmonary dysplasia: Neonatal intensive care unit and developmental outcome. *Pediatrics, 78*, 1123–1132.

Avery, G.B. (1994). Neonatology: Perspective in the mid-1990s. In G.B. Avery, M.A. Flecther, & M.G. MacDonald (Eds.), *Neonatology: Pathophysiology and management of the newborn* (4th ed., pp. 3–7). Philadelphia: J.B. Lippincott.

Barker, R.G. (1968). *Ecological psychology.* Stanford, CA: Stanford University Press.

Bennett, F.C. (1987). The effectiveness of early intervention for infants at increased biological risk. In M.J. Guralnick & F.C. Bennett (Eds.), *The effectiveness of early intervention for at-risk and handicapped children* (pp. 79–112). Orlando, FL: Academic Press.

Bennett, F.C. (1990). Recent advances in developmental intervention for biologically vulnerable infants. *Infants and Young Children*, 3(1), 33–40.

Brown, W., Pearl, L.F., & Carrasco, N. (1991). Evolving models of family-centered services in neonatal intensive care. *Children's Health Care*, 20, 50–55.

Bucciarelli, R.L. (1994). Neonatology in the United States: Scope and organization. In G.B. Avery, M.A. Flecther, & M.G. MacDonald (Eds.), *Neonatology: Pathophysiology and management of the newborn* (4th ed., pp. 12–31). Philadelphia: J.B. Lippincott.

Cardinal, D.N., & Shum, K. (1993). A descriptive analysis of family-related services in the neonatal intensive care unit. *Journal of Early Intervention*, 17, 270–282.

Cohen, J. (1960). A coefficient of agreement for nominal scales. *Educational and Psychological Measurement*, 20, 37–46.

Cole, J.G., Begish-Duddy, A., Judas, M.L., & Jorgensen, K.M. (1990). Changing the NICU environment: The Boston City Hospital model. *Neonatal Network*, 2(3), 15–22.

Dobbins, N., Bohling, C., & Sutphen, J. (1994). Partners in growth: Implementing family-centered changes in the neonatal intensive care unit. *Children's Health Care*, 23, 115–126.

Duxbury, M.L., Armstrong, G.D., Drew, D.J., & Henly, S.J. (1984). Head nurse leadership style with staff nurse burnout and job satisfaction in NICUs. *Nursing Research*, 33, 97–101.

Duxbury, M.L., Henly, G.A., & Armstrong, G.D. (1982). Measurement of nurse organization climate of NICUs. *Nursing Research*, 31, 83–88.

Education of the Handicapped Act Amendments of 1986, PL 99-457, 20 U.S.C. §1400 et seq.

Ensher, G.L., & Clark, D.A. (1986). *Newborns at risk: Medical care and psychoeducational intervention*. Rockville, MD: Aspen Publishers.

Fleiss, J.L. (1981). *Statistical methods for rates and proportions*. New York: John Wiley & Sons.

Gabriel, M., Grote, B., & Jonas, M. (1981). Sleep-wake patterns in preterm infants under two different care schedules during four day polygraphic recording. *Neuropediatrics*, 12, 366–373.

Gilkerson, L., Gorski, P., & Panitz, P. (1990). Hospital based intervention for preterm infants and their families. In S.J. Meisels & J.P. Shonkoff (Eds.), *Handbook of early childhood intervention* (pp. 445–468). Cambridge, England: Cambridge University Press.

Glass, B., Gretz, J., Fisher, L., & Speaks, S. (1985). A nurse colleague program: One solution to nurse turnover. *Neonatal Network*, 3, 16–21.

Glass, P. (1994). The vulnerable infant and the neonatal intensive care environment. In G.B. Avery, M.A. Flecther, & M.G. MacDonald (Eds.), *Neonatology: Pathophysiology and management of the newborn* (4th ed., pp. 77–94). Philadelphia: J.B. Lippincott.

Glass, P., Avery, G.B., Subramaniou, K.N.S., Keys, M.P., Sostek, A.M., & Friendly, D.S. (1985). Effect of bright light in the hospital nursery on the incidence of retinopathy of prematurity. *New England Journal of Medicine*, 313, 401–404.

Gorski, P.A. (1984). Premature infant behavioral and physiological responses to caregiving intervention in the intensive care nursery. In J.D. Call, E. Galenson, & R.L. Tyson (Eds.), *Frontiers in infant psychiatry* (pp. 142–169). New York: Basic Books.

Gorski, P.A., Hole, W.T., Leonard, G.H., & Martin, J.A. (1983). Direct computer recording of premature infants and nursery care: Distress following two interventions. *Pediatrics*, 72, 198–203.

Gottfried, A.W. (1985). Environment of newborn infants in special care units. In A.W. Gottfried & J.L. Gaiter (Eds.), *Infant stress under intensive care: Environmental neonatology* (pp. 23–54). Baltimore: University Park Press.

Gottfried, A.W., & Gaiter, J.L. (Eds.). (1985). *Infant stress under intensive care: Environmental neonatology*. Baltimore: University Park Press.

Gottfried, A.W., Wallace-Lande, P., Sherman-Brown, S., King, J., Coen, C., & Hodgman, J.E. (1981). Physical and social environment of newborn babies in special care units. *Science*, 214, 673–675.

Gottwald, S.R., & Thurman, S.K. (1990). Parent-infant interaction in neonatal intensive care units: Implications for research and service delivery. *Infants and Young Children*, 2(3), 1–9.

Gottwald, S.R., Thurman, S.K., Cornwell, J.R., & Korteland, C. (1992, November). *Communicative relationships in the neonatal intensive care environment*. Paper presented at the American Speech-Language-Hearing Association, San Antonio, TX.

Gribbons, R., & Marshall, R. (1982). Nurse burnout in a NICU. In R.E. Marshall, C. Kasman, & L.S. Cape (Eds.), *Coping with caring for sick newborns* (pp. 123–145). Philadelphia: W.B. Saunders.

Harrison, H. (1993). The principles for family-centered neonatal care. *Pediatrics*, 92, 643–650.

Hodgman, J.E. (1985). Introduction. In A.W. Gottfried & J.L. Gaiter (Eds.), *Infant stress under intensive care: Environmental neonatology* (pp. 1–6). Baltimore: University Park Press.

Jacobson, S. (1978). Stressful situations for neonatal intensive care nurses. *American Journal of Maternal/Child Nursing, 3,* 144–150.

Jones, C.L. (1982). Environmental analysis of neonatal intensive care. *Journal of Nervous and Mental Disease, 170,* 130–142.

Klaus, M.H., & Kennell, J.H. (1976). *Parent-infant bonding.* St. Louis: C.V. Mosby.

Korones, S.B. (1985). Physical structure and functional organization of neonatal intensive care units. In A.W. Gottfried & J.L. Gaiter (Eds.), *Infant stress under intensive care: Environmental neonatology.* Baltimore: University Park Press.

Lawhon, G., & Melzar, A. (1988). Developmental care of the very low birth weight infant. *Journal of Perinatal Neonatal Nursing, 2*(1), 56–65.

Lawson, K., & Turkewitz, G. (1985). Relationships between the distribution and diurnal periodicities of infant state and environment. In A.W. Gottfried & J.L. Gaiter (Eds.), *Infant stress under intensive care: Environmental neonatology* (pp. 157–170). Baltimore: University Park Press.

Linn, P.L., Horowitz, F.D., Buddin, B.J., Leake, J.C., & Fox, H.A. (1985). An ecological description of neonatal intensive care unit. In A.W. Gottfried & J.L. Gaiter (Eds.), *Infant stress under intensive care: Environmental neonatology* (pp. 83–112). Baltimore: University Park Press.

Mann, N.P., Haddow, R., Stokes, L., Goodley, S., & Rutter, N. (1986). Effect of night and day on preterm infants in a newborn nursery: Randomised trial. *British Medical Journal, 293,* 1265–1267.

Marshall, R.E., Roberts, J.L., & Walsh, J.H. (1985). The impact of the environment on the NICU caregiver: Perspectives of the nurse, pediatric house officer, and academic neonatologist. In A.W. Gottfried & J.L. Gaiter (Eds.), *Infant stress under intensive care: Environmental neonatology* (pp. 227–250). Baltimore: University Park Press.

Marton, P.M., Dawson, H., & Minde, K. (1980). The interaction of ward personnel with infants in the premature nursery. *Infant Behavior and Development, 3,* 307–313.

Murdoch, D.R., & Darlow, B.A. (1984). Handling during neonatal intensive care. *Archives of Disease in Childhood, 59,* 957–961.

Norbeck, J.S. (1985). Perceived job stress, job satisfaction and psychological symptoms in critical care nursing. *Research in Nursing and Health, 8,* 253–259.

O'Brien, M., & Dale, D. (1994). Family-centered services in the neonatal intensive care unit: A review of research. *Journal of Early Intervention, 18,* 78–90.

Peabody, J.L., & Lewis, K. (1985). Consequences of newborn intensive care. In A.W. Gottfried & J.L. Gaiter (Eds.), *Infant stress under intensive care: Environmental neonatology* (pp. 199–226). Baltimore: University Park Press.

Rao, H.K.M., & Elhassani, S.B. (1981). Iatrogenic complications of procedures performed on the newborn. *Perinatology/Neonatology, 5,* 23.

Ross Laboratories. (1990). *Survey of neonatal intensive care centers.* Columbus, OH: Author.

Rushton, C. (1990). Family-centered care in the critical care setting: Myth or reality? *Children's Health Care, 19,* 68–78.

Sammons, W.A.H., & Lewis, J.M. (1985). *Premature babies: A different beginning.* St. Louis: C.V. Mosby.

Schoggen, P. (1989). *Behavior settings: A revision and extension of Roger G. Barker's ecological psychology.* Stanford, CA: Stanford University Press.

Thurman, S.K. (1991). Parameters for establishing family-centered neonatal intensive care services. *Children's Health Care, 20,* 34–39.

Thurman, S.K. (1993). Intervention in the neonatal intensive care unit. In W. Brown, S.K. Thurman, & L.F. Pearl (Eds.), *Family-centered early intervention with infants and toddlers: Innovative cross-disciplinary approaches* (pp. 173–209). Baltimore: Paul H. Brookes Publishing Co.

Thurman, S.K. (with commentaries by D.C. Bauman and J.D. Rapacki). (1994). Family-centered care in the neonatal intensive care unit. In S.L. Hostler (Ed.), *Family-centered care: An approach to implementation* (pp. 213–249). Charlottesville: University of Virginia, Children's Medical Center, Kluge Children's Rehabilitation Center.

Thurman, S.K., Cornwell, J.R., & Korteland, C. (1989). The Liaison Infant Family Team (LIFT) Project: An example of case study evaluation. *Infants and Young Children, 2*(2), 74–82.

Thurman, S.K., & Gonsalves, S.V. (1993). Adolescent mothers and their premature babies: Responding to double risk. *Infants and Young Children, 5*(4), 44–51.

Thurman, S.K., & Widerstrom, A.H. (1990). *Infants and young children with special needs: A developmental and ecological approach* (2nd ed.). Baltimore: Paul H. Brookes Publishing Co.

Volpe, J.J. (1990). Intraventricular hemorrhage in the premature infant. In S.M. Pueschel & J.A. Mulick (Eds.), *Prevention of developmental disabilities* (pp. 197–215). Baltimore: Paul H. Brookes Publishing Co.

Wolke, D. (1986, July). *The neonatal intensive care environment: Developmental support for preterm infants.* Invited address at the International Symposium on The Biopsychology of Parent-Infant Communication, Lisbon, Portugal.

Wolke, D. (1987). Environmental and developmental neonatology. *Journal of Reproductive and Infant Psychology, 5,* 17–42.

... 8

. . .

The Home Environment

Donald W. Mott

Just as the family is now viewed as the center of early intervention, the home is viewed as the center of family life. Professionals privileged enough to be allowed into families' homes have the opportunity to observe and participate in some of the most intimate moments of their lives, entering into their inner circle, the primary micro-system (see Bronfenbrenner, 1979; also see Chapter 1 of this book). The home is more than a physical place; it is an emotional and social place that reflects the family's values, beliefs, customs, and attitudes. All these variables interact and change across time, and, taken together, these variables provide a setting for early intervention efforts and frequently become a focus of those interventions.

This chapter briefly summarizes major research findings related to home-based services; identifies key characteristics of the home environment, including physical, social, and emotional characteristics; describes major implications for providing early intervention in the home, including interpersonal and logistical aspects; and describes a variety of strategies to address child and family needs through home-based services. The chapter concludes with a case study that illustrates many of the points made in the chapter.

The importance of the home has roots in Judeo-Christian traditions, American culture, and law and is reflected in contemporary paradigms within the field of developmental disabilities, such as normalization, deinstitutionalization, the least restrictive environment concept, and the family support movement. For example, the Administration on Developmental Disabilities (1990) began its list of family support principles with the following: "Children, regardless of the severity of their disability, need families and enduring relationships with adults in a nurturing home environment" (p. 7) (cited in Bradley, Knoll, & Agosta, 1992, p. 4). Before the civil rights movement and the implementation of the Education for All Handicapped Children Act of 1975 (PL 94-142), the ease with which society removed people with disabilities from their homes and communities was frightening (see Scheerenberger, 1983).

There is considerable evidence for the value of home-based services, especially in the United States. For example, the Portage Project (Shearer & Shearer, 1972) was a home-based model of early intervention and was the first of many that demonstrated the effectiveness of providing services in the home. Other models are described in Davis and Rushton (1991); Dunst (1985); Feldman, Sparks, and Case (1993); Krantz, MacDuff, and McClannahan (1993); and Vitulano, Nagler, Adnopoz, and Grigsby (1990). Bailey and Simeonsson (1988) reported that home-based child development programs are more likely to involve the family than center-based programs (cited in Dawson et al., 1990).

Other studies support the efficacy of a combined model, where home-based services are combined with other modes, such as center-based services, or where home-based services are offered as one option in an array of services available to the family (Dore, Wilkinson, & Sonis, 1992; Dunst, Trivette, & Deal, 1988, 1994; Karnes, 1977; Parry, 1992). Fewell and Neisworth (1991) pointed out that the "key to the success of all home-based services is the relationship between the professional and the family" (p. xi). Numerous others have stressed this point as well, including Dunst and colleagues (Dunst et al., 1988; Dunst, Trivette, & Deal, 1994) and Turnbull and colleagues (Turnbull, Summers, & Brotherson, 1986).

For infants with biological risk factors, Sandall (1990) pointed out that "home-based services are often the preferred service delivery method" (p. 3) due to the medical issues involved, as well as logistics such as transportation and families' schedules. Similarly, Sandall noted that the "quality of home environment of premature/low birth weight infants predicts developmental outcome better than any single or set of biological factors" (p. 3). Sandall reviewed research studies on the efficacy of home-based intervention for infants with biological risk factors and found that the "evidence of the effectiveness of home-based intervention programs . . . is encouraging but not unequivocal" (p. 4). Sandall found that "the effectiveness of early home-based interventions is best demonstrated by differences in the home environment, increased responsivity and sensitivity by mothers on interaction measures, and to a lesser degree increased scores on cognitive measures" (p. 7). She pointed out, however, that long-term positive effects of home-based interventions are less certain, that the optimal length of intervention is not clear, and that "certain infant and family characteristics may be more important than others for the assessment of receptivity and need for early intervention" (p. 7). Sandall concluded that the reason for positive changes is often hard to determine with certainty because many studies used a variety of interventions simultaneously.

Dawson et al. (1990) described a home-based program using paraprofessionals (i.e., mothers of school-age children) and found positive effects in terms of mother–child interactions, which were partly attributed to the fact that the "paraprofessionals were effective in forming relationships partly because they saw women in the home rather than in the office" (p. 41). The authors felt that three specific factors were important in this process, including the visitors' personality assets, the flexibility of the visitors' roles, and the natural affinity that developed between the visitors and the mothers. Wayman, Lynch, and Hanson (1991) also stated that the

> home is the ideal setting to gather information about family concerns and priorities, to demonstrate and plan interventions with families, and to provide family members with information and education about their child's special needs. Practical considerations are also associated with home-based models. Home-based models can be used in rural or remote rural areas where it is impractical for families to travel long distances or with populations of children for whom group care is contraindicated, such as those who are chronically ill or infection prone. In some instances, a home-based approach may be more economical in that the costs of maintaining a center and purchasing equipment are avoided. (p. 57)

Hanson and Lynch (1989) described the functionality of "teachable moments" that occur during home-based interventions (cited in Wayman et al., 1991, p. 57). Wayman et al. (1990) discussed the issue of cultural diversity as it relates to home-based intervention and provided guidelines for the home visitor, such as considering the family's perceptions of health and healing, language and communication issues, and child-rearing practices. They pointed out, however, that

> although cultural differences should help shape interventions and make them more appropriate, one caveat should be observed—families, like individuals, have their own characteristics that may or may not reflect what is considered to be typical for their culture . . . therefore, culturally sensitive interventions can only occur when each family is viewed and treated as a unique unit that is influenced by its culture but not defined by it. (p. 59)

Bryant, Lyons, and Wasik (1990) discussed ethical considerations for home-based interventionists and suggested that, although there are no commonly accepted ethical guidelines for home-based practitioners, existing guidelines, such as those of the National Association of Social Workers, may be useful. They also discussed ethical guidelines developed by Reamer (1990) in the context of home-based services and specific issues such as confidentiality, honesty, and terminating services. Bryant et al. (1990) pointed out that values issues are also crucial. May (1991) highlighted that fathers' roles are very important during early intervention and can be addressed in creative ways during home visits. McConachie (1991a) discussed the importance of flexibility and varying expectations of families based on parents' energy and philosophy about family life and child rearing. Similarly, parents' perceptions of their roles affect their responses to services (McConachie, 1991b).

Although the research support for the efficacy of home-based early intervention is still evolving, it is clear that home-based services are of great value to children and families. The remainder of this chapter examines key aspects of home-based services and focuses on practical issues of concern to early interventionists.

KEY CHARACTERISTICS

Key physical characteristics of the home include location within the community, material resources (e.g., furniture, toys, books), accessibility to the community, accessibility to people with disabilities, space available, temperature control, noise level, cleanliness, arrangement of available resources, and health and safety. Each of these characteristics can have a significant impact on the family's ability to benefit from the resources offered by the early interventionist.

The location of the home is important from both a safety and logistical point of view. If the home is in a densely populated area, there may be other families nearby who receive services from the early intervention agency, thus making scheduling visits more cost-efficient from a staffing perspective. By contrast, homes in rural areas may require relatively higher amounts of travel and may also require travel on unpaved roads. (An extreme example of the effect of the location of a home on home visitors occurs in Alaska, where some early interventionists travel by plane to areas above the Arctic Circle and have spent weeks at a time in small villages because of weather conditions.) There is a degree of risk in any home visit, but some homes are in high crime areas that even police or sheriff department personnel may be reluctant to visit. As noted later in this chapter, all early intervention agencies should have policies and procedures for safety based on the factors in their areas.

The material resources available in each home vary widely and include all the physical contents of the home, such as furniture, appliances, toys, books, educational materials, clothing, and other essential resources such as food, water, and medicine. The physical characteristics of the home itself can also be considered part of this category. Each of these resources can be a target of early intervention efforts and can affect the development of the child and the overall quality of life of the family members. Material resources also affect the ability of the early interventionist to interact effectively with the child and family during home visits. Issues to consider include seating arrangements and availability of toys during home visits. The interventionist may bring toys to a home visit but should consider doing so only if the toys can be loaned to the family or if the family has sufficient financial or other resources to obtain toys or educational materials that are used successfully during home visits. The space available in the home should also be considered, both in terms of its impact on the family members' interactions with one another and on the home visit itself. For example, if space is limited, there may be distractions from siblings, telephone calls, or other interruptions. The noise level may be high, and there may be visual distractions that affect the child's ability to attend to developmental activities during the visit.

The home's accessibility to the community and accessibility to people with disabilities are also important considerations. Many families struggle to obtain needed resources that are available in their communities but are not near their homes. For example, families who qualify for the Women, Infants and Children Program (WIC) may have difficulty getting to the health department to continue to qualify for the program. Sometimes transportation can be arranged or the early interventionist may be able to arrange for the necessary resources to be offered in a location closer to the family's home. Other examples include providing specialized therapies in homes (rather than in center-based programs) and development of neighborhood family resource centers, which help families obtain access to a variety of informal and formal resources at a location convenient to their homes.

Other characteristics to be considered include the cleanliness of the home; health and the safety of the home; and the availability of basic resources such as heat, electricity, and water. All of these can be legitimate targets of intervention during home visits, if they reflect the family's concerns directly or indirectly.

Social and emotional characteristics of the home are also crucial factors to be considered by the early interventionist. Social characteristics include the people who live in the home, the interpersonal patterns of the individuals who live there or frequent there, the schedule followed by those same individuals, and the skills and abilities of those individuals. Emotional characteristics include the beliefs, values, mores, and customs of the individuals who reside there or frequent the home as well as the "ownership" of the home (from both a legal and functional point of view). These issues are reflected in the next section and case study later in this chapter.

Sometimes a family's "home" is not really a home at all. A family may be living in a car, a bus, a barn, an attic, an office building, a condemned building, or a shelter. Other families may be homeless or may frequently be in transition between homelessness and various forms of shelter (see Grant, 1990). Early interventionists need to be prepared to respond to families and children where they are and to recognize that living conditions may be very different from those to which the interventionist is accustomed. An example is an early interventionist who refused to make home visits to a family living near a farm because he could not tolerate the smell of the cow manure and other fertilizer nearby and was irritated by the flies that occasionally entered the family's home. Such responses by interventionists are hoped to be rare exceptions; nevertheless, each interventionist must know his or her own limitations and should be encouraged to turn service delivery responsibilities over to others when those limits are exceeded.

A variety of methods exist to assess home environments, including direct observation, interview of family members, and instruments such as the Preschool Home Observation for Measurement of the Environment Inventory (HOME) (Caldwell, 1978). The HOME is a widely used instrument and measures "stimulation through toys, games, and reading materials; language stimulation; physical environment (safe, clean, and conducive to development); pride, affection, and warmth; stimulation of academic behavior; modeling and encouragement of social maturity; variety of stimulation; and physical punishment" (cited in Barrera, Kitching, Cunningham, Doucet, & Rosenbaum, 1990, p. 20). Various scales also exist to measure characteristics of family members and family needs and resources, such as the Parent Needs Inventory (Fewell, Meyer, & Schell, 1981) and those developed by Dunst and colleagues, which are described in Dunst et al. (1988) and Dunst, Trivette, and Deal (1994).

Early interventionists should conduct assessments to further the goals and interests of the child and family and should be as family friendly as possible. Assessment of the home should result in functional intervention ideas that are consistent with the family's values, lifestyle, and priorities and that relate to the family's goals. As with all assessment procedures, home assessment should focus on strengths as well as needs. Additionally, family members should be informed of the reasons for the assessment, should be active participants, and should choose or approve any assessment procedures used. This is especially important when formal assessment procedures, such as scales, are used. Because professionals inherently make "observations" of the home environment whenever they make home visits, they have the opportunity to develop functional intervention options based on their ongoing observations. Early interventionists need to develop a communication style that allows them to give positive and constructive feedback to families and avoids making the family feel like they, or their home, are under scrutiny.

IMPLICATIONS FOR PROVIDING EARLY INTERVENTION SERVICES

A number of significant issues must be addressed for home-based services to be successful. These fall into two main domains: interpersonal aspects and logistic aspects, each of which is discussed in this section. Although these issues are described sequentially, they often occur concurrently and in an ongoing manner that is more like a continuous spiral than a linear sequence.

Interpersonal Aspects

Interpersonal aspects related to home-based services include partnerships between providers and families, needs of the families, roles each person will play in the delivery of services, and strengths of family members.

Partnerships Although Chapter 6 of this book discussed partnerships in depth, they are discussed briefly here in relation to the home context. Partnerships are necessary for effective early intervention, with identified roles and mutually agreed-upon goals. In developing partnerships with family members, it is especially important that the early interventionist develop clear expectations with family members regarding what role the interventionist will play during home visits. Some parents, for example, initially expect the interventionist to provide hands-on "tutoring" or therapy during home visits and are surprised to learn that the interventionist's primary role is to help parents (and other family members) learn how to interact with the child with a disability. Parents also sometimes expect the interventionist to be the expert and tell them what to do. It is important to emphasize to parents that *they* are the experts on their own children, although the interventionist has expertise in his or her particular discipline. In the partnership with each family, the expertise of both the family and the interventionist will be blended to result in the best outcomes for the child and family.

Needs It is essential that early interventionists focus their energies on helping families to identify, express, and address needs and concerns that are important to the families. However, it must be the *family* who determines the needs as well as the relative importance or priority of each need. An interventionist may enter a home and immediately observe numerous interpersonal or physical needs, including developmental or health needs of the child; learning needs of the caregivers; or basic material needs such as heat, food, or safety items. However, as pointed out by McKillip (1987) and elaborated by Dunst et al. (1988), something is not a need unless it has the following four characteristics: 1) psychological awareness, 2) value influence, 3) need recognition, and 4) solution identification. This means that for something to be a need, the issues must be perceived by an individual (psychological awareness), the individual must care about the issue (value influence), the individual must become aware that a possible resolution for the issue exists (need recognition), and the individual must believe that the resolution is actually possible for him or her (solution identification). This perspective on needs is particularly useful if the interventionist identifies needs that the family does not seem to recognize or care about. It may be that the family has learned to live with a situation because they do not know of a solution or do not believe the solution is within their grasp. Often simply informing the family that resources exist and are available to them helps the family acknowledge that a need exists.

Sometimes, however, the family may not be ready to deal with a certain situation because there are other issues or concerns that are higher priority or because of the emotional cost that might be involved. This is often the reason that some parents are absent at home visits or do not follow through with suggestions made by the early interventionist. For example, parents who have not yet accepted that their child has a motor disability may not follow through with physical therapy. Similarly, parents who are struggling with values issues related to discipline or their emotional relationship with the child may have a difficult time implementing certain behavior management strategies consistently (e.g., time-out). Interventionists need to recognize these kinds of caregiver responses as legitimate issues rather than as uncooperative or noncompliant behavior. The interventionist's focus can then turn to assisting the family to clarify needs by providing objective information, developing intervention options from which the family can choose to address needs, and engaging the family in problem-solving strategies to help them set priorities. This should be done in a respectful, nonjudgmental manner that communicates respect for the family members and acknowledgment of their right and ability to make decisions that affect their lives. Table 1 lists several steps for helping families identify needs.

Roles As the family identifies and agrees on needs to be addressed, it then becomes essential to discuss the possible roles that each person in the partnership will play. Will the interventionist spend time each visit directly working with the child, or will he or she "coach" one of the family members? Who will actually interact with

Table 1. Steps in identifying needs

1. State clearly the reason and purpose of the meeting (visit, call, etc.).
2. Make sure the family knows that you will be exploring what their needs are and that you will follow through on this by helping to plan ways to meet the needs.
3. If possible, let the family choose the setting for the session (home, office, etc.).
4. Consider whether communication will be interrupted by children, telephone calls, and so forth.
5. Know that you cannot rush this process. More than one visit may be needed.
6. Involve the key people in the family. Who makes the decisions? Who is legally responsible? Don't overlook involving husband/wife or extended family members. (Keep in mind this is not your decision . . . but the family's.)
7. If you have a definite time frame for the meeting, let the family know this *up front.*
8. Start the session by summarizing/reviewing the purpose and then asking the member(s) to "tell their story." Allow TIME.
9. Use empathic listening skills.
10. Summarize the family's needs from their point of view. Clarify and begin slowly the process of *REFRAMING* needs into 1) specific attainable goals and 2) positive outcomes based on family strengths/available resources.
11. Use observation skills and ask general questions around the areas in the "taxonomy of needs."
12. Consider using the Family Needs Scale or other instrument, *if necessary* (e.g., Family Needs Survey, Goldfarb et al., 1986; Parent Needs Inventory, Fewell et al., 1981; Personal Projects Scale, Little, 1983).
13. Keep in mind that many factors come into play in recognizing/identifying and expressing needs. A "critical" need now may be unimportant in a month, when an area completely unrecognized or unexpressed may be identified as a major need.

the child? Which caregivers will be present during visits, and what will their roles be? If there is a father living with the child, or involved with him or her, will the father be present and what will he do during visits? Will siblings, cousins, neighbors, friends, or extended family be involved, and if so what will be their roles? Such individuals are often present in the home and may or may not be introduced to the interventionist by the parent or other caregiver. These individuals may be important parts of the family's informal network, and their presence can be turned into a positive aspect of the home visit if the interventionist is comfortable with engaging these individuals and viewing them as potential resources.

Strengths   A key to the success of early intervention in the home is focusing on strengths of family members. Among others, Bowman (1983), Curran (1983), Stinnett and DeFrain (1985), and Turnbull et al. (1986) have written extensively about family strengths. Dunst, Trivette, and Mott (1994) proposed that family strengths consist of values, competencies, and interactional patterns, which combine to form each family's unique "functioning style" (p. 119). When interventionists view families from a value-free perspective, they help create a proactive process that acknowledges and builds on existing competencies and views deficiencies as opportunities for growth and learning. Conversely, interventionists can become reactive rather than proactive during home visits, especially when they see firsthand some of the problems and issues confronting the family. For example, an interventionist visited the home of a single mother who had been in an abusive relationship with her children's stepfather. Her children (a 2-year-old boy and a 3-year-old girl) were noisy, extremely active, aggressive, and generally out of control during most of the visit, and the mother was on the verge of tears throughout the hour-and-a-half visit. She frequently put the older child in time-out and physically restrained the younger child. Her efforts were clearly well-intentioned, but she made a number of "mistakes" in the behavioral procedures she used (e.g., talking with the older child frequently while she was in time-out; offering the younger child food to get him to become quiet). Although the interventionist acknowledged the obvious difficulties the mother had with her children, rather than focusing on the "mistakes" she made the interventionist gave her positive feedback about her efforts, her successes (the children did eventually become quiet for a time), and her obvious affection for the children. The interventionist also made an effort to engage the children in appropriate play and redirected them before they engaged in some of their more destructive behavior. By the end of the visit, the mother asked for feedback about her strategies and imitated some of the techniques the interventionist used with the children. Focusing on the positive enhanced the mother's self-esteem, and communication was opened for further discussion of the children's behavioral and emotional issues. Had the interventionist focused on the negative, the outcomes may have been much different.

Resources One of the most important roles of early interventionists is assisting families in identifying and obtaining a wide variety of resources from their informal and formal networks. An advantage of providing early intervention in the home is the clarity with which interventionists can observe the family's strengths as well as needs. The interventionist could be overwhelmed by the level of need that often exists, especially if the interventionist tries to single-handedly address all the needs. Instead, the interventionist must help the family identify a multiplicity of resources to meet their needs. These resources should include the family members themselves; extended family, friends, neighbors; and other resources from the informal network, when feasible and appropriate. In many cases, these informal resources should be used in combination with formal resources but not as a substitute for formal resources.

Figure 1 illustrates one way to conceptualize resources available to families. For any given need identified by the family, there are potentially six types of resources that may be used to meet the need:

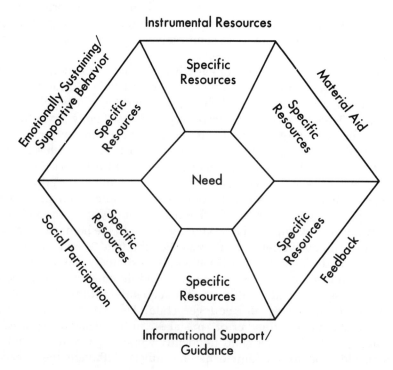

Figure 1. A format for conceptualizing resources.

- Emotionally sustaining/supportive behavior refers to resources such as emotional support from others, spiritual or religious beliefs, counseling or therapy, and other resources that are useful to the person coping with the emotional aspects of a situation.
- Instrumental resources include direct "hands-on" resources, such as specialized therapy, tutoring, babysitting, respite care, housecleaning, and transportation.
- Material aid includes tangible resources, such as books, toys, games, food, clothes, shelter, vehicles, and equipment, as well as cash or other financial assistance to obtain resources.
- Feedback includes information about another person's satisfaction with resources or evaluative information about outcomes or progress related to an existing need. Examples include parents' comments about their experiences with specific doctors, teachers' reports about children's progress on individualized education program goals, and child care staff's reports about children's responses in the child care environment.
- Informational support/guidance refers to information that is more general in nature and that focuses on proactive problem solving. Examples include information about behavior management (e.g., the advantages and disadvantages of using time-out or corporal punishment), information about available resources in the community, recommendations on the best medical procedures available to treat a specific condition, or suggestions for motor activities that will help a child learn to walk.
- Social participation includes resources such as friendships, social gatherings, recreational events, concerts, or parent-to-parent meetings, where the purpose is fun, recreation, or social affiliation as opposed to decision making, problem solving, or personal development.

Figure 2 gives a specific example of resources used to assist a family with respite services. All six types of resources were necessary for the need to be met, and the resources were from both the formal and informal networks. The case coordinator and the respite provider represent the formal network, and the other parents and extended family represent the informal network. Both the mother and father are listed as resources because they provided the opportunity for social affiliation for each other, which was the reason that respite was desired. The use of both formal and informal network resources to meet needs is frequent and ongoing, as is the use of multiple types of resources, as depicted in Figures 1 and 2. Although early interventionists may frequently provide instrumental assistance, such as hands-on work with children, often the most important role they play may be helping families become proficient at identifying and managing resources to meet their needs. Providing home-based services often makes this task easier as the early interventionist is literally in the center of the action and can both observe and participate in the family's resource network.

Logistical Aspects

Logistical issues related to home-based services include scheduling, policy issues, and staff safety. Social conventions and courtesies must be considered, as well as the phenomenon of the professional being perceived by the family members as a guest or a friend. The interventionist must also decide whether to bring toys, books, or other materials into the home or to rely on materials available in the home. Additionally, the interventionist must be able to constructively handle potential conflicts between family members and must be aware of the special importance of the beginning and

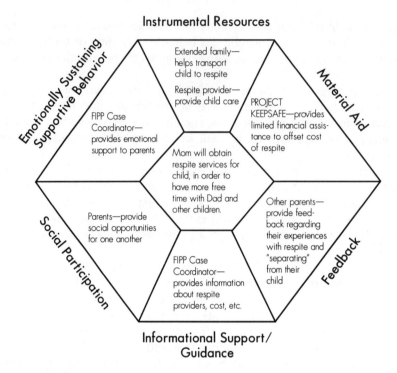

Figure 2. An example of resources used to meet a need.

the end of each home visit. The issue of accountability and completion of paperwork also must be addressed.

Scheduling Home visits should be convenient for families and should consider the schedules of the primary caregiver and any others who may be involved. It is especially important that fathers be involved in the early intervention process; unfortunately, they are often left out, sometimes because home visits are scheduled while they are at work. May (1991) suggested that family stability suffers when fathers are excluded from direct involvement with their children. Consequently, the early interventionist may need to make special arrangements for visits when the father is available and may need to be creative in engaging the father in the planning and intervention process. Fathers may prefer taking action, such as adapting toys, roughhousing with the child, or building a ramp, but their need to talk about their feelings and experiences and to be involved in the decision-making process regarding their child and family should not be discounted.

Policy Issues Policy issues, such as responses to "no-shows," are important considerations in early intervention. Caseload demands are often high, and many programs operate with waiting lists, making no-shows frustrating, especially when substantial travel time is involved. The agency's policy for no-shows should be explained to families, and interventionists should leave a note or follow up with a telephone call after a no-show. It is important to examine the reasons that families are not home for a scheduled visit. This may occur because the family has conflicting time demands, has poor time management skills, or is forgetful, all of which may then be addressed in the intervention planning process. However, missed visits also may be a sign that the family does not value the services being provided or does not feel that their needs are being addressed. Families are more likely to be present when they are highly invested in the needs assessment and intervention process and when they view their relationship with the interventionist as a partnership. Consequently, missed home visits should be signals to the interventionist to examine the relationship with the family and to ask the family for feedback on their satisfaction with the services they are receiving.

Staff safety is another important policy issue. Despite taking a positive and strengths-based approach with families, early interventionists who make home visits must also take reasonable precautions. Whether services are provided in rural or urban areas, home visits often involve women traveling alone, sometimes in unknown or dangerous neighborhoods. Each agency should have a policy addressing this issue that reflects the specific characteristics of the area served by the agency. Some strategies to consider include sending two individuals on each visit, especially during the early phases of a relationship with a family; providing cellular phones to staff, especially when they visit families with no phone or who live in especially dangerous neighborhoods; arranging to visit families in center-based settings or in public places, particularly if threatening behavior has been encountered during a home visit; ensuring administrative knowledge of the whereabouts of each staff member; providing administrative support to staff who may have encountered difficulties during home visits; and training staff on the agency's policies as well as strategies to defuse potentially confrontational or difficult situations.

Responding to Abuse or Neglect Early intervention staff who make home visits may become aware of family situations suggestive of abuse or neglect that might need to be reported to social services departments. Establishing trust is such a crucial element of the working partnership with families that reporting abuse or neglect situations may be especially difficult for early intervention workers, and there should be sufficient emotional and policy support within the agency to assist workers in discussing their experiences and in deciding on the best course of action. When abuse or neglect have occurred, it is often constructive to inform the family of the legal and ethical reporting requirements, as well as what to expect in terms of an investigation and follow-up. This process can be a trust-building one that enhances the partnership and empowers family members, if it is handled openly, honestly, and respectfully. It is also imperative that the early interventionist take a nonjudgmental approach and emphasize that he or she is committed to working with the family to mobilize necessary resources to resolve the issues that originally led to the neglect or abuse.

Bringing Toys and Materials Early interventionists must decide whether to bring toys or other materials on home visits. There is an advantage to bringing materials to demonstrate play skills and teaching strategies or to assess children's abilities. However, if the toys and materials leave with the interventionist, the child and family may feel frustrated or resentful. An alternative is to use materials that families have around the house or to assist families in identifying ways to obtain needed toys and other materials. Additionally, home-based programs may want to establish a toy and material library so that families can borrow or barter for items they need.

Paperwork Early interventionists who provide home-based services must decide how to integrate paperwork demands into the home visit. The amount of paperwork required varies from agency to agency and state to state, but regardless of the amount of paperwork required the interventionist's goal should be to keep the process as family friendly as possible, while meeting agency, state, and federal regulations. Some interventionists find it convenient to take a few minutes at the beginning and end of each home visit to complete paperwork, and others integrate the paperwork process throughout the visit. Some interventionists are uncomfortable with the formality and intrusiveness of the paperwork process and prefer to complete paperwork in the office. When this occurs, it is essential that the family be aware of and receive copies of documents such as the individualized family service plan (IFSP), which is meant to be the family's document.

Friendships   Another issue to be considered by home-based early intervention-ists is the phenomenon of being viewed by family members as a family friend. The act of welcoming someone into one's home on a regular basis and participating in common goals in an emotionally supportive and respectful manner signifies friendship to many people. That the early interventionist is getting paid to be there and can be reassigned or transferred to another family is often obscured by the power of the context and the relationship. One mother at a panel discussion made the comment, "My home visitor would come every week, bring doughnuts, and sit on the floor of my son's room playing with him and just talking about life. She was my lifeline to the real world. She was my best friend." Because families often view home-based visitors as friends, it is essential that the parameters of the relationship be explicit and acknowledged. To some extent, each interventionist needs to decide these parameters for himself or herself, sometimes on a case-by-case basis. Issues to consider include giving out a home telephone number, responding to family emergencies or crises, sharing personal information about self or family, and responding to invitations to social or recreational events in the family's life. The boundaries that are established are not always easy to determine, but early interventionists can become overwhelmed and burned out in their personal lives if they do not set such boundaries. This is not to say that true friendships cannot or should not develop between family members and early interventionists, but that these should be the exception rather than the rule.

RECOMMENDATIONS AND SOLUTIONS

No one strategy or specific set of strategies will be successful in every situation; con-sequently, a variety of approaches is necessary. For example, one family may benefit from weekly home visits, or even from 24-hour-a-day services, such as those provided through home-health nursing or some family preservation programs. Other families may only want periodic visits to check on the child's progress. The services provided by the interventionist during home visits may also vary greatly and should be based on the child's and family's needs. In some cases, the interventionist may primarily share information with the family about resources, while in others he or she may provide emotional support. The role that the interventionist plays will vary across time, and often the interventionist will play numerous roles during one visit.

Meeting IDEA Requirements in the Home

Early interventionists must be prepared to address the primary service components required by the Individuals with Disabilities Education Act (IDEA) of 1990 (PL 101-476). These include assessing the child's strengths and needs, assessing the family's strengths and needs (if desired by the family), developing an IFSP, providing or mo-bilizing services (or resources) needed to meet the goals identified in the IFSP, and ensuring a smooth transition from early intervention services when the child reaches his or her third birthday.

Assessment   Assessing child and family needs and strengths is often facilitated by making home visits, through the direct observation of the home and family mem-bers. For example, instruments such as HOME (Caldwell, 1978) must be implemented in the home. Assessment of children can also be conducted in the home, depending on the instrument or procedure used. For example, play-based assessment procedures can be conducted in the home, as can certain standardized tests such as the Battelle Developmental Inventory (Newborg, Stock, Wnek, Guidubaldi, & Svinicki, 1984) and Griffiths' Mental Development Scale (Griffiths, 1979). Implementing such instruments in the home may have advantages or disadvantages, depending on the characteristics of the home and child. Advantages may include increased cooperation by the child, increased parent participation and acceptance of the assessment results, and increased opportunities to see how the child functions in his or her "natural" environment. Disadvantages may include distractions, space limitations, and difficulty implementing the instruments according to standardized procedures. Some assessment instruments require administration in a structured setting, sometimes without the parent present. Further discussion of this issue is beyond the scope of this chapter, but *Assessment for Early Intervention: Best Practices for Professionals* (Bagnato & Neisworth, 1991) is an excellent resource for information about the assessment of young children.

Developing the IFSP There are a variety of approaches to the actual planning and development of the IFSP. Many professionals distinguish between the IFSP process and the written product. Ideally, the process and product should be intertwined, and the writing of the IFSP should be an integral part of the planning process. For most families, the planning process occurs in the home, in face-to-face discussions with the early interventionist. Often, the writing of the IFSP occurs in the home as well, but at times the IFSP is physically written at the office and then given to the parent on the next home visit. In some cases, parents themselves write the IFSP. The IFSP conference, another component required by IDEA, can also occur in the home. For many families, it might not be feasible for a large group of professionals to come to their home, but many families prefer this to meeting with those same professionals in an office environment. There are also times when the IFSP conference may only include two or three professionals, in addition to the parent(s). When this is the case, it is quite feasible for the IFSP conference to be in the home. As with other aspects of early intervention, decisions on the specific time and place of IFSP planning meetings and the IFSP conference should be made by the parent, in collaboration with the early interventionist.

Providing or Mobilizing Services Once the initial IFSP has been developed, the early interventionist must ensure that the goals of the family are addressed. At times, the family's concerns may focus on the child and specific issues related to his or her health or development. The early interventionist may be the primary resource for the family to address these goals, and the primary context may be the home. For example, if the early interventionist is a teacher and the parents' goals are to promote the child's social and cognitive development, the interventionist may visit weekly in the home, discuss and demonstrate ways to interact with the child, leave reading material for the parents, and have occasional contact by telephone to answer questions and schedule visits. Between visits, the parents should be applying what they learned during the home visit, by playing with the child appropriately, developing reasonable expectations, and showing others in the family's support system (e.g., grandparents) how to promote the child's development. There are other situations in which a single early interventionist working with the family in the home provides most, if not all, of the services documented on the IFSP. For example, an early interventionist might provide information and emotional support in the home to parents of a newborn child with Down syndrome. However, there also are situations in which the early interventionist is not the actual service provider but serves more as a case manager or service coordinator, helping the family navigate the system and obtain needed resources. In these instances, the contacts between the early interventionist and family may or may not occur in the home, depending on the child's and family's needs. For example, in the case study presented later in this chapter, there were times when the interventionist met with the family in the home to discuss needs, and other times when the interventionist attended meetings, visited other agencies, or met with the family in other settings.

Transition   As with IFSP development and implementation, transition planning may occur in the home but frequently also will involve contacts with the family in other settings. The early interventionist may attend meetings with the family in local school settings and may visit classroom settings with the family as part of the transition planning process. The case study presented at the end of this chapter illustrates this process.

The Home as a Target of Intervention

It is often essential to explicitly identify the home as one of the targets of intervention. Both the interventionist and the family members should be aware of this. An assessment of "strengths and needs" of the home should be part of the overall assessment of family strengths and needs. As with all assessments, this should only be done with the family's understanding, permission, and participation. The assessment of the home should be based on concerns and needs identified by the family members, and it can be either formal or informal in nature. Regardless of how the home is assessed, functional intervention options based on a realistic assessment of the home characteristics should occur.

When home-based services are offered, if possible they should be offered in conjunction with other types of services such as drop-in centers, center-based services, child care, respite, and so forth. Interventionists must be proactive and strengths based and must promise or offer only what can actually be delivered. Nevertheless, interventionists need to be careful not to avoid issues related to the home environment. They should develop a style that is comfortable for them, in which they can ask questions such as "What would it take?" or "Is that something you would like to work on?" when sensitive issues related to the home context are raised. In developing IFSPs (or other intervention plans), family members and interventionists must consider the various resources required to meet a particular need and determine whether the home context provides one or more of these resources or whether additional resources will be required to meet the need.

Early interventionists must also be sensitive to issues of cultural diversity and must be prepared to recognize and respect the values and traditions of people from different ethnic, social, cultural, and religious backgrounds (see Chapter 4 of this book for more detail on culture as a context for early intervention). Wayman et al. (1990) developed guidelines for consideration when working with culturally diverse populations, which are included in Table 2. These strategies will be useful in working with all families, not just culturally diverse families. Examples of considerations specific to home-based services include customs (e.g., seating arrangements, wearing shoes, sleeping arrangements), religious beliefs (e.g., talking about death in the home, scheduling visits on holy days or after dark), and sanitation (e.g., in some rural or mountain cultures). Additionally, consideration should be given to the issue of gender or race differences between the interventionist and the family.

Table 2. Guidelines for working with culturally diverse families

Part I—Family structure and child-rearing practices
- Family structure
  - Family composition
    - Who are the members of the family system?
    - Who are the key decision makers?
    - Is decision making related to specific situations?
    - Is decision making individual or group oriented?
    - Do family members all live in the same household?
    - What is the relationship of friends to the family system?
    - What is the hierarchy within the family? Is status related to gender or age?
  - Primary caregiver(s)
    - Who is the primary caregiver?
    - Who else participates in the caregiving?
    - What is the amount of care given by mother versus others?
    - How much time does the infant spend away from the primary caregiver?
    - Is there conflict between caregivers regarding appropriate practices?
    - What ecological/environmental issues impinge upon general caregiving (i.e., housing, jobs, etc.)?
- Child-rearing practices
  - Family feeding practices
    - What are the family feeding practices?
    - What are the mealtime rules?
    - What types of foods are eaten?
    - What are the beliefs regarding breastfeeding and weaning?
    - What are the beliefs regarding bottle feeding?
    - What are the family practices regarding the transition to solid food?
    - Which family members prepare food?
    - Is food purchased or homemade?
    - Are there any taboos related to food preparation or handling?
    - Which family members feed the child?
    - What is the configuration of the family mealtime?
    - What are the family's views on independent feeding?
    - Is there a discrepancy among family members regarding the beliefs and practices related to feeding an infant/toddler?
  - Family sleeping patterns
    - Does the infant sleep in the same room/bed as the parents?
    - At what age is the infant moved away from close proximity to the mother?
    - Is there an established bedtime?
    - What is the family response to an infant when he or she awakens at night?
    - What practices surround daytime napping?
  - Family's response to disobedience and aggression
    - What are the parameters of acceptable child behavior?
    - What form does the discipline take?
    - Who metes out the disciplinary action?
  - Family's response to a crying infant
    - Temporal qualities—How long before the caregiver picks up a crying infant?
    - How does the caregiver calm an upset infant?

Part II—Family perceptions and attitudes
- Family's perception of child's disability
  - Are there cultural or religious factors that would shape family perceptions?
  - To what/where/whom does the family assign responsibility for the child's disability?
  - How does the family view the role of fate in their lives?
  - How does the family view their role in intervening with their child? Do they feel they can make a difference or do they consider it hopeless?
- Family's perception of health and healing
  - What is the family's approach to medical needs?
    - Do they rely solely on Western medical services?
    - Do they rely solely on holistic approaches?
    - Do they use a combination of these approaches?

(continued)

Table 2. (*continued*)

> • Who is the primary medical provider or conveyer of medical information?
>> • Family members? Elders? Friends? Folk healers? Family doctor? Medical specialists?
> • Do all members of the family agree on approaches to medical needs?
> • Family's perception of help-seeking and intervention
>> • From whom does the family seek help—family members or outside agencies/individuals?
>> • Does the family seek help directly or indirectly?
>> • What are the general feelings of the family when seeking assistance—ashamed, angry, demand as a right, view as unnecessary?
>> • With which community systems does the family interact (educational/medical/social)?
>> • How are these interactions completed (face-to-face, telephone, letter)?
>> • Which family member interacts with other systems?
>> • Does that family member feel comfortable when interacting with other systems?

Part III—Language and communication styles

> • Language
>> • To what degree:
>>> • Is the home visitor proficient in the family's native language?
>>> • Is the family proficient in English?
>> • If an interpreter is used:
>>> • With which culture is the interpreter primarily affiliated?
>>> • Is the interpreter familiar with the colloquialisms of the family members' country or region of origin?
>>> • Is the family member comfortable with the interpreter? Would the family member feel more comfortable with an interpreter of the same sex?
>> • If written materials are used, are they in the family's native language?
> • Interaction styles
>> • Does the family communicate with each other in a direct or indirect style?
>> • Does the family tend to interact in a quiet manner or a loud manner?
>> • Do family members share feelings when discussing emotional issues?
>> • Does the family ask the home visitor direct questions?
>> • Does the family value a lengthy social time at each home visit unrelated to the early childhood services program goals?
>> • Is it important for the family to know about the home visitor's extended family? Is the home visitor comfortable sharing that information?

From Wayman, K.T., Lynch, E.W., & Hanson, M.J. (1990). Home-based early childhood services: Cultural sensitivity in a family systems approach. *Topics in Early Childhood Special Education, 10*(4), pp. 65–66; reprinted by permission.

Collaboration with Other Agencies and Professionals

One of the most exciting aspects of early intervention is the opportunity to collaborate with professionals from numerous disciplines and with providers from the private and public sector. IDEA requires collaboration between publicly funded agencies as well as true family involvement in decision making for their child and family.

When the primary context of early intervention is the home, there are numerous ways in which collaboration can occur, including joint home visits by representatives of different agencies, participation in IFSP development and transition planning meetings by members of different agencies, and consultation "behind the scenes" by numerous professionals. For example, an early interventionist may consult with an occupational therapist or nutritionist from a different agency before making a home visit with a family to discuss feeding methods or nutritional concerns. Similarly, a parent may consult with a neurologist about behavior issues or sleep patterns and share information about these topics with the interventionist during the next home visit. It is important to note that the early interventionist may or may not be the person collaborating with other professionals. One of the outcomes of early intervention should be helping parents become more skilled in and comfortable with making contacts themselves with a variety of professionals and other resources.

Collaboration should be viewed more broadly than simply interagency coordination. Rather, collaboration should be thought of as the mutual effort of all the individuals involved in the child's life who are working together toward a mutually agreed-upon goal or goals. Thus, the family should be in the center of the collaborative process, not the early interventionist. Instead, the early interventionist is one player in the collaboration with the family. Although the early interventionist often functions as the service coordinator legally, ideally the family will eventually be comfortable assuming this role themselves, particularly once the transition from early intervention services has occurred. The following case study includes several examples of collaboration.

Case Study

This case study includes two sections: The first is a summary of the major characteristics of the family involved and the events that took place over 2 years; the second is a brief discussion of these events in the context of the concepts presented earlier in this chapter. The case study is based on a real family and all significant elements presented are accurate, but names and details have been changed to preserve confidentiality.

Case Summary

The Ervins The Ervin family included Elmer and Virginia and their grandchildren, Daryl and Katrina. The children had been abandoned by their mother, who was the Ervins's daughter. Later, she was arrested on drug charges and relinquished guardianship of the children to the Ervins. She lived about 100 miles away and had inconsistent and infrequent contact with the family. The Ervins also had an adult son, who had moved to California to work in construction and who communicated with the Ervins occasionally by letter. Elmer worked as a roofer, but his health prevented him from working regularly. However, he also worked making wooden crafts representative of the Appalachian culture, including dulcimers for which he had won awards at local shows. Virginia worked in a local factory and had done so since she dropped out of high school in the 11th grade.

The Home One of the major issues in working with the Ervins was the home. It was the nucleus of the family's life, especially because Elmer did most of his woodwork in one of the outbuildings and because Daryl became upset whenever he was taken out of the home. Consequently, everyone but Virginia spent most of their time in the home, and Virginia rushed to get shopping done after work so she could get home and relieve Elmer. The house was a small frame house, with four rooms of about 10 feet by 12 feet, each room taking up one corner of the house, with a small vestibule in the center area between all four rooms. Doorways with no doors connected each room to its two adjoining rooms. There was a lot of furniture present, including a very large upright piano with a mirror above the keyboard, and many fragile figurines. The house had a basement accessible from the vestibule, with extremely steep steps with no handrail. There was a storage area, a laundry area, and a very small bathroom area in the basement. A covered porch with wooden rocking chairs ran the length of the front of the house and looked out on the paved road, the edge of which was about 10 feet from the front porch. In addition to the living room and kitchen, there were two bedrooms, one of which was used for storage. The other bedroom had two beds, one for Elmer and Virginia, one for Daryl and Katrina. More frequently, Virginia slept with Katrina and Elmer slept with Daryl.

Material Resources The Ervins's material resources included the small frame house with several outbuildings, which they owned, and an old sedan and an even older pickup truck. Their home was in a rural, mountainous area but on a narrow two-lane paved road, which was a highly traveled route between two mountain communities. The house had been built on the sloping side of a small mountain, and their back yard descended eventually into a wide valley, with streams, forest, and farmland.

Intangible Resources The Ervins also had a variety of intangible resources, including longstanding relationships with neighbors and church members, a strong value system, and a commitment to each other and to their grandchildren. Additionally, despite their limited education, they were intelligent and capable people who were effective in communicating their needs and desires.

Initial Concerns The Ervins's involvement in an early intervention program began shortly after they received custody of their two grandchildren. At the time, Daryl was 19 months old and Katrina was 4 years old. Although Katrina was often "moody" and "feisty," they felt she was developing typically and "would be okay, once she gets over missin' her mama." They had serious concerns, however, about Daryl, who they described as "a wild child," who "runs wide open all day long, and half the night, too." They were becoming exhausted keeping up with Daryl and were worried that he didn't talk, although he made "lots of strange sounds, like he's talking to someone on another planet." They had also noticed some "peculiar" behaviors, especially related to eating, drinking, and interacting with others. For example, Daryl would not eat or drink anything until he had sniffed it, and then he would laugh or giggle before tasting it carefully with the tip of his tongue. He also became very agitated at times if food was prepared different from the usual way. When he interacted with Elmer and Virginia, he was often very affectionate, hugging them and touching them gently on the face. But his moods would often suddenly change from affectionate to sullen and withdrawn, to "silly and wild," to tearful, and then back again to affectionate. He also became extremely agitated and would scream and hit himself if taken outside of the house.

Elmer and Virginia had at first thought that Daryl, like Katrina, was simply having difficulties adjusting to his mother's departure, and they had decided to focus their energies on "making him feel secure." They held him frequently, offered him numerous foods until he was satisfied, let him stay up and play in the middle of the night, and arranged their work schedules so one of them could supervise him at all times. They also encouraged Katrina to "be a good big sister and help your brother." They soon realized that he was "getting worse, not better," and that their lives were revolving around him. In some ways, they had become prisoners in their own home. That is when they called the early intervention program and asked for help.

The Initial Home Visit Within a few days of the Ervins's telephone call, a social worker and a nurse from the local early intervention program visited the home and spent about 2 hours talking with Elmer and Virginia, playing with the children, and observing the environment. They explained the resources available, including the services offered by their agency, as well as major resources available in the community (e.g., respite care, Supplemental Security Income benefits). Most of the discussion, however, consisted of Elmer and Virginia "telling their story." This included details about Daryl and Katrina but also considerable discussion about the Ervins's two children. They described strong anger and resentment toward their daughter for abandoning the children and for what they described as neglect that had occurred for months before she actually left. They also expressed frustration that their daughter lived so far away from them and their children. They said that they blamed themselves for the problems their daughter had and that they were determined to "do better" with Katrina and Daryl. During the visit, Katrina sat quietly near one of her grandparents, often physically touching them or sitting in one of their laps. Daryl spent about half the time wandering around the room, climbing up and down off the back of the couch, occasionally sitting on one of his grandparents' laps. He grinned and laughed spontaneously at times, did not speak, and resisted the social worker's and the nurse's attempts to engage him in interactions. He spent the other half of the visit slowly nibbling an apple while standing on his head with his legs leaning against the couch.

The Emerging Partnership   The social worker and nurse returned to the office after the initial home visit and immediately consulted with the team psychologist, Bill, who became the Ervins's "family resource coordinator." Bill began making weekly home visits within a few days after the initial home visit. During these visits, he continued the work begun on that visit, by providing additional information about resources available and explaining how he and other early intervention staff could be helpful to the family. He also encouraged Elmer and Virginia to again "tell their story" so that he could hear their concerns firsthand. The focus in this early stage was on establishing a trusting relationship and on identifying the issues that were Elmer's and Virginia's primary concerns. It was also important to begin addressing some of these concerns immediately. Elmer, particularly, was skeptical: First, he was still hopeful that Daryl would eventually "come out of it and be okay," and second, he was accustomed to taking care of himself and was not sure that he and Virginia really needed help.

During Bill's first visit, Elmer made a point of showing that everything was "under control" by telling Daryl to sit and watch television while Elmer sat nearby with a hickory switch in hand. He waved the switch around if Daryl began to move from his spot on the floor near the television. Bill was tempted to explain the pros and cons of corporal punishment but instead used this as an opportunity to point out to Elmer that his involvement with Daryl was accomplishing several important things. For example, it was getting Daryl used to the idea of someone structuring his environment and placing demands on him, it was allowing Virginia to have time to get household chores done and have a little time to herself, it gave Katrina a break from the responsibility of keeping Daryl occupied, and it encouraged Daryl to attend to an activity for more than a few seconds at a time. By focusing on the positive aspects of Elmer's behavior, rather than criticizing Elmer for the use of the hickory switch, Bill set a tone for future discussions and opened the lines of communication regarding behavior management strategies. This led quickly to the development of a plan to make some minor rearrangements of the position of furniture in the living room so that Elmer could sit in his favorite chair while supervising Daryl and physically prevent him from leaving the room. This functionally eliminated the need for the switch and created a more appropriate play opportunity for Daryl while achieving Elmer's primary objective, which was to have some control of the situation while giving Virginia a break.

Assessment and Intervention Planning   About 1 month after Bill's first visit, an assessment and intervention planning day was conducted at the early intervention office, with participation by Virginia, Daryl, Bill, the team social worker who had visited in the home, a speech-language pathologist, an educator, a pediatrician, a nurse, and a physical therapist. During this day, standardized tests were implemented, but much time was also spent interacting with Daryl in play situations and observing Virginia and Daryl play and interact together. Unfortunately, Elmer did not feel comfortable attending this day and chose to stay home with Katrina. The major goal of the assessment and intervention planning day was to develop functional intervention strategies to assist the Ervins in achieving their goals for their family. This included clarifying Daryl's diagnosis, and the team agreed that Daryl had developmental delays and autism.

Home-Based Resources   Over the next 2 years, a working partnership between Elmer and Virginia and the early intervention program was solidified. Bill was the primary liaison with the family and visited weekly for most of that time. Other staff members also visited the family, including the speech-language pathologist, the social worker, and the nurse. Each of these individuals visited to provide information or demonstrate strategies to supplement those shared by Bill. Additionally, a psychologist from a program that specialized in working with children with autism and their families visited on two occasions to assess Daryl and to describe the resources that could be offered by that program once Daryl entered public school.

During this period, numerous strategies were implemented to promote Daryl's communication skills, cooperation, self-help skills, fine motor skills, socialization skills, and self-regulation. (His gross motor skills were excellent, as was his general health.) At the same time, strategies were implemented to help the Ervins have some time to themselves, meet their financial obligations, increase their understanding of autism and mental retardation, and develop a more pleasant and satisfactory family routine (including everyone in the family sleeping at approximately the same time). Additional strategies were implemented to assist Katrina in adjusting to her mother's departure; to help her with kindergarten readiness; to develop friendships with other children; and to develop a more age-appropriate sense of responsibility toward Daryl, for whom she felt very protective and overly responsible. It is beyond the scope of this case study to elaborate in detail on all of these strategies, but those that relate most specifically to working with families in the home context are discussed below.

Sleep Patterns and Arrangements   One of the first concerns presented to Bill by the Ervins was Daryl's sleep pattern. He tended to stay awake much of the night and sleep 4 or 5 hours during the day. A pattern had developed in which Elmer and Virginia let him sleep during the day because it was their only opportunity for rest. But they had reached a point where he began sleeping less and less at night and more and more during the day. Most of their efforts had focused on trying to get Daryl to sleep at night, and Bill suggested that they switch their efforts to focus on getting him to stay awake during the day. Because medical problems had been ruled out by the pediatrician, Bill asked the Ervins to describe Daryl's sleep pattern specifically and made arrangements to visit around the time that Daryl was likely to fall asleep so that he could participate in their efforts to keep him awake. This proved to be a challenging experience for everyone and involved keeping Daryl moving, engaging him in his most preferred activities, giving him snacks and drinks, taking him outdoors, and occasionally washing his face and neck with a cool washcloth (which he enjoyed). The Ervins had initially felt that they were "being mean" to Daryl to keep him awake during the day, but with Bill's encouragement and direct involvement they decided to set a goal of gradually increasing his awake time during the day in the hope that this would increase his asleep time at night. This plan was successful and allowed the Ervins to regain some of their energy and then focus on other issues. It is important to note that, until this sleep pattern was changed, the Ervins had virtually no interest or energy to address any other issues.

Communication and Cooperation   As Daryl's sleep pattern began to regulate toward nighttime sleeping, the Ervins's interest gradually shifted toward his communication and cooperation. These two areas were intertwined because Daryl tended to move around and do what he wanted most of the time, eliminating the need for much communication. Although Elmer had moved some furniture so that he could supervise Daryl more efficiently in the living room, this was not convenient most of the time. It seemed clear to Bill that the living room needed to be adapted so that it could be a safe play area for Daryl, with the other areas of the house off-limits. He suggested that doors be put in the doorways, with a hook on the front door, and that age-appropriate toys and household objects be made available to Daryl in the living room. He also suggested that Elmer and Virginia spend some time with Daryl playing with toys appropriately and assisting in Daryl's learning how to play with toys, work simple puzzles, look at books, and so forth. Many of these ideas were the result of the assessment and intervention planning day that had occurred at the program office. The Ervins thought most of these ideas made sense, and they provided a variety of materials and moved fragile objects out of the way. However, they did not like the idea of doors or a latch on the front door. This created a dilemma for Bill because at each visit Elmer and Virginia would express their frustration and concern about Daryl's behaviors but would consistently object to the environmental changes that Bill suggested. This became such a pattern that Bill and the Ervins discussed it explicitly and "agreed to disagree" on this issue. Bill stressed that his role was to provide ideas for the family to consider and that he respected their decision on this point and supported their right to make this decision. They then focused on areas that did not involve doors or latches and on using Bill's time in ways that they all felt were productive.

The Sister One of these areas of focus involved Bill spending time with Katrina at each visit, which he did regularly throughout his involvement with the Ervins. They played board games, took walks, worked on prereading workbooks that Virginia had purchased, and played together with Daryl. The Ervins had noticed that Katrina could get Daryl to do things that no one else could, especially when physical guidance was necessary. Bill helped Katrina teach Daryl how to put shapes into a shape ball and make marks on a paper with a crayon. However, Bill also encouraged Katrina to pursue her own interests and have times every day when she played with friends and was not "responsible" for Daryl.

Respite Care Bill also helped the Ervins obtain respite care for Daryl, beginning with an hour at a time in the home and eventually allowing the Ervins to take a long weekend together, without the children. Much of Bill's role involved allowing the Ervins time during home visits to express their feelings about leaving the children with someone else and assuring them that this was all right.

Other Resources In addition to the home visits provided by Bill and others, the Ervins used resources in several other settings. For example, they participated in a monthly support group meeting for family members of children with disabilities. This included a covered dish meal with the children followed by a breakout time where the adults talked or listened to a speaker while the children participated in play activities in another room. These monthly outings were some of the initial opportunities that Katrina had to get out of the house, meet other children, and learn that many children have brothers and sisters with disabilities.

When Katrina began kindergarten, the Ervins enrolled Daryl in a child care program, where he was included with the other children. Elmer, Virginia, and Bill all spent time at the child care center during the first weeks of Daryl's enrollment, and Bill continued to make home visits during this time. Because Daryl still struggled with changes in his routine, meeting new people, and changes in meals, this was a very challenging time for everyone. Meals were especially difficult, as Daryl would scream and fall on the floor, sometimes staying agitated for 30 minutes or more. Eventually, Virginia began sending food from home so that the food would be familiar to Daryl, and Bill went to the child care center during lunch time on several occasions to show the staff the techniques that were used in the home to encourage Daryl to eat. This strategy was successful and Daryl eventually learned to eat with the other children and to eat the food provided by the child care program.

Daryl gradually made substantial increases in his social cooperation and began to use a few words and signs functionally. He also increased affectionate behavior and seemed to adjust more quickly to changes in his routines, although this was still challenging for him. Shortly after adjusting to his child care environment, he became more daring in his explorations, both at child care and at home. Once, at home, he got out the front door and was found playing in the street a few minutes later, and on one or two occasions he succeeded in sneaking through the gate at the child care center. One day shortly after this, when Bill arrived for a home visit, he found that the Ervins had put a hook on their front door and had arranged to have their yard fenced in. A few months later they rearranged their bedroom areas so that Daryl and Katrina could have a room of their own. With input from Bill, they also began to focus more on teaching Daryl to stay within boundaries, in the home as well as outdoors.

Transition   About 6–9 months before Daryl became eligible for public school services, Bill began discussing the available options with the Ervins. Although he continued to make regular home visits, the Ervins felt that visits were only needed about twice per month; however, they continued participation in the support group. Elmer, Virginia, and Bill all visited the public school and met with Daryl's prospective teacher on several occasions before Daryl's first day of school. Bill also made several follow-up visits to consult with the teacher and her staff regarding Daryl's developmental and social-emotional development and to suggest specific strategies to use in the classroom.

Case Discussion   The Ervins's case illustrates many of the issues presented throughout this chapter. The home itself was a focus of many of the intervention efforts. Although a standardized assessment of the home did not occur, observation and discussion of the home environment were integral to the early intervention focus, and changes to the home environment were crucial to the outcomes attained. These changes occurred only when the family was ready to make them and then only in a manner consistent with their values. For example, the fence was installed only when the family felt that this would help meet their goals for Daryl's safety. Similarly, sleeping arrangements were changed only when the family decided that this would suit their lifestyle and when they felt they had the energy to make the change.

Bill's role was not limited to providing resources within the home but included involvement in multiple settings, including child care, public school, and the agency's office. He also played a major role in mobilizing many of the other resources used by the family. A proactive, strengths-based approach was used, which identified family members' existing strengths and promoted development of additional strengths. Bill used a flexible and responsive style to visit when convenient for the family, which allowed interventions to occur in a functional way, and both primary caregivers were included in the process. Bill was always respectful of the family's values and priorities, even when there were differences of opinion between him and the Ervins. Nevertheless, the relationship was a partnership, in which all the Ervins and Bill played key roles. The roles each played changed during individual home visits, and across time, and were explicitly discussed and agreed upon during the relationship.

The initial home visit was made by two staff members, ensuring that ample attention could be paid to the family and also ensuring staff safety. Transition planning began 9 months before Daryl's actual transition to public school, and then several resources were used on a follow-up basis. Although Bill had a very positive relationship with the Ervins, it was clear all along that there would be an "end" to the relationship, and when home-based resources were no longer needed, a smooth transition occurred.

A variety of resources were used to meet the family's needs. These included informal and formal resources and all of the different resources that were described in Figure 1. Initially, most of these resources centered around the family home and included the family's own resources, as well as instrumental assistance, emotional support, and information provided by Bill in the home itself. Although most of these efforts focused on Daryl, time and energy were also spent addressing the needs of the other family members. Eventually resources from the community were used to supplement the resources being provided in the home, and gradually these community-based resources eliminated the need for home visits.

SUMMARY

This chapter focused on the home as a context for early intervention. Major research findings indicate that these services generally result in positive outcomes, often for families as well as children. Findings also suggest that home-based resources are often most effective when provided in combination with other resources.

Key physical, social, and emotional characteristics of each home environment must be identified in order to provide the best service possible. Interpersonal aspects and logistical aspects must also be considered. Interpersonal aspects include establishing partnerships with families, focusing on families' needs and strengths, and identifying and mobilizing multiple resources to assist families in meeting needs. Logistical aspects include scheduling visits at times convenient to families, involving all primary caregivers, including fathers, and addressing policy issues such as paperwork and safety.

A variety of strategies must be used while providing early intervention in the home. These include addressing issues of cultural diversity, using effective communication techniques, actually focusing on the home as a target of intervention, and many others. Only by selecting among various techniques based on the individual characteristics of each family can the best results be obtained for both child and family.

REFERENCES

Administration on Developmental Disabilities. (1990). *Educating policymakers: A nine state perspective*. Washington, DC: Mayatech.

Bagnato, S.J., & Neisworth, J.T. (1991). *Assessment for early intervention: Best practices for professionals*. New York: Guilford Press.

Bailey, D.B., & Simeonsson, R.J. (1988). Home-based early intervention. In S.L. Odom & M.B. Karnes (Eds.), *Early intervention for infants and children with handicaps: An empirical base* (pp. 199–215). Baltimore: Paul H. Brookes Publishing Co.

Barrera, M.E., Kitching, K.J., Cunningham, C.C., Doucet, D., & Rosenbaum, P.L. (1990). A 3-year early home intervention follow-up study with low birthweight infants and their parents. *Topics in Early Childhood Special Education, 10*(4), 14–28.

Bowman, T.W. (1983). Promoting family wellness: Implications and issues. In D. Mace (Ed.), *Prevention in family services: Approaches to family wellness* (pp. 39–48). Beverly Hills: Sage Publications.

Bradley, V.J., Knoll, J., & Agosta, J.M. (Eds.). (1992). *Emerging issues in family support*. Washington, DC: American Association on Mental Retardation.

Bronfenbrenner, U. (1979). *The ecology of human development: Experiments by nature and design*. Cambridge, MA: Harvard University Press.

Bryant, D., Lyons, C., & Wasik, B.H. (1990). Ethical issues involved in home visiting. *Topics in Early Childhood Special Education, 10*(4), 92–107.

Caldwell, B.M. (1978). *Preschool Home Observation for Measurement of the Environment Inventory*. Little Rock: University of Arkansas.

Curran, D. (1983). *Traits of a healthy family*. Minneapolis, MN: Winston Press.

Davis, H., & Rushton, R. (1991). Counseling and supporting parents of children with developmental delay: A research evaluation. *Journal of Mental Deficiency Research, 35*(pt 2), 89–112.

Dawson, P.M., Robinson, J.L., Butterfield, P.M., van Doorninck, W.J., Gaensbauer, T.J., & Harmon, R.J. (1990). Supporting new parents through home visits: Effects on mother–infant interaction. *Topics in Early Childhood Special Education, 10*(4), 29–44.

Dore, M.M., Wilkinson, A.N., & Sonis, W.A. (1992). Exploring the relationship between a continuum of care and intrusiveness of children's mental health services. *Hospital & Community Psychiatry, 43*(1), 44–48.

Dunst, C.J. (1985). Rethinking early intervention. *Analysis and Intervention in Developmental Disabilities, 5*, 165–201.

Dunst, C.J., Trivette, C.M., & Deal, A.G. (1988). *Enabling and empowering families: Principles and guidelines for practice*. Cambridge, MA: Brookline Books.

Dunst, C.J., Trivette, C.M., & Deal, A.G. (Eds.). (1994). *Supporting and strengthening families: Vol. 1. Methods, strategies and practices*. Cambridge, MA: Brookline Books.

Dunst, C.J., Trivette, C.M., & Mott, D.W. (1994). Strengths based family-centered intervention practices. In C.J. Dunst, C.M. Trivette, & A.G. Deal (Eds.), *Supporting and strengthening families: Vol. 1. Methods, strategies and practices* (pp. 115–131). Cambridge, MA: Brookline Books.

Education for All Handicapped Children Act of 1975, PL 94-142, 20 U.S.C. §1400 *et seq*.

Feldman, M.A., Sparks, B., & Case, L. (1993). Effectiveness of home-based early intervention on the language development of children of mothers with mental retardation. *Research in Developmental Disabilities, 14*(5), 387–408.

Fewell, R.R., Meyer, D.J., & Schell, G. (1981). *Parent Needs Inventory*. Unpublished scale, University of Washington, Seattle.

Fewell, R.R., & Neisworth, J.T. (Eds.). (1991). Foreword. *Topics in Early Childhood Special Education, 10*(4), x–xii.

Goldfarb, L.A., Brotherson, M.J., Summers, J.A., & Turnbull, A.P. (1986). Family Needs Survey. In L.A. Goldfarb, M.J. Brotherson, J.A. Summers, & A.P. Turnbull (Eds.), *Meeting the challenge of disability or chronic illness: A family guide* (pp. 77–78). Baltimore: Paul H. Brookes Publishing Co.

Grant, R. (1990). The special needs of homeless children: Early intervention at a welfare hotel. *Topics in Early Childhood Special Education, 10*(4), 76–91.

Griffiths, R. (1979). *The abilities of young children*. London: Child Development Research Center.

Hanson, M.J., & Lynch, E.W. (1989). *Early intervention: Implementing child and family services for infants and toddlers who are at-risk or disabled*. Austin, TX: PRO-ED.

Individuals with Disabilities Education Act (IDEA) of 1990, PL 101-476, 20 U.S.C. §1400 *et seq*.

Karnes, M.B. (1977). Exemplary early education programs for handicapped children: Characteristics in common. *Educational Horizons, 56*(1), 47–54.

Krantz, P.J., MacDuff, M.T., & McClannahan, L.E. (1993). Programming participation in family activities for children with autism: Parents' use of photographic activity schedules. *Journal of Applied Behavior Analysis, 25*(1), 137–138.

Little, B.R. (1983). Personal projects: A rationale and method for investigation. *Environment and Behavior, 19*, 273–309.

May, J. (1991, Spring). What about fathers? *Family Support Bulletin*, p. 19. Washington, DC: United Cerebral Palsy Associations.

McConachie, H.R. (1991a). Home-based teaching: What are we asking of parents? *Child: Care, Health & Development, 17*(2), 123–136.

McConachie, H.R. (1991b). What parents think about parenting and teaching. *Journal of Mental Deficiency Research, 35*(pt 1), 58–65.

McKillip, P. (1987). *Need analysis: Tools for the human services and education*. Beverly Hills: Sage Publications.

Newborg, J., Stock, J.R., Wnek, L., Guidubaldi, J., & Svinicki, J. (1984). *The Battelle Developmental Inventory.* Allen, TX: DLM/Teaching Resources.

Parry, T.S. (1992). The effectiveness of early intervention: A critical review. *Journal of Pediatrics & Child Health, 28*(5), 343–346.

Reamer, F.G. (1990). *Ethical dilemmas in social service.* New York: Columbia University Press.

Sandall, S.R. (1990). Developmental interventions for biologically at-risk infants at home. *Topics in Early Childhood Special Education, 10*(4), 1–13.

Scheerenberger, R.C. (1983). *A history of mental retardation.* Baltimore: Paul H. Brookes Publishing Co.

Shearer, M., & Shearer, D. (1972). The Portage Project: A model for early childhood education. *Exceptional Children, 39*, 210–217.

Stinnett, N., & DeFrain, J. (Eds.). (1985). *Secrets of strong families.* New York: Berkley Books.

Turnbull, A.P., Summers, J.A., & Brotherson, M.J. (1986). Family life cycle: Theoretical and empirical implications and future directions for families with mentally retarded members. In J.J. Gallagher & P.M. Vietze (Eds.), *Families of handicapped persons: Research, programs, and policy issues* (pp. 45–66). Baltimore: Paul H. Brookes Publishing Co.

Vitulano, L.A., Nagler, S., Adnopoz, J., & Grigsby, R.K. (1990). Preventing out-of-home placement for high-risk children. *Yale Journal of Biology & Medicine, 63*(4), 285–291.

Wayman, K.I., Lynch, E.W., & Hanson, M.J. (1991). Home-based early childhood services: Cultural sensitivity in a family systems approach. *Topics in Early Childhood Special Education, 10*(4), 56–75.

... 9
.
:
.

Family Child Care

Susan L. Golbeck and Susan Harlan

There is growing public appreciation of the importance of early intervention for children with special needs. At the same time, the need for quality child care is urgently felt by families as increasing numbers of mothers with small children work outside the home. This chapter focuses on family child care as a setting for early intervention with children who have special needs. It begins with an overview of family child care as a context for young children's development, referred to as the ecology of family child care. Subsequently, the chapter discusses the unique concerns that emerge when children with special needs are cared for in family child care and elaborates on the ways early intervention and family child care intersect. Obstacles to optimal service delivery are also discussed, and recommendations are given for overcoming them. The chapter concludes with a case study of one child with special needs in a family child care home.

WHAT IS FAMILY CHILD CARE?

Family child care is a child care arrangement in which up to six children are cared for in the home of a nonrelative (Kontos, 1992). Family child care stands in contrast to center-based care, which serves larger numbers of children in a child care center. Within the family child care setting, the caregiver's own preschool children are counted as part of the group of six or fewer children, although state guidelines actually vary in the group size permitted. In some states, the maximum allowable group size is contingent on the ages of the children. In 12 states, the maximum number of children allowed for one caregiver is greater than 6 (7–12); in 36 states, homes with more than 6 children are required to have a second adult present and are called group homes or large family child care homes (Kontos, 1992).

Family child care has been the most frequently used form of out-of-home child care in the United States (see Hofferth & Phillips, 1987, 1991; Kahn & Kammerman, 1987). Despite its popularity, family child care has received less attention from researchers than center-based care. Furthermore, the studies that have been conducted on family child care are less likely to be disseminated in scholarly journals. As a result, the professional community and the general public know less about family child care than center-based child care.

Why Choose Family Child Care?

As previously noted, family child care is the most frequently used form of out-of-home child care. Why do families choose this kind of care for their young children? The home setting, the more flexible hours, affordability, and the convenience of neighborhood location are frequently cited (Hofferth & Phillips, 1991; Kahn & Kammerman, 1987; Kontos, 1992). Although these factors may explain the popularity of family child care, the empirical evidence supporting these assumptions is scarce (Kontos, 1992).

Research does suggest that parents with children under age 3 and those in need of part-time care are more likely to choose family child care (see Kontos, 1992, for discussion). The increased usage of family child care by these groups may reflect parental preferences or simple availability. Perhaps parents of infants and toddlers feel more comfortable leaving their children in a home setting than in a more school-like child care center.

Parents seeking part-time care, or evening care, typically have a difficult time finding it in a child care center. In most communities, it is very difficult to locate part-time care within a child care center without paying full-time tuition. These parents must rely on family child care because there are no alternatives.

Who Are Family Child Care Providers?

Family child care providers may form the largest single group of home-based workers in our economy (Nelson, 1990). Child care, as a profession, is dominated by women. Caring for other people's children at home transforms a woman's traditional caregiving role into self-employment. Who chooses this work and why?

The National Day Care Home Study (NDCHS) provides some answers to these questions. The typical family child care provider is in her mid-30s to mid-40s and has children of her own (Fosberg, 1981). Kontos (1992) characterized the typical family child care provider in this way:

> [She] earns $10,000 or less, contributing one-fourth to one-third of her family's total income. She became a family day care provider because she likes to work with children, wanted to be home with her own children, and/or needed the money. She likes her work and is committed to staying in family day care although perhaps not permanently. What she likes best about her work is her interactions with children; she least likes her interactions with parents. She does not feel isolated as a family day care provider and perceives herself as having an ample social support network. She is not formally trained but has some informal training experiences, primarily workshops and conferences. Her motivation for training is low since her work is perceived as an extension of mothering. (p. 58)

Although the typical family child care provider may report that she is committed to continuing her work in child care, the rate of turnover in family child care is extremely high, almost 50% a year (National Association for the Education of Young Children [NAEYC], 1985). This instability of the work force undermines the quality of the caregiving environment. When a staff member leaves, or a family child care provider discontinues her work, the relationships she has established with the children in her care are lost, and the continuity of caregiving is disrupted for each child and his or her family. Such continuity in relationships is essential for healthy emotional and intellectual development in the child.

How Is Family Child Care Regulated?

Regulation of child care refers to licensing, registration, and compliance with various zoning, local fire, and sanitation codes and business permits (Save the Children, n.d.). All states require child care centers to meet licensing standards. However, regulation of family child care homes varies considerably across locales (Phillips, Lande, & Goldberg, 1990). Thirty-nine states, the District of Columbia, and the military mandate regulation. Six states regulate only subsidized family child care, three states encourage voluntary registration of family child care homes, and two states do not regulate family child care at all.

However, a large number of family child care providers fail to abide by regulatory guidelines. Estimates of unlicensed or unregistered providers are difficult to establish, but a 1991 study reported that only 10%–18% of family child care homes were licensed or registered (Willer et al., 1991). A number of explanations have been offered for this low level of compliance. Parents and caregivers vary in their knowledge of regulations and in their attitudes toward governmental regulation. Caregivers with small group sizes may view themselves as exempt from regulation. Zoning regulations can prohibit and discourage small businesses such as family child care. Finally, the nature of the regulations themselves and the overall regulatory climate may discourage compliance (Kontos, 1992).

Whatever the reasons, regulatory systems in family child care are not working as well as they might to protect young children from harmful care (Kontos, 1992). Given the overall low level of compliance, simply because a provider is unlicensed or unregistered does not necessarily mean she is providing poor care. (For an in-depth discussion of this issue, see Nelson, 1990.)

Supervision of providers is not an aspect of regulation (Belsky, Steinberg, & Walker, 1982). Licensing standards generally focus on group composition (i.e., staff–child ratio) and basic health and safety measures. Licensed homes are visited by local officials who review the health and safety of the environment. In contrast, providers in sponsored or supervised homes belong to networks or organizations of child care providers. These groups of licensed or registered caregivers are organized to receive referrals and training and other support materials. Support may include individualized consultation and supervision. Research suggests that providers who participate in support networks and receive individual supervision provide higher quality care (Rosenthal, 1990).

FAMILY CHILD CARE AND CHILDREN WITH SPECIAL NEEDS

Parents of children with special needs have at least as great a need for child care as parents of children without disabilities. For example, in a statewide survey of parents of children with special needs conducted in New Mexico, 40% of the parents surveyed used some form of child care in addition to the early intervention services their children received from the state. Children spent an average of 26 hours per week in a variety of settings for supplemental care. An important factor in choice of services was the number of hours per day and days per week the settings were open (Klein & Sheehan, 1987). Elsewhere, Fewell (1986) noted that family child care is the most widely used form of child care by families with children with special needs.

Arranging child care can be a challenge for any parent. However, parents of children with special needs encounter unique problems. Child care providers often lack confidence in their ability to care for children with special needs, they worry about effects on their own family and the other children in their care, and they are concerned about insurance (Deiner, 1992).

Yet family child care providers usually expect to work with children of varying developmental levels, and this type of care can be flexible and individualized. Such a context can be optimal for accommodating the child with exceptional needs. Unfortunately, there are relatively few data on family child care providers who care for children with special needs. In an effort to understand who takes on this care and why, the authors of this chapter interviewed family child care providers in New Jersey and Pennsylvania serving children with special needs. Providers were located through resource and referral agencies and a newsletter for family child care providers. These providers, who had all cared for at least one child with special needs for more than 1 year, were highly motivated and committed to their work. They took pride in their ability to care for their children with special needs and were eager to talk about their experiences (Golbeck & Harlan, 1994). Throughout this chapter reference is made to these providers and what was learned from them.

ECOLOGY OF FAMILY CHILD CARE

Family child care is a unique setting for caring for children. It is home based and the number of children in the group is small. Children are typically of mixed ages, like a family. In some ways this setting resembles a home setting. However, the number of children in regulated family child care homes is larger than the typical American family, and the age mix in family child care homes is not characteristic of typical families. Family child care shares features with home care and center care, but is different from both (Goelman, 1986; Kontos, 1992). This section discusses the defining features of the family child care setting and provides an overview of the processes characterizing this unique child care environment.

Quality in the Family Child Care Setting

Defining quality in child care is not an easy task. Experts agree that quality is multi-dimensional and incorporates aspects of both the social and the physical setting. Furthermore, the family child care home is a system that includes the provider, the families she serves, and the provider's own family. To function effectively, components of the system must work together (Kontos, 1994). The family child care provider engages in a difficult balancing act, meeting the needs of her own family as well as those of the children for whom she is paid to provide care.

Conceptions of quality in child care have changed since the beginning of the century. In the 1950s, high-quality care was defined in terms closely resembling the warm, nurturing care parents provide to their own children. In the 1960s and 1970s, quality care was redefined in terms of factors leading to cognitive gains for children. In the 1980s, this conception broadened. In the 1990s, quality is based on factors believed to be related to developmental outcomes in children. The changing definitions of quality reflect the values of society at large and, more specifically, the interpretation of those values by professionals (Clifford, Harms, Pepper, & Stuart, 1992).

Several tools for measuring quality in family child care have been developed. The most widely used is the Family Day Care Rating Scale devised by Harms and Clifford (1989), which provides a global assessment of the family child care environment and includes six subscales evaluating each of the following: space and furnishings for care and learning, basic care, language and reasoning, learning activities, social development, and adult needs. Different criteria are specified for infants/toddlers and children older than 2 years of age. Supplementary items for use in homes with a child with special needs are also included (see Clifford et al., 1992, for discussion of other instruments designed to measure quality). Other tools useful for assessing quality have been developed in conjunction with the Child Development Associate (CDA) credential and the National Associate for Family Day Care Credential. (For a comparison and discussion of these and other assessment tools in family child care, see Modigliani, 1994.)

What Happens within the Setting?

A typical day in a family child care home can take many forms. Ideally, the daily routine incorporates a variety of activities that are developmentally appropriate for the child. There is a balance of experiences enhancing cognitive, linguistic, social, emotional, and physical development (Bredekamp, 1985; Deiner, 1992). The routine is predictable but flexible and responsive to children's needs. There is adequate time for sensitive and responsive adult–child interaction as well as opportunities for peer interaction and play. The routine includes some contact with the community beyond the family child care provider's home through walks to the playground, trips to the library, or visits from special guests.

These ideals can be expressed in different ways. Some caregivers function with daily routines similar to typical family life. According to Wandersman, "Caregivers of fewer and younger children seem to view their role as 'mother' and report the emotional drain and role strain that comes of caring for a large family of young preschoolers" (1981, p. 98). The daily routine is likely to include cleaning and housekeeping as well as child-oriented activities. In contrast, caregivers with larger numbers of older children tend to model their daily routine after a child care center. They view their role as director of a small, personal child care center and structure more of the children's activities and environment on a center model. These caregivers are more likely to have a separate playroom for the children and devote their attention primarily to child care, supervision, and teaching.

These two approaches are illustrated by the providers we have interviewed. When asked what a typical day is like, some caregivers sounded like mothers with large families. Jennie said:

> Oh, about quarter after seven I get up. The first kid comes at 7:30 . . . [the kids] watch "Barney" and "Sesame Street." Most of the time they want to play and watch cartoons. Sometimes they watch the older kids play . . . Today, since you were coming it was a little different. I straightened up and they clean up when I'm doing that and then they go outside and then we draw and color. We play squirt with the hose, they like that. We watch tapes—they're learning tapes. And then, they follow through with whatever the tape did. I ask them questions. (Golbeck & Harlan, 1994)

Others used the language and terminology of teachers. For example, Debbie said that her routine is centered around weekly themes and includes field trips and guest visitors (Golbeck & Harlan, 1994).

Physical Setting

A family child care home must meet minimum safety standards. Stairways must be protected, outlets must be covered, and so forth. However, concern for the physical setting should extend beyond safety. For young children, opportunities to actively explore and manipulate the environment are essential (Greenman, 1988; Weinstein, 1987). Within family child care, the presence of a well-organized play space that includes appropriate toys has been related to children's cognitive gains (Clarke-Stewart & Gruber, 1984). The availability of such a play space also has been related to more positive and less negative affect among caregivers. Caregivers working with less child-designed space were more restrictive (Howes, 1983). Howes (1983) also found children to be more positively engaged when the environment was child centered.

An ideal family child care home provides a play area with an appropriate number and range of toys for the children using the space. Materials are organized and appropriately accessible to children. Both outdoor and indoor play space is available. Play space is roomy, light, and aesthetically pleasing. There are soft and comfortable places, as well as places to be safely alone. Children have opportunities to engage in activities promoting language and reasoning, literacy, dramatic play, and creative expression. Infants and toddlers should have plenty of space to crawl and test newly developing motor skills (see Greenman, 1988; Prescott, 1981, 1987; Weinstein, 1987).

The home-based nature of family child care creates some unique demands on the physical environment. In family child care, the setting is also the provider's home. An absence of child-designed space may result from a provider's failure to resolve her conflicts about transforming her family's living space into children's play space. Resolving such dilemmas is essential to the creation of a high-quality environment for children (see Johnson & Dineen, 1981).

Social Setting

The social setting in family child care includes the children, the caregiver, the children's families, the caregiver's family, the community, the cultural backgrounds of all participants, and the sociopolitical climate. The social environment has a profound influence on children's development. Bronfenbrenner (1979) called for viewing the environment as nested systems of influence ranging from the most proximal (i.e., the family and the immediate child care setting) to the most distal (i.e., the cultural and political context in which the immediate setting is embedded). This section focuses on the immediate systems of influence within family child care, the children and the caregiver. Subsequent sections discuss relationships with the children's families and the early intervention community.

Are Parenting and Professional Caregiving Synonymous?   Child care providers perform many of the same functions as parents, yet it is probably inappropriate to assume that parenting is a model for professional caregiving. Continuities in home and family child care were explored in a literature review by Long, Peters, and Garduque (1985). Across home care, family child care, and center-based care, adult–child interactions differed on a number of dimensions. However, the relationships were often complex and counterintuitive. For example, family child care providers demonstrated less negative affect than parents. However, when family child care providers cared for their own children, they demonstrated more negative affect *and* more positive affect to their own children than to the other children in their home. This finding makes sense in light of the emotional attachment between child and caregivers. Parents have a stronger emotional investment in their own children and respond to them more intensely.

These findings suggest that it is inappropriate to expect family child care providers and parents to interact with children in the same way. Parents and professional caregivers have different kinds of relationships with children. Behaviors characterizing good parenting and good professional caregiving are overlapping; they are not identical (for further discussion of this issue, see Howes & Sakai, 1992).

What Factors Influence Interactions Between Children and Caregivers? Factors influencing caregivers' behavior with children are vitally important to assessing the quality of the child care environment. Research has shown that the size of the group and the age of the children are particularly important in eliciting optimal caregiving behavior. This section discusses the research evidence on these and other factors important to the child–caregiver interaction.

Group size refers to the number of children cared for by a single caregiver. The NDCHS showed that, as group size increases, the frequency of caregivers' interactions with individual children decreases (Divine-Hawkins, 1981). Howes (1983) also found that caregivers caring for more children talked less, expressed more negative affect, were more restrictive, were more likely to ignore a request, and were less likely to respond positively to a toddler's social bid. In another study (Howes & Stewart, 1987), it was shown that the greater the number of children, the fewer the positive caregiver behaviors (e.g., positive affect, contingent responses to stress). The research shows that caring for children in large groups with a single caregiver is likely to be detrimental to children's well-being.

Age of the children has also been related to caregiver behavior. Caregivers do less teaching, playing, and watching television with older children when infants are present. In homes with toddlers, caregivers are more directive and less likely to provide messy materials such as playdough or paint. When there are more preschool children, caregivers provide more language stimulation (Divine-Hawkins, 1981; Stallings, 1981). In another study, adults caring for more younger children reported more role strain and emotional drain from caregiving than caregivers with more older children (Wandersman, 1981).

In addition, contact hours per day, the presence of child-designed space, and intensity of supervision also seem to influence the quality of caregiving behavior in family child care. Howes (1983) found that more contact hours per day and more time spent engaged in housework were associated with ignoring toddlers' requests. Howes also found that adults who worked in a more child-designed space were more likely to express positive affect and less likely to express negative affect or to restrict toddler activity. Rosenthal (1990) found that caregivers receiving weekly supervision engaged in higher quality interaction.

In sum, group size, children's age, contact hours per day, intensity of caregiver supervision, and the presence of child-designed space are all related to the quality of caregiving behavior (see Kontos, 1992, for further discussion). Interestingly, family child care providers often refuse to consider caring for a child with special needs because they believe it will be too much work. Yet virtually nothing is known about how the presence of a child with special needs actually influences the ecology of the family child care environment.

What Factors Influence Interactions Between Children? Early childhood educators recognize that the social world of peers is one of the most important contexts for learning and development (Damon, 1977; DeVries & Kohlberg, 1987). The opportunity for peer interaction is one of the main reasons middle-class parents offer when asked why they enrolled their child in preschool (Hyson, 1991).

Quality of peer interaction in child care has often been studied through observations of children's play. Patterns in children's play normally change with development and as a function of the ages of other children in the group. It seems reasonable to think that children's play might also be influenced by adults. In a study of toddlers in family child care homes, Rothstein-Fisch and Howes (1988) found that caregiver activity (interacting with children or participating in child care-related tasks [e.g., housework, leisure, interviewing a new parent]) was related to complexity of peer play. However, toddlers actually engaged in more complex play when the caregiver was not interacting with them. Similar findings were reported by Dunn and Kontos (1989).

Although caregiver involvement in peer play does not seem to facilitate its complexity, high levels of involvement in other areas, such as language, may indirectly influence the quality of children's social interaction. Caregivers may also indirectly influence social interaction through the organization of the physical environment. Howes and Rubenstein (1981) found that toddlers in family child care had higher levels of interactive play when they were able to use features of the home environment, such as hallways, corners, and connecting rooms, in play and when they were allowed greater freedom of movement across such areas. Howes and Unger (1989) argue that objects and space shape complementary actions and prevent children from intruding on one another's play space.

Much less is known about the social environments of homes accommodating children with special needs. The social environment of the family child care home would seem to provide an excellent opportunity for a child with disabilities to interact with children without disabilities. Guralnick (1990) argued that most children with disabilities experience a peer interaction deficit. They have difficulties in child–child social interactions beyond what would be expected given their developmental level. Drawing on research conducted in preschool settings, Guralnick further noted that, when children with disabilities are placed in normalized, mainstreamed settings, they receive far more social stimulation and participate in more responsive interactions. More demands for appropriate social behaviors are placed on children and more advanced play is supported. The family child care home would seem like an excellent setting to enhance the social development of young children with special needs.

The Child, the Family, and Family Child Care

Family dynamics, parenting style, and family stress can have direct influences on children's development. However, families indirectly influence their children's development when they choose a child care setting or move to a new neighborhood. These indirect influences can have important consequences for children's development. Research shows that families under greater stress—specifically, those who are more socioeconomically disadvantaged—may indirectly influence their children's development by choosing lower quality child care arrangements. These families may not be able to afford higher quality programs, or those programs may not even exist in their communities. Such child care arrangements include both center-based and family child care settings (Howes & Hamilton, 1993).

Another example provided by research findings is the stability of child care arrangements. Although low rates of stability in care arrangements can result from child characteristics and high rates of turnover, they also result from particular family features. Children of divorced parents are more likely to experience multiple child care arrangements. Children with insecure maternal attachments are also more likely to experience unstable child care arrangements as infants (Howes & Hamilton, 1993).

That family and child care play complementary roles in child outcomes is consistent with the work of Bronfenbrenner (1979, 1989). Bronfenbrenner described the family child care home and the family as two separate microsystems within which the child functions. A microsystem is a "pattern of activities, roles, and interpersonal relations experienced by the developing person in a given setting with particular physical and material characteristics" (Bronfenbrenner, 1979, p. 22). Infants and toddlers in out-of-home care experience multiple microsystems very early in life. (For a detailed description of the microsystem, see Chapter 1 of this book.)

Throughout development, individual functioning is enhanced when there is overlap between microsystems (Bronfenbrenner, 1979). Overlap occurs when participants from one microsystem share experiences with participants of a second system. For example, a parent–teacher conference brings together the microsystems of home and school, or a conversation between a parent and child care provider creates overlap between home and child care. Young children are dependent on others to create linkages in microsystems because they lack the representational and communication skills that older children and adults use to facilitate linkages autonomously.

Family child care has unique potential for mutuality between the microsystems of home and child care. Unlike typical interactions between parents and teachers in child care centers, those between parent and family child care provider are more personal. The parent is in the caregiver's home daily, meets her family, and perhaps chats in the living room or kitchen at the end of the day. Typically, there is a relaxed, neighborly relationship supporting an easy exchange of information and ideas (see Golbeck, 1992, for further discussion).

This relationship between the caregiver and the parent can serve the parent's emotional needs as well the child's. In a study of caregivers in Vermont, Nelson (1990) described caregivers who acted as supports to parents. These providers offered advice about child care and served in a motherly role to the mothers of the children they cared for. Here the provider is acting as part of a social support network to the parent. In other contexts, such direct support of the mother has been shown to positively influence the child (Crockenberg, 1981; Garbarino & Sherman, 1980).

The role of the family child care provider as parental support may be especially salient for providers of children with special needs. Some of these families may be in a state of crisis. Interviews with providers of children with special needs support this concept (Golbeck & Harlan, 1994). This is also illustrated by the case study presented at the end of this chapter.

Connections with the Community

Family child care providers run small businesses within their homes. Often they have a strong network of personal supports within the community. However, providers vary tremendously in terms of their linkages with other child care professionals. Providers who are licensed or registered have one level of contact with the larger child care community. They are informed of state regulations and are likely to receive information about informal and formal training in their communities. Providers who work with a resource and referral network within their community are also likely to have access to information about training. Local and state family child care associations also provide support and information to providers. Some states provide financial reimbursement for training. Unlicensed or unregistered providers may be less knowledgeable about these resources and lack access to information about them.

A higher level of support for family child care providers can be provided through a network of "supervised" homes (Belsky et al., 1982). In such a network, a supervisor visits the family child care home and offers support and supervision to the provider.

Access to a toy library and professional training can also be incorporated into this arrangement. In some locales such supervised networks are run by private corporations, usually providing care at a higher cost than do nonparticipating providers.

Bronfenbrenner (1979) refers to forces influencing the child, but not directly experienced by the child, as the mesosystem. (For a detailed description of the mesosystem, see Chapter 1 of this book.) The regulatory climate of the state and the availability of professional support are both features of the mesosystem of family child care. For a child with special needs, the mesosystem becomes considerably more complex. The provider's access to information relevant to the child's special needs is critical. The climate of the early intervention service delivery system will influence the provider's ability to create an optimal environment for the child.

IMPLICATIONS FOR PROVIDING EARLY INTERVENTION SERVICES

The Education of the Handicapped Act Amendments of 1986 (PL 99-457) and its reauthorization mandate services to children with special needs and their families, the provision of choices, and support to families (Bryant & Graham, 1993; McCollum & Maude, 1993). The child care needs of families with children with disabilities are not specified in the legislation. As noted previously in this chapter, almost 50% of the children being served in specialized early intervention programs are also being cared for in child care settings (Klein & Sheehan, 1987). Unfortunately, mechanisms for supporting child care providers in homes as well as in centers are often poorly delineated.

Children with special needs have been cared for in family child care for many years, and it is reasonable to assume that this practice will continue. This section explores the linkages between child care services and early intervention. Undergirding this discussion are three assumptions: 1) it is in the child's best interests to create overlap among the various microsystems within which the child functions (home, child care, and the early intervention center); 2) child care is an important support to family functioning; and 3) the family child care provider is a child care professional who plays an important role in optimizing the development of the child.

The Child with Special Needs in Family Child Care: Some Examples

A family child care setting can be an ideal child care arrangement for a child with special needs. Furthermore, a parent's ability to return to work can be an important step in securing the family economically and emotionally. But what happens when a parent of a child with special needs begins to look for child care?

As stated previously, many family child care providers are hesitant to care for a child with a disability. Providers are afraid they lack the requisite skills, and they worry about effects on other children, time, and insurance. Given the background of the typical family child care provider, these concerns are not surprising. Most providers lack formal training for their work and they use their own mothering experience as the knowledge base for their job. In light of these factors, Golbeck and Harlan (1994) were particularly impressed by the providers interviewed who were caring for children with special needs. They approached their work with enthusiasm and self-confidence. The authors asked them about their work and the resources they relied on to help care for their children with special needs.

Robyn cares for a child with a hearing impairment. She reported that she took sign language classes, received copies of the individualized education program (IEP), and talked to the parents. Debbie cares for a child with mild developmental delay.

She described an impressive search for services and supportive cooperative relationships with the intervention team:

> I sought help from everywhere . . . eventually, he began having a half-hour session with an itinerant teacher in my home once weekly. This was not started until May and ended in June when the school year was over. He then went to the 5 day A.M. preschool. In September he will attend kindergarten. . . . The local intervention team helped me tremendously, especially his itinerant teacher. I was able to call her with any questions I had. She included me in the child's IEP team conference and has offered help from the rest of the team. (Golbeck & Harlan, 1994)

Jeannette cared for Abby, who has congenital abnormalities. Abby also attended a half-day early intervention program in the mornings. Abby stayed at Jeanette's 1½ hours in the morning before school and 5 hours after school. Although Abby's mother was very familiar with what is happening with Abby at the program, it was to Jeannette's home that both Abby's teacher and her sign language teachers come each week. Abby's teacher comes often because in Jeannette's home Abby is doing more and different things (e.g., talking, signing, playing with toys) than she was initially at the program. Since her teacher started visiting at Jeannette's home, Abby is more cooperative at school. The sign language teachers also saw Abby at school and came to Jeannette's so that everyone working with Abby would be able to communicate with her. Jeannette reported that the other children picked up the sign language quickly and use it with Abby. There was an attempt to include Jeannette in the IFSP meeting, which even included an offer to hold the meeting at Jeannette's house, but this has not yet been accomplished.

Several points are worth noting about these providers. First, they are resourceful and committed providers. All seemed strongly invested in "their" children and worked hard to optimize the care the children in their charge received. Whether these providers are typical of those caring for children with special needs is unknown, but all appeared to enjoy contact with professionals in the child care and special education community. This is consistent with findings from a study in Montana showing that family child care providers taking children with disabilities were more likely to have had professional training in the field. Massey (1992) reported that family child care providers with training in special education and related fields were more likely to accept children with disabilities. Massey also noted that providers with workshop experience in special education and child development were more likely to care for children with special needs.

Second, all providers relied on parents as a source of information and as a support. Parental input was critical for these providers to learn how to care for their children. However, this does not mean that interactions with parents were always smooth and easy.

Third, there was variation in the role the family child care provider played in early intervention and the level of suppport she received from the early intervention team. This is supported by available research (Deiner, 1992) on training family child care providers. Approaches vary in the level of direct support to the provider and the degree to which she functions as an early interventionist.

Finally, social inclusion seemed to occur in all the settings identified. This is not surprising given that a family child care provider has no choice but to modify the environment and her routine to include the child with disabilities. Typically, family child care occurs in contexts with only one adult. Providers talked about how they had acquired the strategies they used to achieve integration. They talked about times when integration seemed difficult. For example, one provider described problems that occurred when a child with special needs arrived at her house at lunch time and required catheterization. At the time the child was dropped off, the other children in her care were eating lunch. However, this transition was resolved because it was in everyone's best interest (Golbeck & Harlan, 1994).

Three approaches can be taken to family child care as an early intervention setting. These approaches differ in the degree of coordination and integration among the parents, the family child care provider, and the early intervention team. These are not distinct conceptual orientations but categorizations of recommended practice as it is understood.

Providers and Parents Alone as Caregivers: Informal Early Intervention

In this form, family child care as an early intervention is very informal and unplanned. Early intervention occurs at the early intervention center or special needs preschool. The early intervention specialists have no involvement in child care. Golbeck and Harlan (1994) interviewed two providers who fit this category. These providers viewed themselves as responsible for caring for the children in their charge. Their goals focused on adapting the environment to allow the child with disabilities to participate in regular ongoing activity. They were not responsible for providing an educational program or linking their care with other interventions their children were receiving.

Providers and parents always rely on each other as mutual supports (Galinsky, 1988; Powell & Bollin, 1992). However, in the case of a child with special needs, the caregiver is more likely to need new and specialized information to manage child care. If no other professionals are involved, parents must assume the full responsibility of this task. Yet parents are likely to need extra support, reassurance, and assistance in child care. Once a caregiver has acquired the specialized skills needed to care for a child with disabilities, parents may ask her to care for the child on weekends or "off hours" as relatively few adults possess this specialized knowledge.

In light of the legislative mandates, it may seem surprising that parents and caregivers are left to manage child care alone. Yet the support the providers received from the early intervention community or other specialists varied considerably (Golbeck & Harlan, 1994), and legislation is not clear on support for child care (Rose & Smith, 1994). Family child care providers often work alone and have minimal contact with the early intervention specialists.

Child Caregiver as Early Interventionist

A very different child care situation is illustrated by the child caregiver as early interventionist. In the most extreme form, the provider has the primary responsibility for implementing the educational component of the early intervention program. She does this with the support of an individual consultant, individualized supervision, and workshops targeted to specific skills important in working with children with special needs and their families. This approach is especially appropriate in rural areas where it is not feasible for a family to travel long distances to reach an early intervention center. Similarly, in such areas it also may not be feasible for a child to travel long distances to attend a part-time preschool program.

The best examples of this approach to early intervention are provided by several federally funded projects designed to train family child care providers as early interventionists (e.g., Jones & Meisels, 1987; Kontos, 1988; see also Bryant & Graham, 1993). These projects have generally made use of a consultation model for training and program delivery. Caregivers volunteered to participate in these projects, and training included both workshops and individual consultation and supervision. Consultation provided the opportunity to individualize instruction to meet the specific needs of the child, the family, and the caregiver.

Project Neighborcare   Project Neighborcare, developed by Susan Kontos (1987, 1988), is an example of a program designed to train family child care providers as early interventionists. Project Neighborcare was based on an ecological framework and a consultative approach, and it was conducted in a primarily rural area. The goals of training focused on 1) enhancing child care providers' knowledge and skills and 2) maintaining the advantages of the family child care home environment that have been documented in the research (e.g., flexible scheduling, individual attention) while increasing the rigor of programming standards to ensure credibility as an early intervention setting.

Participants in Project Neighborcare were assessed for initial skills in early intervention and for the quality of their family child care home. Workshops were designed to increase caregivers' knowledge and awareness of special needs, quality child care, program planning and tracking progress, teaching strategies, behavior management, and working with parents. Consultation and supervision included weekly visits to family child care providers' homes, during which time information, support, and technical assistance were provided. At the outset of the consultation, the consultant and the provider developed a list of training objectives based on the initial skills assessment. This plan helped consultants individualize training and recognize and reward behavior change when it occurred.

Following 10 months of training, Kontos (1988) reported that providers showed meaningful improvement in both the quality of the child care environments and in their early intervention skills. Providers unanimously agreed that the workshops, weekly visits, and toy-lending library had helped prepare them for providing early intervention services. They felt confident in their ability to work with children with special needs, with two reservations: 1) They believed they needed the continual support and assistance provided by their consultant, and 2) they were unsure of their ability to work with children with severe disabilities. Kontos (1988) noted that several children with severe disabilities had been successfully placed in the program and suggested that "severe" must mean more severe than what they had experienced. The providers saw the program for children as beneficial to all, not just to the child with the disabilities. They also saw improvements in the quality of the care they were providing and elevations in their own self-esteem as a result of their success and the support of the consultants.

Family Child Care Provider as Partner in Early Intervention

A third approach to family child care as a setting for early intervention focuses on the family child care provider as a true member of the early intervention team. The child care provider is one of several professionals working together to support children and families. The total early intervention program incorporates a combination of services, including participation at an early intervention center or preschool program and family child care. The family child care provider is supported by specialists on the early intervention team; such support might also include home visits. Because parents and providers often need similar information about the child, home visits might be designed to include the parent as well as the provider.

Debbie and Jeannette, described previously, provided child care under this approach. As Jeannette noted, visits from the specialists also engaged other children in the family child care home. This facilitated social interaction as well as the particular language, motor, and cognitive skills the teacher and therapist were directly addressing. The home visits from the preschool teacher also enabled the teacher to observe the child with special needs, Abby, in a context other than school (Golbeck & Harlan, 1994).

Interaction Between the Family Child Care Provider and Early Intervention Specialists

The third approach to family child care with the provider as partner implies a high level of interaction among family, child care providers, and early intervention professionals. Regardless of the situation, there will be a high level of interaction between parents and providers. It benefits everyone if there is interaction between the early intervention team and the family child care provider. Such interaction occurs when the child care provider talks with members of the early intervention team, visits therapy sessions, and is included in the development of the individualized family service plan (IFSP). For a variety of reasons, coordinating this relationship can be complicated.

Many factors can block productive relationships between early intervention personnel and family child care providers. The political climate, philosophical orientations, level of professional education, and differences in working conditions can make interactions a challenge. This section discusses some of these factors.

Confusions About Child Care as a Service to Families One problem concerns the status of child care as a service to families. Child care services have, at best, an ambiguous status under the Education of the Handicapped Act Amendments of 1986 (Bryant & Graham, 1993; McCollum & Maude, 1993). Although an array of services to children and families are required under Part H, developmental child care is considered optional. Educational programming for preschool children is specified by law, but typically this occurs through local education agencies or the public schools. Early intervention professionals are committed to working with families directly. However, supporting families indirectly by supporting child care providers in general community programs and family child care homes is yet to be well accepted. The importance of respite care for families of children with disabilities is recognized, although it too is an optional service.

Preschool versus Child Care A second problem is the ambiguous status of community-based child care as an option for families of children with special needs (see Rose & Smith, 1994). Increasingly, programs for 3- to 5-year-old children with disabilities have been criticized for creating artificial environments of exclusively or predominantly children with special needs (Guralnick, 1990). One solution to this problem is inclusion in community-based nursery school and child care programs as well as family child care programs. Yet special educators bemoan the low quality of services available in the community.

The majority of preschool programs serving children without disabilities are not publicly funded. Teachers are paid less, work longer hours, and have fewer benefits than teachers working for public schools. Because community-based programs are mostly financed by parents, not taxpayers, physical facilities are less elaborate, and materials and supplies are purchased more frugally. Bryant and Graham (1993) noted that the major barrier to expansion of inclusion in community settings is the lack of quality programs in the community. Certainly, these factors make some components of some community settings lower in quality. However, early childhood special educators need to become more sensitive to the strengths of good teachers in community-based settings.

Family child care offers the opportunity for a group experience in a normalized setting. This opportunity has gone largely unrecognized. Guralnick (1990) noted that research strongly suggests that substantial benefits in peer-related social competence of children with disabilities can occur in those programs consisting primarily of children without disabilities, that is, fully inclusive programs. This resource in family child care settings needs to be used.

Locales maintaining early intervention centers and publicly funded preschool special education programs will still have many families requiring additional care for their children. Most of these early intervention and preschool programs are half-day or 1-day-a-week programs. Parents need additional wraparound care while they work. Whether this care occurs in homes or centers, caregivers and parents will need information and support from early intervention specialists to optimize children's development.

Skepticism About Child Care Providers   A third area of concern is the skepticism expressed by early intervention professionals about the quality of care provided by child care providers in the community. Special educators often express reservations about the ability of family child care providers to understand what children with special needs require and how to reach the goals set for them. Kontos (1988) documented this in her evaluation of Project Neighborcare: "One person encapsulated this thinking by asking how family day care providers could be trained to do in six workshops what she had obtained a college degree to do" (p. 10). Kontos also noted that the perception that training was limited to workshops without consultation and supervision was common. Furthermore, when professionals spoke favorably about the program, they perceived the consultants, rather than the providers, as the key to the program's success.

Logistical Problems   A fourth factor concerns simple logistical problems in coordinating meetings between the family child care provider and other members of the early intervention team. Even when a positive climate exists between the provider and the early intervention team, arranging meetings can be a struggle, as there is a limited amount of time available. Meetings must be scheduled during children's nap time, or coverage for the other children in the family child care home must be arranged.

Unrealistic Expectations   A fifth problem can be unrealistic expectations by all parties involved. Some additional insights into relationships between child care providers and early intervention specialists are provided by a report from the PACT Day Care Project in Maryland (Maryland Committee for Children, Inc., n.d.). This project was designed to facilitate the inclusion of children with special needs in child care settings through the provision of consultation and support services. Although the majority of child care settings were in centers, a few children were placed in family child care; however, results are not broken down by type of setting. In cases where children's disabilities were overtly physical, child care staff seemed to be more receptive and willing to carry out targeted interventions. Difficulties were encountered with children whose problems were in the social and emotional areas. Unrealistic expectations that consultant-trainers would "fix" the child and make him or her less difficult to manage were described. Golbeck and Harlan (1994) did not see evidence of this, but providers unable to manage a child's behavior problems may have been unwilling to participate in the interviews.

Fostering Cooperation

Despite these obstacles, early intervention professionals must take the lead in devising strategies for working with family child care providers. Parents and providers share many of the same concerns. Both need similar types of information, training, and support (Klein & Sheehan, 1987). Also, both parents and child care providers offer valuable information about children's development. This information is likely to be useful to other early intervention professionals working with the child and the family.

Because the child spends so much time in family child care, the early intervention team should be in contact with the provider on a regular basis. The provider should be informed of the services the family and child are receiving and included in the development of the IEP or IFSP. Although the family child care provider may have less formal education than other professionals involved in the delivery of early intervention services, she spends more time with the child and the family than any other member of the early intervention team. This experience should be effectively used. The child benefits from the increased skill and knowledge the provider acquires from the early intervention professionals.

The Provider as Support to a Family in Crisis

Families with children with disabilities are more at risk for experiencing crisis. The mutually dependent relationship between parents and caregivers was emphasized previously in this chapter (Galinsky, 1988). However, the significance of child care as a stabilizing force for families cannot be overstated. A child care arrangement with which the parent feels confident and comfortable can enable the parent to function optimally at work. A positive experience in the workplace can influence parental functioning at home.

Support networks have been shown to be important to family functioning. For example, families in similar economic situations have been shown to differ markedly in the incidence of child abuse as a function of their informal supports networks in the community (Garbarino & Sherman, 1980). The family child care provider functions much like friends or family as a support. Although parents pay for her services, her schedule is flexible, she is available at unusual hours, and a friendly, if not close, personal relationship exists. Caregivers working in centers are unlikely to serve as a support in this manner.

The Family Child Care Provider Who Identifies a Problem

Few family child care providers are trained in screening children for developmental disabilities. Yet providers can be the first to recognize a problem. As experienced caregivers of young children, they are often knowledgeable about normative behavior in infants and children. As secondary caregivers (as opposed to parents), they are emotionally more detached and better able to accept the possibility of a developmental problem. Golbeck and Harlan (1994) interviewed several providers serving children with special needs who expressed concerns about children to parents and encouraged the parents to discuss the child's behaviors with the pediatrician. The children were later identified as in need of special services.

Many providers may feel uncomfortable sharing their concerns about a child with a parent. However, all family child care providers should have access to information about Child-Find programs and professional assistance for handling such concerns.

OPTIMIZING FAMILY CHILD CARE
AS A SETTING FOR EARLY INTERVENTION

The need for coordination and interaction between the child care provider and the early intervention team has been emphasized in this chapter. This coordination can occur in many ways and should vary depending on the needs of the child, the family, and the services available in the community. However, several obstacles block the optimization of family child care as an early intervention setting. This section identifies these obstacles and provides some recommendations for change.

Failure to Recognize Importance of Child Care

Young children spend a great deal of time in child care. For young children with special needs, child care provides an important opportunity for them to participate in a normalized, inclusive environment. Child care is not only an opportunity to enhance children's development; it is a vital support to families. Parents *need* child care arrangements to supplement early intervention services. This is not a frill; it is an economic necessity. Parents need good child care arrangements to be able to work, to maintain their own sense of competence, and to provide for their children.

To overcome this obstacle, the early intervention community needs to be educated about the significance of child care and the potential for family child care. The significance of the family for meeting the needs of young children with disabilities has been recognized by the professional community and implemented into social policy through the Education of the Handicapped Act Amendments of 1986 and IDEA. Now it is time to recognize the importance of child care in the lives of young children and their families as well.

Access to Family Child Care

Helping families locate appropriate child care arrangements is an important support to children and to parents. As previously noted, many child care providers, both family and center based, are unwilling to accept children with disabilities. Deiner (1992) reported that a child care database in Maryland found only 673 family child care providers in the state who were willing to accept children with disabilities. Deiner also noted that there were wide differences in the children they were willing to accept. Half of the family child care providers were willing to accept children with delayed development, hearing loss, learning disability, speech and language delay, or vision loss, but less than 5% were willing to accept children with AIDS or respiratory problems (Salkever & Connolly, as cited in Deiner, 1992).

Two actions are needed to change this situation: Early intervention professionals must 1) identify more family child care providers interested in working with families and children with special needs and 2) work with early intervention centers to link providers with families in need of care. Concerted efforts must be made to recruit providers. Providers attending supplemental training workshops, those seeking credentials not mandated by law (e.g., the CDA), and those with exceptional backgrounds, such as experience in education or social services, could be good candidates for recruitment. An approach that emphasizes the significance of child care to families with special needs and the rewards inherent in the work would be important because these providers might feel they lack needed skills to be successful.

This effort should be coordinated through local child care resource and information agencies (e.g., National Association of Child Care Resource and Referral Agencies), which typically ask providers if they are willing to accept a child with special needs (e.g., through use of *Childfinder*, a software program developed by Work/Family Directions, 1984/1990). This could be a good opportunity to identify caregivers seeking the additional challenge and gratification associated with this work.

Providers who have been successful in caring for children with special needs can be especially good advocates. When Golbeck and Harlan (1994) asked one of the providers they interviewed (Debbie) how the experience had changed her views about child care and children in general, she answered, "It has taught me the value of individuality and different approaches to child care. Diversity is now very much a part of my approach to child care. . . . I guess I have found that I really do make a difference."

Access to Support Services for Providers

Regardless of the climate created by the early intervention community and the willingness of family child care providers to care for children with special needs, a system for supporting family child care providers needs to be created. Caregivers need specific skills in caring for children with disabilities, for working with parents, and for managing the impact of this work on other children in their care.

There are two solutions to address this lack of support. First, local support systems for family child care providers serving children with special needs should be created. Second, these providers should have increased opportunities to receive training.

Partnerships among families, child care providers, and early intervention specialists are needed. Support systems must be designed to achieve this goal. Systems will vary depending on the particular needs of the community. These systems must be flexible and provide specialized training in skills needed to successfully work with children with disabilities. Furthermore, such systems must integrate child care and early intervention. In this model, family child care providers would have ready access to early intervention personnel and would be involved in the development of the IFSP or IEP. Early intervention personnel would work with family child care providers to optimize children's experiences in the child care setting. A model of child care including visits by a consultant or supervisor is also an ideal arrangement. As providers gain experience working with a child with special needs, they will be more likely to continue caring for children with special needs.

Several experimental programs yielded similar findings regarding the most effective types of support and training for family child care providers. Three of these programs are Project Neighborcare (Kontos, 1988), the Michigan Project (Jones & Meisels, 1987), and Delaware FIRST (Deiner, Whitehead, & Peters, 1989). Training targeted toward specific skills, such as basic listening and peer counseling, is especially important for providers caring for infants and toddlers with disabilities. Training needs to be practical and useful. Deiner (1992) claimed that providers need guidance in matching activities to the developmental levels of children as well as general information about child development. Consultants or supervisors and additional resource support (e.g., toy-lending library) can help achieve this goal.

Klein and Sheehan (1987) described a community-based training model for child care providers in Cleveland. This program employs a special education/early childhood consultation arrangement for enhancing the professional development of child care providers. In this grass roots approach, an early childhood/special education program is identified as responsible for planning, implementing, and evaluating staff development for child care providers. Assessment of the needs of individual centers and family child care providers is the first step in the training process. The content, methods of training, and follow-up training were developed by the early childhood special education program. The training procedures include on-site consultation, demonstrations, and discussion of individual children. This approach could be used to support caregivers of children with special needs and to prepare providers planning to enroll a child with special needs.

Lack of Awareness of Social Environment in Family Child Care

Participation in inclusive settings is important for the development of skills needed for peer relationships. Productive relationships with peers constitute an essential task of childhood and have important benefits for language and communicative development, the development of prosocial behaviors, social-cognitive development, and the socialization of aggressive tendencies (Guralnick, 1990). As discussed earlier in this chapter, the family child care home provides a unique setting for fostering such social skills.

Early intervention personnel and family child care providers need to be educated about the significance of the social environment in family child care. Guidelines for optimizing the social experience also should be clarified to facilitate awareness of the social environment.

Promoting social competence in young children with special needs is an area particularly appropriate for the family child care provider. Child care providers are likely to be very invested in helping children master these skills, although they may need support in implementing specific strategies. One way to educate family child care providers about strategies for enhancing children's social development is to include social skills in the IEP or IFSP and to involve the provider in the development of the IEP. This involvement would underscore the importance of family child care as a context for social development, help family child care providers optimize children's development in this domain, and create a collaborative relationship between the family child care provider and the early intervention team.

Deiner (1992) believed that the provider should be involved in the development of the IFSP or IEP and not simply handed a list of tasks. Participation in the planning process helps to develop the provider's skills. Deiner also argued that if a family child care provider is responsible for carrying out aspects of the IFSP or IEP, she should have technical assistance, as many providers have limited access to toys, games, and learning materials.

Social skills relevant to successful functioning within the peer group could be identified in the IFSP or IEP. These would be consistent with goals of inclusion. Murphy and Vincent (1989) studied teachers' perceptions of social skills needed for success in child care. Items such as greeting familiar people, asking for help, taking turns, and cooperating are behaviors valued by teachers and no doubt by child care providers as well. Providers probably have an "implicit" set of social goals for children. Working with early intervention professionals to formalize some of these goals could benefit children, parents, and providers. Providers would need help with strategies for observing and recording as well as teaching such skills.

High Costs of Working with Children with Special Needs

Until financial support is offered to child care providers working with children with disabilities and their families, family child care cannot be fully used as an early intervention setting. Child care must be viewed as a support to families. It must be recognized that child care for families with children with special needs, as opposed to families with children without disabilities, is a more costly undertaking for all involved.

The solution is to create financial incentives to ensure support to family child care providers working with children with special needs. These incentives could be created in many ways. In North Carolina, family child care providers of children with special needs whose care is state and federally subsidized can receive up to 70% more than the typical fee. These funds should allow the provider to operate profitably with one fewer child, therefore creating a better adult–child ratio (Bryant & Graham, 1993). More programs such as this one are essential.

CASE STUDY

Shelly has been a family child care provider for 19 years. She presently operates a group child care home in the basement of her large home in a suburban neighborhood. She serves 12 children from 6 weeks to 5 years of age. Shelly has three part-time assistants in her home.

Shelly has a 4-year degree and had worked in a doctor's office. She began her work in child care so she could stay home with her four children. She has been working on an associate's degree in early childhood education at night for 5 years and needs only six more credits to complete it. As part of her coursework she has taken four credit-bearing and several noncredit courses in early childhood special education at the two area community colleges. Shelly's experience caring for children with special needs includes one child who was deaf. She began taking these classes because of this experience, her background in the medical field, and a general interest in children with special needs.

Shelly's Initial Concerns   Adam's mother was still pregnant with Adam when she approached Shelly about child care, and Shelly agreed to enroll the child in her home. Because of this, Adam's "problems" were not a factor she considered in agreeing to care for him. Shelly stated that there was never a time during the 5 years she cared for him that she felt she could no longer continue to do so.

Adam came to Shelly's home when he was 6 weeks old. Shelly saw a difference in Adam immediately because he did not have the muscle tone she knew a child his age should have. She did a lot of reading, took notes on his development, and talked to several doctors before talking to Adam's parents. She was advised to wait until he was 6 months old to approach the parents. At 6 months she shared her concerns with the parents. They got very angry and did not return the next day.

Eventually, however, they did return and took Shelly's concerns and her notes to their pediatrician. He agreed that Adam should be tested and referred him to a developmental pediatrician for blood tests and magnetic resonance imaging. Nothing was found. The parents told Shelly that the doctors indicated that he would outgrow his problems by the time he was 3 years old. (Shelly reflected that she went through 3 years of "he'll be fine when he's 3" with the parents.)

However, Adam was eventually diagnosed as developmentally delayed. During his time in her care, he also attended numerous therapy sessions and a preschool early intervention program. He is presently in a special class with two other children in the public schools. He is now diagnosed as emotionally disturbed. Shelly believes he has autism.

Learning to Help Adam   Shelly continued to seek help for Adam. From one of her courses she learned to adapt a car seat so he could sit and so she could put him in a wagon. She also adapted a wheeled toy so that he could get around using his arms instead of walking. She spoke to a speech therapist who was a guest lecturer in one of her classes about Adam's eating problems. (He stuffed food into his mouth and did not chew it.) The therapist gave her suggestions that worked very well.

At age 1, Adam went to a rehabilitation hospital for physical therapy. His mother decided to go once a week even though Shelly recommended every day. Later, Adam's mother went to visit one of the early intervention programs at the hospital. When she came back to Shelly she said, "Have you ever walked in a room where there are all children with special needs? Can you imagine having to put your child there?" She decided not to enroll him in the program because she wanted him with typical children as much as possible.

Shelly visited Adam's therapy sessions to see how the physical therapist was helping Adam to sit up and later to walk. Adam's parents have always given her permission to go to therapy sessions and to talk with the doctors or therapists. They have also told the doctors and therapists to contact Shelly as well.

Adam learned to walk when he was 2. Although Adam seemed to be overcoming some of his physical delays, Shelly remained concerned about his language and social development. She came to believe that Adam had autism based on her reading and observation.

Adam as a Preschooler   At age 4, Adam went 5 half days a week to the early intervention program to receive physical, occupational, and speech therapy. Shelly wanted to know what the specialists were doing to help Adam talk. The parents visited the program and wanted her to go, so she did. Shelly was very impressed with the early intervention specialists. She said they were very accepting of her. She noted that teachers and therapists had to do things one-to-one with Adam. It made her feel better to know that they also had no magic answer but experienced the same problems interacting with Adam that she did. Shelly would call the therapists and teachers whenever she had a concern or a question about Adam or his program. She also called them if he had not progressed for a while to see if others were seeing progress.

When Adam left Shelly's child care at age 6, he was not toilet trained. He was not able to hold a conversation, his language was mostly imitative, he did not interact with the other children, and he could not sit at circle time. He roamed the room instead. Adam liked to engage in repetitive behaviors, such as running around the room, talking to himself in the mirror (in "another language"), putting lids on and off, turning door knobs, opening and shutting doors, and pounding on the piano. Even though he was wandering the room during circle time and did not participate in songs and fingerplays with the group, Shelly would later observe him repeating them into the mirror.

Adam could not sit very long at meals and took things from other children's lunches. Shelly preferred to keep him in a high chair, but the parents objected so she put him in a regular seat and had to work hard on keeping him there. Shelly believes that because she served a mixed-age group there was greater flexibility and it was easier to accommodate Adam's "toddlerlike behavior."

Supporting Adam's Family   Despite the special therapies and classes, Shelly feels that to this day the parents deny there are problems and speak of Adam as if he were a typical child and as if he was going to be all right. However, Shelly reported that the mother often cried at her home, knowing that there was something wrong with her baby but not really having a clear diagnosis.

Most of the other parents did not acknowledge Adam when they came into Shelly's home. Shelly said she thought they were afraid of him and did not know what to say to him. One father, who had some professional training in counseling, did make a fuss over him, and Adam would run to him each day when he came. Shelly also noticed that it was hard for Adam's mother to interact with the other parents. Shelly arranged a meeting with those parents. She told them that they should speak to Adam's mother. She also encouraged them to talk to Adam, even though he would not answer.

Shelly felt that the other children accepted Adam and were very nice to him. They might tell the adults some of the things he was doing, such as banging the door repeatedly. She said that, although they seemed to accept him, they didn't ask questions about him. However, at times they ignored him, and there was very little interaction between the other children and Adam.

Shelly noted the difference between what the early intervention teachers were saying about what Adam was doing and what he was really able to do without assistance. Adam's mother thought at first that he was really doing much more at the program than at Shelly's. This turned out not to be true when the teachers admitted that everything was done with a great deal of assistance.

Shelly reported that she constantly worried about Adam. Adam's mother said to her, "It would be the worst day of my life if you couldn't care for him anymore." The parents seemed to be very socially isolated and never left Adam with babysitters in the evening. When Shelly was sick or on vacation, she arranged for another family child care provider to take Adam.

Shelly and her husband once had Adam sleep overnight at their home so his parents could go out for their anniversary. Adam's grandparents live far away. One grandmother, however, made books of pictures of Adam's favorite things, such as vacuum cleaners and washing machines.

Adam's parents came to view Shelly as one of the family. They still keep in touch by telephone. The parents asked Shelly if they could have other people in Adam's life call her as a reference. Shelly felt very honored because they originally had questioned her right to make statements about their son's development and seemed to think she was trying to hurt them. Through the years she cared for him, Shelly feels that the parents continued to resist her concerns. However, they did read the book on autism that she gave them. They attended a seminar and as a result Adam's father has adapted several computer programs for Adam and spends more time with him. They invited Shelly to their home to see Adam and Dad working on the computer.

Shelly's Recommendations   Shelly stressed the need for family child care providers to continue their education, especially if they are caring for children with disabilities. The courses she took in special eduction increased her "comfort level" in dealing with Adam and with the early intervention specialists.

Comments   This case illustrates how family child care can serve as a setting for early intervention. Shelly played a critical supporting role to Adam and his family. She recognized Adam's atypical behavior and development and encouraged the family to seek help. She worked with the early intervention team and the various professionals involved in Adam's care. She integrated Adam's experiences in therapy and early intervention with the care he was receiving at her home. While in her home, he was in a normalized setting with other children and their parents. Shelly made every effort to include Adam and his family fully in the ongoing activities within her home.

Shelly was also an unusual family child care provider. She had professional training in special education and some previous medical training. This background may have helped her feel more confident about seeking the help she needed or in coping with some of the very difficult problems presented by Adam and his family.

SUMMARY

This chapter provided an overview of family child care for infants and young children with disabilities and an introduction to family child care as a setting for infants and young children, emphasizing the unique role family child care providers can play in the lives of families. Family child care can be an especially good setting for young children with special needs because programs are usually small, can be individualized, and can enhance children's social development, and the relationship between caregiver and parent can be close and supportive. However, many family child care providers need additional guidance and training. Better mechanisms must be articulated for helping parents of children with disabilities meet their child care needs and for helping family child care providers optimize their caregiving practices.

REFERENCES

Belsky, J., Steinberg, L., & Walker, A. (1982). The ecology of day care. In M.E. Lamb (Ed.), *Nontraditional families: Parenting and child development* (pp. 71–116). Hillsdale, NJ: Lawrence Erlbaum Associates.

Bowlby, J. (1969). *Attachment and loss: Vol. 1. Attachment.* New York: Basic Books.

Bredekamp, S. (Ed.). (1985). *Developmentally appropriate practice in early childhood programs serving children from birth through age 8.* Washington, DC: National Association for the Education of Young Children.

Bronfenbrenner, U. (1979). *The ecology of human development.* Cambridge, MA: Harvard University Press.

Bronfenbrenner, U. (1989). Ecological systems theory. In R. Vasta (Ed.), *Annals of child development* (Vol. 6, pp. 187–251). Greenwich, CT: JAI Press.

Bryant, D., & Graham, M. (1993). Models of service delivery. In D. Bryant & M. Graham (Eds.), *Implementing early intervention: From research to effective practice* (pp. 183–215). New York: Guilford Press.

Clarke-Stewart, K.A., & Gruber, C.P. (1984). Day care forms and features. In R.C. Ainslie (Ed.), *The child and the day care setting: Qualitative variations and development* (pp. 35–62). New York: Praeger.

Clifford, R., Harms, T., Pepper, S., & Stuart, B. (1992). Assessing quality in family day care. In D.L. Peters & A.R. Pence (Eds.), *Family day care for informed public policy* (pp. 243–265). New York: Teachers College Press.

Crockenberg, S. (1981). Infant irritability, mother responsiveness, and social support influences on the security of mother-infant attachment. *Child Development, 52,* 857–865.

Damon, W. (1977). *The social world of the child.* San Francisco: Jossey-Bass.

Deiner, P. (1992). Family day care and children with disabilities. In D.L. Peters & A.R. Pence (Eds.), *Family day care for informed public policy* (pp. 129–145). New York: Teachers College Press.

Deiner, P., Whitehead, L., & Peters, D. (1989). *Delaware FIRST: Family/Infant Resources, Supplemental Training: Final report to the Handicapped Children's Early Education Program* (Project No. 024MH70006, Grant No. GOO8630267). Washington, DC: U.S. Department of Education.

DeVries, R., & Kohlberg, L. (1987). *Constructivist early education: Overview and comparision with other programs.* Washington, DC: National Association for the Education of Young Children.

Divine-Hawkins, P. (1981). *Family day care in the United States: Executive summary* (Final report of the National Day Care Home Study) (Report No. DHHS-OHDS-80-30287). Washington, DC: Administration of Children, Youth & Families. (ERIC Document Reproduction Service No. ED 211 224)

Dunn, L., & Kontos, S. (1989, April). *Influence of family day care quality and childrearing attitudes on children's play in family day care.* Paper presented at the biennial meeting of the Society for Research in Child Development, Kansas City, MO.

Education of the Handicapped Act Amendments of 1986, PL 99-457, 20 U.S.C. § 1400 *et seq.*

Fewell, R. (1986). Child care and the handicapped child. In N. Gunzenhauser & B. Caldwell (Eds.), *Group care for young children* (pp. 35–47). Skillman, NJ: Johnson & Johnson Baby Products Co.

Fosberg, S. (1981). *Family day care in the United States: Summary findings and final report of the National Day Care Home Study* (Vol. 1). DHHS Pub. No. 80-30282. (ERIC Document No. ED 211 218)

Galinsky, E. (1988). Parents and teacher-caregivers: Sources of tension, sources of support. *Young Children, 43,* 4–12.

Garbarino, J., & Sherman, D. (1980). High-risk neighborhoods and high-risk families: The human ecology of child maltreatment. *Child Development, 51,* 188–198.

Goelman, H. (1986). The language environments of family day care. In S. Kilmer (Ed.), *Advances in early education and day care* (Vol. 4, pp. 153–179). Greenwich, CT: JAI Press.

Golbeck, S. (1992). The physical setting: Ecological features of family day care and their impact on child development. In D.L. Peters & A.R. Pence (Eds.), *Family day care: Current research for informed public policy* (pp. 146–169). New York: Teachers College Press.

Golbeck, S., & Harlan, S. (1994). *Caring for children with special needs in family child care: Perspectives from providers.* Manuscript in preparation. New Brunswick, NJ: Rutgers University, Graduate School of Education.

Greenman, J. (1988). *Caring spaces, learning places.* Redmond, WA: Exchange Press.

Guralnick, M. (1990). Major accomplishments and future directions in early childhood mainstreaming. *Topics in Early Childhood Special Education, 10*(2), 1–17.

Harms, T., & Clifford, R. (1989). *Family day care rating scale.* New York: Teachers College Press.

Hofferth, S., & Phillips, D.A. (1987). Child care in the United States, 1970 to 1995. *Journal of Marriage and the Family, 49,* 559–571.

Hofferth, S., & Phillips, D.A. (1991). Child care policy research. *Journal of Social Issues, 47,* 1–13.

Howes, C. (1983). Caregiver behavior in center and family day care. *Journal of Applied Developmental Psychology, 4*(1), 99–107.

Howes, C., & Hamilton, C. (1993). Child care for young children. In B. Spodek (Ed.), *Handbook of research on the education of young children* (pp. 322–336). New York: Macmillan.

Howes, C., & Rubenstein, J. (1981). Toddler peer behavior in two types of day care. *Infant Behavior and Development, 4,* 387–393.

Howes, C., & Sakai, L. (1992). Family day care for infants and toddlers. In D.L. Peters & A.R. Pence (Eds.), *Family day care: Current research for informed public policy* (pp. 115–128). New York: Teachers College Press.

Howes, C., & Stewart, P. (1987). Child's play with adults, toys and peers: An examination of family and child care influences. *Developmental Psychology, 23*(3), 423-430.

Howes C., & Unger, O. (1989). Play with peers in child care settings. In M.N. Bloch & A.D. Pellegrini (Eds.), *The ecological context of children's play* (pp. 104–119). Norwood, NJ: Ablex.

Hyson, M. (1991). Building the hothouse: How mothers construct academic environments. In L. Rescorla, M. Hyson, & K. Hirsch-Pasek (Eds.), *Academic instruction in early childhood: Challenge or pressure?* (pp. 31–37). San Francisco: Jossey-Bass.

Johnson, L., & Dineen, J. (1981). *The kin trade.* New York: McGraw-Hill.

Jones, S.N., & Meisels, S.J. (1987). Training family day care providers to work with special needs children. *Topics in Early Childhood Special Education, 7*(1), 1–12.

Kahn, M., & Kammerman, S. (1987). *Child care: Facing the hard choices.* Dover, MA: Auburn House.

Klein, N., & Sheehan, R. (1987). Staff development: A key issue in meeting the needs of young handicapped children in day care settings. *Topics in Early Childhood Special Education, 7*(1), 13–27.

Kontos, S. (1987). *Training manual for family day care.* Lafayette, IN: Purdue University, Department of Child and Family Studies.

Kontos, S. (1988). Family day care as an integrated early intervention setting. *Topics in Early Childhood Special Education, 8*(2), 1–14.

Kontos, S. (1992). *Family day care: Out of the shadows and into the limelight.* Washington, DC: National Association for the Education of Young Children.

Kontos, S. (1994). The ecology of family day care. *Early Childhood Research Quarterly, 9,* 87–110.

Long, F., Peters, D.L., & Garduque, L. (1985). Continuity between home and day care: A model for defining relevant dimensions of child care. In I. Sigel (Ed.), *Annual advances in applied developmental psychology* (Vol. 1, pp. 131–170). Norwood, NJ: Ablex.

Maryland Committee for Children, Inc. (n.d.). *The PACT Day Care Project: Mainstreaming disabled children into child care programs.* Baltimore: Author.

Massey, L. (1992). *Willingness of day care providers to accept handicapped children.* Unpublished doctoral dissertation, Montana State University.

McCollum, J., & Maude, S. (1993). Portrait of a changing field: Policy and practice in early childhood special education. In B. Spodek (Ed.), *Handbook of research on the education of young children* (pp. 353–371). New York: Macmillan.

Modigliani, K. (1994). *Assessing the quality of family child care: A comparison of five instruments.* New York: Bank Street College of Education.

Murphy, M., & Vincent, L. (1989). Identification of critical skills for success in day care. *Journal of Early Intervention, 13*(3), 221–229.

National Association for the Education of Young Children (NAEYC). (1985). *In whose hands? A demographic fact sheet on child care providers.* Washington, DC: Author.

Nelson, M. (1990). *Negotitated care.* Philadelphia: Temple University Press.

Phillips, D., Lande, J., & Goldberg, M. (1990). The state of child care regulation: A comparative analysis. *Early Childhood Research Quarterly, 5,* 151–179.

Powell, D., & Bollin, G. (1992). Dimensions of parent-provider relationships in family day care. In D.L. Peters & A.R. Pence (Eds.), *Family day care: Current research for informed public policy* (pp. 170–187). New York: Teachers College Press.

Prescott, E. (1981). Relationship between physical setting and adult/child behavior in day care. In S. Kilmer (Ed.), *Advances in early education and day care* (Vol. III, pp. 129–158). Greenwich, CT: JAI Press.

Prescott, E. (1987). The environment as organizer of intent in child care settings. In C.S. Weinstein & T. David (Eds.), *Spaces for children: The built environment and child development* (pp. 73–88). New York: Plenum.

Rose, D., & Smith, B.J. (1994). Providing public education services to preschoolers with disabilities in community based programs: Who's responsible for what? *Young Children, 49*(6), 64–68.

Rosenthal, M.K. (1990). Social policy and its effects on the daily experiences of infants and toddlers in family day care in Israel. *Journal of Applied Developmental Psychology, 11,* 85–104.

Rothstein-Fisch, C., & Howes, C. (1988). Toddler-peer interaction in mixed age groups. *Journal of Applied Developmental Psychology, 9,* 211–218.

Save the Children. (n.d.). *A history of family day care.* Atlanta: Save the Children, Child Care Support Center.

Stallings, J.A. (1981). *A description of caregivers and children in family day care homes.* Paper presented at the biennial meeting of the Society for Research in Child Development, Boston.

Wandersman, L. (1981). Ecological relationships in family day care. *Child Care Quarterly, 10*(2), 89–102.

Weinstein, C.S. (1987). Designing preschool classrooms to support development: Research and reflection. In C.S. Weinstein & T. David (Eds.), *Spaces for children: The built environment and child development* (pp. 159–186). New York: Plenum.

Willer, B., Hofferth, S., Kisker, E., Divine-Hawkins, P., Farquhar, E., & Glantz, F. (1991). *The demand and supply of child care in 1990.* Washington, DC: National Association for the Education of Young Children.

Work-Family Directions. (1984/1990). *Childfinder* [computer software for child care referral programs]. Boston: Author.

... 10

Child Care Centers

Susan E. Craig

The benefits of integrating preschool-age children with disabilities into programs with peers without disabilities, as well as strategies for implementing this type of model, are well documented in the early childhood special education literature (Brault, 1992; Guralnick, 1990; McLean & Hanline, 1990; Odom, 1989; Peck, Odom, & Bricker, 1993; Strain, 1990). Less attention has been given to integrated programs for infants and toddlers with disabilities. Until 1986, there were no federal funds available to states to develop early intervention programs for children ages birth to 2. However, with the passage of Part H of the Education of the Handicapped Act Amendments of 1986 (PL 99-457), states were encouraged to develop systems of integrated service delivery for these children.

The problem then became identifying settings where inclusion could occur because there are very few places, other than their homes, where children under age 3 are likely to spend large amounts of time. Public school programs and, until recently, Head Start programs were not options for this age group. As a result, early intervention programs looked to center-based child care programs as a resource in developing integrated programs for infants and toddlers (File & Kontos, 1992).

This chapter describes the center-based child care setting and how it can be used in cooperation with early intervention to meet the needs of infants and toddlers with disabilities and their families. Obstacles to service delivery in the child care setting also are discussed as well as recommendations for overcoming them.

THE CHILD CARE SETTING

The inclusion of infants and toddlers with disabilities into center-based child care programs is driven by a model that assumes the relational nature of child development

This chapter was prepared as part of a Handicapped Children's Early Education Program (now referred to as Early Education Program for Children with Disabilities) model demonstration project titled Successful Integration of Infants and Toddlers with Disabilities through Multidisciplinary Training, which was funded by the U.S. Department of Education, Office of Special Education Programs, Grant No. HO24B0097. The opinions expressed herein do not necessarily reflect the position or policy of the funding agency.

(Bronfenbrenner, 1979; Stryker, 1980). Connections between individuals and environments are transactional, each influencing the other in a dynamic, ongoing process. For children with disabilities, environmental factors affect the extent to which specific skill deficits have an impact on participation and success in natural settings. Similarly, participation by children with disabilities changes child care programs and the interactions that occur within them (Peck et al., 1993).

Understanding the child care environment can help early intervention staff use it effectively to care for young children with disabilities. Appreciating the expectations child care providers have about how inclusion may change the child care environment and their role in it can facilitate the development of meaningful cross-training and collaboration between child care providers and early intervention staff.

Bronfenbrenner's four systems of ecological analysis—macro, exo, meso, and micro—provide a framework for describing child care as a service delivery system. (For a more detailed explanation of these systems in general, see Chapter 1 of this book.) A description of the history of center-based child care and its relationship to young children, families, and other early childhood professions helps identify potential linkages between center-based programs and early intervention.

Macrosystem Characteristics

Macrosystem characteristics are the cultural beliefs and values that underlie the organizational structure of child care, professional expectations, and daily interactions with children and families. Center-based child care is committed to individualized care of children in safe, socially rich settings. It is organized around curriculum, patterns of social interaction, and a daily schedule of activities and routines that reflect the child's developmental age.

Historically, center-based care was developed in the 1940s in response to the needs of working mothers and widows. These day nurseries offered supervision, supplementary food, and health care to families with limited alternative resources (Scarr & Weinberg, 1986). During the 1980s, child care became more closely aligned as an educational early childhood model emphasizing its benefits to children's cognitive and social development (Bredekamp, 1987; Burton, Hains, Hanline, McLean, & McCormick, 1992). However, child care's roots in respite services for poor families, coupled with significant interstate variation in certification requirements, continue to plague its professional image and, to a large extent, its credibility as a viable setting for early intervention services (Green & Stoneman, 1989; Winton, 1993). This is especially true in terms of infant and toddler programs, whose benefits for even typical children have been debated (Belsky, 1988; Belsky & Steinberg, 1978; Clarke-Stewart, 1988).

As a result, the role of professional child care provider carries a set of mixed expectations. Within the child care community and its national organization, the National Association for the Education of Young Children (NAEYC), providers are expected to be knowledgeable child development practitioners. However, high rates of turnover, low pay, and minimal educational requirements in many states continue to evoke an image of child care providers as day care workers or babysitters who are only able to provide for children's custodial needs. In most cases, this image is incorrect.

Two national studies (Willer, 1992; Willer et al., 1991) of child care completed since 1990 indicated that roughly half of the teachers in center-based child care programs have at least a 4-year degree and an additional 13% have an associate's degree. Fewer than 8% of the child care workers surveyed reported having had no training specifically related to young children (Willer, 1992; Willer et al., 1991), although training specific to the needs of infants and toddlers with disabilities continues to be an issue (Bureau of National Affairs [BNA], 1991; Kontos & File, 1993).

In most states, training requirements are standardized. As of 1994, all but four states required the Child Development Associate (CDA) credential of all licensed child care providers. To qualify, staff must complete 150 hours of in-service training in specified components of child care, including 13 functional areas: safety, health, learning environment, physical, cognitive, communication, creative, self, social, guidance, families, program management, and professionalism. More than 50,000 child care providers have received the CDA credential since 1975.

Families with young children rely on center-based child care both for its ability to care for children in the parents' absence and to provide social and intellectual stimulation (Olmsted & Weikart, 1994). Center-based child care programs are important resources for respite care, information about child development, and networking with other families of young children. The dilemma for families with infants and toddlers with disabilities is that child care is not available for their children. Less than 10% of these families who desire child care have it, resulting in increased stress on the family and fewer opportunities for satisfactory participation in the workplace (Fewell, 1993).

Exosystem Characteristics

Exosystem characteristics are defined by Bronfenbrenner (1979) as "settings that do not involve the developing person as a participant, but in which events occur that affect, or are affected by, what happens in the setting containing the developing person" (p. 25). There are several exosystem characteristics of center-based child care that need to be addressed as infants and toddlers with disabilities are integrated into these programs.

Traditional early childhood service delivery models that separate children by category have conveyed the message to child care providers that children with disabilities are *qualitatively* different from other children and can benefit only from specialized care. As a result, providers feel unable to care for these children and therefore resist their integration into center-based programs (BNA, 1991). Policy initiatives to provide educational services and support to families of young children with disabilities have failed to involve the child care community. A 1992 survey of child care directors in Maryland, New Hampshire, Massachusetts, and the Department of the Army International Child Development System indicated that, although children with disabilities were enrolled in several programs, less than 10% of the directors knew what an individualized family service plan (IFSP) was, and none of them had participated in an IFSP meeting (Craig & Eshoo, 1992).

Center-based programs often have policies and procedures that inadvertently limit the enrollment of children with disabilities. For example, some programs prohibit food being brought from home. If a child can only eat certain kinds of food, this policy could keep him or her out of the program. If participation in the toddler program requires that a child be toilet trained or walking, children with developmental disabilities may never be allowed in because they may never be toilet trained or able to walk.

Mesosystem Characteristics

Mesosystems are the web of relationships that exist across interfacing social systems. In child care these have traditionally included relationships between the child care programs and families. Center-based child care fosters close communication between families and staff members. Drop-off and pickup times offer providers opportunities to answer questions parents have about their children, as well as to make suggestions about coping with them at home. Center-based child care encourages networking between families by offering parenting courses, support groups, and social programs, such as potluck suppers and fund-raising activities.

Microsystem Characteristics

Microsystems are "the patterns of activities, roles and interpersonal relations experienced by the developing person in a given setting with particular physical and material characteristics" (Bronfenbrenner, 1979, p. 22). In child care, microsystems consist of the physical and social environments that characterize the setting as well the curriculum and daily schedule of activities and routines.

Physical Environment   Child care classrooms are rich in stimulating materials with a variety of textures and levels. Rooms are set up in a homelike, comfortable fashion and frequently contain materials found in the child's home (e.g., pots and pans, rocking chairs, pillows). Infant rooms are divided into sections similar to those in a home: one for playing, one for eating, one for diapering. Quiet spaces that allow caregivers to spend time with a child who needs to be away from the day's activities are also available. The furniture and equipment in toddler rooms are arranged so that children can safely move around. Toddler rooms have several small, clearly defined interest areas where children can play. Multiples of popular toys and materials are available so that children do not need to wait too long for their favorites.

Child care centers are restricted in the number of children who can be cared for in one room or child care environment. States regulate the number of square feet that must be available per child. Similar regulations exist concerning the number of available bathrooms, the quality of cooking facilities, and the type of outdoor area available to the children. Each child care center must develop a plan that outlines the intended use of center space for child activities. Provisions for napping and toileting space must be included. If centers receive any type of surplus food from the Department of Agriculture, they must also have menus on file for all meals provided.

The intent of these regulations is to ensure the safety and physical comfort of all children. The regulations also foster the creation of classroom environments that are attractive to children and encourage their active exploration. For example, NAEYC recommends that infant room floors be covered with rugs or other soft materials so that children can crawl and sit comfortably without fear of injury.

Quality child care programs restrict the amount of time infants and toddlers can be left in high chairs or cribs and prohibit feeding children by propping bottles on a pillow. The intent is to foster ongoing interaction between children and providers. This interaction, as well as continual movement and exploration, is characteristic of all quality child care.

Social Environment   Building healthy relationships between children and providers and promoting positive social relationships with peers are important parts of the curriculum in center-based child care (Galinsky, 1990). In infant and toddler programs, services are provided in such a way that strong bonds can develop between the primary caregiver and the young child. Empathy is fostered among the children through modeling and acknowledgment of their feeling states and temperamental differences.

Ratios and group sizes are regulated by state standards. Although there is variation across states, a national study completed in 1990 (Whitebrook, Howes, & Phillips,

1990) indicated that the average child–staff ratio for infants (younger than 1 year) in center-based care is 4:1. For toddlers (1-year-olds only) the average ratio is 6:1. Average ratios for 2- and 3-year-olds are 7:1 and 9:1, respectively.

The average ratios for infants and 3-year-olds are at the upper end of the range recommended by NAEYC. The average group sizes and ratios for 1- and 2-year-olds exceed NAEYC recommendations (Willer, 1992). The higher-than-recommended child–staff ratios reflect increased demands for child care as well as the difficulty in retaining staff. In a profession where annual salaries average $11,500, an annual turnover rate of 25% is not surprising (Willer, 1992).

Curriculum   The program curriculum in a center-based program is play based and adapted to the characteristics and learning styles of the children being cared for (Bredekamp, 1987). Emphasis is placed on developing children's cognitive understanding of the world, as well as building their social skills through exploration of the environment and self-initiated discovery. Classrooms are typically organized around activities that involve gross and fine motor movement and the ability to explore and discover new experiences and relationships. Activities are concrete and relevant to the lives of the children who participate in the center's program.

Programs for infants and toddlers help children develop their sense of wonder and exploration in an environment that is both safe and challenging. Children develop a sense of safety and belonging and appropriate language and motor skills through interactions with caregivers and participation in routines. Children's play experiences are used to develop cognitive concepts such as object constancy and choice making.

Daily Schedule of Activities and Routines   Child care programs are busy places. The daily schedule offers children opportunities to creatively explore the world around them within the security of an established routine. Schedules are very flexible, so that providers can attend to the needs of each infant and toddler. Generally, they include arrival periods, meal and nap times, indoor and outdoor play times, activity periods (for toddlers), and departure periods. Routines such as diapering, washing, and feeding are used to build relationships and to promote development.

Activities in infant and toddler rooms vary with the age of the children. In general, however, they allow children to be active participants in routines and self-selected activities with a variety of safe toys and materials. Turn taking, choice making, and self-expression are important communication skills that are stressed during each activity. Physical comfort, safety, and a nurturing atmosphere help children acquire a sense of competence in managing the world around them.

RECOMMENDATIONS

Center-based child care settings have great potential for serving the early intervention needs of infants and toddlers with disabilities and their families. To do so successfully, programs must be collaborative, building on the strengths of both child care and early intervention. Neither service can supplant the other; rather, both need to work together to use their resources for agreed-upon priorities.

Child care administrators are in a good position to lead this cooperative effort. They can change policies that deny access to young children with disabilities. They can actively recruit infants and toddlers with disabilities and collaborate in their care. Collaboration with other professionals can result in better services for all children. However, to be successful, administrators must win the support of child care providers. Providers must understand their role in caring for young children with disabilities and their families. This is best accomplished through training that builds on skills they already possess, such as the ability to create safe, nurturing environments for all children (Craig, Eshoo, & Haggart, 1993).

Using center-based care to support early intervention services to young children with disabilities can enhance the capacity of early intervention to respond to the needs of an increasingly higher number of families requesting services. To successfully use this alternative structure, early intervention therapists must broaden the scope of decentralized service delivery and shift its emphasis from direct treatment to consultation. Applying clinical skills in ongoing child care routines may require some release of control and preferred patterns of behavior. Research in integrated service delivery at the preschool level indicates that many professionals have a vested interest in maintaining the status quo based on the fears of losing control (Peck, Hayden, Wandschneider, Peterson, & Richarz, 1989). Shifting from a direct service model to a consultative model can threaten therapists' self-confidence by requiring skills they do not have. Therapists may also resist integrated therapies because they feel the model "waters down" clinical treatment. They may also question the ability of child care providers to implement services. Despite these concerns, the documented shortage of therapists working in early intervention (Yoder, Coleman, & Gallagher, 1990) and the realization that infants and toddlers are better served by one or two primary caregivers require that alternative models of service delivery be considered.

Joining other systems and working on other people's turf requires personal flexibility and a strong commitment to inclusion. It also requires knowledge of the child care setting and childhood environments. Preservice and in-service programs for related-services providers need to prepare graduates to work effectively with infants, families, and child care providers within these natural settings.

Structured Communication

When early intervention services are provided in a clinic or family setting, staff usually have time allotted to review goals and objectives and modify program implementation as needed. It is critical that this type of program monitoring continue as early intervention providers move into decentralized service delivery in child care settings. Regularly scheduled meetings between child care providers and therapists offer opportunities to exchange information and create avenues for supporting and training one another in the new competencies required in an inclusive setting. For example, a physical therapist can demonstrate the use of adaptive equipment with which child care providers are unfamiliar. Child care staff can offer strategies for working with groups of young children rather than in a more traditional one-to-one therapy situation. Planned opportunities for cross-training build team cohesion and encourage the development of mutual respect and shared visions of success.

Mutual Respect   Child care providers and early intervention therapists offer important services to young children and their families. Both professional groups bring knowledge, skills, and competencies to the process of inclusion. Child care providers are knowledgeable about developmentally appropriate practices and typical children's reactions to the child care setting. Early intervention therapists are experienced in a variety of disciplines related to the growth and development of young children with disabilities. Both must recognize the unique contribution they make to the successful inclusion of young children with disabilities. Their task is not to compete with one another but to join forces for the benefit of all children and their families.

Shared Vision   Collaboration between child care and early intervention providers encourages consensual decision making about the skills children need to be successful in typical environments. A careful assessment of the natural routines of the child care setting can help early intervention therapists identify clinical evaluation data most relevant to the child's participation and functional independence. Similarly, when opportunities to practice targeted goals and objectives are identified, child care personnel can address them throughout the child's day, rather than limiting interventions to when the therapist is on-site. A commitment to inclusion should inform the shared vision developed by early intervention therapists and child care providers. This commitment can ensure the delivery of services in age-appropriate settings and safeguard the child's continued inclusion in his or her family and community.

CASE STUDY

Paul is a 2-year-old boy who attends a community child care program 3 days a week. Paul lives with his mother, who is a social worker; his dad, who is a corporate executive; and his 3-year-old sister, Amy.

Paul was pronounced dead at birth. His mother and father recall in vivid detail how they were told of his death, only to find out minutes later that "there'd been a mistake" and that their son was breathing. His mother said, "It was so confusing. I was exhausted, struggling to accept that Paul was dead, only to be told seconds later that he was breathing. It was like a miracle. Of course we were thrilled, but also appalled that this type of mistake had occurred."

Paul experienced some loss of oxygen at birth. As a result he has mild cerebral palsy, which affects both his upper and lower extremities. He has poor head control and is unable to sit without support. He often reaches for familiar objects but lacks the hand strength to grasp them. Paul's oral-motor control has also been affected by the cerebral palsy. His utterances are unintelligible and appear to be random.

Although Paul attends to voices and activities in his environment, because of his lack of motor control and speech, it is difficult to assess how much he comprehends of what is going on around him. His mom and dad feel that he can anticipate familiar routines because he gets excited and laughs when they tell him that they're going for a ride or that Gramma's coming. He is also beginning to laugh at appropriate times when they play simple games with him such as "peekaboo."

Paul's parents cared for him at home until he was 6 months old. His mother remembers that time as a haze of therapist and doctors appointments:

> We were so stressed out, running from here to there. Everyone was wonderful, but I felt like I was losing my baby to hospital and therapy schedules. Our life at home was also suffering. It was "chopped up," with little time to just be together and enjoy one another. I missed my job and time to be with our daughter. My husband and I decided we needed to get some normalcy back into our lives. Paul's disabilities were going to be a part of our lives together from now on. We needed to figure out how to make that work.

Paul's mother liked the staff at the child care center that her daughter, Amy, attended. She and her husband spoke with the director about enrolling Paul. They brought the director a copy of Paul's IFSP, which they reviewed together. The director explained that the center staff had recently completed a training program to prepare them to care for children with disabilities:

Altogether we had 20 hours of training. Each session was based on one of the Child Development Associate training modules that we use for in-service orientation of new staff. We learned how to modify the recommended practices described in each module to accommodate the needs of infants and toddlers with disabilities. It was great. The training built on what we knew and gave us confidence in our ability to care for children with special needs. Since then, we've been meeting with the local early intervention program to get technical assistance on the care of specific children.

The director offered to get in touch with the early intervention program to review Paul's case and set up his program. Paul began attending the child care center the following week. Early intervention staff consultation with child care staff allowed Paul's therapy objectives to be integrated into the child care program's daily schedule.

At first, the child care providers worried whether Paul was getting enough stimulation in the infant program. As he grew older, they feared that he would get hurt as the other children began to crawl and walk. Maybe he should stay with the younger children until he caught up with them. And what about toileting? How would they explain why Paul was still in diapers, as the other children mastered toilet training?

The early intervention therapists had their own set of worries: Were they doing enough for Paul? Would the other children make fun of him as he failed to keep up with their development? Would he get more from a clinical program?

The center director and Paul's parents addressed the concerns of staff. They were convinced that child care was the best program for Paul and for his family. They answered questions and solved problems as they came up, one by one, time after time. They also took data. Believing that "a picture's worth a thousand words," the director and Paul's father videotaped him at home and at the center at least twice a month. Paul's mother said, "The videotapes were amazing. Every time we got discouraged, the director would sit us down and let the tapes roll! It was incredible what this little boy was learning to do. That kind of reinforcement and support kept us going. It made us a team."

Within the first few weeks, Paul started lifting his head, visually tracking movements in his environment, and trying to grasp familiar objects. After 4 months of center-based care, he could sit in a high chair with support. He was eating finger food and babbling to familiar adults and children. He showed increased interest in his environment, exploring it through crawling and mouthing toys.

Paul has been at the child care program since he was 6 months old. He is now 2 years old and has moved into the toddler group at the same child care program. Although he still has delays in speech and language, his parents continue to be satisfied with the progress Paul is making. The child care staff think of him as one of their success stories. They are proud of the work they have done with the early intervention team to help Paul. When asked to define his success, to explain their satisfaction, their responses are similar: "exposure to other children," "being treated like a normal kid," and "being allowed to be at child care." Clearly, for Paul's team the child care setting has made the difference.

SUMMARY

As early intervention and child care professionals learn to work together in their support of young children with disabilities and their families, a shift from early intervention as direct service to a consultation model can be anticipated (Odom & McEvoy, 1990). This means that training, program accommodations, and resource development will be important components of early intervention services.

The release of therapeutic control of many aspects of direct implementation may be difficult for therapists, in much the same way that child care providers may have difficulty releasing control of physical space or preferred ways of managing classrooms. Well-developed communication skills and an ability to work with a variety of community service providers will be required competencies of both early intervention therapists and child care providers.

Shifting intervention from direct service to consultation in center-based child care environments may change the priorities teams set for young children. An emphasis on helping children achieve functional independence through the use of adaptive equipment and environmental supports can be expected. This shift in intervention presents a challenge for parents, child care providers, and early intervention therapists. Although consultation responds to the need to create alternative service delivery systems and provide infants and toddlers with disabilities opportunities for inclusion, it dramatically changes expectations of the therapist's role and the process of intervention. Emphasis is placed on environmental accommodations rather than clinical treatment. Strategies that can be implemented in the therapist's absence are a critical component of this service delivery system.

The challenge of using center-based child care to support early intervention for infants and toddlers with disabilities is to create a service delivery system that uses the context of child care routines to intervene with children with disabilities. Within this new system, child care professionals are not asked to become therapists nor are therapists asked to become child care providers. Rather, both groups are asked to collaborate to make something new. Neither group can expect to remain unchanged.

The expected benefits of this type of service delivery system include a better use of resources to serve all children and an increased participation of infants and toddlers with disabilities in age-appropriate activities and routines. It can also increase the involvement of parents of young children with disabilities in the work force and community.

REFERENCES

Belsky, J. (1988). The "effects" of infant day care reconsidered. *Early Childhood Research Quarterly*, 3(9), 235–272.

Belsky, J., & Steinberg, L. (1978). The effects of day care: A critical review. *Child Development, 49*, 929–949.

Brault, L. (1992). Achieving integration for infants and toddlers with special needs: Recommendations for practice. *Infants and Young Children, 5*(2), 78–85.

Bredekamp, S. (1987). *Developmentally appropriate practices in early childhood programs serving children from birth through age 8* (expanded ed.). Washington, DC: National Association for the Education of Young Children.

Bronfenbrenner, U. (1979). *The ecology of human development*. Cambridge, MA: Harvard University Press.

Bureau of National Affairs. (1991). *Caring for children with special needs (Work and Family #43)*. Washington, DC: Author.

Burton, C.B., Hains, A.H., Hanline, M.F., McLean, M., & McCormick, K. (1992). Early childhood intervention and education: The urgency of professional unification. *Topics in Early Childhood Special Education, 11*(4), 53–69.

Clarke-Stewart, K.A. (1988). "The 'effects' of infant day care reconsidered" reconsidered: Risks for parents, children and researchers. *Early Childhood Research Quarterly, 2*(9), 293–318.

Craig, S., & Eshoo, M. (1992, November). *Building collaborative teams of early intervention and child care personnel*. Paper presented at NAEYC conference, Altanta, GA.

Craig, S.E., Eshoo, M., & Haggart, A.G. (1993). *Including all children: An administrator's guide*. Hampton, NH: AGH Associates.

Education of the Handicapped Act Amendments of 1986, PL 99-457, 20 U.S.C., §1400 *et seq.*

Fewell, R. (1993). Child care for children with special needs. *Pediatrics, 91*(1), 193–198.

File, N., & Kontos, S. (1992). Indirect service delivery through consultation: Review and implications for early intervention. *Journal of Early Intervention, 16*(3), 221–233.

Galinsky, E. (1990). Government and child care. *Young Children, 45*(3), 27–30.

Green, A., & Stoneman, Z. (1989). Attitudes of mothers and fathers of nonhandicapped children. *Journal of Early Intervention, 13*(4), 292–304.

Guralnick, M.J. (1990). Major accomplishments and future directions in early childhood mainstreaming. *Topics in Early Childhood Special Education, 10*(2), 1–17.

Kontos, S., & File, N. (1993). Staff development in support of integration. In C.A. Peck, S. Odom, & D. Bricker (Eds.), *Integrating young children with disabilities into community programs: Ecological perspectives on research and implementation* (pp. 169–186). Baltimore: Paul H. Brookes Publishing Co.

McLean, M., & Hanline, M.F. (1990). Providing early intervention services in integrated environments: Challenges and opportunities for the future. *Topics in Early Childhood Special Education, 10*(2), 62–77.

Odom, S. (1989). *LRE, mainstreaming and integration for young children with disabilities: A decade of research.* Chapel Hill, NC: National Early Childhood Technical Assistance System.

Odom, S., & McEvoy, M. (1990). Mainstreaming at the preschool level: Potential barriers and tasks for the field. *Topics in Early Childhood Special Education, 10*(2), 48–61.

Olmsted, P., & Weikart, D. (1994). *Families speak: Early childhood care and education in 11 countries.* Ypsilanti, MI: High/Scope Press.

Peck, C.A., Hayden, L., Wandschneider, M., Peterson, K., & Richarz, S. (1989). Development of integrated preschools: A qualitative inquiry into sources of resistance among parents, administrators, and teachers. *Journal of Early Intervention, 13*(4), 353–363.

Peck, C.A., Odom, S.L., & Bricker, D.D. (Eds.). (1993). *Integrating young children with disabilities into community programs: Ecological perspectives on research and implementation.* Baltimore: Paul H. Brookes Publishing Co.

Scarr, S., & Weinberg, R.A. (1986). The early childhood enterprise: Care and education of the young. *American Psychologist, 41*(10), 1140–1146.

Strain, P.S. (1990). LRE for preschool children with handicaps: What we know, what we should be doing. *Journal of Early Intervention, 14*, 291–296.

Stryker, S. (1980). *Symbolic interactionalism.* Cambridge, MA: Harvard University Press.

Whitebrook, M., Howes, C., & Phillips, D. (1990). *Who cares? Child care teachers and the quality of care in America. Executive Summary, National Child Care Staffing Study.* Los Angeles: Child Care Employee Project.

Willer, B. (1992). An overview of the demand and supply of child care in 1990. *Young Children, 47*(2), 19–22.

Willer, B., Hofferek, S.L., Kisker, L.E., Divine-Hawkins, P., Farquhar, E., & Slantz, T.B. (1991). *The demand and supply of child care in 1990.* Washington, DC: National Association for the Education of Young Children.

Winton, P.J. (1993). Providing family support in integrated settings: Research and recommendations. In C.A. Peck, S.L. Odom, & D.D. Bricker (Eds.), *Integrating young children with disabilities into community programs: Ecological perspectives on research and implementation* (pp. 65–80). Baltimore: Paul H. Brookes Publishing Co.

Yoder, D., Coleman, P., & Gallagher, J. (1990). *Personnel needs: Allied health personnel meeting the demands of Part H, P.L. 94-457.* Chapel Hill: University of North Carolina, Frank Porter Graham Child Development Center, Carolina Policy Studies Program.

··· 11

Early Intervention Centers

Rosemary Karabinos

Note from the Editor (J.R.C.):

The early intervention center as a setting is the focus of much question and discussion in the field of early intervention today. We have included this chapter, written by the director of an early intervention center from her personal perspective and experience, to consider the reality of this setting as it fits within the concepts of early intervention as a system. The primary issues to be considered within the context of this setting include the issue of family-centered services, service delivery in natural environments, and the use of family and community resources in service delivery.

Numerous questions arise when examining the early intervention center as a setting. Can early intervention services through a center model provide resources and supports to families that meet the intent of the conceptual framework of early intervention, one that evolves from the family and fits within the family's sense of their needs and resources? Or does it by neccessity fit the family to the program and work toward a child-centered rather than a family-centered model, continually attempting, as described in this chapter, to include or involve the family? Is the concept of "family centered" not able to be incorporated fully into an "early intervention–centered" setting?

Can the setting of an early intervention center fit into the complexity and community perspective needed for providing early intervention in "natural environments"? Or does it by necessity offer a segregated perspective, one that only exists because of children's differences and need for special services? When typically developing children are integrated into the setting, as described in this chapter, does that change the setting to a more community-based, more natural environment, or does that goal remain elusive?

An additional issue to be considered when examining the early intervention center as a setting is the shifting focus of early intervention from service delivery, especially as children and families are offered a menu of therapeutic and educational services, to resource enhancement, as considered in Chapter 5. How does this system design fit into the setting of an early intervention center?

These issues are all essential questions to the field of early intervention. In areas of the country where early intervention centers have provided a majority of early intervention services in the past, there is much discussion as to their viability as early intervention settings in the future. The setting of early intervention centers has a historic value and a current reality. Therefore, it is a setting that is described in this chapter.

The traditional early intervention center is a setting that offers educational, developmental, and therapeutic services to children below school age who have a diagnosed disability, exhibit a developmental delay, or are classified as at risk. This chapter presents a brief history and purpose of early intervention centers and describes a comprehensive early intervention center model that is family focused, reflecting the philosophies and recommended practices in the field in the late 1990s.

Concurrent with the initiation of Head Start in 1965, early intervention programs began to develop. Many of these early center-based programs were modeled after traditional school-age educational programs. Others were designed only as child care centers, a concept just beginning to gain in popularity. For many years, and even in the 1990s, some early intervention programs are licensed as special needs child care centers even though their primary purpose is not to provide child care but to teach new behaviors and develop independent functioning in young children. When early intervention programs were first developed, most mothers of young children were not employed outside the home. According to the Bureau of the Census, (1994), only 18.6% of women with children under the age of 6 were working in 1960, compared with 59.6% in 1993. When children were born with disabilities, parents were led to believe that they could not adequately provide for their children's care and development at home. Consequently, they were told that they should enroll their children in a full-time center-based program with specially trained staff who could maximize their children's development. Babies and young children were literally put on a bus early in the morning and returned in the late afternoon while their mothers stayed at home. Parents were not involved in or even consulted about their children's programming. Programming was left up to the "professionals."

Despite their relative lack of sophistication, early intervention centers met with success. Progress in development was documented in children who attended programs at these centers, and this success created a greater demand for these services. Early intervention was expanded and improved when the federal government passed the Handicapped Children's Early Education Act of 1968 (PL 90-538) (currently Early Education of Children with Disabilities Program), and money became available to fund model preschool programs for children with disabilities. Professionals then began to recognize that parental involvement was instrumental in promoting the development of their children. The act funded programs only when applicant programs stressed the involvement and training of the parents or primary caregivers of the children to be enrolled and when they showed that the program could be replicated in other parts of the country. Some of these early federally funded model programs are responsible for the advances made into the 1990s in the field of early intervention.

THE EARLY INTERVENTION CENTER AS A SETTING

The comprehensive early intervention center in the late 1990s is a specially equipped facility with trained professionals who work with young children with special needs. These specialists generally include early intervention teachers, speech-language pathologists, occupational therapists, physical therapists, nurses, social workers, coordinators, and managers. Most early intervention centers primarily or exclusively serve infant, toddler, and preschool-age children who meet predetermined eligibility criteria. Due to the separate funding sources for different age levels, some centers limit their services to children younger than age 3 and others exclusively serve children older than 3 years of age. Still others use dual funding sources to serve the full range of children from birth to school age. A child is frequently identified as having a delay by a parent, guardian, or physician and is then referred to the early intervention center for services. Children are evaluated in all developmental areas by a team of staff members at the center with the involvement and input of the parents. Goals and objectives are established based on the child's and the family's needs, with the parents and other family members taking an active part in this process.

Once the initial assessment is completed, the team, including the parents, meets to determine what outcomes the family would like to see accomplished based on their concerns and priorities. The types and locations of early intervention services, as well as the support services, counseling, information, and other resources needed by the family to reach these outcomes, are also determined. These identified services, in addition to the anticipated goals for the following 6 months, are written into a program plan referred to as an individualized family service plan (IFSP) for children under 3 years or an individualized education program (IEP) for 3- and 4-year-old children.

The classroom options in early intervention centers frequently include a parent–infant class or a specialized class. In the parent–infant class, the parent or primary caregiver (this can include a grandparent, babysitter, or foster parent) attends along with the child one or two mornings per week. In this model, an early intervention teacher, speech therapist, or occupational therapist are also in the room—moving from child to child, instructing the child, and demonstrating techniques to the caregiver for follow-through at home. There are some group interactive activities, but the majority of the time is spent in individualized activities with the child by the teacher, therapist, or parent.

In a specialized class, six to nine eligible infants, toddlers, or preschool-age children attend the program 3–5 half days per week with a teacher and one or two aides. Therapists sometimes work directly in the classroom or are available for consultation. A speech therapist, for example, might engage in a group language activity with the class, demonstrate to the teacher how to best expand expressive language, or work with an individual child on articulation. The physical therapist might accompany the class to the gym or playground and demonstrate activities that develop gross motor skills or might suggest to the teacher alternative ways of encouraging a child with spina bifida to participate in classroom activities. However, it is the teacher who is generally responsible for planning each day's program and carrying out the children's intervention plans.

Parents or caregivers are often invited to attend a program intermittently with their child to learn developmentally appropriate activities, proper positioning, feeding techniques, and other skills that they can use at home. There are several "at-home" suggested activities that are sold commercially, such as the *Portage Guide to Early Education* (Bluma, Shearer, Frohman, & Hillard, 1976), The Learning Activity Program Learning Activities Cards (Miller, 1982), the Hawaii Early Learning Profile at Home (Parks, 1984), and the Home Program Instruction Sheet for Infants and Young Children (Jaeger, 1987). Teachers can also develop their own activities, known as intervention plans, which complement the goals identified on the IFSP or IEP, for classroom and home use. Figure 1 shows a sample teacher-made intervention plan, and Table 1 gives examples of daily schedules for the various age groups.

To provide appropriate role models and produce a more natural environment, some centers have invited typically developing children from the community to join in the class in what might be described as a reversed mainstream program. Others have designed integrated settings where 50% of the children have special needs and

CHILD'S NAME:	Kathy Jones	CHILDLINK #:	
DATE:	11/9/94	DEVELOPMENTAL AREA (s): Cognitive and Fine Motor	

OUTCOME: Kathy will reach for objects and interact with them.

ACTIVITIES TO ACHIEVE THE OUTCOMES	CHILD'S EXPECTED BEHAVIOR	DATES	
		TARGET	ACHIEVE
Hold a toy in which Kathy is interested in front of her. Position the toy so that the toy and her hand are within view. Encourage Kathy to reach out for the toy. If she does not, make a noise with the toy, bring Kathy's hand to the toy. Encourage and reinforce all efforts.	Kathy will reach out and grab a toy.	12/94	
Once Kathy has the toy in one hand, bring the other hand within view. Encourage her to transfer the toy back and forth. Allow Kathy to play with the toy in any way she likes (e.g., mouthing, throwing it).	Kathy will transfer a toy from one hand to the other.	1/95	
Give Kathy a second small toy and demonstrate how to bang the two together. Take the toys and bang them together yourself, then hand her the toys and placing your hands over hers, bang them together. Have a second set of toys for you to bang while Kathy is holding hers.	Kathy will bang two toys together.	2/95	

DID THE PARENT/LEGAL GUARDIAN TAKE PART IN AND ACCEPT THE INTERVENTION PLAN?	YES X	NO

PREPARED BY:	Susan Smith	DATE ATTACHED TO THE IFSP	11/9/94

Figure 1. Sample intervention plan.

Table 1. Sample daily schedules

Parent–infant class	Preschool class

Circle time
   Greetings/introductions
	Circle time
	   Introductions game
	   Good morning/weather

Individualized activities
   Parents work on child's intervention plan
   Speech therapist, teacher, and occupational
     therapist work with each parent and child to
     demonstrate activities and give
     recommendations
	Small group activities
	   Matching
	   Sorting
	   Puzzles

	Group gross motor
	   Obstacle course
	   Ball toss
	   Playground

Snack time
   Work on self-help skills
	Snack
	   Work on self-help skills

Group activity
   Gross motor play
   Socialization
	Fine motor
	   Stacking
	   Stringing beads
	   Painting
	   Manipulatives

Closing activity
   Music
	Closing activity
	   Music and movement

50% are typically developing. Some early intervention centers have a truly main-streamed environment with 20% or less of the enrolled children having special needs. These program designs are described in more detail later in the chapter.

In addition to participating directly in the development of their children's program, attending parent–child days, and carrying out activities at home with their child, parents are generally given the opportunity to enroll in parent education classes or parent support group sessions. Parent education classes usually focus on specific topics of interest to parents raising a child with a disability. These topics, provided on a weekly or monthly basis, might include child development, positive discipline, communication, the right to education laws, and community resources. Table 2 contains a more expansive list of possible parent education topics. Parent support groups, often facilitated by a counselor or social worker, deal more with issues of acceptance, coping, interfacing with the medical community, and extended family concerns. Table 3 includes sample support group topics. Individual counseling and referral to resources outside of the early intervention center also take place.

Groups for the siblings of children with special needs also have been developed to encourage young children to talk about the unique problems of growing up in a family with a child with a disability (Lobato, 1990). The support from the facilitator and the other children in the group is designed to help young children cope with their situation and prevent resentment toward their brother or sister.

Facilities in which early intervention takes place vary greatly, and, although an impressive building does not necessarily indicate that recommended practices are being implemented, the available resources can affect the quality of services provided, the attitude of the staff, and the staff's feelings about the services they are providing. A well-equipped center will have spacious classrooms that are appropriately furnished and supplied, private meeting rooms, a comfortable place for parents to gather, a large indoor play area, and an accessible playground. A lending library with books, magazines, adaptive equipment, and toys that parents can preview and take home pro-

Table 2. Parent education topics

Unit I: Early intervention	**Unit IV: Managing behaviors**
Early intervention: What is it?	Behavioral development in children
Equipment/toys used in early intervention	Positive guidance techniques
Basic concepts of assessment	Basic behavior management techniques
Assessment instruments commonly used with young children	Reinforcement, extinction, and punishment
Developing an IFSP/IEP	**Unit V: Community resources**
Carrying out an intervention plan	Mental health/mental retardation systems
Unit II: Human development	Infant and preschool programs
Principles of human development	School-age programs
Prenatal behavior	Recreational services
Birth/unlearned behavior	Alternative living arrangements
Maturation	Other resources
Central nervous system	
Motor development	
Sensory development	
Symbolic processes	
Growth of intelligence	
Social and emotional development	
Growth of personality	
Unit III: Speech and language development	
Introduction to speech and language development	
Theories of language development	
Anatomy and physiology of speech and language development	
Oral-motor and feeding development	
Remediation of oral-motor dysfunction	
Cognitive prerequisites of language	
Speech and language development	
Communication disorders	
Remediation of communication disorders	
Augmentative communication systems	

Topics are adapted from the PEERS Early Intervention and Parent Education Program. (1994). Special People in Northeast, Inc., Philadelphia.

vides families with a valuable resource. Specialized equipment and toys may be needed by families for only months at a time, but their price may prohibit many families from buying them. Even items that parents are interested in purchasing are best tried out before making the investment.

IMPLICATIONS FOR PROVIDING EARLY INTERVENTION SERVICES

Center-based early intervention, by efficient use of resources, can provide a setting with a multitude of service options for children with special needs and their families. When children are provided services in group situations they are given the opportunity to develop socialization skills (e.g., learning how to get along with other children, cooperating during group games, taking turns, following directions) that will serve children their entire lives. Language development is enhanced when other children who are verbally expressive serve as role models. Staff can readily set up situations that stimulate the desire to communicate. Positive reinforcements can be given frequently for appropriate behaviors, and inappropriate behaviors can be ignored and therefore extinguished when a child is regularly attending a center-based program. Data collection and record keeping can be best accomplished when the teacher has regular contact with the child. Progress can be monitored and adjustments can be made in intervention plans as necessary.

For parents, the center-based option gives them the opportunity for contact with other parents, both formally and informally, which reduces feelings of isolation and

Table 3. Sample support group topics

September: "Introductory Session." Introductions will be made. A discussion will be held to help determine which topics the group feels would be important to discuss over the course of the year.

October: "Dealing with Professionals." This session will look at how to locate sympathetic and knowledgeable pediatricians, neurologists, and other professionals. Ways to interact assertively with these essential people will be a part of this session.

November: "The Extended Family." This session will include interactions with those other important people in our lives: parents, grandparents, best friends, neighbors, and so forth.

December: "Siblings of the Child with Special Needs." This session shows that siblings also have special needs. Research has some interesting things to say about these children and how we can help them handle their unique situation.

January: "Impact on the Family of Having a Child with a Developmental Delay or Disability." This session will look at what happens to the total family in this situation. What happens to the parents' involvement with friends? Does their social life go on hold? What can they do to continue to grow themselves?

February: "Overprotection versus Letting Them Go." We all know that children must take a certain number of "bumps" while they learn to handle their bodies, use implements, and deal with other children and the world outside. At the same time, it is natural for parents to want to spare them these hurts. What is the happy medium? Enough protection to prevent serious harm, yet enough freedom to permit them to grow?

March: "The Couple with a Special Needs Child." This topic will deal with the additional stresses on the relationship when your child has special needs. At this session, the group members will share the ways they have found to enrich their lives together and to deal with some of the normal conflicts that may arise as they care for their child.

April: "Topic of Group's Choice." The last meeting will be reserved for a topic selected by the group. It may be something that has been discussed and needs to be talked about again, or it may be a totally new topic that the group has identified.

Topics developed by Margaretta Bigley, Ed.D., Family Therapist, Special People in Northeast, Inc. (1990).

is valuable in the support that families gain from each other. Even the most empathetic professional cannot fully understand what parents of young children with special needs confront. Other parents, however, can be empathetic because of their firsthand experience. Just knowing that they are not the only ones in these circumstances can lift some weight off parents' shoulders. A parent from an early intervention program said it best, after attending a parent training class for the first time, by responding:

> I was devastated when I learned that my baby was disabled. I felt so alone. I thought I would never smile again. After attending my first parent training session and meeting other parents I was simply amazed. They smiled and laughed and talked openly about the problems they were facing. I felt that if they could do it, so could I. I can't remember what the topic of the session was but I remember leaving that church basement feeling that I could go on.

Lasting friendships are often developed from such encounters, which can provide sustenance for a lifetime.

In a center-based program, parents also have immediate access to the professional staff with questions about their child's program or development. Techniques can be demonstrated, questions answered, and individualized objectives quickly revised; even services indicated on individualized plans can be changed when parents and staff have frequent contact with each other. Other team members also can consult with each other and work closely together in a center-based program. Efficient use of staff time and ease of supervision are two advantages from a management perspective.

The therapy staff can use the center-based environment for integrating therapies into a child's daily schedule and demonstrating to teachers and parents how they can play a role in the child's therapy throughout the day. In this way, "therapy" is not limited to the time that the child is having a one-to-one session with the therapist but is going on throughout the day, where appropriate. The benefits to a child of being properly positioned during his or her hour of physical therapy are totally negated if that same child is not properly positioned during the rest of the day. A half hour of speech therapy is far more beneficial if the teacher and parent learn the therapist's methods and implement them throughout the day. Ideally, parents can be encouraged to carry out recommended activities at home to reinforce skills learned in the center and to generalize these skills to other situations. However, if a parent is unable or unwilling to follow through on the program at home, the child at least has the advantage of intervention during the time he or she is in the program.

If the early intervention center is well equipped, the availability of adaptive equipment and supplies can be advantageous in meeting each child's special needs. Therapists can try different pieces of adaptive equipment for a child until they find one that best suits the child. Therapists can regularly consult with the teachers directly to help design programs and activities to meet the individual needs of the children. Teachers have a variety of toys and supplies available for motivating children. If one item is not effective with a child, the teacher can find another method or material. New teachers and therapists can rely on the advice and experience of the senior staff members because everyone is in the same location and easily accessible.

Although the center-based option may be efficient and can offer a variety of services, it is usually limited in its ability to provide a natural environment for the children that includes interaction with typically developing children. The least restrictive environment has been a standard in the provision of educational services since the passage of the Education for All Handicapped Children Act of 1975 (PL 94-142). With the passage of the Education of the Handicapped Act Amendments of 1986 (PL 99-457) (and later the Individuals with Disabilities Education Act [PL 101-476] and its amendments [PL 102-119]) this principle has been extended to children ages 3–5. In providing services to children from birth to 3, early interventionists are mandated to consider the child's natural environment.

Arguments for and against integration have been previously published (Thurman & Widerstrom, 1990), and, whether for ethical, legal, or developmental reasons, the advantages of integration clearly outweigh the disadvantages. However, children enrolled in early intervention centers are generally in segregated classes with no opportunity for observing and modeling typical behavior, which early research has found to be an advantage of mainstreaming. Thurman and Widerstrom noted Guralnick's conclusion that peers without disabilities "can provide a linguistic environment for children with handicaps that is sufficiently complex to stimulate language development and still remain at the appropriate development for the listener" (Thurman & Widerstrom, 1990, p. 39).

Specialized centers also reinforce the erroneous notion that children with disabilities should be separated from their peers. Professionals, parents, organizations for people with disabilities, and advocates speak of normalization and inclusion as a philosophical imperative that must be embraced; however, in practice, this is generally not occurring in segregated early intervention centers.

During the mid-1990s, as school districts are looking for ways to include their special education children in general classrooms and supported employment initiatives are preferred to sheltered workshop placements, it appears that the era of the traditional center-based, segregated early intervention center is coming to an end. Rather than attempt to reintegrate the adult with disabilities into the community, why not make the change at the point of diagnosis by not separating the child with the disability from other children in the first place? If there is to be a commitment to the concept of inclusion it must begin at the point at which a child with a disability is born, and the necessary services must be provided in whatever environment that child would be in had the disability not occurred.

RECOMMENDATIONS AND SOLUTIONS

To provide optimal services to children with special needs and their families, center-based early intervention needs to be viewed in a broader sense than it has traditionally been. As long as professionals insist on "specialized" segregated services for eligible young children, true inclusion will never be reached.

At a time when working parents are clamoring for quality child care for their young children, many early intervention centers have opened their doors to typically developing young children. They have capitalized on a growing need while providing a natural environment for children with disabilities. The children with special needs then have appropriate role models to imitate and are challenged to develop their skills. The typically developing children can also benefit greatly from the involvement with trained staff, a developmentally appropriate curriculum, and a well-equipped facility. This notion is supported by Odom and McEvoy (1988), who, after reviewing the literature, concluded that "the cumulative evidence suggests strongly that normally developing children are not adversely affected by enrollment in integrated classes, and in fact benefit developmentally from the curriculum and instructional strategies." (Odom & McEvoy, 1988, p. 259).

Another advantage of inclusive education is that these typically developing children may also learn early in life to accept people with disabilities and carry this acceptance throughout their lives. Esposito and Peach (1983) administered the Primary Student Survey of Handicapped Persons to typically developing children enrolled in an inclusive kindergarten and found that "the children exhibited generally more positive attitudes towards handicapped persons during the course of the year" (Odom & McEvoy, 1988, p. 261).

This inclusive education is philosophically best achieved when services are provided directly in the locations where children are typically cared for, such as child care centers, preschools, church or synagogue programs, and recreation centers. Research has shown that general early childhood centers are receptive to serving children with special needs at their sites (Odom & McEvoy, 1988). Gallagher (1987) found that parents have "expressed a willingness to have children with handicaps enroll in their children's program" (Odom & McEvoy, 1988, p. 244). Although this practice is appropriate and supports current recommended practices of inclusion, it tends to be used primarily for children with mild to moderate delays. Experience has shown that frequently the class size and the lack of staff training make it less than optimal for children with severe and profound disabilities. The provider of the support services does not have sufficient control over elements of the general environment to ensure that the needs of these children are met.

However, if traditional early intervention centers converted to comprehensive early childhood centers, they would have the ability to design the environment more specifically to accommodate the needs of children with severe and profound disabilities. The number of children in a classroom can be adjusted, support personnel can be available, daily schedules may be modified, and therapy can be integrated into a child's daily routine. Early intervention staff and parents can determine the appropriate staff–child ratio and the ratio of children with special needs to those who are typically developing. They can also decide if a child would benefit best from an inclusive setting (where 80% or more of the children are typically developing) or an integrated setting (where the class is 50% typically developing and 50% with special needs) and then create these settings within the center. Traditional specialized classes could also be continued for those children for whom this setting is determined to be most appropriate or to give families a choice in the type of education that their children receive.

By their very nature, early intervention centers have all of the basic components necessary for this transformation. First, staff who are trained to work with children with special needs generally have the skills necessary to work with children who are typically developing. Properly prepared early intervention staff have knowledge of typical development and developmentally appropriate practices and are trained to meet the needs of individual children. They are familiar with assessment instruments and when to refer a child who is having difficulty in any area of development. Second, the physical environment of a good early intervention center would certainly be appropriate for children who are typically developing. Aside from the specialized adaptive equipment required by some children with special needs, the rest of the furniture, equipment, toys, supplies, and materials should be the same as that found in a quality early childhood center. An additional advantage for families with more than one preschool-age child is that all their children could attend the same program. Knowing that the staff are specially trained, that child development specialists and therapists are available, and that state-of-the-art practices are implemented can be attractive to the parents looking for quality child care or a preschool, whether their child is typically developing or has special needs.

In an effort to support inclusion, some early intervention programs offer child care and preschool on a fee-for-service basis to typically developing children in their communities. For example, an early intervention center in Philadelphia, Special People in Northeast, Inc. (Losinno, n.d.), when expanding its early intervention center also opened a child care and preschool program. This enabled the program to provide more center-based time in a natural environment to the children with special needs. The program was also able to offer child care to their staff and provide a service to the community. The children with special needs had the option of a specialized, integrated, or inclusive class setting and could attend the program from 3 half days to 5 full days per week, depending on the child's need for programming and the family's needs for child care.

The concept of transforming a traditional specialized early intervention center that provides services exclusively to children with special needs into a comprehensive early childhood center for all children certainly has challenges to be overcome. The most obvious obstacle is the number of children with special needs who can be served in this design. Local regulations generally require a certain number of square feet of floor space per child, usually between 35 and 45 square feet. If a center is filled to physical capacity with children with special needs, then there is no room to admit children who are typically developing unless children with special needs are denied entrance. For example, an early intervention center, required by local regulations to have 45 square feet per child, has 4,500 square feet of classroom space and is currently providing services to 100 children with disabilities. If this center became integrated it would still only be able to serve 100 children, but half of them would be typically developing; therefore, 50 children with special needs would go unserved. Until there are more alternatives in the community for children with special needs, early intervention centers may be reluctant to admit children who are typically developing when it means denying services to children with special needs.

A second obstacle to this conversion is the issue of funding. Although funding is generally available for early intervention, parents of children who are typically developing are expected to pay for child care or preschool for their children. Parents of children who have special needs must also pay for that which is considered child care and not early intervention as defined in a child's IFSP or IEP. This is not a problem in areas where parents can afford the tuition or when subsidized child care is available for low-income families. It can become a problem when classroom enrollment is reduced to accommodate the children with special needs and no funds are identified to offset the decrease in income that this causes. Also, when children with moderate to profound disabilities are integrated or included in classes with children who are typically developing for 8–10 hours per day, they often require additional staff for the full time they are in attendance. Because much of the day would be considered child care and not early intervention, it is likely that it would not be reimbursable through early intervention funds. Yet neither the family nor the center could be expected to incur the expense of the additional staff person. There needs to be a funding base that allows early intervention centers to design inclusive settings without fear of loss of income.

Thus far in this chapter, legal (e.g., PL 99-457) and ethical reasons have primarily been cited as arguments for inclusion. There also are developmental reasons why this should occur. Research has shown that both children with special needs and their typically developing peers do at least as well in an integrated setting as they do in segregated environments. It is not conclusive, however, that children perform better in inclusive settings (Thurman & Widerstrom, 1990). It can therefore be argued that as long as both groups of children do at least as well in either setting, then the ethical and legal reasons are sufficient to encourage inclusive environments. However, PL 99-457 and PL 102-119 mandate that children be served in a natural environment, which needs to be defined for each individual child. The natural environment can be quite different depending on the age and needs of the child and the family's need for child care.

CASE STUDY

The following case study demonstrates a family's use of an early intervention center over a period of 4 years and how the evolution of the center met the family's changing needs.

When Nancy McBride gave birth to her second child, she received the devastating news that her beautiful new daughter, Megan, had Down syndrome and a congenital heart defect. While still in the hospital, Nancy received a visit from a social worker who explained the value of early intervention and gave Nancy literature about a local program, SPIN, that provided weekly home visits by an infant development specialist with consults from a physical therapist.

When Megan was just 4 weeks old, her family received a visit from the infant development specialist who assessed Megan and discussed with them their need for more information. They also expressed the desire to talk with another family whose child had the same heart defect, as they knew they might soon be faced with open heart surgery for Megan. Nancy was pleased with Megan's progress, and she found the visiting staff to be very helpful and supportive. The specialist demonstrated developmental activities for the parents to do at home, and the physical therapist showed them how they could help increase Megan's muscle tone and encourage her motor development.

After 1 year of home visits, Nancy and her husband, Tom, discussed with their service coordinator their feeling of isolation and their need to meet with other families in similar situations. They visited the center-based program and felt good about having Megan interact with other children and being able themselves to talk to other parents of children with Down syndrome.

When Megan was 18 months old, Nancy enrolled in the parent–infant component of the program. Nancy attended once a week with her daughter, and Tom attended a monthly fathers' group. Megan's individual program objectives were updated regularly, and Nancy was given ideas on how she and Tom could carry out some activities at home. Each week Nancy received instruction from the classroom teacher, and monthly she was able to consult with the speech therapist and physical therapist about any concerns she had. Nancy was feeling very confident with her skills as a parent of a baby with Down syndrome and very comfortable with the early intervention center and staff. This confidence and comfort level prompted Nancy to enroll Megan in the traditional early intervention class with other children with disabilities when she was about 2 years old. Yearly assessments occurred, Megan's individual objectives were updated quarterly, and home activities were suggested. Megan's parents were particularly pleased with the progress Megan made in understanding what was said to her and in her ability to get along well with other children. They also found her to be more independent now that she was not always with her mother.

When Megan was about 3 years old, Nancy and Tom were delighted to hear that the early intervention center was opening a child care center that would accept both children with special needs and their typically developing peers. Nancy had been considering returning to work, but she and her husband were reluctant to enroll Megan in their local child care center. When they visited their neighborhood center they found 20 children per class with a teacher and an aide. The child care manager expressed a reluctant willingness to accept Megan into the center, but she voiced concern about meeting her needs and explained that the staff were not trained to worked with children with special needs and they were also not certified in CPR.

Nancy and Tom felt much more confident enrolling Megan and her 4½-year-old brother, Tommy, in the integrated child care class at the early intervention center. Nancy was able to return to work full time. According to Megan's IEP, she was eligible for early intervention three mornings per week; her parents paid for the additional hours of the program as child care. Megan and her brother are part of a very typical preschool child care class. The only difference was that the number of children was limited to 15 (traditional child care centers in their area have 20 children in a class), and there were 4 other children in the class who have disabilities. Although the teacher was not certified in special education, she was well trained, was certified in first aid and CPR, and had consultation with a speech therapist and physical therapist on a weekly basis. Tom continued to enjoy attending his fathers' group meeting, and Nancy took off from work occasionally to participate in a parent–child day or attend a parent conference. She was also an active member of the center's advisory board.

Tom and Nancy attribute Megan's progress and their acceptance of her disability to their early referral to early intervention, their active involvement from the beginning, the quality program she attends, and Megan's interactions with her typically developing peers.

CONCLUSIONS

The concept of an early intervention center is no longer limited to classrooms full of young children with special needs who attend full-time programming. It is more likely to be a facility where various types of early intervention services are available to a child and family based on individual needs and preferences. One early intervention center might include any or all of the following options for families:

- Home visits by a child development specialist or therapist to work directly with the child and provide education and guidance to the parents
- Participation in a one-session-per-week parent–infant class instructed by a therapist and teacher who work with both the child and the parent
- Participation in a Saturday morning early intervention and parent education class
- Weekly visits by any member of the child's assessment team to a community program that the child attends (this can be at a family child care provider, child care center, recreation program, or other type of early childhood center in the community)
- Enrollment in a weekday specialized class consisting of all children with special needs and a 1:3 staff-to-child ratio
- Enrollment in a half day preschool class with approximately 12 children, half of whom are typically developing and half of whom have special needs
- Enrollment in the early intervention center's typical child care program as a mainstreamed child with support services

All options should address the needs of the child and family, and none should usurp the family's role in the child's life but rather should offer the parents the skills they will need to raise their child as well as additional supports and resources they desire. And when the choice is to bring the child into a traditional early intervention center, the challenge to that program will be to provide the child with a natural environment with opportunities for interacting with her typically developing peers.

Traditional center-based early intervention programs may efficiently provide a variety of quality services, but if they cannot overcome the obstacles to inclusion that are inherent in traditional segregated early intervention centers they will not be able to provide state-of-the-art services and therefore will become extinct. There will continue to be dialogue in the field of early intervention about the early intervention center as a setting and how it fits within the concepts and philosophy of family-centered early intervention in natural environments.

REFERENCES

Bluma, A., Shearer, M., Frohman, A., & Hillard, J. (1976). *Portage guide to early education.* Portage, WI: Cooperative Educational Service Agency.

Bureau of the Census. (1994). *Statistical Abstract of the United States–1994* (114th ed.). Washington, DC: Author.

Education for All Handicapped Children Act of 1975, PL 94-142, 20 U.S.C. § 1400 *et seq.*

Education of the Handicapped Act Amendments of 1986, PL 99-457, 20 U.S.C. § 1400 *et seq.*

Esposito, B.G., & Peach, W.J. (1983). Changing attitudes of preschool children toward handicapped persons. *Exceptional Children, 49*, 361–363.

Gallagher, T.A. (1987). *Assessing the needs of families of preschool children.* Unpublished master's thesis, Vanderbilt University, Nashville, TN.

Handicapped Children's Early Intervention Act of 1968, PL 90-538, 20 U.S.C. §621 *et seq.*

Individuals with Disabilities Education Act (IDEA) of 1990, PL 101-476, 20 U.S.C. §§ 1400 *et seq.*

Individuals with Disabilities Education Act Amendments of 1991, PL 102-119, 20 U.S.C. §§ 1400 *et seq.*

Jaeger, L. (1987). *Home program instruction sheets for infants and young children.* Tucson, AZ: Communication Skill Builders.

Lobato, D.J. (1990). *Brothers, sisters, and special needs: Information and activities for helping young siblings of children with chronic illnes and developmental disabilities.* Baltimore: Paul H. Brookes Publishing Co.

Losinno, A.K. (n.d.). *The PEERS Program: An overview.* Philadelphia, PA: Special People in Northeast, Inc.

Miller, P. (1982). *LAP learning activities for the young child: Chapel Hill Training Outreach Project.* Winston-Salem, NC: Kaplan Press.

Odom, S.L., & McEvoy, M.A. (1988). Integration of young children with handicaps and normally developing children. In S.L. Odom & M.B. Karnes (Eds.), *Early intervention for infants and children with handicaps: An empirical base* (pp. 241–267). Baltimore: Paul H. Brookes Publishing Co.

Parks, S. (1984). *HELP At Home: Hawaii Early Learning Profile.* Palo Alto, CA: VORT Corp.

Thurman, S.K., & Widerstrom, A.H. (1990). *Infants and young children with special needs: A developmental and ecological approach.* Baltimore: Paul H. Brookes Publishing Co.

... 12

Public Schools

Sheryl Ridener Gottwald and P. Alan Pardy

With the mandates of the Education of the Handicapped Act Amendments of 1986 (PL 99-457) now fully operable, public schools are developing program options designed to provide a free and appropriate public education to children with disabilities ages 3–6 (Barnett & Frede, 1993). The challenges posed by program development at the preschool level provide public schools with opportunities to design creative intervention options that reflect the mandates of the federal legislation while being molded by the requirements and resources of each local education agency (LEA).

HISTORY OF EARLY INTERVENTION IN PUBLIC SCHOOLS

The imperative need for publicly supported early intervention at the preschool level and younger was defined by the passage of the Handicapped Children's Early Education Act of 1968 (PL 90-538). States were provided with funds to develop model education programs for young children with disabilities (Safer & Hamilton, 1993). This landmark legislation stimulated related developments in the following years. Head Start began servicing youngsters with disabilities from low-income families in 1972. Regulations specified that no less than 10% of Head Start enrollments be for children with disabilities. The Council for Exceptional Children established a new division, the Division for Early Childhood, in 1973. In 1974, federal grant money was allocated to state education agencies (SEAs) to review and begin developing early childhood special education programs.

In 1975, the Education for All Handicapped Children Act (PL 94-142) provided incentive money for states to voluntarily develop education programming for children under age 6. The mandates of this national legislation formally endorsed public education programs for preschoolers with disabilities. Even with such accreditation, it was not until passage of PL 99-457 in 1986 that all young children with special learning needs were considered eligible for publicly funded early intervention services.

Part B, Section 619, of PL 99-457 and its 1990 counterpart, the Individuals with Disabilities Education Act (IDEA, PL 101-476) direct states to extend all of the special education provisions of PL 94-142 to children ages 3–6. If states did not comply with

215

this national mandate by 1992, they would lose all federal funds for preschool special education services. Although some states were providing special education services to this group of children as early as 1973, it was not until the 1992–1993 school year that all 50 states and 8 U.S. jurisdictions ensured a free and appropriate public education to eligible 3- to 6-year-old children (Heekin, 1993).

The preschool special education legislation encouraged states to move away from labeling educational disabilities to provide early intervention services (Smith & Schakel, 1986). Family involvement evolved from a supportive to a primary role in the design, implementation, and evaluation of the child's education plan. States were also directed to develop interagency coordination procedures to more efficiently use existing services and streamline early intervention service delivery. Fifty U.S. states and jurisdictions reported interagency agreements with agencies such as Head Start, developmental disabilities, mental health, and health and human services (Heekin, 1993).

PUBLIC SCHOOL CONTEXT FOR EARLY INTERVENTION

Preschoolers who are developing as expected for their age receive early education in a multitude of ways. Some children remain at home learning from interactions with siblings, playmates, and relatives. Others attend preschools, Head Start programs, child care at home or school, or publicly funded kindergarten programs. Therefore, when public schools become involved in planning special education for preschoolers in the least restrictive (most "normalized") environment, a variety of program options from full inclusion in a local early childhood program to participation in a self-contained classroom in the public school will need to be considered (Strain, 1991).

The public school special education team must choose the most appropriate and least restrictive options for providing special education to identified preschoolers. There is continuing debate regarding the characteristics of an inclusive education program at this level (Guralnick, 1990). By June 1993, only seven SEAs across the country had policies or guidelines readily available that specifically addressed inclusive program options for preschoolers (Heekin, 1993). Nevertheless, teams must match the child and his or her family's strengths, priorities, and needs with the resources available in the child's community, including the local public school (Treusch, 1989).

In a Division for Early Childhood White Paper, McLean and Odom (1988) described four potential options for providing integrated programming at the preschool level. Public schools may use one or more of these options as they develop early childhood special education procedures. These alternatives are summarized in the following sections.

Mainstreamed Educational Programs

In mainstreamed educational programs (MEPs), preschoolers with disabilities are enrolled in classes for peers who are developing as expected for their age. The educational needs of the child with disabilities are cooperatively addressed by the early childhood and public school special education staff. Private preschools, Head Start programs, and early childhood centers are possible MEP sites. This approach allows preschoolers with learning problems to receive interventions designed to address their difficulties while being contributing members of their community peer group (Diamond, Hestenes, & O'Connor, 1994).

Several limitations must be noted when evaluating this option for preschool programming by the public schools. Public school special educators may need to spend a significant amount of travel time providing itinerant services. Services may become fragmented and less comprehensive unless appropriate time allocations are made. Itinerancy may also limit collaborative work between the general and special education staff if conference time, consultation strategies, and classroom responsibilities are not considered. If LEAs decided to use the "principle of natural proportions" to determine the ratio of students with special needs to general education students (Salisbury, 1990, p. 3), local preschools would only be able to incorporate students with disabilities up to approximately 10% of their total enrollment. Consequently, there would be a limited number of available slots in the community for children with identified learning needs. Finally, some identified preschoolers will have multiple developmental needs that may not be satisfactorily managed in the mainstream environment (Carta, Schwartz, Atwater, & McConnell, 1991; Diamond et al., 1994). Other placement options must be made available to meet these needs.

Mainstreamed Child Care Programs

Preschoolers with special needs may attend a home-based or community child care program for part of their day. Although special education interventions would not be the focus during this part of the day, the setting would allow opportunities for interaction with typical peers. Research has repeatedly supported the positive impact of mainstreamed settings on the educational competence of preschoolers with disabilities (Guralnick, 1990). However, educational gains in integrated settings cannot be guaranteed without education plans that specifically address the learning needs of the identified preschoolers (Lamorey & Bricker, 1993; McLean & Hanline, 1990).

Integrated Special Education or Reverse-Mainstreamed Programs

Children who are developing as expected are enrolled in classes for young children with disabilities, providing an opportunity for interaction between the two groups of children. The level of integration in this option varies across school districts (Odom & McEvoy, 1988). The choice of curriculum and the quality of teaching also vary extensively and will significantly affect the value of this integration option (Jenkins, Odom, & Speltz, 1989). One interpretation of this option is the establishment of an integrated preschool classroom in the local public school. Children with special education plans would receive individualized interventions while benefiting from inclusion in a classroom with community peers without disabilities.

In this kind of classroom, children from the community and children with special education plans would regularly take part in learning activities in a classroom in the local public school. Depending on the philosophical orientation of the LEA and the preschool staff, the children may participate in circle time, small group projects, free choice (play) time, outdoor activities, and snack or lunch time. Although the children without special education plans would be transported by their families, busing would be provided for those children with identified learning needs who required transportation assistance. The classroom staff would most typically consist of a special education teacher with academic or clinical experience at the preschool level and a teacher assistant with some training or experience in working with young children. Related-services professionals, most likely those already on the school district payroll, also would work with some or all of the class.

This option has several advantages. Because both general and special education staff would be school district employees, administrative and scheduling problems would be lessened. Increased consultation time, shared ownership of teaching materials, and a history of integration in the elementary school may all contribute to successful programming in the public school. Transition from preschool to elementary school would be enhanced; preschoolers attending an integrated classroom in the LEA and their families would have an opportunity to become familiar with the public school context and the elementary school staff. Administrators and elementary teachers also would have an opportunity to get to know the children who might be included in their classrooms in the following years.

Nonintegrated Special Education Programs in the LEA

In this setting, young children with disabilities receive special education in a self-contained classroom in the public school. Preschoolers with special needs become familiar with the public school environment and are exposed to typical children but on a more remote level. They have limited opportunity to profit from ongoing interactions with their age-appropriate peer group. Therefore, this may be the least desirable option described by McLean and Odom (1988) because inclusive classrooms have been shown to be more favorable to social and communicative growth and at least as beneficial in all other areas of development (Guralnick, 1990).

An alternative context not discussed by McLean and Odom (1988) that public schools may identify for providing special education to preschoolers is the home (Treusch, 1989). Home-based services may be chosen if the child's education needs can be satisfactorily met there and if the family and special education team identify that setting as the least restrictive option. When an intervention team works in the home, the development of functional intervention goals is facilitated. Family involvement is enhanced as family members are more likely to be accessible in their own home. Of the contexts discussed thus far, working in the home may be the least familiar environment for public school staff because traditionally all education during the school day was generally conducted in a public school building. The limitations posed by itinerancy, including service fragmentation and limited intervention time, will need to be considered when this option of intervention is chosen.

Unique Characteristics of the Public School Context

The public school context for providing special education for preschoolers represents a variety of settings, as described in the preceding section. Depending on the education options available in the community, the child's individual needs, the preferences of the child's family, and the recommendations of the education team, the environments in which public school early intervention may take place will range from classrooms in the LEA to community preschools to the child's home. Individual needs can be met more efficiently if the setting in which services are implemented best matches the needs and expectations of the people served. The more options available to public school staff, the more likely a fine-tuned match can be made.

At the elementary level, parents play a supportive role in the development, implementation, and evaluation of their child's individualized education program (IEP). In preschool programming, however, the focus on family takes precedence. Family priorities and preferences play an integral role in the development of an education plan for preschoolers. In a 1993 Part B, Section 619, profile conducted by the National Early Childhood Technical Assistance System (NEC*TAS) (Heekin, 1993), it was reported that 23 states used or were considering using the individualized family service plan (IFSP) for preschool service provision in addition to or in replacement of the IEP. Such a choice clearly broadens the primary unit of focus from the child to the family.

School-age special education plans concentrate on improving an identified child's performance in the academic domain. However, inclusive special education programming for preschoolers is likely to be focused on helping the child to satisfactorily participate in and belong to the community peer group. Naturalistic teaching strategies and activity-based interventions provide a learning environment different from the typical elementary classroom (McEvoy, Fox, & Rosenberg, 1991).

To receive special education services at the elementary level, the specific area of disability must be labeled. Alternately, preschool teams have been encouraged to use broad-based identification categories instead. SEAs were given the option of using the category of "developmental delay" as an alternative to the more specific labels, such as speech-language disability, used at the elementary level. Such noncategorical identification has the potential for avoiding the stigmatizing effects that labels can sometimes have on children (Smith & Schakel, 1986).

IMPLICATIONS OF EARLY INTERVENTION IN PUBLIC SCHOOLS

LEAs have addressed an array of issues in their attempt to implement the mandates of IDEA at the preschool level. Although considerable variations in policy on issues such as integration, teacher qualification, and eligibility continue to exist across school districts (Barnett & Frede, 1993), a number of noteworthy accomplishments have been realized.

Benefits

Development of inclusive preschool programming run by the public schools occurred in a context already familiar with the principles of mainstreaming. Early childhood inclusion efforts were thus able to incorporate the lessons learned at the school-age level to create service delivery models that more closely represented the least restrictive environment option. In light of experience with PL 94-142, SEAs and LEAs were aware of difficult issues such as service coordination and classroom management that needed to be addressed before program implementation at the preschool level (Guralnick, 1990).

The benefits of early intervention (Mahoney & Powell, 1988) and the positive effects of integrated programming for preschoolers with disabilities (Guralnick & Groom, 1988; Odom & McEvoy, 1990; Strain, 1983) have been well documented in the literature. Research also has suggested that children without disabilities fared at least as well in integrated settings as in nonintegrated ones (Bricker, Bruder, & Bailey, 1982; Lamorey & Bricker, 1993) and that parents and teachers expressed favorable opinions about integrated preschool programs once they had experienced that type of setting (Diamond et al., 1994). When inclusive preschool programs are established by LEAs, the positive effects previously noted have the potential of increasing community awareness of and support for inclusive early intervention. Communities are more likely to support programs that provide successful results. Efficacy data on the positive effects of early intervention and inclusion provide the strong evidence school boards and administrators need to justify financial support of such programs.

A major component of Part B legislation is that community agencies, including the public schools, collaborate and coordinate services to efficiently provide preschool education. If school districts use already existing services in the community, they may save time and money in their efforts to develop appropriate preschool program options. Community programs such as private preschools can expect to benefit from a partnership with the LEA as their services may be more fully used.

Challenges

Public schools continue to face numerous challenges as they formulate free and appropriate public education in the least restrictive environment for preschoolers with identified learning needs (Salisbury & Vincent, 1990). Community perceptions of early intervention and inclusion may be less than positive if the public is unaware of the financial, educational, social, and ethical benefits of inclusive special education programs for preschoolers. At a time when financial support for special education services in general is being severely criticized, it is easy to understand how requests for additional monies for new programs could be viewed with skepticism by school administrators and the public at large if information about program efficacy has not also been disseminated (Peck, Furman, & Helmstetter, 1993).

Because most public schools do not have preschool programs for children without disabilities readily available, they must look to the community to find appropriate placements for preschoolers identified with learning needs (McLean & Hanline, 1990). As the number of children requiring early intervention grows, the availability of program space may become more limited. The problem is magnified in rural areas where there are fewer preschool programs for LEAs to access. School districts not only must locate community early childhood programs but also must have some means for evaluating the appropriateness of these settings (i.e., staff preparedness, quality of the education program, availability of resources, family involvement) for individual children. Once a community program has been chosen and deemed satisfactory, the various issues of service coordination, travel time, and transportation of equipment and supplies will need to be addressed (Odom & McEvoy, 1990).

Once early intervention programs are in place, they risk criticism again from people unfamiliar with the principles and practices associated with early intervention curricula. Preschool classrooms are generally activity based and children learn in a variety of ways, including interaction with play materials (McEvoy et al., 1991). Someone unfamiliar with the theoretical support for developmentally based and functional procedures at this level may wonder why public funds are being used to support a program where all the children do is "play" (Peck et al., 1993).

Developing inclusive programs for special education at the preschool level is yet another challenge for SEAs. The options for inclusive programming for preschoolers are more varied than for the school-age child. A comment added in 1989 to the regulations for the Education of the Handicapped Act Amendments (PL 99-457) directed LEAs to use a range of placement choices for preschoolers, including full- or part-time placement in public or private preschool programs (Salisbury, 1990). School districts are being asked to provide services to an age group of children who would not otherwise have been served by the district and in inclusive programs that school districts may have had little or no participation in before this law. As of June 1993, 19 of 53 SEAs had developed policies or guidelines specifically addressing the least restrictive environment for the preschool population (Heekin, 1993).

The extent of family-centered practice in preschool programming also varies from state to state. School districts will need to structure service delivery so that families and not children only are the focus and must also develop methods for ensuring satisfactory family participation (McLean & Hanline, 1990). As of June 1993, only 12 of 50 states had developed preschool policies and procedures to include parent counseling and training on their preschooler's IEP (Heekin, 1993).

Some states have begun to report the availability of a range of services for families of preschoolers with disabilities. For example, a survey of early childhood programs administered by public schools in Massachusetts in 1993 indicated that eight different family services, including parenting workshops, support group meetings, home visits, and parent conferences, were offered by more than half of the LEAs represented in the study. However, less than 25% of the services offered were actually used by parents (Barnett & Frede, 1993). A lack of family involvement may have reflected problems such as a mismatch between services offered and family needs, scheduling conflicts, or inadequate advertising that failed to motivate family participation (Barnett & Frede, 1993).

RECOMMENDATIONS

With the implementation of IDEA at the preschool level, public schools have had the opportunity to create unique program options that reflect the strengths and needs of each community. Because existing systems for special education in the public schools are not easily extended to the preschool level, LEAs have had the freedom to interpret federal legislation to best mesh with their philosophies and with the resources available to them as they create new programs (Barnett & Frede, 1993). As with any change, public school personnel have confronted numerous obstacles in their attempts to provide early intervention services. The following recommendations address some of the urgent issues that will need to be considered as publicly supported early intervention evolves.

Educate the Public

An educated consumer can advocate for funding to support effective programming at the preschool level. Information about preschool curriculum, the efficacy of early intervention and inclusion, and strategies used to intervene with preschoolers must be made available in meaningful contexts to taxpayers, families of children with disabilities, and public school administrators and staff (Salisbury, 1990).

Redefine Eligibility Criteria

Part B criteria for identifying school-age children with disabilities are not easily transferable to or comprehensive enough for the preschool-age child. In response to this lack of appropriate identification criteria, 42 of 51 SEAs incorporated a preschool-specific category by June 1993 that supplemented or, in the case of 9 states, substituted for the Part B school-age categories (Heekin, 1993). In addition, educational ability for preschoolers encompasses much more than academic skill alone. A preschool child's ability to negotiate with peers, play interactively, and manipulate fine and gross motor systems for task accomplishment contributes to educational ability. School districts will need to examine the standards by which preschoolers with special education needs are identified. The definition of educational disability requires elaboration because "academic" performance can be viewed as only one of numerous contributors to educational ability at the preschool level. New means for formally assessing educational competence in early childhood is also an area of urgent need.

Identify Inclusive Program Options

The possibilities for special education in the least restrictive environment for identified preschoolers are much broader than those available for school-age children. Individual communities can use existing services to ensure that each child's and family's needs and preferences are satisfied in as typical a setting as possible. In some cases options can be combined so that children in need spend time with special education professionals while also attending a community child care or preschool program (McLean & Hanline, 1990). Regardless of the individual plans that are constructed, an underlying commitment to integration must precede any attempt to outline placement options.

Involve Families

PL 94-142 instructed teams to fully inform parents about the special education evaluation, placement, and review process and to secure parent consent for testing and intervention procedures. Early intervention legislation expands the role parents play in their child's special education plan. The focus is no longer solely on securing parent approval but on enhancing the vital role families play in ensuring their child's continued growth and development. Not only are the child's strengths and needs pertinent to special education planning at the preschool level, but public policy now acknowledges the integral role families play in their child's educational development (McLean & Hanline, 1990). Schools will need to develop policies and procedures to ensure meaningful and ongoing involvement of families.

Develop Certification Standards

There is a critical need for personnel who have been trained to address special education needs in the context of general education for preschoolers (Odom & McEvoy, 1988). Part B amendments implemented in April 1987 required states to develop standards that would ensure adequately trained personnel (Treusch, 1989). SEAs have interpreted this directive broadly. In the 1993 NEC*TAS Section 619 Profile (Heekin, 1993), only 5 states reported using both preschool special education certification and general early childhood certification requirements. Nine states had no certification criteria directly related to provision of early intervention services at the preschool level other than general special education certification. However, 17 states had developed procedures to prepare LEA preschool providers to work within integrated community settings using an itinerant-consultative model (Heekin, 1993).

Recommendations for the characteristics of a qualified early childhood special educator will need to be translated into certification or endorsement criteria that SEAs can use to ensure quality staff. Personnel preparation programs will need to integrate training in early childhood education with early childhood special education to develop a "mainstreamed professional" (Odom & McEvoy, 1990, p. 54) who can address the individualized needs of all children in the mainstream. A national survey of general early education faculty members revealed that many preservice early education training programs required students to take at least one course in special education at the bachelor's level; however, 65% of the training programs did not require students to take a course in preschool inclusion (Wolery et al., 1993). In addition, less than 25% of the programs required field experiences in inclusive settings. Current and future preschool service providers should receive direct instruction designed to strengthen their ability to work collaboratively with professionals from a variety of disciplines to most efficiently meet the child's and family's needs.

Support Collaboration and Consultation

For integrated programming at the preschool level to materialize, early childhood general and special educators, administrators, and families will need to pool their resources and skills. The tenets of inclusive preschool programming may be most closely implemented under the guidelines of a transdisciplinary service delivery model. Such an approach necessitates that team members work cooperatively in teaching each other how to expand current roles and in being supportive as they assume responsibilities previously implemented by a single discipline. Issues revolving around ownership of the child and responsibility for the child's progress can be more easily resolved if staff and administrators are committed to supporting integrated programming.

Effective implementation of this method, especially in an inclusionary context, requires time and resources for consultation and collaboration (Odom & McEvoy, 1990; Salisbury & Vincent, 1990). Few schools have the organizational resources available to support this model of intervention (Peck et al., 1993). Regularly scheduled time must be set aside for team collaboration and consultation if this model of intervention is to be successful (Odom & McEvoy, 1988). Regular opportunity for debriefing the team process will also be critical for all team members in identifying and resolving barriers to inclusive preschool program development.

Use Resources Efficiently

Public schools will want to develop a number of strategies in creating program options for identified preschoolers while efficiently allocating public funds. Some LEAs have arranged liaisons with community preschool programs; young children with disabilities attend the private preschool classroom and then receive special education services from public school staff. Although the school district is responsible for paying the child's tuition and the special education service time, it has bypassed the expense and management issues that accompany developing a new preschool classroom to meet free and appropriate public education in the least restrictive environment for this age group. Other LEAs have developed more intensive partnerships with preschool programs in the community; the school district sponsors one or more special education staff to work in the preschool classroom, team teaching with the early childhood educators and ensuring that the needs of the identified children are met (Guralnick, 1990).

Operate Integrated Preschools in Public School Buildings

The number of preschool-age children served under Part B of IDEA has grown considerably. From the 1990–1991 to 1991–1992 school year alone, 72,400 additional preschool children were served by LEAs across the country (Heekin, 1993). As caseloads continue to grow, school districts may find it financially advantageous to use existing space in a local public school building to run an integrated preschool program. The LEA could collect tuition monies from the nonidentified preschoolers who attend the classroom. Such a program may be more visible in the community and have the potential for increasing awareness of the importance of both early intervention and inclusion.

The physical space in an elementary school may be inappropriate for preschool-age children, however. Existing furniture, toilets, sinks, playground equipment, transportation, and other miscellaneous items (e.g., coat hooks, blackboards) may be too large or too high to accommodate the young child. School districts may need to allocate money in an already tight budget to retrofit existing space and to purchase educational materials appropriate to this younger age group. With a classroom run by the school district, LEA administrators will need to address programmatic issues such as staff hiring and evaluation, securing ongoing funding for supplies and equipment, and managing student records and tuition billing. However, many of those systems are already in place in the public school and merging the needs of a new preschool classroom with an existing public school system may save time and money for the LEA.

Create Transition Plans

Some school districts have outlined procedures for ensuring a smooth transition into and out of preschool early intervention services. However, by 1993 only seven states had information ready to share describing their policies for transition from preschool to kindergarten or first grade (Heekin, 1993). SEAs and LEAs will want to incorporate guidelines that ensure that teams develop a transition plan that satisfactorily addresses the child's education needs in the new setting. Times of transition can be stressful for everyone involved. Families will need time to get to know and trust an unfamiliar education team. They also may need to learn about new identification labels (e.g., "developmental delay" changing to "speech-language impaired" or "learning disabled") and different categories for the provision of services (e.g., "individualized programming" changing to time in the "resource room"). Preschool teams will need time to carefully match children's and families' strengths, priorities, and concerns with the services available at the next level of intervention.

Establish Program Evaluation Procedures

Procedures for assessing a LEA's ability to maintain quality early intervention programming must be established. Criteria available to teachers of school-age children such as quarterly report cards and nationally standardized tests are not necessarily available to preschool early intervention teams. However, SEAs have been directed to develop and implement monitoring procedures to ensure that preschool programs meet state and federal requirements (Treusch, 1989). As of June 1993, only 12 of 53 SEAs reportedly used the National Association for the Education of Young Children Accreditation Program, Self-Study Project, or a state-developed preschool accreditation process to evaluate program effectiveness. Less than half of the 53 states and U.S. jurisdictions surveyed had developed data collection tools to monitor the provision of preschool services in the least restrictive environment (Heekin, 1993).

At one level, measuring the progress of children as they accomplish IEP goals and objectives is an indication of program effectiveness. However, other levels of evaluation might include the degree to which the program meets and/or exceeds federal requirements, the quality of classroom curriculum and instruction both for children with identified needs and those without, and the degree to which the program satisfies family and community needs and expectations (McLean & Hanline, 1990). In addition, if local preschool programs are used as sites for special education programming, the LEA must determine what constitutes an appropriate early childhood setting as well as the qualifications required for adequately trained staff (Odom & McEvoy, 1990).

CASE STUDY

Bethany was born in November 1988, and soon after a diagnosis of Down syndrome was made. Early intervention services were initiated when Bethany came home from the hospital. Throughout her first 3 years of life, Bethany received individualized speech-language, occupational, and physical therapies and participated at various times in small groups at the early intervention center with other children with developmental disabilities. Bethany's parents participated in both individual and group sessions, learning much about early intervention and inclusion.

As Bethany approached her third birthday, the LEA began the process of assuming responsibility for Bethany's early intervention program. Following observation and formal evaluation as well as numerous team conferences, Bethany began attending a regional, self-contained preschool program when she turned 3. Bethany's parents expressed hope that the specialized interventions available at this center would facilitate skill mastery for Bethany. Bethany's school district agreed to pay not only the program tuition but also extensive transportation costs, as the specialized preschool program was more than 30 minutes from Bethany's home.

Bethany's parents soon became aware that Bethany's behavior at school was much less appropriate than the behavior she displayed when playing with cousins and neighborhood pals without disabilities. They began to feel that the models provided by Bethany's classroom peers who had disabilities were not encouraging the best performance from Bethany. With the parents as strong advocates and with the support of a community children's center, the school district agreed to transfer Bethany from the specialized, self-contained regional program to a preschool classroom at the community children's center. The director of the children's center, who was strongly committed to inclusive programming, was instrumental in ensuring that Bethany's education needs could be adequately met in that setting.

Bethany's preschool programming occurred at the same time that the school district was beginning to develop service options at this level. Speech-language, occupational, and physical therapy staff who worked with children at the elementary school volunteered to provide related services to Bethany at the children's center. One of the elementary-level special education teachers also consulted with the teachers at the children's center to help modify the curriculum for Bethany and design a behavior plan. Because this was a new service option for the school district, time was set aside to solve problems as they arose and to periodically evaluate the implementation of the education plan.

Bethany's parents were much more satisfied with their daughter's behavior and the rate with which she learned new skills at the community preschool program. They especially valued Bethany's increasing ability to be a contributing member of her neighborhood peer group. School district special educators valued the opportunity to use their knowledge and skills in this new setting. The related-services professionals taught with the children's center staff, having the opportunity to share their own expertise while learning about preschool curriculum and methodology. The school district taxpayers ultimately spent less money with this new service option; the special education staff were already on the school district payroll and the children's center tuition was less expensive than that of the specialized, self-contained program that was initially chosen for Bethany.

One final benefit of Bethany's preschool programming at the community children's center should be noted. Bethany had developed skills to participate effectively in activities with her same-age peers. The neighborhood children who attended the children's center accepted Bethany as one of the group, understood her needs, and appreciated her friendship. The elementary school special education team had worked with Bethany and was familiar with her strengths and needs firsthand. It was an expected outcome that Bethany would enter a general first-grade classroom with an adapted education plan when she turned 6 years of age.

Bethany is now a member of a general third-grade classroom in the local elementary school. She is learning to read and has the assistance of a tutor-aide during academically focused portions of the school day. However, she independently participates in class projects, recesses, lunch, music, and art periods. When observing from the periphery, it is clear that in this typical setting Bethany is an active contributor rather than an onlooker. The preparatory groundwork laid during Bethany's inclusive preschool program contributed greatly to Bethany's, her family's, and her community's readiness for effective participation in the elementary school mainstream.

SUMMARY

There is a substantial history, supported by research and rationale, that forms the basis for programs designed specifically for preschool children with disabilities. Beginning with the federal mandates of the Education for All Handicapped Children Act of 1975, and subsequent legislation at both the state and federal levels, preschool-age children with disabilities were finally ensured the right to a free and appropriate education in all 50 states and 8 U.S. jurisdictions by 1992.

As with any educational innovation, a number of ways for the public school system to achieve the stated objectives quickly surfaced, resulting in various program options based in private and public settings. Paralleling the mainstream concept developed in public elementary and secondary schools, preschool programs provided youngsters with disabilities varying degrees of opportunities to receive schooling with their same-age peers in their neighborhood schools. Over time, practitioners realized that the public school settings benefited preschool children in a variety of ways, including interaction with other children without disabilities. Additionally, program coordinators began to realize the cost savings and other efficiencies of operating programs under one roof. Although public elementary or secondary program staff and administrators may begin from a somewhat different philosophical basis than do early intervention proponents, there has been a collaborative effort now reflected in the number of early intervention programs housed within public school settings.

Considering the history and evolution of early intervention programs as required by public policy and as developed by practitioners, a number of recommendations have emerged. Public education stressing the benefits and efficacy of these early intervention programs should be provided at the state and local level. Eligibility criteria need to be examined to accurately assess educational competence and potential. Continuing dialogue on the least restrictive alternative will ensure provision of services in appropriate settings at the preschool level. Family involvement must continue to be a priority. Certification standards and preparation programs for early intervention as well as early childhood personnel need to continue to be reviewed and refined at the state level. New methods for preparing all teachers to work in integrated settings must be developed. Administrators and families must support collaboration and consultation across traditional professional discipline lines. Program evaluation must include a review of the use of resources to ensure the wise use of time, money, and personnel. Transition plans for moving from early intervention programs into general elementary settings need to be continually refined to ensure as smooth a change as possible. Finally, program evaluation procedures need to be clearly stated to all of those involved in program implementation, with creative review and refinement as part of continuous improvement.

REFERENCES

Barnett, W.S., & Frede, E.C. (1993). Early childhood programs in the public schools: Insights from a state survey. *Journal of Early Intervention, 17*(4), 396–413.

Bricker, D.D., Bruder, M.B., & Bailey, E. (1982). Developmental integration of preschool children. *Analysis and Intervention in Developmental Disabilities, 2,* 207–222.

Carta, J., Schwartz, I., Atwater, J., & McConnell, S. (1991). Developmentally appropriate practice: Appraising its usefulness for young children with disabilities. *Topics in Early Childhood Special Education, 11*(1), 1–20.

Diamond, K.E., Hestenes, L.L., & O'Connor, C.E. (1994). Integrating young children with disabilities in preschool: Problems and promise. *Young Children, 49*(2), 68–75.

Education for All Handicapped Children Act of 1975, PL 94-142, 20 U.S.C. §1400 *et seq.*

Education of the Handicapped Act Amendments of 1986, PL 99-457, 20 U.S.C. §1400 *et seq.*

Guralnick, M.J. (1990). Major accomplishments and future directions in early childhood mainstreaming. *Topics in Early Childhood Special Education, 10*(2), 1–17.

Guralnick, M.J., & Groom, J.M. (1988). Peer interactions in mainstreamed and specialized classrooms: A comparative analysis. *Exceptional Children, 54*(5), 415–425.

Handicapped Children's Early Education Act of 1968, PL 90-538, 20 U.S.C. §621 *et seq.*

Heekin, S. (1993). *Section 619 profile* (4th ed.). Chapel Hill, NC: National Early Childhood Technical Assistance System.

Individuals with Disabilities Education Act (IDEA) of 1990, PL 101-476, 20 U.S.C. §1400 *et seq.*

Jenkins, J.R., Odom, S.L., & Speltz, M.L. (1989). Effects of social integration of preschool children with handicaps. *Exceptional Children, 55,* 420–429.

Lamorey, S., & Bricker, D.D. (1993). Integrated programs: Effects on young children and their parents. In C.A. Peck, S.L. Odom, & D.D. Bricker (Eds.), *Integrating young children with disabilities into community programs: Ecological perspectives on research and implementation* (pp. 249–270). Baltimore: Paul H. Brookes Publishing Co.

Mahoney, G., & Powell, A. (1988). Modifying parent-child interaction: Enhancing the development of handicapped children. *Journal of Special Education, 22,* 82–96.

McEvoy, M.A., Fox, J.J., & Rosenberg, M.S. (1991). Organizing preschool environments: Suggestions for enhancing the development/learning of preschool children with handicaps. *Topics in Early Childhood Special Education, 11*(2), 18–28.

McLean, M., & Hanline, M.F. (1990). Providing early intervention services in integrated environments: Challenges and opportunities for the future. *Topics in Early Childhood Special Education, 10*(2), 62–77.

McLean, M., & Odom, S.L. (1988). *Least restrictive environment and social integration: Division for Early Childhood White Paper.* Reston, VA: Council for Exceptional Children.

Odom, S.L., & McEvoy, M.A. (1988). Integration of young children with handicaps and normally developing children. In S.L. Odom & M.B. Karnes (Eds.), *Early intervention for infants and children with handicaps: An empirical base* (pp. 214–267). Baltimore: Paul H. Brookes Publishing Co.

Odom, S.L., & McEvoy, M.A. (1990). Mainstreaming at the preschool level: Potential barriers and tasks for the field. *Topics in Early Childhood Special Education, 10*(2), 48–61.

Peck, C.A., Furman, G.C., & Helmstetter, E. (1993). Integrated early childhood programs: Research on the implementation of change in organizational contexts. In C.A. Peck, S.L. Odom, & D.D. Bricker (Eds.), *Integrating young children with disabilities into community programs: Ecological perspectives on research and implementation* (pp. 87–205). Baltimore: Paul H. Brookes Publishing Co.

Safer, N.D., & Hamilton, J.L. (1993). Legislative context for early intervention services. In W. Brown, S.K. Thurman, & L.F. Pearl (Eds.), *Family-centered early intervention with infants and toddlers: Innovative cross-disciplinary approaches* (pp. 1–20). Baltimore: Paul H. Brookes Publishing Co.

Salisbury, C.L. (1990). *The least restrictive environment: Understanding the options. Policy and practice in early childhood special education series.* Pittsburgh, PA: Alleghany-Singer Research Institute.

Salisbury, C.L., & Vincent, L.J. (1990). Criterion of the next environment and best practices: Mainstreaming and integration 10 years later. *Topics in Early Childhood Special Education, 10*(2), 78–89.

Smith, B.J., & Schakel, J.A. (1986). Noncategorical identification of preschool handicapped children: Policy issues and options. *Journal of the Division for Early Childhood, 11*(1), 78–86.

Strain, P.S. (1983). Generalization of autistic children's social behavior change: Effect of developmentally integrated and segregated settings. *Analysis and Intervention in Developmental Disabilities, 3,* 23–34.

Strain, P.S. (1991). Least restrictive environment for preschool children with handicaps: What we know, what we should be doing. *Journal of Early Intervention, 13*(4), 315–328.

Treusch, N. (1989). *Placement of preschool aged children with handicaps in the least restrictive alternative.* (Preschool grants memorandum.) Washington, DC: U.S. Department of Education.

Wolery, M., Brookfield, J., Huffman, K., Schroeder, C., Martin, C., Venn, M., & Holcombe, A. (1993). Preparation in preschool mainstreaming as reported by general early education faculty. *Journal of Early Intervention, 17*(3), 298–308.

... 13

The Interrelationship of Contexts in Early Intervention

Wesley Brown and Maureen Conroy

Each child and his or her family experiences a unique combination of the multiple contexts for early intervention. Four systems—family, economic, sociopolitical, and cultural—influence the family and child as they interact with the delivery of early intervention services and resources in their community. (For a detailed description of each of these systems, see Chapters 6, 3, 2, and 4, respectively.) As these systems change, internal and external changes occur for each child in a family and community. Children may receive single early intervention services in isolation or multiple services that may also occur in isolation from one another. More desirably, they may receive such services collaboratively from one or more service providers. These might be delivered in a linear or sequential manner or concurrent with each other with service coordination and transition occurring between services.

As discussed in Chapter 1, the ecological perspective can be used to facilitate understanding of interrelationships of context and settings in early intervention. The work of Bronfenbrenner (1979) is seminal in its capacity to provide a frame of reference for understanding and organizing the complex services that are interrelated and a critical part of early intervention.

Figure 1 illustrates the interrelationships of the contexts discussed in this book. The child is embedded in the family, which is embedded in the community, ordinarily at the heart of Bronfenbrenner's (1979) microsystem. These are influenced by cultural, economic, and sociopolitical factors, the primary components of the macrosystem (see Chapter 1 for an explanation of these systems). Early intervention settings are shown as represented in this book. The two mediators, service coordination and the individualized family service plan (IFSP), join the systems and settings. These mediators must respond individually and flexibly to the systems to enable the family's linkage with resources and services in a variety of settings.

The authors would like to acknowledge the assistance of Dr. Lynda Pearl and the Tennessee Early Intervention System staff for their assistance with the case studies included in this chapter.

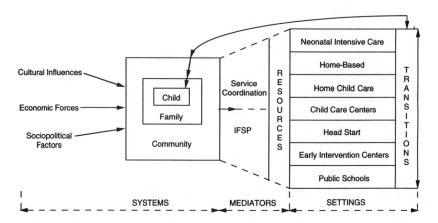

Figure 1. The interrelation of contexts for early intervention.

Service coordination, collaboration, and transition become the critical mediators in early intervention services and resources for young children and their families. This design focuses on the mediating influence of these factors within the portrayal of systems and settings that otherwise would be viewed concentrically, as commonly portrayed by Bronfenbrenner (1979).

This chapter explores how systems and settings come together in unique combinations for the child and family and examines the interrelationships among settings in the provision of early intervention. Several child and family scenarios are provided to illustrate changing systems in a chronological context of concurrent and sequential services. Finally, from these ecological roots, implications for future practice are given.

INTERRELATIONSHIP OF SETTINGS

Services and resources should be provided in an individualized manner for each child and family. This delivery should be needs driven and family centered in a flexible, collaborative manner. A variety of approaches and solutions are required to respond in a culturally sensitive manner to the different paths portrayed by families (see also Chapters 4 and 6). Such individualistic flexibility requires partnerships and collaborative methods for the concurrent delivery of resources and services.

In Chapter 1, Thurman illustrated the complexity and dynamic nature of systems and explored the concept of "fit." While the complex, mutual influence of systems is taking place, individuality must be accommodated to achieve a fit that is truly responsive to the family's needs. Mott (Chapter 8) found the home setting most likely to involve the family and to be offered in combination with other settings, services, or resources. The home setting was found to have particular strengths with young children and families who may have difficulty obtaining services (e.g., those with complex health care needs, individuals living in rural areas). In contrast, Gottwald and Pardy (Chapter 12) suggested that the public school is not a setting at all but rather a provider of a continuum of services, responding across a variety of settings to meet its responsibilities.

The findings on early intervention centers (Chapter 11) illustrate the shortcomings of past segregated models of centers, which are now in transition to become part of the natural ecology of communities under the expectation for services in family-centered, natural environments. Karabinos (Chapter 11) advocated for early intervention centers to become part of comprehensive early childhood centers in communities. Child care, both in centers and in family settings (see Chapters 10 and 9, respectively), represents a new setting in the delivery of early intervention. Golbeck and Harlan (Chapter 9) pointed out the negative professional opinion of family child care for the purpose of early intervention. Some professionals view funding requirements as necessitating separation of the child care nature of the services from the early intervention aspects; others find these features inseparable. These settings often use consultation models and are now evolving in partnership with early intervention centers.

RESOURCE-BASED VERSUS SERVICE-BASED PRACTICES

Traditionally, services have been defined by the type of professional services available for the child and the family; that is, they tend to be based in terms of formal services provided by professionals only (e.g., occupational therapy, physical therapy, respite care). This view limits the availability of services for children and families. When a service-based approach is taken, the need for these services usually outweighs the availability of the services, leading to a shortage of available resources for children and families.

As Trivette, Dunst, and Deal discuss in Chapter 5, a resource-based approach provides additional opportunities for children and families by using a range of resources, both informal and formal, within the community. The authors redefine early intervention services as supports and resources, both informal and formal, to children and families that affect directly and indirectly the parents, family, and child's functioning. Included in a resource-based approach are social networks, associations, community programs and professionals, and specialized professional services.

The service-based approach is more limiting, formal, and professionally centered; the resource-based approach is varied, flexible, and community centered. The resource-based approach may provide an improved framework for coordinating and expanding early intervention services for children and families. This approach would require an ecological assessment of the resources within the community and support for families to have access to these resources. A major component appears to be the need for community collaboration and training so that community services and supports are accessible and appropriate for young children with disabilities and their families. This would entail the dedication of families and supporters to advocate for and provide technical assistance to community members, associations (e.g., YMCA), and professionals to coordinate efforts and provide opportunities.

CASE STUDIES

This section provides five case studies that may be used to examine the interrelationship of contexts of early intervention services within individual families.

The McGough Family:
Individual Home-Based Therapy to Child Care with
Integrated Early Intervention Services to Segregated Public School Services

The McGough family is a young, two-parent family with local southern Appalachian traditions and a large extended family. Mr. McGough does seasonal factory work, but is regularly unemployed and on Medicaid. When he does work, the family eats out and lives well, but does not develop savings. The McGoughs have one child, an attractive, blue-eyed son named George who was born with severe health needs. At 2 months of age, George experienced many rehospitalizations, home health care, and surgeries. His health was not stable enough for many interventions; however, assistance in feeding was provided in the home with Part H funding and assistance.

The McGoughs were familiar with community resources (e.g., WIC) and used them often; however, they were highly anxious about the medical aspects of caring for their son. When George was 18 months old, an IFSP was developed by his early intervention service coordinator. The IFSP goals included providing early intervention services for George in a group setting (in response to concerns about the family system). A strong child care setting was viewed as appropriate, but the parents preferred to have George attend only a few days a week. George was to receive speech-language and occupational therapy at the child care center. A part-time aide was included for his program to assist with feeding and health care needs. Part H funded tuition for the center and provision of the aide. A service coordinator worked to establish Supplemental Security Income (SSI) eligibility for George, as the family's eligibility was constantly changing due to Mr. McGough's varying work status.

When George turned 3, his parents wanted him to continue to receive early intervention in a child care setting. The school system refused and placed him in a preschool segregated setting.

The Selby Family:
Initial Home-Based Clinical Services
Extended to Home-Based Developmental Studies

The Selby family consists of June, a single mother attending high school, her daughter Loretta, and her parents, who are the primary caregivers for Loretta and who provide the resources for the family. At 6 months of age, Loretta was diagnosed with developmental delays and immune deficiency. Her developmental pediatrician referred Loretta for early intervention. Loretta needed a physical therapist for positioning and home health. By 1 year, Loretta's health was good, and she was moving and interacting well, although she still needed the services of the physical therapist. At this time, an IFSP was developed whose goals included improving motor, language, and cognitive skills. Loretta could not leave the home setting because of her immune difficulties. These services were funded through Medicaid and Part H services. Loretta's grandparents provided additional financial support as needed.

At 2 years of age, Loretta continues to receive physical and speech-language therapy and work on her cognitive goals at home. Her early interventionist considers her a good candidate for a consulting model of service delivery.

The Koslowski Family:
Custodial Child Care to Developmentally Appropriate Child Care
with Integrated Speech and Language with a Concurrent Home-Based Program

The Koslowski family is a two-parent working-class family. Their son, Stephen, was 18 months old when he contracted encephalitis, which led to a profound hearing impairment. At that time, he was enrolled in a community child care center that provided predominantly custodial services. After discovery of his hearing impairment, he was enrolled in a statewide home-based program for young children with hearing impairments. However, the Koslowski family wanted better services for Stephen, and the administrators of the home-based program wanted more intensive speech-language therapy for him.

Stephen's IFSP was reviewed and revised to specify that he should have developmentally appropriate child care oriented toward learning (the child care was funded by a child care block grant) and a speech-language therapist (funded by Medicaid) who would provide services at the child care center daily for 2–3 months to assist both the child and child care staff. The IFSP also specified family counseling for the Koslowskis to assist them in learning how to cope with Stephen's disability. Finally, the IFSP called for the following measures after 3 months of therapy: hiring a classroom assistant (funded by Part H), continuing home visits (funded by a state early intervention program), and reducing speech-language therapy to once every other week.

The Esquivel Family:
Home-Based Services with Related Services Supports

The Esquivels are a Spanish-speaking family whose third child, José, is a friendly and affectionate boy with Down syndrome. When he was born, his family was referred to a Part H service coordinator. This coordinator hired a local homemaker who was a Mexican citizen to translate during medical assessment and IFSP services.

The Esquivels preferred home-based intervention and soon outgrew the need for a translator because the father (the primary collaborator in intervention) was making rapid gains in English competency. José needed early intervention services and physical therapy. Because a Spanish-speaking physical therapist was not available, he received services from a Spanish-speaking occupational therapist with physical therapy consult. An early interventionist through Part H made weekly visits to the family. Again, the father implemented the consultation and translation services needed.

Recently, state health care reform efforts have endangered funding of related services for José. The family is unable to fund these services on their own. With the assistance of the IFSP service coordinator, the family is seeking alternative funding sources.

The Bates Family:
Extensive Service Coordination and Eventual State Custody

The Bates family lives in a rural community and consists of the parents, a grandmother who lives with the family, a young daughter, Susan, and her older brother Jeff. Both parents have mental retardation and emotional difficulties. The father, although employed initially in low-income jobs, also has difficulties with alcohol and other drugs. Jeff is often truant from school and has limited supervision. The grandmother has poor health and emotional difficulties, and the mother provides the primary stability of the family.

Susan was born with a rare syndrome requiring multiple surgeries to maintain the potential for typical development. These surgeries were unavailable within 150 miles of the Bates's home and thus required the relocation of the family for extended periods. The first surgery Susan underwent required service coordinators from both the home and community sites, a home health nurse, a family support liaison, respite caregivers, Medicaid-funded transportation, family support funds from the local Ronald McDonald house, and a hospital social worker.

Susan's initial surgeries were unsuccessful. The family continued to receive home health assistance from an early interventionist, and the father began to receive SSI. Mrs. Bates began counseling, and family support and training home visits were initiated to help with medical provision and appointments.

After a short time, however, the family stopped cooperating with medical providers and refused to allow more surgeries for Susan. The family was then reported for abuse and neglect. Mr. Bates's drinking began to escalate, and eventually both children were removed from the home. Susan was placed with a foster family, one of whose members was involved with her medical care. Eventually, Susan was placed in foster care nearer to her surgery site.

ANALYSIS OF CASE STUDIES

The McGough Family

This case study shows how one family received a number of services concurrently and across time: home-based early intervention assistance with feeding, hospital care, home health care, child care services in a center setting with provision of related services, and eventually segregated preschool services. Important influences on care for this family included the changing employment status of the father and the good use of community resources by the family. The family was able to use a variety of resource and service providers in a collaborative, natural environment setting until the public school transition provided conventional, segregated preschool services, against the wishes of the family. This case demonstrates the importance of transitions and the need to offer a variety of service delivery options for preschool-age children. Economic issues included the use of Part H funds and the need to establish SSI eligibility for the child as a solution to inconsistent family eligibility.

The Selby Family

This family received early intervention services at home, including physical therapy, health, and eventually speech and cognitive services. The child was limited to home services because of an immune deficiency, and service delivery alternated between day and evening hours to accommodate the various caregivers. Important influences within this family included the caregiving and support role of the grandparents. Economic issues included the funding of services through Medicaid, Part H, and family support.

The Koslowski Family

Initially, this family's child attended a custodial child care center. When he developed a hearing impairment as a result of encephalitis, he was enrolled in a statewide home-based program in which home-based speech-language therapy was provided. Additional supports were provided at the child care center, including a classroom assistant funded through Part H and speech-language services funded through Medicaid. Later, family counseling was provided. Important influences in this family's service provision included the need to coordinate a complex set of services delivered in two natural environments coordinated through the IFSP. Economic issues included the coordination of four different funding sources for the funding of child and family support services.

The Esquivel Family

This family needed a translator to assist with service provision, which was partially limited by available bilingual providers. In addition, early intervention services and physical therapy services were needed and provided. Important influences in this family's services included the family's changing linguistic competency. Economic issues included the change in state-funded health-related services and early intervention services. This scenario is another example of flexible and changing service provision and funding.

The Bates Family

This case study provides a highly simplified perspective of a child with complex medical needs and a family with various health and disability needs. Service coordinators were active at both the home and the hospital where the child often required surgery. Important influences in this family's service provision included the temporary inability of the family to cope with the complex needs of their child and the distance of the hospital from the family's home. Although the transition of the child to state custody was an unfortunate, if necessary, measure, the family was eventually reunited when the child's medical condition was resolved. Economic issues in this section were minimal compared with the social influences.

COLLABORATION, SERVICE COORDINATION, AND TRANSITION

Collaboration, service coordination, and transition should be incorporated across settings and cannot exist within a single setting. As outlined in the case studies, each topic plays a critical role within the provision of early intervention services. This section provides background on each topic, examines the state of the practice for each area, and concludes with promising practices and how these practices may be promoted across settings and within systems.

Collaboration

With the development of services for young children with disabilities, the concept of collaboration has gained attention in the literature (e.g., see DeWeerd, 1992; Dunst, Johanson, Rounds, Trivette, & Hamby, 1992; Johnson, Jeppson, & Redburn, 1992; Kaplan-Sanoff & Nigro, 1988). As suggested in the early intervention literature and stated in the Education of the Handicapped Act Amendments of 1986 (PL 99-457), there is a need for service providers and families to develop interagency, collaborative relationships to provide appropriate comprehensive services for families and young children with disabilities. Dunst, Trivette, Hamby, and Pollock (1990) stated that a single agency, working in isolation, cannot provide all the necessary services needed to educate and enable families who have young children with disabilities. As a result of this premise, the law challenges local communities to develop collaborative programs that include many systems and settings to address a variety of needs for these children and their families.

Although collaboration has often been discussed, the concept has been difficult to define and explain. Collaboration in the early intervention literature is often referred to as the cooperative effort of a group of individuals who problem-solve and work together toward a common goal (Bishop, Woll, & Arango, 1993; Dunst et al., 1990). It is about families and professionals working together to help the family and child develop and grow (Bishop et al., 1993). Collaboration is characterized by the following: 1) mutual respect among individuals (e.g., both service providers and families); 2) a desire to problem-solve toward a common goal; 3) shared responsibility in achieving goals; 4) trust, honesty, and communication; and 5) full disclosure of information that is critical to the goal. The important component of collaboration is the role of the parent(s) as the final decision maker when solving problems to achieve common goals for the child and family.

Collaboration is a process. It is an outcome and develops when people work together toward a common goal. The initial step toward collaboration is coordination among service providers and families. Eventually, these individuals develop "cooperative" relationships, which lead to "collaborative" relationships. Dunst et al. (1990) suggested that the process continues and a final step, "partnership," occurs after collaboration. The collaborative approach is different from the traditional role in which most professionals and service providers have been trained. It includes a shift in attitudes, philosophy, beliefs, communication style, and actions (Dunst et al., 1990).

The concept of collaboration is one of the most essential features of early intervention services. Collaboration is how systems, mediators, and settings can be intertwined to provide the critical services needed by families and young children. As discussed, families who have young children with disabilities interact with a variety of services and ecological systems. As illustrated in the preceding case studies, these services may be medical, educational, economic, or support. Having different agencies work with a family can be devastating to families unless these services are provided in a collaborative manner. During the Part H hearings, families testified that services were often fragmented due to a lack of communication among service providers. The end result of fragmented services is additional stress, confusion, and isolated care for children and families. Therefore, collaboration should occur among parents and all service providers to provide the most appropriate services for the child.

There are a number of barriers that make collaboration difficult for service providers and families. Often individual agencies have different policies, goals, and eligibility requirements (DeWeerd, 1992). In addition, service providers have not been trained to collaborate with families. They have been trained in the professional role and to be the "expert" making decisions for the family. Barriers such as logistics, scheduling, role definitions, and responsibilities also can prevent collaboration among service providers and families (Kaplan-Sanoff & Nigro, 1988). Through mutual problem solving and focusing on the common goal of the child and family, these barriers can be overcome.

Collaboration occurs throughout the case studies previously presented. For example, in the first case study, collaboration occurred among the service coordinator, family members, and health care agency around feeding therapy. In addition, collaboration occurred among the assistant, speech and language therapist, and occupational therapist. Each agency representative worked collaboratively with the others and the family to provide the optimal services for the child.

The ultimate result of collaboration is to improve the outcomes for children with disabilities and their families. When collaboration occurs between families and service providers the outcome is shared ownership, responsibility, and successes (Bishop et al., 1993).

Service Coordination

Another critical component of early intervention is the concept of service coordination. As outlined in PL 99-457, the medium for service coordination is the IFSP. Service coordination and the IFSP are presented in Figure 1 in this chapter as the mediators for interrelating contexts for early intervention.

The traditional approach for providing services to families with children with disabilities was a case management approach, in which the professional or service provider determined the services to be offered and coordinated them for the family and child. This approach viewed the family on a deficit basis. The family played a minor role in the coordination of services and, as a result, participated very little in the planning and provision of services for their child. With the progress in early intervention, the traditional case management approach has evolved into a service coordination and family-centered approach.

Family-centered service coordination includes jointly coordinating the provision of services that address the goals and intervention plans that meet the family's and child's needs. The needs of the family and the child should be the focus of service coordination, and the family should be the decision maker in the provision of the types of services needed (McBride, Brotherson, Joanning, Whiddon, & Demmitt, 1993). The services coordinated should provide the interventions needed to strengthen and enable the family to meet the needs of their child. Services may include social services such as financial, emotional, and information support to family members as well as direct services for the child (e.g., health, educational). The service coordinator also helps coordinate assessments, parent and family contact, direct intervention services for the child and the family, transition planning, and follow-up services. This individual should empower the family to coordinate and choose services. There should be a partnership between the family and the service coordinator and a relationship of mutual regard and problem solving (Cardinal & Shum, 1993).

There are a number of impediments to family-centered service coordination. As discussed by Brown, Pearl, and Carrasco (1991), one impediment is the lack of service coordinators within communities to individually assist a family in coordinating needed services. The caseloads of service coordinators are often too heavy. Another impediment is training. Most service coordinators have received training in traditional case management approaches. There is a need to teach service coordinators a new role and philosophy. Finally, the logistical barriers previously outlined in the collaboration section also apply here. There are often many individuals and agency regulations to coordinate with little time and resources.

Although there are challenges, service coordination is critical in the provision of early intervention services, as was illustrated in this chapter's case studies. In the case of the Koslowski family, service coordination played a critical role in the first three settings. The service coordinater assisted in coordinating financial, educational, therapy, and counseling services for this child and family. The result was an ecological approach that met not only the needs of the child but also of the family. With the Esquivel family, the service coordinator was able to coordinate assessment and direct intervention services as well as translation services and financial support for the intervention services. This coordination improved the quality of services the family and child received.

The transition of service coordination to a family-centered model is evolving, as is collaboration into a partnership model, where families and service providers work together to enhance the services for the child. This is a changing role for service providers and for families, but the outcome is improved transitions between services for children.

Transition

Transition is the final component that is critical when providing early intervention services for children across a variety of settings and contexts. Transition is the process that occurs (or does not occur) when a child moves from one early intervention setting to the next. As illustrated in the case studies, transition may occur from neonatal intensive care units to home-based services. Transition also occurs when a child leaves an early intervention center and enters a public school setting. There are many types of transitioning processes that may occur, from no planning and support for the child and family to a well-planned transitioning process between settings that appropriately focuses on the family and the child.

A well-planned transition between settings is important for several reasons. First, a transition means change. Changes can be stressful, and families have indicated that the transition out of early intervention can be a very stressful time for both the family and the child (Spiegel-McGill, Reed, Konig, & McGowan, 1990). This transition results in different roles and expectations for everyone involved in the child's development, including the child and the family (Hamblin-Wilson & Thurman, 1990; McDonald, Kysela, Siebert, McDonald, & Chambers, 1989). In addition, transition planning can provide consistency and continuity in the services provided for the family and the child. As outlined in the case studies, the transition was critical when the context of the services was being changed. For example, for the McGough family, the transition occurred when the child was moving from the child care center to the public preschool setting. Although this setting was not the family's first choice, a collaborative effort between the family, early intervention network, and public school staff occurred that facilitated the transition of the child into the program. Family's and child's needs continued to be addressed without an interruption in the services being received. In the case of the Bates family, no transition planning occurred. This resulted in additional stress for the child and family and an interruption and fragmentation in services. The effects of this may have been prevented or lessened if transition services had been provided.

Because the concept of transition between early intervention settings is so critical, many researchers have examined this topic. McDonald et al. (1989) outlined several steps for making transitions successful. First, transition planning should occur at least 6 months before the change. Next, family input and collaboration should also occur. Transition goals should be added to the IFSP. Families and service coordinators should begin planning for future environments. A time line should be established and goals should be addressed. Finally, after the transition, follow-up should occur. This process allows for planning, education and information, and adjustment to the new context. An ecological approach for transitions can help prepare the service providers, the family, and the child. Service providers and families should evaluate and visit the new and existing contexts, develop a liaison between the two contexts, plan family conferences, exchange information, and collaborate among each other to facilitate the transition process (Thurman & Widerstrom, 1990).

Parents have indicated that information is important for successful transitions (Hanline & Knowlton, 1988). Spiegel-McGill et al. (1990) outlined several topical areas that may provide information to parents whose children are making the transition into the public school setting. These include the knowledge of 1) the effects of the transition, 2) the child's skills, 3) program options and services, 4) effective communication, 5) educational rights, and 6) the "puzzle pieces" (e.g., multidisciplinary teams).

As with collaboration and service coordination, transitions avoid weaknesses in the traditional isolated model of service delivery. It requires individuals to collaboratively plan and coordinate services to meet the needs of the child. As Hamblin-Wilson and Thurman (1990) suggested, transitions are critical for families and children to move between one early intervention context and the next. However, it involves the continual efforts of agencies and families working toward a common goal of meeting the needs of the child.

SUMMARY

This book has provided extensive presentations of the contexts and settings for early intervention services. This chapter illustrated and discussed the interrelationships between these settings and contexts in existing and evolving practices. Resource-based practices and early intervention should be needs driven, flexible, family centered, culturally competent, individualized, in natural environments, and, most of all, enabling for families and their children.

This chapter also focused on evolving practices in three important areas—collaboration, service coordination, and transition—as they respond to the interrelationship of context and settings. There is a great need for better use of child care as an early intervention setting, for shifts away from segregated early intervention centers as unnatural settings, for greater financial flexibility in the delivery of services, and for shifts in professionals' roles and philosophies in relationship to families and intervention.

Early intervention providers must pay particular attention to context, setting, and expanded collaboration to continue to improve intervention systems for families and their children.

REFERENCES

Bishop, K.K., Woll, J., & Arango, P. (1993). *Family/professional collaboration for children with special health care needs and their families*. Burlington, VT: Family/Professional Collaboration Project.

Bronfenbrenner, U. (1979). Ecology of the family as a context for human development. *Developmental Psychology, 22*, 723–742.

Brown, W., Pearl, L.F., & Carrasco, N. (1991). Evolving models of family-centered services in neonatal intensive care. *Children's Health Care, 20*(1), 50–55.

Cardinal, D.N., & Shum, K. (1993). A descriptive analysis of family-related services in the neonatal intensive care unit. *Journal of Early Intervention, 17*(3), 270–282.

DeWeerd, J. (1992). Head Start/preschool collaboration. *Early Childhood Report, 3*(7), 11–12.

Dunst, C.J., Johanson, C., Rounds, T., Trivette, C.M., & Hamby, D. (1992). Characteristics of parent-professional partnerships. In S.L. Christenson & J.C. Conoley (Eds.), *Home-school collaboration: Enhancing children's academic and social competence* (pp. 157–174). Silver Spring, MD: National Association of School Psychologists.

Dunst, C.J., Trivette, C.M., Hamby, D., & Pollock, B. (1990). Family systems correlates of the behavior of young children with handicaps. *Journal of Early Intervention, 14*(3), 204–218.

Education of the Handicapped Act Amendments of 1986, PL 99-457, 20 U.S.C. §1400 *et seq.*

Hamblin-Wilson, C., & Thurman, S.K. (1990). The transition from early intervention to kindergarten: Parental satisfaction and involvement. *Journal of Early Intervention, 14*(1), 55–61.

Hanline, M.F., & Knowlton, A. (1988). A collaborative model for providing support to parents during their child's transition from infant intervention to preschool special education public school programs. *Journal of the Division for Early Childhood, 12*(2), 116–125.

Johnson, B.H., Jeppson, E.S., & Redburn, L. (1992). *Caring for children and families: Guidelines for hospitals*. Bethesda, MD: Association for the Care of Children's Health.

Kaplan-Sanoff, M., & Nigro, J. (1988). The education in a medical setting: Lessons learned from collaboration. *Infants and Young Children, 1*(2), 1–10.

McBride, S.L., Brotherson, M.J., Joanning, H., Whiddon, D., & Demmitt, A. (1993). Implementation of family-centered services: Perceptions of families and professionals. *Journal of Early Intervention, 17*(4), 414–430.

McDonald, L., Kysela, G., Siebert, P., McDonald, S., & Chambers, J. (1989). Parent perspectives: Transition to preschool. *Teaching Exceptional Children*, 22(1), 4–8.

Spiegel-McGill, P., Reed, D.J., Konig, C.S., & McGowan, P.A. (1990). Parent education: Easing the transition to preschool. *Topics in Early Childhood Special Education*, 9(4), 66–77.

Thurman, S.K., & Widerstrom, A.H. (1990). *Infants and young children with special needs: A developmental and ecological approach* (2nd ed.). Baltimore: Paul H. Brookes Publishing Co.

Index

Page numbers followed by t *or* f *indicate tables or figures, respectively.*